Andrew Jukes

TYPES in GENESIS

Books by Andrew Jukes

Four Views of Christ
The Names of God
The Law of the Offerings
Types in Genesis

Andrew Jukes

Types in Genesis

kregel PUBLICATIONS

Grand Rapids, MI 49501

Types in Genesis, by Andrew Jukes, © 1976 by Kregel Publications, a division of Kregel, Inc., P.O. Box 2607, Grand Rapids, Michigan 49501. All rights reserved. First paperback edition, 1993.

Cover Design: Alan G. Hartman

Library of Congress Cataloging-in-Publication Data

Jukes, Andrew John, 1815-1901.
  Types in Genesis

  (Andrew Jukes Reprint Series)
      p.   cm.
  Reprint. Originally published: The Types of Genesis. London: Longmans, 1898.

  1. Typology (Theology). 2. Bible. O.T. Genesis—Criticism, interpretation, etc. 3. Bible. N. T.—Relation to the Old Testament. 1982. 4. Bible—Criticism, interpretation, etc. I. Title. II. Series: Jukes, Andrew John, 1815-1901. Works. 1982.

ISBN 0-8254-2959-5 (pbk.)

3 4 5 6 7 8 Printing/Year 97 96 95 94 93

Printed in the United States of America

CONTENTS

INTRODUCTION

THE WORK AND REST OF GOD

Chapters 1, 2

		PAGE
I.—The Work of God	. . . .	. 5
II.—The First Day	. . . .	. 11
III.—The Second Day	. . . .	. 14
IV.—The Third Day	. . . .	. 18
V.—The Fourth Day	. . . .	. 25
VI.—The Fifth Day	. . . .	. 32
VII.—The Sixth Day	. . . .	. 36
VIII.—The Seventh Day	. . . .	. 42

PART 1

ADAM, OR HUMAN NATURE

Chapter 3

I.—Adam, or Man	. . . .	. 63
II.—Man's Way	. . . .	. 69
III.—The Fruit of Man's Way	. . . . . .	. 76
IV.—The Remedy for Man	. . . .	. 80

PART 2

CAIN AND ABEL, OR THE CARNAL AND SPIRITUAL MIND

Chapters 4, 5

I.—Cain and Abel, or the First and Second Birth	. . .	. 88
II.—The Carnal and the Spiritual	. . . . .	. 94
III.—Their Lives	. . . .	. 97

V

PART 3

NOAH, OR REGENERATION

Chapters 6-11

PAGE

i.—Noah on the Ground of the Old Man 105
ii.—Noah in the Waters 115
iii.—Noah on the Earth beyond the Flood 122
iv.—Noah's Sons 131
v.—Noah's Failure 142

PART 4

ABRAHAM, OR THE SPIRIT OF FAITH

Chapters 12-20

i.—Abram's Separation from his Country and his Father's House . 163
ii.—Abram's Separation from Lot 181
iii.—Abram's Conflicts to deliver Lot 192
iv.—Abram's Trials through the Word of God and Prayer . . 202
v.—Abram's Efforts to be fruitful by Hagar 210
vi.—The true Way for Abram to be fruitful 218
vii.—The End of Lot 228
viii.—Abraham in the Philistines' Land 239

PART 5

ISAAC, OR THE SPIRIT OF SONSHIP

Chapters 21-26

i.—The Birth of Isaac, and its Results 251
ii.—The Offering up of Isaac 258
iii.—Sarah's Death, and Isaac's Union with Rebekah . . 265
iv.—Keturah, and Isaac at Lahai-roi 277
v.—The Trials of Isaac respecting Seed 285
vi.—Isaac's Two-fold Seed, the Elder and the Younger . . 291
vii.—Isaac in the Philistines' Land 301

Contents

PART 6

JACOB, OR THE SPIRIT OF SERVICE

Chapters 27-36

PAGE
I.—Jacob's Carnal Means to gain God's Ends 315
II.—The Motives to Service, and Encouragements by the Way . 324
III.—The Service for Wives and Flocks 332
IV.—The Departure from Laban 346
V.—The Journey to Canaan, and Change of Name . . . 351
VI.—The Sojourn in Succoth, and Dinah's Fall . . . 357
VII.—The Return to Bethel. 364
VIII.—The Seeds of Jacob and Esau 369

PART 7

JOSEPH, OR SUFFERING AND GLORY

Chapters 37-50

I.—Joseph's Dreams, and Suffering from his Brethren . . . 381
II.—Judah's History 386
III.—Joseph in Potiphar's House 394
IV.—Joseph in Prison 399
V.—Joseph exalted over all Egypt 408

INDEX 415

PREFACE

I wish, by way of Preface, to throw together a few thoughts on the mystic character of Scripture, and on other kindred matters.

Many are aware that the Books of Moses deal largely in typical representations, that is, figures of spiritual things, both facts and doctrines, of the Christian dispensation. We cannot read St. Paul without perceiving that he saw far more in Genesis than the mere letter. The creation with him is the figure of another work, which God accomplishes in every saved sinner. " God, who commanded the light to shine out of darkness, hath shined into our hearts." Then, " If any man be in Christ, he is a new creature: old things have passed away; behold, all things are become new." As much as to say, that just as God began to work upon this earth, when all was dark and without form and void, and worked upon it, step by step, bringing forth fruits and forms of life, until the image of God, the man created in righteousness, was seen to rule it all; so is it with the soul of man, from " Let there be light,

and there is light," till the new man in us rules every
faculty. The story of Hagar and Sarah too, as is well known,
has with St. Paul a sense far deeper than the mere letter.
Melchisedek is another example, the import of whose
name and acts is familiar to all readers of the Epistle to
the Hebrews. These and St. Peter's allusion to the flood,
as a figure of that judgment of the first creation which
baptism declares, are too well known to need comment.
In every age they have witnessed to the most unwilling
that Genesis has treasures richer than those upon the surface, secrets of God's purpose and of man's ways, which
the spiritual man may search, for the Spirit searcheth all
things, yea the deep things of God.

But though many have a general notion that Genesis
contains types, few have any idea of the immense extent or
depth of this hidden wisdom. Just as in nature the distinct
orders under which plants are found to range are quite
beyond the conception of any but a botanist, though
every one must have generally noticed their great differences, or marked some peculiarity of this or that flower.
Just as it needs the patient study of years to make an
astronomer, though every educated man understands something of the phenomena of the heavenly bodies. So is it
with the Word. And in this book of Genesis, diligence and
prayer and God's Spirit will bring to light worlds of truth
infinitely beyond the conception of the carnal mind ; and
humble faith will discover systems of wisdom as complete
and wondrous in the Word, as science with all her researches
has found in the material universe. We may indeed read
the Scriptures, as men cultivate the earth, simply to find

food to support the life which God has given. But we may also read with higher views, to know the ways of God. He who has given us the earth to bring forth food, has shewn us vast and mysterious heavens above, the contemplation of which is fitted to raise and humble and spiritualise us. In the Word are not only fruitful fields, but heavenly depths full of unnumbered lights. Often as we regard them must we confess our ignorance. Why should we scruple to do so, when even in nature the keenest eye, and the mightiest mind, is baffled on every hand. Errors even may mingle with views in the main correct, as men have erred in studying the phenomena of the heavens, and indeed must err until they have learnt to correct the readings of sense by the conclusions of a higher faculty. Yet diligence reaps its fruits, which, though open to abuse, may also be an offering to God's glory.

The form of the Word, however, and the wisdom of its form, is a subject which yet waits to receive that attention which is its just due. Four Gospels have forced some in every age to notice the distinct purpose of God in each Gospel. But for the rest of Scripture, why its form is what it is,—why like a man, and with man, it grew from age to age,—why it looks and is so human,—what connection all this has with the mystery of the Holy Incarnation,—these are questions seldom asked, or, if asked, rarely answered as befits His dignity from whom we say the Scripture came.

I do not attempt here to enter on the reasons for this form; but I notice one fact, namely, that the Word is given to us in many books or sections, each of which, I am assured, is a divine chapter, with one special end, illustrating something in God and man, or the details of some relation between the Creator and the creature.[1] As in the Gospels, one is to shew Christ as David's Son; the next to reveal Him, not so much as the King, as the meek and true Servant; the third, to set forth the Son of Adam; the fourth, the Son of God; each giving a distinct view of the various relationships of the same One Lord: so it is in the rest of Scripture; each book has its own end, and the order and contents of all, as they describe the progressive ways of God with man, answer to His ways in every soul, for within and without His ways are one, and His work the same from age to age.

As a base or ground for what is to follow, we first are shewn what springs from man, and all the different forms of life, which either by nature or grace can grow out of the root of old Adam. This is the book of Genesis. Then we see, that be it bad or good which has come out of Adam, there must be redemption; so an elect people by the blood of the Lamb are saved from Egypt. This is Exodus. After redemption is known, we come to the

[1] As to the form of the Old Testament, Jerome notices that the number of the books, according to the Jewish division, (five books of the Law, eight of the Prophets, and nine Hagiographa,) answers exactly to the twenty-two letters of the Hebrew alphabet; and that as there are five double letters in the Hebrew, so there are five double books, namely, two Samuels, two Kings, two Chronicles, two Ezras, (which we call Ezra and Nehemiah,) and two Jeremiahs, (that is, Jeremiah and the Lamentations.) The fact that part of the Book of Proverbs, (chap. xxxi. 10—31,) the whole of the Lamentations, and seven Psalms, (namely, the xxv. xxxiv. xxxvii. cxi. cxii. cxix. and cxlv.,) are acrostics, founded on the Hebrew alphabet, leads him to suppose that there is some mystery in these twenty-two sounds, which form all words, connected with the comprehensive character of the Word. *Prol. Galeat.* 1–8. Modern criticism may smile, but there is far more in this than appears at first sight.

experience of the elect as needing access, and learning the way of it, to God the Redeemer in the sanctuary. This we get in Leviticus. Then in the wilderness of this world, as pilgrims from Egypt, the house of bondage, to the promised land beyond Jordan, the trials of the journey are learnt, from that land of wonders and man's wisdom, to the land flowing with milk and honey. This is the book of Numbers. Then comes the desire to exchange the wilderness for the better land, from entering which for a season after redemption is known the elect yet shrink; answering to the desire of the elect at a certain stage to know the power of the resurrection, to live even now as in heavenly places. The rules and precepts which must be obeyed, if this is to be done, come next. Deuteronomy, a second giving of the law, a second cleansing, tells the way of progress. After which Canaan is indeed reached. We go over Jordan : we know practically the death of the flesh, and what it is to be circumcised, and to roll away the reproach of Egypt. We know now what it is to be risen with Christ, and to wrestle, not with flesh and blood, but with principalities and powers in heavenly places. This is Joshua. Then comes the failure of the elect in heavenly places, failure arising from making leagues with Canaanites instead of overcoming them. This is Judges. After which the different forms of rule, which the Church may know, pass in review in the books of Kings ; from the first setting up of rule in Israel down to its extinction, when for their sin the rule of Babylon supersedes that of the elect. When this is known with all its shame, we see the remnants of the elect, each according to its measure, doing what may be done, if possible, to restore Israel; some like Ezra returning to build the temple, that is, to restore the forms of true worship; and some coming up like Nehemiah to build the wall, that is, to re-establish by Gentile permission a feeble imitation of the ancient polity; while a third remnant in Esther is seen in bonds, but faithful, providentially saved, though God's name (and this is characteristic of their state) never appears throughout the whole record.

This subject would of itself fill a volume. I touch it here, not only to shew that each book has its own peculiar end, each being but the illustration of some one truth or fact, on which a revelation from God was needed by us; but to call attention also to their order and gradation, answering so exactly to the steps by which truth is ever apprehended by us in the world of thought within. In this light the position of Genesis is most suggestive. Its purport is to shew what Adam is, and what can spring out of him. And just as in our souls the Spirit of God first comes to shew us ourselves, that so " coming to ourselves," like the Prodigal, we may then " come to our Father " also; so does the Word open with the same, with Adam and his seed, that is the fruit of human nature. This, as it is the ground of all that follows, is not only an introduction : it is also an abridgment or summary of all the books. For what is the series but a revelation of God, shewing His resources by the very wants and failure of the creature. Genesis, in shewing us Adam and his outcome, man by grace and nature, reveals in embryo the whole mystery of grace and nature in the creature. It is thus an abstract of the Bible, with the long sum of the Divine counsels worked out and expressed in God's algebra.

Genesis then reveals to us all that can spring out of Adam. In the letter it gives us the story of Adam and his sons. Here we may read how Adam behaved, and what races and peoples sprung out of him. In spirit we may learn how old Adam behaves, what the old man is in each of us, and all the immense variety which can grow out of him. And what an outcome it is. Some forms of life there are which spring out of Adam or human nature, simply by nature, according to the course of nature; and some forms of life there are which spring out of Adam by grace, which are the result of a divine seed sown in that poor soil, contrary to nature, and to the common course of nature. It is a wondrous tale, yet within and without it is but one. For the development of Adam or human nature in the great world without, has its exact image and counterpart in the little world within; I call it " little," though indeed it is not little; for if "the kingdom of God is within us," there must be room enough. And what confusion it seems: life and death, evil and good, love and hate, and pride and meanness everywhere: men praying, cursing, blessing; palaces and hovels, churches and armies, schools and markets, jails, cities, asylums, unions; such are some of the fruits of old Adam, in whom all this was before it was seen, and is only seen without because it was and is within him.

But whether within him or without, man finds it hard to unravel all this tangled skein of life and being; for man looks only on the outward appearance; God who looketh upon the heart only knows and can trace out the whole development. In the book of Genesis He tells the story, how both human society and divine spring by grace or nature from the same root. To illustrate this subject is my aim in this volume, the details of which I will not here anticipate, further than to say that there are seven very distinct forms of life, owned by God, which this book of Genesis fully reveals to us; first Adam, then Abel, then Noah, then Abraham, then Isaac, then Jacob, then at last Joseph. These seven are the various shades of the true light of life, as it appears when refracted through body, soul, and spirit, the triangular prism of human nature; from the red of Adam on the one hand, up to that regal purple, in which he may he said to shine who completes and is over all the rest. Connected with all these are other forms of life disowned of God, various shades, that is, and degrees of darkness; but these seven lives give us all the light which beams through this book. These are all representative men. In Adam we see the old man, human nature as it is in itself, ready to trust the tempter, and to distrust God and rob Him of His glory; then hiding from His presence, and covering its nakedness with fig leaves, and laying the blame on the very gifts which God has given it; yet pitied and visited with a promise and a gift,—a promise that, weak as he is, the Seed of the woman shall at length prevail,—a gift by which, naked as he is, his nakedness may be covered. All that can be said of mere human nature,—of man as man,—is set forth in the history of poor, fallen, yet pitied and redeemed Adam. Soon we have another stage or picture. In Adam's sons, the elder and younger, a type is given us of the two seeds, the flesh and spirit, the natural and spiritual, which have grown by nature or by grace out of the root of old Adam. That is not first which is spiritual, but that which is natural. Both are seen here in all their main outlines. Then comes Noah who is more than the spiritual man; for there may be spiritual men who have not passed the mystic waters. Noah is a type of the regenerate, of those who know what it is to be taken out of one world and placed in another. His seed shew us all the works which may be, and have been, wrought by those who are regenerate. Then Abraham, Isaac, Jacob, and Joseph, set forth those four great forms of life, which are known and enjoyed after regeneration has been fully reached by us; Abraham being the life of faith, shewing how the man of faith goes forth, not knowing whither, yet seeking to go to Canaan; Isaac, revealing the life of sonship in the land, dwelling by wells of water, with many joys and few conflicts; Jacob, the life of service, begotten on resurrection ground, and going down into the far country, to win a bride and flocks, whom he may bring back to share his joy in heavenly places; Joseph, the last, most perfect life, the life of suffering, which first dreams of rule, and ends with all things brought into subjection to it.

How the order of these lives answers to the development of Adam in us is sufficiently known to all who understand much of that development. First, we learn old Adam; then the difference of flesh and spirit; then the way through the flood, that is, regeneration: after which faith begets sonship, and sonship service, and service that life of suffering, which now, as then, ends in glory. The series never changes, nor do its stages come by chance. Abraham or faith now and ever precedes sonship, even as sonship will ever precede that evangelic service of which Jacob is the figure. All the path we may not know, but as far as we know it, the order will be that set forth in Genesis. In each newborn man is some portion of this history fulfilled, from the day when he knows not that he is naked, when the thing which is true for him in fallen Adam is not yet realised, (for as things are true for us in Christ before we experimentally know them, so is it in old Adam,) until stage by stage the things which have been realised by man, both the old man and the new man, are all part and parcel of his own experience. Thus Genesis and its history becomes again incarnate. He, in whom man is developing after God, will have lived as in the world before the flood. He has known, because he is by nature in Adam, what it is to live in the old world, in the first creation, before its judgment. He has known too, like Noah, the judgment of the first creation, and that there is a way of safety through the deep waters. And he may know, if he is faithful, the walk and life in the new creation, and the many developments there, from sonship to service, and from service to glory; if unfaithful, other developments, the forms of which are foretold, and which though partaking of some of the blessings of the elect are not elect.

The measure therefore in which these truths will be apprehended will depend on the difference of spiritual experience or growth of different souls. Experience is proving the truth; and just in proportion as we have proved these truths, so far shall we be able to enter into the lives here depicted. Thus I can foretell that, inasmuch as all know something of human nature, all will have some understanding and apprehension of the parable set forth in Adam's life. Those who can discern the flesh and spirit will decipher Cain and Abel: those who have reached to regeneration will understand Noah; those who know the path of faith will be at home in Abraham's trials; while the spirit of sonship will open Isaac's path. In like manner, service will explain Jacob, and suffering, Joseph; the likeness in each case being easily to be recognised by those who know and love the original. If we will do the works, we shall know of the doctrine.

But is not this all mere imagination? What proof have we that there is anything but fancy to support all this? I am not careful to answer this; first, because I write for those, who, though requiring help, fully believe that some such secrets are treasured here; and also because the spiritual sense is its own proof, as a key by opening a complicated lock sufficiently proves that it has been designed for it; a proof indeed which requires some capacity in the observer, and some exercise and intelligence in the things of God, but which will, I am assured, be increasingly satisfactory to those who will test it in the daily study and meditation of the Word of God.

Do I then despise the letter? God forbid. With sincerest faith I receive it, and thank God for it, throughout Scripture. Most precious is it, speaking to all in words of truth, shewing how the outward daily life on earth may be sanctified, and is watched and cared for by God. Especially now, when so many act as if the earthly calling were a path of which God took no notice, and in which faith availed us nought, most precious is the letter, as shewing God, for He changeth not, in all His providence over the outward path of those who love and fear Him; shewing how the path of lonely men, if they walk with Him, their wells, and sheep, and feasts, and wars, are all His interests; that not a marriage, birth, or death,— not the weaning of a child, or the dismissal of a maid,— not the bargain for a grave, or the wish respecting the place of burial,— but He watches and directs it. Thus precious is the letter; a daily guide and comfort to us as dwellers here.

But holding this, I see much more,—that while the letter is a guide for things on earth, in spirit it veils and yet reveals to us the things of heaven; in this like the world around us, which, while supplying means for this life, in those very supplies sets before the opened eye the secrets and treasures of the world within the veil; in this too like the Lord, coming under our hands in human form, under that lowly form veiling yet revealing the glory of the eternal Son. Christ, the Incarnate Word of God, seems to me, not an illustration only, but a proof, both of the preciousness of the letter, and of the deeper spirit which everywhere underlies the letter throughout the Word of God. He was man, but He was God. There was the human form of the Word, the outcome of David and Abraham, for He sprung out of Judah. This was the humble form which men despised; but besides and under this was the Divine, full of the unspeakable depths of the wisdom of Almighty God; giving forth draughts of that wisdom, emitting rays of that light, to as many as had capacity to receive of His fulness; and yet in mercy hiding from others awful depths which they were unfit to know; being, like the world His hands had made, an "open secret" to all around Him.

Such also is the Written Word. Coming to us in human form, as the outcome of David or of some other Israelite, and judged by most as Joseph's son, it has a higher birth, truly human indeed, and yet no less divine; in its letter, in its human form, coming down to teach men upon the earth, full of lessons of love and truth for us as pilgrims here; in its spirit to shew us the things within the veil, and to lift us up to live and walk and dwell above; in the letter, even as the flesh of Christ, "never to see corruption," though rejected; and in spirit to be seen as shining with unearthly glory. • I have known Christ after the flesh. I can never cease to adore the God and Father of our Lord Jesus Christ for the grace of the mystery of His Holy Incarnation, by which He has come as a man to speak to men; but I have also seen His glorious resurrection and ascension, and the coming of the Holy Ghost. So have I known the Word in the letter. Most sweetly has it spoken. When I walked, it led; when I slept, it kept; when I awaked, it talked with me.[2] It has been my guide, my staff, my bread, my counsellor, my comfort, all through this lonely pilgrimage. But I have also felt its spirit, and seen the depth within the veil, where I could but fall down, and cry, Holy, Holy, Holy, Lord God Almighty.

[2] Prov. vi. 22.

And to turn from God's Word to man's, our own words, which in their very form confess that human language can only speak of spiritual things under outward images, might prepare us to find that God, who is a Spirit, in speaking of outward things, in them is teaching spiritual things. All our words for spiritual things are, if we mark them, figures. We take something from outward nature and apply it morally. The language which forms the medium of our intercourse with heaven, is constituted out of the forms of this world, and if we look at its letter only points us to the outward world around. Thus sin ($\dot{\alpha}\mu\alpha\rho\tau\dot{\iota}\alpha$) is simply missing the mark; grace is outward beauty; right is straight; wrong, twisted: spirit is wind: transgression is a stepping over: error is only wandering. The same is true of countless other words, which, originally forms of outward life, through that mysterious correspondence which exists between all the works of the Divine Word, have come to express the relations of the mind and the world within. For, indeed, His works are words. There is a word in the forms of things, by which they are prepared to represent what is inmost in our souls. There is a word in all nature, in light and darkness, cold and heat, in summer and autumn, in fruits, in storms, in sunshine. There is a word in the lives of men, yea, even in beasts and birds, each saying somewhat to us, not unintelligibly. Day unto day uttereth speech, and night unto night sheweth know-ledge. Their line is gone out through all the earth, and their words unto the end of the world. Surely "there are many kinds of voices in the world, and none of them is without signification."

Wondrous, therefore, as it is, that the facts of man's first and natural development should figure the growth and progress of his spiritual life, — that a chain of events, such as Genesis records, should spiritually express all the manifold history of man's inward life in every age, — it is but the wonder which meets us everywhere, that all we see, and far more than any see, — every law of nature, the seasons, the days, every tree in its laws of growth, each beast and creeping thing, — speak to our souls of other higher things, and have been so felt to speak by man in every age. We do not make these things significant. Light, darkness, cold, warmth, spring, and winter, are in themselves significant. Why they are so, few may understand. The fact remains still undeniable. And as the growth of seeds is to the eye of Paul a silent yet sufficient witness of higher things;[3] so the growth of the human tree, as it is drawn in Genesis for us by One who knows it perfectly, tells of another higher growth in man, in which God's spiritual image may be discerned yet more perfectly.

But it is not a point for debate. He who walks as becomes his calling, will sooner or later, if he can bear it, have all the proof before him. From others it may be wisely hid. Arguments are of little service here. He who saw Christ as the Eternal Word, whose eye, divinely taught, discerned in that human form, not so much the Son of Abraham or Adam, as the Only Begotten Son, characterises himself as " the disciple which testifieth;"[4] agreeably to

---

[3] 1 Cor. xv. 35, 36.   [4] John xxi. 24.

which his Gospel, and his only, is peculiarly marked by the reiterated, " Verily, Verily ; " for testimony, not proof, is all that disciples can offer to the world, on those subjects which eye hath not seen, but which are revealed by God's Spirit. Paul may argue, if he will ; but John, though he tells what he has seen and handled of the Word of Life, only testifies. The "Verily, Verily," has spoken to him. He relies on its finding its own witness in other hearts.

To brethren, therefore, who love the Word, who have seen cure upon cure wrought by it, but have not yet seen how its very form may be transfigured and shine with heavenly glory, I say,—Yet love and abide by the Word ; it may be you shall not taste death, until you see something of this transfiguration ; and if you see not here on earth, you shall see it in heaven, where He who loves you is gone to prepare a dwelling. Yet if we walk with Christ, daily walking by the Word, (for of His disciples all do not follow all His steps, and therefore see not His transfiguration,) — if we will not leave Him, no not for a day, but will yet walk with Him, — not by what this or the other man saith, but by the simple Word alone, living by it hour by hour, — we may see it changed before us. Then the raiment of the letter shall be filled and beam with heavenly glory ; the human form, which we have so long taken for a true prophet indeed, but only as the outcome of David, will shew with unearthly glory that it is something far higher ; and we shall see Moses and Elias, law and prophets, not in the flesh, but transfigured also, shining like Him of whom they bear witness ; no longer a mere letter, much less a dead letter, but full of God and, radiant with His brightness. We must indeed come down again from thence; for though, as Peter says, " it is good for us " to be there, it is better for others that we descend to those who stay on lower ground; but they who have seen the glory there, even if they come down from that mount, at once to meet a devil,[5] will not forget the glory, or the shining raiment of Moses and Elias, or the voice from heaven, witnessing to Him, who, though He veiled Himself, was the Only Begotten Son.

Others there are, hoping in the Word, who may see their likeness in that blind man who sat beside the way by Jericho;[6] like him in darkness, nigh to that cursed and mystic city, whose walls, once blown down by the blast of rams' horns, have been rebuilt to tempt some Israelites again to seek a dwelling there.[7] And there they sit, both poor and blind; yet they sit " by the way." They have not rightly seen the Word, even in the flesh or letter. They cry, " Thou Son of David," little thinking that the Word which is so nigh them has glories greater than those of David's Son. And some disciples, whose eyes are open to see and confess the Son of God, bid the blind to hold their peace, because they give not the Son His due title. Not so the living Word. Such as seek Him shall be healed. They may not see His transfiguration, but with opened eyes they shall follow in the way.

I would that all who touched the Word were thus

---

[5] See Matt. xvii. 1–18.

[6] Mark x. 46–52.

[7] Joshua vi. 26. The man, also, who fell among thieves, but was cared for by the good Samaritan, was "going down from Jerusalem to Jericho."—Luke x. 30.

climbing the holy mount, or having blind eyes opened by the wayside near Jericho. There are, alas, many more who say and think they see,—who see the letter, even as the Jews saw the flesh of Christ,—who yet nor love nor follow His ways, and yet can sit and judge, and justify to themselves their own narrow views of the eternal Word. To them the Word is Joseph's son. They know exactly whence it is. They have never seen that human form transfigured; therefore it cannot be. With such souls, all that is above them is " imagination ; " all that is below them is " carnal formalism." What they see,—where they are,— that is right. What they cannot receive is, if not downright error, at least questionable. Such souls, instead of trying to understand what others speak, try rather to make others speak only what they understand. Thus their ignorance measures all things. But they too shall see one day, when the veil is taken away, and the Truth returns to judge all things.

The question is one of fitness to receive the Word ; for He who is THE TRUTH, because He knows all men, and knows what is in man, will not commit Himself to all men, because all are not prepared to receive Him.[8] If He has told us earthly things, and we believe not; how shall we believe if He tell us of heavenly things. But just as we can receive Him, so will He reveal Himself; shewing Himself after the flesh to fleshly men ;[9] in the glory of His resurrection only to the elect and spiritual.[10] But whether He veils or unveils, all is love. If He

---

[8] John ii. 24, 25.　　　[9] Psalm xviii. 25, 26.　　　[10] Acts x. 40, 41.

unveils, it is that we, with open face beholding as in a glass the glory of the Lord, may be changed into the same image. If He veils Himself, it is because He knows that His brightness would destroy us; therefore He tempers for us the glory through the cloudy veil. We cannot yet bear the best things. He has many things to say, which, for a season His children cannot bear. Isaac, the seed of promise, has but milk till he is weaned: when he is weaned, a great feast is made in Abraham's house; [11] even as to this day there are fat things on the lees for weaned souls, which unweaned souls receive not, only because they cannot bear them. For the spiritual man may say with Paul, "For me to depart, and be with Christ,"—for me to pass away from earthly things to the Word within the veil, to Christ out of sight of men in His heavenly glory, where Moses and Elias witness of Him,—"this is far better. Nevertheless to abide in the flesh,"—in that which the world can apprehend, in outward forms of truth,—"for others, this is more needful." So Paul abides on earth, saying little of what he had seen when he was caught up into Paradise; while John is permitted to record some of the wonders which an opened heaven had revealed to him.

All this, because unaccustomed, may to some seem strange. Then " as a stranger give it welcome:" receive the stranger; "for thereby some have entertained angels unawares." What is foreign to our notions, or to the notions of our age, may to us be new, while yet not new to saints. It is mere folly to condemn, because what

---

[11] Gen. xxi. 8.

meets us is new to us, and greater folly to mock things as
mere dreams or fancies because we cannot see them. The
wisdom of man is as nothing to a beast; so is the wisdom
of God counted as nothing by carnal animal men. The
chariots of fire were round Elisha, though his servant saw
them not, until in answer to prayer the young man's eyes
were opened to see what to the seer had all along been
open vision.[12] A voice may come from a cloud, understood
by sons of God, although scoffing Jews, who have no ears
to hear, " said it thundered." [13] Even a prophet may be
blind, and animal natures, like Balaam's ass, see more
than those who ought to guide them.[14] Not without reason therefore is the prayer, " Open thou mine eyes, that I
may behold wondrous things out of thy law." For " the
natural man receiveth not the things of the Spirit, neither
can he know them, for they are spiritually discerned; but
he that is spiritual discerneth all things, while he himself
is discerned of no man." [15]

For the views here given, there is the authority, not of
one or two, but of many saints through many hundred
years. And though these things were not first shewn me
by the Fathers, but opened in solitary communings with
the Word of God; yet I am thankful to see that I am in
the same great circle and in the same spirit with the
Church of other days. With them I see the letter, and
within it what I call an inward, an outward, and a dispensational application. They may call these moral, allegoric,
and anagogic senses; but the thing meant remains the

[12] 2 Kings vi. 13–17.
[13] John xii. 28, 29.
[14] Numb. xxii. 23, 31.
[15] 1 Cor. ii. 14, 15.

same, namely, a perception of the same work of God on different platforms. For they saw how God's work is reflected in many spheres, in the world within, and without, and through extended ages ; His work on earth shadowing forth still higher forms of the same work of the same unchanging Lord.[16] Thankful am I that brethren gone before had eyes to see and hearts to apprehend all this. For what I owe them too I am thankful, thus proving that the members of the body from age to age are not independent of one another. Besides, some will not take truth for authority, but want authority for truth. Such may hearken to the witness of saints of other days. The spiritual sense has indeed a witness far higher than holy men : its works will prove from whence it is : but as the Son of God received John's witness, so may the spiritual sense, while possessing a higher testimony, refer to the witness of the burning and shining lights of other days. I have, therefore, added a few quotations from the Fathers. Some may hearken to Augustine, who would not receive truth as truth on its own authority. Such, having first heard the witness of men, may at length hear the witness

---

[16] Readers of the Fathers know, that these different senses or applications of Scripture were generally received, and the principle of them apprehended, by the Church in earlier days. What I have called the *inward* application, they call *moral* or *tropologic*; what I call the *outward* or historic spiritual fulfilment, they call *allegoric*; while the future or *dispensational* fulfilment they call *anagogic*, (from ἀνάγω, to lead upwards or onwards,) according to the well-known lines,—

"Litera gesta docet; quod credas, allegoria;
Moralis, quod agas; quò tendas, anagogia."

Any one who cares to see the ground or principle of this triple interpretation of Scripture, will find the question briefly but clearly stated by Thomas Aquinas; *Summ. Theol.* pt. i. qu. i. art. 10. Nicholas Lira also, in the *Prologue* to his Notes on the Bible, goes fully into this subject.

of the Truth itself. But such lights shew where those are who need them ; for the light of the heavenly city and its inhabitants is the Lamb.

Meanwhile He that hath the key of David is not far off. He can shut so that none can open, and open that none can shut. And my prayer is, that, where these things should be hidden, they may be hidden, and where they can be opened, they may be yet more opened. The book, though sealed with seven seals, opens to the once slain Lamb. And if we, as members of His body, reach to participation in His cross and resurrection, — if with Him we are accounted as sheep for the slaughter, daily dying that we may live another higher life, — things once sealed will open, being opened by the Lamb to those who are partakers with Him in His death and resurrection. For it is the death of nature, not its improvement, which takes us through the veil. Improved nature will only better shew us the things of nature. But let nature die, — let the flesh be judged, — the spiritual world will dawn with glories never to pass away.

I now submit these notes to my brethren, in a deep sense of their imperfectness. I have written the things which I have seen ; and they are the things which are, and the things which shall be. But I am assured that my view is but one of many, and if it is definite, it is only because I have not touched what is infinite. Of this view I have attempted to trace the fulfilment, not only within, but without, and in the dispensations. For in the world-fulfilment of some of the scenes of man's development, every eye will see the figure, which few will have eyes to discern in the little sphere of their own soul. In a larger sphere we may see what is beyond us in a smaller. In a globe of quicksilver we see the whole horizon reflected; but if this drop be shaken or sublimated so as to divide and form a hundred or a thousand smaller spheres, in each one of the globules every object will be reflected as perfectly as in the larger globe, though now the reflection on each is quite beyond the range of our unaided vision. Thus the world-fulfilment of the outcome of Adam will be perceived by many, who cannot see the same fulfilment as wrought within themselves. Let each learn what he may. The lengths and depths of this ocean are all unfathomed and unfathomable.

For myself, as one has said, to whom I am a debtor, " I now return from the utterance of words, to the chamber of my heart, to examine myself, whether in attempting right things I have spoken the truth in a wrong way. For a thing is rightly spoken, when he who speaks it, seeks by what he says to please Him alone from whom he has received it. And though I am not conscious of having said wrong things, I do not maintain that there are not any. If I have said any true things by a gift from above, it is my own fault that they are spoken so imperfectly. Yet when I look closely at the very root of my intention, I find that in this work I wished to please God; and yet the desire of human praise in some secret way may have crept in; and when at last and slowly I discern this, I find that I do a thing in one way, which I know I began in another. I believe it is worth my while to disclose this to my brethren; for since in my writing I have expressed my better thoughts, in this my confession I would not hide my failings. And because in the Church there are not wanting little ones, whom I may teach, nor yet great ones, who may pity and help my weakness, when made known to them, from the one I withdraw not the help of my words, from the other I conceal not the pain of my infirmities ; by my words seeking to confer assistance on some at least of my brethren, by my confession hoping to receive aid in return from them. I therefore beg every one who reads this book, to give me before the Holy Judge the solace of his prayers, and with tears for me to wash away every filthiness he may discover in me. My reader will surpass me in his recompense, if, where he receives words by my means, he gives me tears in return." [17]

[17] Greg. M., *Moral. in Job*, l. xxxv. c. 16.

INTRODUCTION

THE WORK AND REST OF GOD

Chapters 1, 2

" If any man be in Christ, he is a new creature: old things are passed away; behold all things are become new."   2 Cor. v. 17.

" God, who commanded the light to shine out of darkness, hath shined in our hearts, to give the light of the knowledge of the glory of God in the face of Jesus Christ."

2 Cor. iv. 6.

THE WORK AND REST OF GOD

Chapters 1,2

GENESIS, like all the other books of Scripture, has its own special end. Its object is to shew us the outcome or development of Adam or human nature — to trace all the different forms of life, which, either by grace or nature, can grow out of the root of old Adam. In the letter we are shewn here how old Adam acted, and what races and peoples sprung out of him. In spirit we see how the "old man" acts in us, and all the immense variety which can and does grow out of him. Thus some forms of life are presented to us which spring out of Adam or human nature, simply by nature, according to the course of nature; and some forms of life there are which spring out of Adam by grace, which are the result of a divine seed sown in that poor soil, contrary to nature and to the course of nature. It is a wondrous tale throughout, but all its secrets are here, told out by Him from whom no secrets are hid.

As a divine preface to this book, which shews us what man is, and the fruit which his earthy nature can produce under the creative word and will of God, we are shewn what this earth was, and the gradual steps of its adorning, from the time when it was " without form and void," with

"darkness upon the face of the great deep," until after
light and life and fruit, "the image of God," the man
created in righteousness, is seen to rule it all. A fit
preface; for in a man or world the work is one; and,
indeed, man is himself a world, with realms within him
vast and affluent.[1] Darkness and light, and a great deep,
and earth and heaven, are in him. Passions move him
as the storms: volcanic fires rage or smoulder in him.
Thoughts too, as the work of God proceeds, stir in him,
and the realms within are peopled by them, as the air
with birds, the sea with fish, and the earth with living
creatures. Lest, therefore, our blindness should be unable
to trace God's work in the inner world of man, God writes
it in creation on the broad platform of an outer universe.
Lest we should be perplexed by the long detail of the
gradual development of Adam and his seed, God gives
the outline of it in the work of seven days. In each there
is a work of God upon an earthly creature. In each we
are shewn what in successive stages can be brought by
grace out of the creature. Thus the seven days of creation
are a type of all God's work. Nothing is afterwards
revealed, but the seed of it is to be found in the days of
labour or in the day of rest. For in Genesis is hid all
Scripture, as the tree is in the seed; and in the days of
creation is the seed of all Genesis. We shall see how
exactly the special work of the six days and the seventh
day's rest answer in their order to the stages of development which are depicted in the seven great lives of
Genesis. The tale is one, like Ezekiel's vision, "a wheel
within a wheel," with "rings high and dreadful and full
of eyes on every side."

---

[1] "Est ergo hic mundus divinæ specimen operationis," &c. — *Ambros.
Hex.* l. i. c. 5.

To this tale of creation I would now turn. Each part will amply repay us. We may consider first the outline, then some of the details, as illustrating the new creation or regeneration.

I.—The Work of God

First then there is a creation of God announced—then a partial ruin—then a restoration. " In the beginning God created the heavens and the earth." [1] Of these first " heavens" nothing further is here revealed to us; [2] but of the " earth" we read that it was " without form and void," language used by the prophets to describe a state of judgment and utter ruin. [3] In some way not revealed God's work had been destroyed. God then, in the six days, restores that earth, not made dark by Him, yet now in darkness; and on this ruined earth His work proceeds, till His image is seen, and He can rest there. Thus a creation utterly wrecked is the ground for the six days' work. On this dark and ruined mass appears what God can do.

The nature and state of the mass here worked on—the means of its change—the steps of the work —all speak a lesson not to be forgotten.

For its nature, it is "earth;" its state, " without form and void," with " darkness on the face of the great deep." Nevertheless, it is not uncared for. God's Spirit broods over it:—" the Spirit of God moved upon the face of the waters." [4]

This is yet true of the creature before God's work begins.

[1] Chap. i. 1.
[2] " Cœlum illa creatura invisibilis supereminentium potestatum."— *Aug. de Gen. ad lit. lib. imperf.* c. 3, § 9. We find the same interpretation, *Conf.* l. xii. 13, 17.
[3] Jer. iv. 23. The same original words occur in Isa. xxxiv. 11, there translated "confusion and emptiness." *Cf.* Isa. xlv. 18.
[4] Chap. i. 2. " מרחפת, id est, incubebat vel fovebat, more volucris ova calore animantis."—*Hieron. Q. Heb.* So too *Ambros. Hex.* l. i. c. 8, § 29.

Why it is what we see it to be, is another deeper question
—one here left unsolved—but its state remains a fact. Before God's word is heard, the creature, which is earthy, is
void and formless, with an unknown deep within. Upon
this deep all is darkness; yet God's Spirit is brooding
there. The creature is helpless, but God is very near.[5]

This creature begins nothing, continues nothing, per-
fects nothing. Of its change the agent is throughout the
Word of God. Life and power is in the Word. " God
said : "—this is the means, as in the first, so in the new,
creation. In both the first move is on God's part. When
nothing else moved, " the Spirit of God moved upon the
face of the waters." In both each new transformation is
the work of the Word, and its extent in exact proportion
to the measure in which the creature hears it.

All this is the A B C of Christian experience. Those,
in whom the work goes on, know that each succeeding step
is simply by the Word. From everlasting all the work had
been hid in Christ, the Eternal Word. Then, in time,
that which was in the wisdom of God is wrought actually
in the creature. Whether light, or a heaven, or fruits, or
heavenly lights, or the living creatures, or the man in
God's image,—each form of light and life, once hid in
Christ, is reproduced, manifested in the creature to the
Creator's praise. What was in. Christ is step by step accomplished in the earth by the transforming power of the
same Word of God.[6] Without this no change is or can be
wrought. No saint can grow or live without the Word.
What was in the Word from everlasting, by the Word is
wrought in us, just in proportion as we are subject to it.

---

[5] See *Aug. Conf.* l. xiii. c. 12.

[6] " Cum dicitur, ' *In principio
fecit Deus*,' commemoratio Filii fit,
quia principium est ; sed cum dicitur,
' *Dixit Deus, fiat*,' commemoratio,
quia verbum est. Per principium,

Observe two men, both Christians; one neglects the Word, and can pass day after day, buried in earthly things, without God's Word or meditation. Compare with him the man whose delight is in the law of the Lord, and who meditates therein day and night. The one is barren; there is no aptness to receive, and nothing is received. The other grows like a tree planted by the rivers.

As to the steps of the work, its details must be traced, if we would have anything like a just view of the wonderful stages of regeneration. It may be well, however, to premise a few remarks as to the general character of this amazing work.

I observe then first, that the work was progressive. Not at once, but through six successive days, was the creation perfected. In nature we have first the blade, then the ear, then the full corn: the babe, the child, and then the perfect man. So is it in grace. Days of labour, stage on stage, must intervene, after which those in whom God works may surely look for rest. Further, in spirit as in letter, the work proceeds in all its stages from evening to morning, from growing darkness to growing light, with alternations of either, but ever from night to day, and not from day to night.[7] The evening and the morning make the day. Though the light has come, darkness still at times seems to threaten to resume its ancient reign. The shades of temptation and the light of faith alternate for awhile, till the day of rest comes, without an evening: the one to remind us again and again of what the creature is in itself; the other, what it is in Christ, the Word of

insinuat exordium creaturæ, existentis ab illo: per verbum, perfectionem creaturæ ab illo ad ipsum revocatæ, ut formaretur inhærendo Creatori."

Aug. de Gen. ad lit. l. i. c. 4.
[7] " The evening and the morning were the first day." Chap. i. 5. And so of the other days.

God.[8]   Thus from all things wrong does the work advance
step by step, till all is "very good."   Let none forget this;
for some there are who seeing God's end, to shew His glorious
image in the creature, forgetting the steps to this end,
bitterly judge themselves, because as yet the image of God
is not revealed in them.   Let such wait in patience.   He
who hath begun the good work will perform it unto the
day of Jesus Christ.

Further, each stage, though imperfect, was "good" in
God's eyes.   At each step it is repeated, "And God sàw
that it was good."[9]   To the awakened soul, feeling its imperfections, this is blessed, that from the first God can find
something which He pronounces "good."   Not till the
sixth day is God's image seen.   Then "behold, it is very
good."[10]   But from the first, at every step, "God saw that
it was good."   At first nothing was changed: waters still
reigned everywhere: but the light had broken in.   Darkness at least now had a name: its character was perceived;
and God saw this, that "it was good."

[8]   "Nequaquam in hâc vitâ per exercitationem justitiæ peccatum dese-
ritur, ut in ipsâ inconcussè maneatur,
quia si jam a cordis habitaculo cul-
pam rectitudo eliminat, ipsa tamen
culpa quæ repellitur, cogitationis
nostræ foribus assidens, ut sibi ape-
riatur, pulsat. Quod Moyses spiritualiter innuit, dicens, *Facta est lux*,
atque paulò pòst, *Factum est vespere.*
Creator quippe omnium humanæ
culpæ præscius, tunc expressit in
tempore quod nunc versatur in mente.
Lumen namque rectitudinis umbra
sequitur tentationis.   Sed quia electorum lux tentatione non extingui-
tur, nequaquam nox, sed vespera
facta perhibetur; quia tentatio in
corde rectorum lumen justitiæ abscondit, non interimit."— *Greg. M.*

Moral. in Job l. viii. c. 10, § 21. Augustine's mystic explanation here,
that the *evening* describes what the
creature is in itself, the *morning*
what it is in the Word of God, is
only another view of the same thing.
"Multum enim interest inter cogni-
tionem, rei in Verbo Dei, et cogni-
tionem ejus in naturâ ejus; ut illud
merito ad diem pertineat, hoc ad
vesperam."—*De Gen. ad lit.* l. iv. c.
23, § 40.

[9]   In our version, and in the Hebrew, this is omitted in the work of
the second day; but it is to be found
here in the LXX.   There may, however, be a reason for this omission
on the second day.

[10]   Chap. i. 31.

It is thus with God. When He looks upon us, He ever sees what is of Christ, while a carnal brother perhaps is only seeing the sin and failure in us. It is God-like to see Christ in each other in the first stage of His work. One can scarce fail to see Him when the image of God is come. The thing is to see Him, as God sees Him, in the creature's change from the first. St. Paul in his Epistles always does this. If he reproves the darkness and calls it by its name, he sees the light also. Every Epistle begins with a recognition of what was good in each Church. The same may be seen in the Epistles to the Apocalyptic Churches. So Barnabas, who "was a good man, and full of the Holy Ghost," when he went to Antioch, "saw the grace of God" in the disciples.[11] Pilate would have seen only their weakness. For a devil can mark our faults, but it needs the grace of God to mark the dawn of grace. And even if the fruit is not mature, if the juice be sour, grace yet will say, "The vine with the tender grape gives a good smell."[12]

One thing more I notice here. The work of creation has two great parts; the work of the first three days answering to, and yet remarkably differing from, the work of the last three. In each half the order is alike, and the part of creation touched is the same. The difference is, that in the first three days the work is *bounding* and *dividing;* in the last three, *furnishing* and *adorning.*[13] In the first three days a separation takes place between, or is caused by, that

---

[11] Acts xi. 23, 24.

[12] Canticles ii. 13. "Vidit quia bonum. Vidit mihi, probavit mihi. Quod Deus probavit, tu reprehensibile ne dixeris. Quod Deus mundavit, tu commune ne dixeris. . . . Nec mirum si apud quem rerum perfectio, non in consummatione operis, sed in suæ prædestinatione es voluntatis, laudat singula, quasi convenientia futuris: laudat plenitudinem singulorum venustate compositam."—*Ambros. Hex.* l. ii. c. 5.

[13] "Opus *distinctionis* primis tribus diebus, opus *ornatûs* aliis tribus sequentibus."—*Lira, Postill. in loco.*

which is created of the Lord, and that which is proper to
the creature; by which what is natural to the creature is
restrained and bound: then the character of each is marked
by a name bestowed on each, the creature being thus made
to know the thoughts of God. On the first day light shines
out, and is divided from the darkness. Thus darkness at
once receives a bound. Then the light and darkness have
each a name bestowed:—"God called the light, Day, and the
darkness, Night."[14] On the second, the expanse comes in to
bound and divide the waters: then comes its name:— "God
called it, Heaven."[15] On the third, the earth appears, and
is divided from the seas, both at once receiving a name
from God in like manner.[16] Thus far the work is *dividing*
and *bounding*. In the next three days the order is the
same, but the work is *furnishing*. In these days we do
not find "*God called*," but "*God made;*"[17] this latter half
being throughout *perfecting*.

All this is yet fulfilled in regeneration, and will be apprehended by those who press on to " the perfect man."[18]
Half the process is *bounding*; a dividing in the creature
between that which is of self and that which is of God.
At this stage we are submitting to have what is natural to
us restrained, and thus learning to distinguish His work
from what is ours in us. At the same time we are taught
to call things as God calls them. After this, after the
third day, when resurrection power is known, (for on the
"third day" here as elsewhere resurrection comes out
clearly,) the work is to adorn or perfect rather than to
divide and bound. Light, and heaven, and earth now
are not only distinguished from their opposites; but each
gets furnished with the life or light suited to it. At this

---

[14] Chap. i. 5. [16] Chap. i. 10. [18] Eph. iv. 13.
[15] Chap. i. 8. [17] Chap. i. 16, 21, 25.

stage we perceive "*God made*," for, as the work proceeds, it is more and more seen that all is done by God.[19] From the first God had said, "Let there be," and "It was so:" but now it is seen, not only that "He spake and it was done," but further that "He did it." So true is it that advance in grace shews that all things are of God, and that only of His own do we give Him. We shall see this better as we come to each successive step; best of all, if we experimentally know the work within.

I now turn to the special work of each of the days in order, to trace the progressive steps of the new creation; for though the work has two great parts, first bounding, then adorning, yet each of these has steps, answering to the successive days. In these steps we shall be shewn how all the mind of God, that which was in the Son from everlasting,— whether light, or a heaven, or fruits, or heavenly lights, or the living creatures, or the man in God's image,— each form of light and life, once hid in Christ, is by the Word reproduced and manifested in the creature. The depths here are unfathomed; what is upon the surface will suffice to shew lengths and breadths more than enough for us.

II.— The First Day

THE work begins with light   God said, "Let there be light,"[1] and at once light shone where all before was dark. God says, "Repent ye — the kingdom of heaven is at

---

[19] "Fides autem nostra quodam gressu crescit : ideo primo fecit Deus, postea venustavit . . . . . Et fortasse dicant, cur non simul ornatus congruos donavit elementis ? . . . . . Ne verè increata et sine principio crederentur," &c. —*Ambros. Hexæm.* l. i. c. 7.

[1] Chap. i. 3.

hand:" then our darkness displeases us, and we are turned to light.[2] Thus of all those blessings hid in Christ from everlasting, and which are predestinated to be accomplished in the creature, light is the first that is bestowed: "God shines in our hearts to give the light of the knowledge of the glory of God in the face of Jesus Christ."[3] But the "heaven" announced "at hand" is yet unformed. No sun yet shines, no fruits adorn the creature. Many steps remain before the image of God will come, the man created in righteousness, to rule all things. But the light is come, and it is good: "truly the light is sweet," though as yet we cannot add, "and a pleasant thing it is to see the sun."[4] It is, however, yet "light" rather than "lights;"[5] not defined as it shall be; for as the voice differs from the word, so this light differs from that sun which appears in due season. Whether it is the reflected light of faith resting on the Church's witness, or the direct light of truth from Christ Himself within us, or whether it be something more undefined, is not yet perceived: it is at least "light," and "it is good." "God saw the light that it was good." After awhile the day-star too shall rise within.[6]

Then at once comes a division between what is of God and what is not; between the natural darkness in the creature and the light which God has made.[7] The dark-

---

[2] "Terra nostra antequam acciperet formam doctrinæ invisibilis erat et incomposita, et ignorantiæ tenebris tegebamur. Sed quia Spiritus tuus ferebatur super aquam, non reliquit miseriam nostram misericordia tua, et dixisti, 'Fiat lux,' 'penitentiam agite, appropinquavit enim regnum cœlorum,'" &c.—*Aug. Conf.* l. xiii. c. 12.

[3] 2 Cor. iv. 6.

[4] Eccl. xi. 7.

[5] The word here translated "*light*," is different from that used on the fourth day, and which is rendered "*lights*." The Vulgate translates the first by *lux*, the latter by *luminaria*, thus marking the difference. The LXX. also translate with two different words, using $\phi\hat{\omega}s$ in the third verse, and $\phi\omega\sigma\tau\hat{\eta}\rho\epsilon s$ in the fourteenth.

[6] 2 Pet. i. 19.

[7] Chap. i. 4.

ness is yet unchanged, but it is bounded by the light; each by its nature more clearly shewing what the other is : and these not mingled together, for " what fellowship hath light with darkness ?" but separate, as it is written,— " God divided the light from the darkness." This is a well-known stage. The light shines in darkness, but the darkness comprehends it not. Two conflicting powers are striving each to gain the day, making the old domain of darkness a continually shifting but ceaseless battle field.

Then a name is given by God both to light and darkness ;[8] that is, the character of each is learnt according to the mind of God. It is not yet seen indeed how the creature's darkness, like death, will bring to view still greater wonders of God's work in worlds of light innumerable. This is seen at a later stage, when in our night and darkness, yea even by it, the countless forms of God's light in heavenly places, which the day hides from sight, are made manifest. But now the darkness has at least a name. What God calls it, we call it. His thoughts are not altogether strange to us. Natural as the darkness may seem to the creature, God calls it " *night*," or *deviation*. It is a turning from the right or straight line.[9] The light is " *day*," or *movement* : there is a disturbance of the darkness. Death rules no longer ; life with light is come.[10] Besides in this name there is a form given to both. Until now light and darkness were

---

[8] Chap. i. 5.

[9] The word לילה, *night*, means *deviation*, from a root signifying to wind or turn. See Parkhurst's note on the word.

[10] The day, יום, "from י, *motion*, from the agitation of the celestial fluid, under the influence of the light." " A good telescope (on a hot day, the naked eye) will shew us what a tumult arises in the air from the agitation of the rays of light at noonday," &c. — *William Jones's Principles of Natural Philosophy*, p. 241, quoted by Parkhurst, *sub voce*.

unformed, but "day" and "night" intimate order and distribution. Night is darkness put within limits. So with light; it is not "day," till it is arranged and put in form and order.[11] When thus arranged, we can say, not of night only, but of darkness, "The day is thine, the night is thine also."[12] And though as yet on the face of the creature little is wrought, though as yet salt and barren waters may extend everywhere, a change has been effected by the light, the importance of which none can fully estimate but those who from being once darkness are now light in the Lord, and which shall advance step by step till God's will is done in the earth as it is in heaven.

Of this day I only add, that on it the creature's state is very slightly, if at all, realised. Whether waters cover it, — whether there is or is not a heaven, — (there is, I need not say, no heaven upon the first day,) — whether firm ground exists or not, this is not yet noticed. The second day must come before the tossing waves, which are uppermost everywhere, begin to be perceived. So with us. There is at first a general sense of sin; but what is the exact state of things is not perceived. There is light and darkness; but that no heaven is formed within, no firm earth, this as yet is overlooked. And great mercy is it that we learn what we are and lack by degrees; else surely we should at first despair.

III. — The Second Day

THE second day's work is the forming of an expanse or heaven in the creature, by which the hitherto unbounded

---

[11] "Non enim omnis lux dies, aut omnes tenebræ nox; sed lux et tenebræ certis inter se vicibus ordinatæ atque distinctæ, diei et noctis nominibus appellantur." — *Aug. de Gen. ad lit. lib. imperf.* c. 26.

[12] Psalm lxxiv. 16.

waters are divided from the waters. God then names the expanse.[1] At this stage the state of the creature, that it is drowned in waters, begins to be perceived.

Such is the second state or stage in the new creation. In the midst of the waters a heaven is formed in the once benighted creature. That unstable element, so quickly moved by storms, is the well-known type of the restless desires of the heart of fallen man ; for "the wicked are like the troubled sea, which cannot rest, whose waters cast up mire and dirt."[2] Before regeneration, unquiet lusts everywhere prevail: the whole man or creature is drowned and buried in them. In the progress of the new creation, these waters are not at once removed: indeed, they are never wholly removed till that other creation comes, when there is "no more sea."[3] They are first divided by a heaven ; then bounded on the third day, when the dry land rises up out of them. This heaven represents the understanding opened, as the rising earth upon the third day shews us the will liberated. For till now, "the understanding has been darkened ;"[4] nay, it is written of the natural man that he has "no understanding."[5] But now the heaven is stretched. Christ "opens the understanding" of those who before this had been His disciples.[6] And thus another precious gift, once hid with Christ in God, now by Christ is wrought in us also. A heaven is formed within the creature ; a heaven into which

[1] Chap. i. 6-8.

[2] Isa. lvii. 20. So Gregory the Great,— "Quid est mare, nisi cor nostrum, furore turbidum, rixis amarum, elatione superbiæ tumidum, fraude malitiæ obscurum ; quod mare, quantum sæviat, attendit quisquis in se occultas cogitationum tentationes intelligit. Ecce enim jam perversa relinquimus, jam desideriis rectis inhæremus, jam prava opera foris abscindimus ; sed tamen latenter intus eâ, cum quâ huc venimus, vitæ veteris procellâ fatigamur." *Moral. in Job* l. xxviii. c. 19, § 43.

[3] Rev. xxi. 1.

[4] Eph. iv. 18.

[5] Rom. iii. 11.

[6] Luke xxiv. 45, and compare Col. i. 9, ii. 2, and 1 John v. 20.

darkness may return, and through which clouds shall pour as well as bright sunshine; a heaven which for sin may be shut up and become like brass,[7] but which was made to be the home and treasure-house of sweet and dewy showers; a heaven, like Israel's path through the sea of old, sorely threatened by dark and thick waters, but, like that same path, a step to resurrection power, and worthy to be called "heaven," even by God Himself; influencing the earth in untold ways, here attracting, there repelling; the great means after light of arranging and disposing all things.[8] By it the waters are bounded. Until now, they have flowed hither and thither without a bound, and without a rest also. But the heaven is formed; then a bound is set, where hitherto the restless waters have prevailed.

Then again comes division. A heaven in the creature at once "divides the waters from the waters."[9] Some remain below; some are above or in the heaven. The waters henceforth are rent in twain. Some rise, purged of their saltness, and become the fruitful clouds, in which the bow of the covenant shall be set in due season. Some are yet the barren sea. And so within. Of our desires and affections, some are raised and purified, not without sore rendings; and some are as before, unquiet and unbounded, save by the heaven over them.[10]

After this the expanse receives a name from God. It is called "*heaven*," that is *the arranger*:[11] so called, because

---

[7] Lev. xxvi. 19; 1 Kings viii. 35.

[8] "Hoc nomine firmamenti ipsa tranquillitas et magna pax rerum significari potest; unde illud in Psalmis, 'Et veritas tua usque ad nubes.' Nihil enim firmius et serenius veritate."—*Aug. de Gen. ad lit. lib. imperf.* c. 14, § 45.

[9] Chap. i. 7.

[10] "Retulerint aliqui cœlos cœlorum ad intelligibiles virtutes, firmamentum ad operatorias . . . . Alii quoque purificatorias virtutes interpretati sunt aquas quæ super cœlos sunt."—*Ambros. Hexæm* l. ii. c. 4, § 17.

[11] "Heb. שׁמים, the *placers* or *arrangers*, from שׂם, to set or place;

this heaven, in ways above our thoughts, is the great agent in arranging everything. Little do men now think of the heavens, or perceive what forces around us are at work everywhere. We speak in our wisdom of the " three king-doms,"— the animal, vegetable, and mineral,— as if these three were all. Genesis will shew us yet another, on which all these depend. For as the animal depends upon the vegetable, and that upon the mineral, so the mineral itself depends upon another kingdom, which was yet earlier. Some have called it the meteoric. On this the mineral world depends, as the very names of some of the metals, come down to us from days when there was greater insight, yet testify. Now this " heaven," or meteoric kingdom,— formed of old over the earth, before the mineral, as that before the vegetable and animal,— was called by God *the arranger*, to effect great marvels, by what we now call attraction, repulsion, electricity, or eva-poration. And so the " heaven," which is formed within by the Word, is *the arranger*, and in that inward world must precede the gold and fruits and living creatures. Some have tried without this " heaven " to have gold and fruits and life. What have they got? Not God's work, but Satan's imitation. The heaven must be first within, if we would have true fruits, even as true fruits must precede the living creatures.

because the heavens are the agents in arranging things on earth. "This appellation was first given by God to the celestial fluid or air, when it began to act in *disposing* or *arranging* the earth and waters. And since that time the שמים have been the great agents in *disposing* all material things in their places and orders, and thereby producing all those wonderful effects which are attributed to them in Scrip-ture, and which it has been of late years the fashion to ascribe to *at-traction, gravitation,* &c."— Park-hurst's *Heb. Lex.* sub voce. It is worthy of notice that the ancient Greeks derived θεοὺς from θέσις; for the same reasons.—*Herodot.* l. ii. c. 52.

Further, I observe, on this second day, that the creature's state begins to be discerned. The waters now are not overlooked, as upon the first day. It is now noticed that below the heaven all is buried in them; and this discovery, though painful, is a step to better things. Still, as yet there is no earth, nothing " stablished, strengthened, settled; " [12] but this, too, comes in due season.

IV.—The Third Day

FOR on the third day the earth emerges from the waters.[1] Up to this point the unquiet element, which is naturally uppermost in the creature, has prevailed everywhere. Light has come, and shewn the waste; a heaven is formed within it; but nothing fixed or firm has yet appeared. Just as in the saint there is first light, and a heaven too within, while as yet he is all instability, with nothing firm or settled. But now the firm earth rises. The state desired by Paul,—" that we be no more tossed to and fro with every wind of doctrine, but may grow up in all things into Him who is the Head, even Christ," [2]—here begins to be accomplished. Now the will, long buried and overwhelmed with tossing lusts, rises above them to become very fruitful; and the soul, once lost in passions, emerges from the deep, like " the earth which He hath founded for ever."

This earth rises out of the waters. Above their storms and waves something fixed appears, setting a limit to them. Seas yet may remain; at times they roar against the land; but from this time they cannot overflow it. " He hath set a bound that they may not pass over, that they turn not again to cover the earth." [3]   " He hath

---

[12] 1 Pet. v. 10.   [1] Chap. i. 9.   [2] Eph. iv. 14, 15.   [3] Psalm civ. 9.

placed the sand for the bound of the sea, by a perpetual decree that it cannot pass it ; and though the waves thereof toss themselves, yet can they not prevail; though they roar, yet can they not pass over it." [4] And when we think what a bound it is—the shifting sand ; when we think how, as the wise man says, " all the rivers,—all the torrents of passion,—run into the sea, yet it overflows not ;" [5] when we think how oft it rages under the gales of lust, and yet the dry land fails not, nor sinks before it; we must confess God's hand in its preservation, as in its first appearing, and that it is His word and will that keep the bound. For " He shut up the sea with bars and doors, when it broke forth, as if it had issued out of the womb : He said, Hitherto shalt thou come, and no further, and here shall thy waves of pride be stayed." [6] Nay, more. Here, as in all things, " out of the eater comes forth meat, and out of the strong comes forth sweetness." [7] Not only do the waves not destroy the earth, but the rough gales borne from their vexed bosom are full of health and bracing. We could not afford to lose them. Trying as they are for a while, and most hurtful if we have not some protection, the gales of lust and temptation will strengthen while they move us : by them noxious exhalations are carried far away. In the world to come we shall want no storms; therefore " no sea " is there. Here we need it ; therefore it is left in love to try us. Yea, these seas and their roaring may praise the Lord, for He sitteth King above the water-floods; and all their tempests within, like the wrath of man without, in ways above our present thoughts, yet praise Him. [8] But the work here, the rising

---

[4] Jer. v. 22.　　　　[6] Job xxxviii. 8, 11.
[5] Eccl. i. 7.　　　　[7] Judges xiv. 14.
　　　　　[8] Psalm lxxvi. 10.

earth, is to restrain these waves. Good may come out of their roarings; the greater good, the special work of this day, is to bound them, to form a fixed and quiet habitation. So the earth is freed. Need I repeat the lesson here, that it is by checking our desires—by bounding the unstable element in us—that the man is made free?[9]

There is yet more for us to mark in this emerging earth. Not only does it escape the floods: it comes up also into the expanse of heaven. That creature, so long buried, now mounts up to meet the skies, as though aspiring to touch and become a part of heaven; while on its swelling bosom rest the sweet waters, the clouds, which embrace and kiss the hills. When the man by resurrection is freed from restless lusts; when he comes up from under the dominion of passions into a state of rest and peace; not only is he delivered from a load, but he also meets a purer world, an atmosphere of clear and high blessing; where even his hard rocks may be furrowed into channels for the rain; heaven almost touching earth, and earth heaven.

Not without awful convulsions can such a change be wrought. The earth must heave before the waters are gathered into one place. The Psalmist marks this, when he says, " The waters stood above the hills:" then—" at

---

[9] " Conclusit ostiis mare; quia nisi ab ipso cogitationis primordio cordis fluctus gratia divina retineret, tentationum procellis mare sæviens terram proculdubio humanæ mentis obruisset : ut salsis fluctibus perfusa aresceret, id est, perniciosis carnis voluptatibus delectata deperiret. Solus ergo Dominus ostiis mare concludit, qui pravis motibus cordis claustra inspirata formidinis objicit. Quia verò ea, quæ cernimus, sequi prohibemur, quia a corporearum rerum delectatione retundimur : libet etiam ad invisibilia oculos mentis attollere," &c.—*Greg. M. Moral. in Job*, l. xxviii. c. 19, § 43. The whole passage to the end of the book is very striking, and will amply repay any reader the trouble of turning to it.

thy rebuke they fled; at the noise of thy thunder they hasted away: they go up by the mountains, they go down by the valleys, unto the place which Thou hast founded for them." [10] Some have felt all this within: the earth clean dissolved—the earth broken down and moved exceedingly—the earth reeling like a drunkard, and removed like a cottage—preparatory to binding the host of lusts which have held sway over it; till they are gathered together as prisoners in a pit, and shut up in their prison. Many a soul shews rents and chasms like the steep mountains. Nevertheless, "the mountains bring peace, and the little hills righteousness."

And this is effected on the third or resurrection day; for in creation, as elsewhere, the "third day" always speaks of resurrection. [11] We shall see in the development of Adam or man that the *third* great life, I mean Noah's, is regeneration; for in man, as in the earth, much is wrought ere the flood is passed. The earth rises not before the third day. Just so in the world within: much is done before this day, before we know anything of "the power of resurrection." [12] But "after two days He will revive us; in the third day He will raise us up, and we shall live in His sight. Then shall we know, if we follow on to know the Lord." [13]

Then the earth being raised, and so separated from the waters, a name is bestowed on both by God. "The dry land He called Earth; and the gathering together of the waters, Seas." [14] Here, as elsewhere, the name is characteristic; and, in this instance, it seems easy to trace the

---

[10] Psalm civ. 7, 8.

[11] The "*third day*" is resurrection in one aspect, as *deliverance from the grave*; for there are other aspects of resurrection, as the "*first*" and "*eighth*" day. The book of Leviticus will be unintelligible till we see this. Compare Hosea vi. 2; Luke xiii. 32; 1 Cor. xv. 4.

[12] Phil. iii. 10.

[13] Hosea vi. 2, 3.

[14] Chap. i. 10.

thought intended to be conveyed by these titles. The
word " *seas,*" in the Hebrew, means *tumults* or *agitations.*[15]   The word " *earth,*" like our word " ground,"
describes a substance which will suffer itself to be reduced to powder, and so is fitted to take any form as
God pleases; ready to be framed by the will and wisdom
of the Great Potter, to be animal or vegetable, as He
will.[16]   For, indeed, tree or beast, of earth they are, to
earth they return.   Earth is the pliant clay from which
their forms come.   It is " *earth*;" therefore a creature
meet to be used, ready to be transformed into fruits or
bodies, according to the will of God.   Need I apply this
within ?   Surely, till we are such " *earth*" or " *ground,*"
broken and ready to take what form He pleases, though
the light is come, fruits will be wanting; for to this day it
is " out of the ground that the Lord God makes every tree
to grow." [17]

Then the earth brings forth fruit.[18] Fruitfulness, hitherto
delayed, at once follows the bounding of the waters.   For,
" being made free from sin, we have fruit unto righteousness, and the end everlasting life." [19]   The order of the
produce is instructive; first the grass, then the herb, then

---

[15] Heb. ימים, from ים, tumult.

[16] Heb. ארץ. "Various etymo-
logies have been by learned men
proposed of this word; the most
probable seems to be that which derives it from רץ, *breaking in pieces,
crumbling.* 'The matter of earth,'
says the great Boerhaave, 'appears
friable or crumbling, so long as it
continues under the observation of
our senses, as it always readily
suffers itself to be reduced to a finer
powder.'   And it is manifest, that
on this remarkable property of *Earth,*
its answering the end of its creation,

or its usefulness in continually supplying the waste of vegetable and
animal bodies, must depend.   It is
not improbable that the Greek word
χθὼν, from the Hebrew כת, *to pound
to pieces,* the Latin *terra,* from *tero,
to wear away,* and the English *ground,*
from *grind,* all aimed at the same
etymological reasons."—Parkhurst,
Heb. Lex. sub voc.

[17] Chap. ii. 9.
[18] Chap. i. 11.
[19] Rom. vi. 22. "Si enim istas aquas
quæ sunt sub cœlo non separavimus a
nobis, id est peccata et vitia corporis

the fruit-tree yielding fruit after his kind:[20] as ever, the blade before the ear, the small before the great, from imperfection onwards to perfection. The first thing borne is "grass," the common emblem of the flesh.[21] Is it asked how the risen creature can bring forth fruits, which are, like the goodliness of the grass, of the flesh and carnal? Because for long the regenerate man is yet "carnal," and his fruits are in the flesh, though with sincere desires for God's glory. The development of Adam, as exhibited in the Word, not to say experience, gives proofs on proofs of this. The Corinthians, too, were "carnal," though with many spiritual gifts.[22] But after "grass" comes "herb and tree," with "seed and fruit;" some to feed the hungry, some to cure the serpent's bite; some hid in a veil of leaves, or bound in shapeless husks; some exposing their treasures, as the lovely vine and olive; the one to cheer man's heart, the other to give the oil to sustain the light for God's candlestick. Such is the faithful soul, with many-coloured fruits, "as the smell of a field which the Lord blesses."[23] The form of the fruit may vary; its increase may be less or more—some thirty, some sixty, some an hundredfold; for "the fruit of the Spirit may be love, or peace, or faith, or truth, or gentleness:"[24] but all to the praise of His grace, who bringeth forth fruit out of the earth, "fruits of righteousness, which are by Jesus Christ."[25]

---

nostri, arida nostra non poterit apparere, nec habere fiduciam procedendi ad lucem. (Referring to the connection between this day's work and the lights on the fourth day, to which this third day was a step.) Omnis enim qui malè agit odit lucem, et non venit ad lucem, ut non manifestarentur opera ejus: quæ utique fiducia non aliter dabitur, nisi velut aquas abjiciamus a nobis."—*Origen.in Gen. Hom.* i. fol. 1.

[20] Chap. i. 11.

[21] 1 Pet. i. 24.

[22] Compare 1 Cor. i. 4, 7, with 1 Cor. ii. 1, 4.

[23] Gen. xxvii. 27.

[24] Gal. v. 22.

[25] Phil. i. 11. "At animas sitientes tibi, et apparentes tibi alio

Nor let us forget,—" whose seed is in itself, after his kind."[26] God's fruits all multiply themselves : this is their constitution. The tree propagates itself; every fruit produces more: so every act of charity has in it the seed of other acts. As one lie breeds another, so one truth produces more. Love bears love, anger, anger, and kindness, kindness. There is another and higher fruitfulness, which we get on the last two days; yet this of the third day is lovely in its season. The law of creation cannot change. God has said, " Let the tree yield fruit after his kind, whose seed is in itself." Every act, therefore, will yield its fruits; " the seed is in itself," to propagate itself in increasing measure from age to age, even for ever.

It only remains to notice that at this important stage the state of the creature is no longer unperceived. What it shall be, is not known; but what it is, seems realised on this third or resurrection day. Not till this stage is the creature known. And so throughout the last dispensation, because the creature was not known, resurrection was not apprehended. But after resurrection it is seen what the creature is in itself, and the change which God has wrought in it. On this day the light is seen, the seas are seen, the heaven is seen, and, last in order, the earth is seen with herb and

---

fine distinctas a societate maris, occulto et dulci fonte irrigas, ut et terra det fructum suum, et dat fructum suum, et te jubente Domino Deo suo germinat anima nostra opera misericordiæ, secundum genus, diligens proximum in subsidiis necessitatum carnalium, habens in se semen secundum similitudinem, quoniam ex nostrâ infirmitate compatimur ad subveniendum indigentibus; similiter optitulantes quemadmodum nobis vellemus opem ferri, si eodem modo indigeremus; non tantum in facilibus, tanquam in herbâ seminali, sed etiam in protectione adjutorii forti robore, sicut lignum fructiferum, præbenbo protectionis umbraculam." *Aug. Confess.* l. xiii. c. 17, § 21. So, too, Gregory the Great, *Moral. in Job*, l. vi. c. 35, § 54. So also Origen. *Hom.* i. *in Gen.*, and Ambros. *Hex.* l. iii. c. 7, § 31.

[26] Chap. i. 11.

tree. On this day the separating process ends; for things are known. What is now wanted is *perfecting*; and this is next accomplished.[27]

Such is the work of the first three days, deepening at every step; first *light* upon the deep; then a *heaven* in the midst of the waters, which lie uppermost; then a lifting up and working upon that which was lower still, *the earth*, which until now had been buried and concealed. Some have learnt this deepening process. I observe, too, that the work was comparatively slow until the third day. Upon this day God speaks twice;[28] and the amount of work is equal to or exceeding that of the two preceding days. Surely it is a mighty change. Twice on the third day is it repeated, " And God saw that it was good."[29] If we have reached the third day, we shall know how good it is. If we have not reached it, let us pray and wait for it.

V.—THE FOURTH DAY

HITHERTO we have traced but one half of the work which God accomplishes upon the creature which is subject to His word. Now, having reached "the third day," we pass from the stages in which the work for the most part

---

[27] Augustine thus briefly sums up the inward fulfilment of the work of the first three days:—" Habet etiam unusquisque nostrûm in bonis operibus et rectâ vitâ tanquam distinctos istos sex dies, post quos debet quietem sperare. Primo die lucem fidei, quando prius invisibilibus credit, propter quam fidem Dominus visibiliter apparere dignatus est. Secundo die tanquam firmamentum disciplinæ, quo discernit inter carna-lia et spiritalia, sicut inter aquas inferiores et superiores. Tertio die, quo mentem suam ad ferendos bonorum operum fructus, a labe et fluctibus tentationum carnalium, tanquam aridam terram a perturbationi-bus maris secernit, ut jam possit dicere, Mente servio legi Dei, carne autem legi peccati."—*De Gen. contra Manich.* l. i. c. 25, § 43.

[28] Chap. i. 9, 11.

[29] Chap. i. 10, 12.

is *bounding* and *restraining,* to those where the work
is *adorning* and *perfecting*; when, the distinction being
clearly made between what is of God and what is natural
to the creature, He proceeds to furnish all the various
parts with the forms of light and life suited to each. At
this stage, when the earth is raised into heavenly places,
many seem to think the work is done. But now begins
the perfecting and adorning process, which does not cease
until "the image of God" appears. So St. Paul, writing to
the Colossians, exhorts to growth in grace in language
exactly answering to the stages of creation which we are
now to enter on; starting from, "If ye be risen," and
leading on the Church to "put on the new man, which is
renewed in the image of Him that created him."[1] So he
says, "If ye be risen, seek things above:" look for things
in heaven, to comfort and enlighten you. Lights to guide,
hitherto unknown, will shine upon you, making alternate
seasons rich with blessing. Then again advance: — "Put
on, as the elect of God, bowels of mercies, kindness, humbleness of mind, longsuffering." Put on the graces which
are prefigured in the dove and lamb and ox, which appear
in season upon the fifth and sixth days. And then "put on
the new man, which is renewed in knowledge after the
image of Him that created him." So writes Paul, "without
a veil;" so writes Moses, "with a veil," "which veil is done
away in Christ."[2]

We are then to trace the stages after resurrection-life is
known, through resurrection-lights, till we reach "the
moving creature," first creeping, then walking, but with
face earthwards; and then "the man," with open face,
erect, and looking upward.

---

[1] Col. iii. 1, 10.   [2] 2 Cor. iii. 14.

The fourth day's work is "lights set in heaven:" [3] a mighty work: more glorious far than the "light" upon the first day. Then the light was undefined. Now lights are come; the one with warmth; the other cold but shining: each defined; one direct, the other reflex; but both to rule and mightily affect, not the earth only, but even the wide waters: giving another check, too, to darkness, not only taking from it Day, but invading and conquering it by the moon and stars in its own domain of Night.

And so after that the seas of lust are bounded, and the fruits of righteousness begin to grow and bud, a sun, a mighty light, is kindled in our heaven,—Christ dwells there, God's eternal word and wisdom,—no longer undefined, but with mighty warmth and power, making the whole creation to bud and spring heavenward; while as a handmaid, another light, of faith, grows bright within,— our inward moon, the Church's light, or truth received on testimony; for as men say, Christ is the sun, the Church the moon, so is faith our moon within to rule the night. [4] Of these two, the lesser light must have appeared the first; for each day grew and was measured "from the evening to the morning;" just as faith, with borrowed light, in every soul still precedes the direct beams of the greater light of the Word of Wisdom in us. Now both shine to pour down light. Oft should we err, if, when darkness fell, our moon of faith rose not to rule the night. Yet fair as

[3] Chap. i. 14, 15.

[4] Those instructed in the Word will not only find no difficulty in seeing how the moon, which outwardly is the Church, is faith inwardly, but further know that there must be this double application, as in the well-known case of Hagar and Sarah. Outwardly, Hagar is the Jewish dispensation, which stood on law, and Sarah is the Christian Church, which stands on faith. But these dispensations of God have their course in individual souls, and in this inward application Hagar is law, and Sarah the promise, or the gospel. See Gal. iv. 22, 31.

she is, she but reminds us of present night, making us sigh for the day-star and the perfect day. Thus are "the two great lights" now given by Him who began His work by giving "light." Now He gives the word of wisdom, that is the greater light; and again the word of knowledge or faith, that is the lesser light; then tongues, or discerning of spirits, or healings, like the stars, lesser manifestations of the same one Spirit.[5]

That such lights, so different and so defined, may be within, is never known by some who yet have been enlightened. The first day's light has reached them: perhaps the heaven has come: but the waters are not bounded; the earth as yet is not fruitful. To such the difference of lights and their distinct powers must be unknown. Let it not therefore be unlooked for by them. Not till the earth has brought forth fruit are these bright lights set in heaven.

---

[5] This is Augustine's exposition. Speaking of this fourth day, he says:—"Æterno consilio propriis temporibus bona cœlestia das super terram. Quoniam alii datur per Spiritum sermo sapientiæ tanquam luminare majus, propter eos qui perspicuæ veritatis luce delectantur tanquam in principio diei; alii autem sermo scientiæ secundum eumdem Spiritum, tanquam luminare minus; alii fides, alii donatio curationum, alii prophetia, alii dijudicatio spirituum, alteri genera linguarum; et hæc omnia tanquam stellæ. Omnia enim hæc operatur unus atque idem Spiritus, faciens apparere sidera in manifestatione ad utilitatem. Sermo autem scientiæ, quâ continentur omnia sacramenta, quæ variantur temporibus tamquam luna, et ceteræ notitiæ donorum, quæ deinceps tanquam stellæ commemorata sunt, quantum differunt ab illo candore sapientiæ, quo gaudet prædictus dies, tantum in principio noctis sunt," &c. *Confess.* l. xiii. c. 18, § 23. The place here given to sacraments is worthy of notice. Augustine makes them only parts of the lesser light. They are no part of the sun, which rules the day, but only of the moon, that is, the word of faith or knowledge. See also *Aug. de Gen. c. Man.* l. i. c. 25, § 43. Origen's comment is the same in substance:—"Sicut in firmamento isto, quod jam cœlum fuerat appellatum, jubet Deus fieri luminaria, ita et in nobis fieri potest. Si studeamus vocari et effici cœlum, luminaria habebimus in nobis, quæ illuminent nos, Christum et ecclesiam ejus.... Quæ sunt autem in nobis stellæ, id est in cordis nostri cœlo? Moyses stella est in nobis quæ lucet, et Esaias, et Daniel," &c.—*Hom.* i. *in Gen.*

The lower fruitfulness of action must precede the higher delights of heavenly contemplation. Not till some fruits appear shall we be adorned with heavenly lights. Then not only is the earth blessed with dews and showers, " the precious things of heaven;" but " precious things are now brought forth by the sun, and precious things put forth by the moon also."[6] Now we perceive wherein the borrowed light of faith, resting on witness, differs from the direct light of truth, from Christ Himself within. Henceforward even the night is bright with stars : darkness is conquered even within its own borders. Faith invades the gloom, turning it at times almost to day, an approach to the glory, when " no night is there;"[7] now waxing, now waning, but never to fall or fail, until " our sun shall no more go down, neither our moon withdraw itself."[8] Now we see, too, how the creature's darkness, like death, only brings into view the greater wonders of God's work in heavenly places. Darkness shews us that the earth has a celestial suite, bright companions in heaven night and day waiting on it; moving it with celestial influences, its air, its earth, its tides; giving colour, warmth, motion, life, everywhere. Who can count all that is given from on

[6] Deut. xxxiii. 13, 14. " Bene autem terra germinavit primò, et postea facta sunt luminaria; quia post bona opera venit illuminatio, quâ videtur species supernæ veritatis."—*Isidor. in Gloss. Ordinar.* Augustine notices the same :—" Quibus in terrâ natis fructibus, et erumpat temporanea lux nostra, et de istâ inferiori fruge actionis in delicias contemplationis verbum vitæ superiùs obtinentes, appareamus sicut luminaria in firmamento cohærentes." *Confess.* l. xiii. c. 18, § 22. Again,

" Sed prius lavamini, mundi estote, auferte nequitiam ut appareat arida. Discite bonum facere, ut germinet terra herbam pabuli et lignum fructiferum ; . . . ut fiant luminaria in firmamento cœli," &c. *Id. ibid.* § 24. He goes on to instance the young man in the Gospel, (Matt. xix. 16.) as one who, because he bore not fruit, could not advance to see the heavenly lights.

[7] Rev. xxi. 25.

[8] Isa. lx. 19, 20.

high, when we can see that our wondrous path is not indeed a lone one,—that a heavenly sun attracts,—that a heavenly moon follows,—that, though darkness may visit us, henceforth it does not rule us, but is ruled, and that even in the night which still remains in us, we have the presence of Jesus the mediator of the better covenant, and the Church of the First-born, and the spirits of just men made perfect, and an innumerable company of holy angels, who, like the morning stars, are singing all around? In bright days their quiet song, wherein they tell God's glory, may not be heard; yet they watch and sing and go with us. The gloomy night will bring them into view, still ready to teach us if we have a heart to learn.

These lights are " for signs and for seasons and for years," and " to rule over the day and over the night also."[9] For " signs "—first, of what we are. We have thought this earth is fixed: but sun and moon shew that we are but wanderers here. We have supposed ourselves the centre; that it is the sun that moves. The lights will teach us in due time that he is steadfast: it is we who journey on. Again, these lights are " for a sign " how we stand, and where we are; by our relative positions toward them shewing us, if we will learn, our real situation. For the moon is new and feeble, when, between us and the sun, it trenches on his place, and sets at eventide. So is our faith: put in Christ's place, it must be weak: dark will be our night: we shall move on unillumined. Not so when in her place, not in His, but over against Him, our moon of faith rises at even, as our Sun withdraws Himself. Now she trenches not upon Him; therefore she is full of light, making the midnight almost as the noon-day. So it is

[9] Chap. i. 14, 18.

said, " Blow up the trumpet in the new moon ; "[10] and when the moon is full " eat ye the Paschal Lamb ; "[11] that is, let the trumpet of the gospel sound, when faith is weak : when faith is strong, rejoice together in communion. Thus are the lights " for signs " of what and where we are. Dimmed by mists, they tell also of what remains in us. Turned to darkness and to blood, they forewarn of awful fire, when the earth and the works therein shall be burned up.[12] Signs they are, too, to the man, when at length he walks upon the earth,—the image of God, which after fruits and lights is formed in us,—to guide him through the wastes within the creature, as he seeks to know its lengths and breadths that he may subdue it all.

Thus are the lights " for signs : " but they are " for seasons " also ;[13] to give healthful alternations of cold and heat, and light and darkness. Sharp winters with their frosts, chill and deadness in our affections, and the hours of darkness which recur to dim our understandings, are not unmixed evil. In the coming rest such alternations will not be needed : therefore no summer or winter or shades of night are there. Here, like the gales from the ocean, they remind us of our state, and in that state work in the creature what is really best for it. We could not bear, while as we are, unbroken day. It would, though we know it not, destroy the creature. Ceaseless summer would wear us out : therefore the lights are " for seasons," measuring out warmth and light as we can profit by it. So faith wanes and waxes, and Christ is seen and hid, each change making the creature learn its own dependence ; forcing it to feel, that, though blessed, it is a creature, all whose springs of life and joy are not its own.

---

[10] Psalm lxxxi. 3, 5.

[11] Exod. xii. 6, &c.

[12] Luke xxi. 25, and 2 Pet. iii. 10.

[13] Chap. i. 14.

These lights, too, are " to rule over the day and over the night." To rule the creature, much more to rule such gifts as the day, wrought by God Himself in it, as yet has been unknown. Even to bound the natural darkness hitherto has seemed high attainment. Now we learn that the precious gifts, which God vouchsafes, need ruling ; an earnest this of that which comes more fully on the sixth day. A sun "to rule the day" leads to the man " to have dominion," set to rule, not the day only, but every creature. It is no slight step, when God's aim, hitherto unknown, is learnt ; that in His work this gift is for this, that for the other purpose ; when it is felt that the best gifts may be misused and wasted ; that they need governing, and may and must be ruled. No young Christian feels this ; but as he grows up into Christ, his day not only shines, but is divinely governed. The sun now marks the hours, setting to each their bound : morning is discerned from noon, and noon from evening. O blessed day, when the creature comes to bask in sunshine ; gift on gift poured on it in due order from the God of all grace !

VI.—The Fifth Day

The fifth day's work is the peopling of the sea and air.[1] Animate life now is added to inanimate. The waters swarm with life, and the air with winged tribes, which wake the woods and vales with melody. Thus, too, is it within, when on us the fifth day dawns. Now higher forms of life appear everywhere ; each new form yet more revealing in the creature that which hitherto had only been reasured up in the mind of God for it. For we must

[1] Chap. i. 20, 21.

never forget, that all this wondrous work, which step by step is thus produced in us, is only the developing in the creature of that which had been in Christ, the wisdom of God, from everlasting. For God will stamp Himself upon us. His will is that His fulness should be revealed in us; that as we have borne the image of the earthy, we now may bear the image of the heavenly. We have seen how several glories,—light, a heaven, fruits, and lights,—once hid in Him, by Him are wrought in us. Each of these was a precious gift, and worthy of the Lord, transforming the creature from its natural state of ruin to light and fair order. But now come higher blessings, forms of life unknown before, multiplying first in the air and waters, then upon the dry land.

We have seen what the waters and the heaven are within,—the former the desires, the latter the understanding. With the waters until now little has been done save to bound them. Desires are checked in us, but this is all. Now new life moves in them, the varied fish and fowl, all figuring some of the countless forms of Christ's spirit. For such is Christ's fulness, that no one type can express it; and His will is that of this fulness we should be filled also; " to know the love of Christ which passeth knowledge, that we might be filled with all the fulness of God." [2] The light, or a heaven, or the seed, or sun and moon, each was but some manifestation in the creature of what had been in Him. So the turtle and the eagle, now created, are but types of some fresh gift or grace of Christ's spirit; "diversities of gifts, but the same spirit; differences of administration, but the same Lord." [3] For just as in nature matter is one in all its forms, so in the new creation is the spirit one in all its transformations. The

[2] Eph. iii. 19. [3] 1 Cor. xii. 4, 5.

revelation only widens as the work proceeds. In due time the lion and ox and man are seen also; each a yet further expression of something in God's mind, which by His Word through grace is wrought in us.

But the forms and natures of the creatures made this day, like the light and fruits, will best explain themselves. The dove is the well-known figure of meek innocence. So at Christ's baptism the Spirit "like a dove" came and abode on Him.[4] The eagle's lofty flight and keen vision represent but another form of the same Divine Spirit. He who says, "I bare you upon eagles' wings,"[5] gives us also to "mount up with wings as eagles;"[6] for "of His fulness we all receive, and grace answering to His grace."[7] The other fowls of heaven, as the law shews us, both the clean and the unclean, each taught their own lesson; expressing in the difference of their lives and natures those faculties and emotions which give a form to life.[8] Since the fall these emotions are mostly evil. Hence, in Scripture, birds are generally a type of evil spirits.[9] The dragon and the whale too are used as evil.[10] But they are only evil because fallen. In themselves they simply represent certain forms of life, good if dependent, evil if independent. Just as Satan, once an angel, is now a devil, and all his light and knowledge are accursed; so the powers of the understanding, figured by the birds, are good, and through self-will only become evil.[11] I know the eagle-eye which loves to gaze on light, and the soaring thought which delights to

---

[4] Matt. iii. 16.
[5] Exod. xix. 4.
[6] Isa. xl. 31.
[7] John i. 16.
[8] Lev. xi. 9–23.
[9] Matt. xiii. 4; Rev. xviii. 2.
[10] Ezek. xxix. 3, and xxxii. 2.

[11] This explains how the same type may be either good or bad. Christ is a "lion." Rev. v. 5. But Satan also is a "lion." 1 Pet. v. 8. The same is true also in countless other instances.

mount upward, and the searching spirit which finds a pleasure in fathoming great deeps,—"for the spirit searcheth all
things, yea the deep things of God,"—may all be misused
through self, and so be spoilt; for I know no good gift of
God which may not become a curse to us. But the faculty
as given by the Lord is good, and the thoughts or emotions
which are formed to soar upward, or to dive into that depth
which yet remains in us, may all tell forth the Lord's
glory. Therefore "the dragons, and the beasts, and creeping things, and flying fowl," as much as "sun and moon,
and heaven, and fruitful trees," are called to praise Him.[12]
As formed upon the fifth day they speak His praise, "saying, Glory to Him that sitteth upon the throne, and to the
Lamb for ever."[13]

The details here would open an endless field; for the
natures of these creatures vary, yet cannot be misunderstood. We have seen the dove and eagle, but others
preach also, exhorting us to look for like powers to be

---

[12] Psalm cxlviii.

[13] Rev. v. 13, 14. Augustine explains the "moving creatures" to
be *emotions.* "Pisces maris et volatilia cœli et repentes omnes quæ
repunt super terram . . . rectè in-
telligantur spiritualiter ut omnes
affectiones et motus animi, quos
habemus istis animalibus similes."
De Gen. c. Manich. l. i. c. 20.
Further on in the same book, c. 25,
he says, "Fortior effectus incipit
quinto die operari . . . producere
animarum vivarum reptilia, id est
opera quæ prosint animis vivis, et
cetos magnos, id est fortissimas
actiones, quibus fluctus sæculi di-
rumpuntur, et volatilia cœli, id est
voces cœlestia prædicantes." See
also *Confession.* l. v. c. 3, § 4. Origen says, " Secundum literam jussu
Dei producuntur ab aquis repentia
et volatilia. Videamus quomodo
secundum nostrum firmamentum
cœli, id est mentis nostræ vel cordis
soliditatem, hæc eadem fiant. Arbitror quia si mens nostra illuminata
fuerit a nostro sole Christo, jubetur
postmodum ex his quæ in eâ sunt
aquis producere repentia et volatilia,
id est cogitationes bonas. . . . Si
sit in nobis sensus ut etiam si duo
minuta habeamus, hæc ipsa pro mi-
sericordiâ offeramus in dona Dei,
iste sensus avis est, nihil de terrenis
cogitans. . . . Si ascendat nobis
sensus et cogitatio talis, ut usque ad
mortem pro veritate certemus, avis
hæc, a terrenis ad superna conscen-
dens. Similiter etiam de cæteris,"
&c.—*Hom.* i. *in Gen.*

created in us; some to sing by day, as the thrush; and some, like the nightingale, to wake the dark hours; some with clarion, like the cock, to foretell the morning, and bid the sleepers arise to greet the day; some, like vultures, far-seeing, to seek their meat from far; some, like the swallow, to live as pilgrims here; some, like cranes, to fly in ranks, and know the seasons, and watch while others sleep around; some to care for the aged, as the stork; or, like the turtle, once widowed never so to pair again. Each tells its own story of what God can work, and the rich profusion of form in which the same life may shew itself. And these increase. Some heavenly gifts, as the lights of the fourth day, can never multiply. They may rise and set, and bring round springs and winters; but they do not increase by generation. But when the fifth day comes, the forms of heavenly life then given may increase greatly. For God has said, " Be fruitful and multiply."[14] And just as the fruits formed upon the third day, " whose seed is in themselves," reproduce themselves and grow rapidly, so do the graces of the fifth day spread wondrously. And when this has come, the image of God is near, when the work shall cease, for all is " very good."

VII.—The Sixth Day

To this last stage of the work we now proceed, when the earth also having brought forth its living creatures, man, the image of God, His last and crowning gift, is set to rule as lord of all. This is the sixth day's work. Now the life of the Lamb and Man is added to the likeness of the Dove in the redeemed creature.

[14] Chap. i. 22.

These forms speak for themselves. They are but the continuation, in greater perfection, of the work of the fifth day. Then the work was in the seas and heaven: now the earth, that is the will, brings forth in like manner. I need not here repeat what I have said, upon the fifth day, as to the principle on which these living creatures are to be interpreted; how they represent emotions good in themselves, only evil when fallen and independent; the living creatures of the earth representing the emotions connected with the will; the birds of heaven those connected with the understanding.[1] The instinct of mankind has always read these forms aright, nor has the difference of age or country made any difference in their interpretation. To this day, wherever the primitive language of symbol yet remains, the passions are still characterised by the names of different beasts. And those to whom heaven is opened see "the living creatures" there, in the midst of the throne of God, and round about it,[2] proving that powers like to these creatures, if not in God, may yet be most holy and very near to Him. It was but the perversion of this very truth, seeing in these creatures some trace or glimpse of the Divine, which ended in the worship of the creature, as in Egypt, where the ox and other beasts were deified; just as, to this day, in mystic Egypt, those gifts which are given as witnesses for God are made to take His place; the creature, in whom some trace of God is seen, being worshipped instead of the Creator. Still the gifts are good, each added form expressing but some further fulness which was in Christ Jesus: the ox, the spirit of unselfish toil;[3] the lion, that

---

[1] Respecting the heaven and the earth, as figuring the understanding and will respectively, see above on the second and third days. Both have their own emotions.

[2] Rev. iv. 6, 8.   [3] 1 Cor. ix. 9.

holy wrath in which we may judge and be angry, and yet sin not;[4] the lamb, that meekness which beareth all things, which is oppressed and afflicted, and yet openeth not its mouth.[5] These and like gifts now appear, till at length the man is seen, the "image of God," to crown and perfect all.

What is this image? It is the mind of God; for Christ is that Mind or Word to rule in us. The man is Christ, the perfect mind of God. The light, and heaven, and herb, and moving creature, were all but partial glimpses of Him, preludings of that perfect revelation which should be seen in God's image. That image now is come, to rule all things, itself containing all within itself. O the depth that opens here! Who shall take the measure of that which is the likeness of the immeasurable God? For He made the heaven, and yet He rested not,—the earth and its fruits, and yet He rested not,—the sun, and the moon, and the creatures of the sea, and sky, and of the earth, and yet He rested not. But He made man, His image in the earth, and then He rested; for it was "very good."

This image is the mind of God in us. When this is come, the "man" is formed, erect in walk, and looking upward, able to recognise the mind and will of One above him, with an understanding to know, and a will to love, God. This it is which marks man: a mind able to understand and bow to a superior. Lose this, and we at once become as beasts, incapable of recognising, save by force, the will of One above us; "like the horse or mule which

---

[4] Eph. iv. 26.

[5] Isa. liii. 6. It is well known that the early church applied these figures, the lion, the ox, the man, and the eagle, to the four Gospels, conceiving that these "living crea- tures" were apt representations of those peculiar relations of Christ, which are respectively set forth in the four Gospels. See *Ambros. Prol. in Lucam*, § 8.

have no understanding, whose mouth must be held in with bit and bridle;"[6] or like Nebuchadnezzar, in vain self-exaltation, losing his reason, and with a beast's heart, becoming as a beast.[7] The "man" is not strength, or grace, or piercing sight; but a mind thinking God's thoughts, and in communion with Him. Strength, and grace, and sight, and light, and warmth, are in him; for the inward as the outward man is in himself a little world. But a mind to recognise and hold communion with One above him, is that which, above all, marks and makes the man. And this is the secret of his rule over others; as it is said, " Subdue, and have dominion."[8] For no one can rule who is not ruled. And just as Adam, while subject to God, had power over every living creature, a power he lost as soon as he rebelled, and instead of being subject became independent; so in us the "man" has power over beasts, that is the emotions within, only while it remains subject. Let the reason take God's place, then the beasts will be unruled until God again is recognised. This, I may add, is true on every platform. It is only the recognition of One above which gives power. It is the lack of this that now makes the rulers of this world helpless. Beasts are rebelling against them, because they have rebelled.

And here let none forget the weighty fact, that the best powers in the new creation need ruling. Good as the ox is to labour, he needs a lord; man, therefore, is given to subdue and guide him; as God said, " to have dominion over all fish and fowl, and every living thing that moveth on the earth."[9] Proofs abound on every hand that God's gifts need rule. How often is the "ox,"—the spirit of true

<hr>

[6] Ps. xxxii. 9.　　　[7] See Dan. iv.　　　[8] Chap. i. 28.
[9] Chap. i. 28.

service,—unless subdued by the "man," found wasting its strength, or even grossly misusing it! Have fences never been broken down by strong oxen? Have weak children never been sorely injured? Have sweet vines never been crushed or trodden under feet, which were set as plants to cheer both God and man? These things have I beheld, where the "man" is not yet seen. And so of every blessing; whether lion, lamb, or eagle, all require rule. Without it, the very abundance of gifts will only cause confusion. The Church of Corinth is a proof, enriched with knowledge, but carnal, for the "man" had not yet come. The gifts indeed were there, but the mind of God was wanting. They need one like Paul, in whom the "man" is come, to set them right. Some yet have to learn this, who have reached the fifth day stage, and to whom the eagle's eye and soaring wing are not wanting. They will find the "man" to rule must come at length, God's Mind directing God's Spirit. In a word, that as in nature the powers God gives, strength, speech, or desire, if unruled by reason, become curses; so in grace the higher powers of God's Spirit must be subject to His Mind, or Word, or Reason, that is, Christ, in us.

This man was created "male and female," that so he might be a perfect image of God. God is infinite Wisdom and Love. No image of Him would be complete which did not express both. Man, as His image, is, therefore, male and female, that he may be a figure both of the wisdom and love of God; the man representing the understanding, the woman the will or love-part of the mind, which united make up that inward man or mind, by which we can both know and love, and so commune with, God. The seventh day will shew us more of this, when the taking of the woman out of the man is clearly set forth. But, seen or not, a work is now wrought in us, the type of which is the man and the woman. Saints in bygone days have thought and spoken much of this, though few now care for such matters.[10] As to the food of this man, too, much is taught here.[11] The fruits of the third day sustain the " man" in vigour. Just as faith, which is the mother of all the virtues, is often when weak supported and nourished by her children; so the " man," the highest form of the life of Christ in us, is sustained by the lower acts and fruits of righteousness. But all this, and much more, will meet the prayerful reader, who looks for teaching from above.

At this stage the work ends, and then the seventh day

[10] See Augustine's interpretation of this in his *Confessions*, book xiii. chaps. 24 and 32. Also in his *First Book against the Manichees*, chap. 25, and book ii. chaps. 11-15. The following passage is from his work *De Opere Monach.* c. 32, § 40 : " Illam quippe mulieres significant partem, eo ipso quo mulieres sunt, quæ concupiscentialis dici potest, cui mens dominatur, etiam ipsa subdita Deo suo, quando rectissimè et ordinatissimè vivitur. Quod ergo est in uno homine mens et concupiscentia, (illa enim regit, hæc regitur; illa dominatur, hæc subditur); hoc in duobus hominibus, viro et muliere secundum sexum corporis figuratur." So too *De Civitat. Dei*, l. xv. c. 7, *ad finem.* Origen gives the same explanation, *Hom. in Gen.* i. fol. 4. The following passage, from a modern writer, speaks the same language : " Man, that he might be capable of being an image of God, was endowed with two faculties, designed for the reception of love and wisdom from his Maker. These are known by the names of the will and the under-

standing, the will being designed for the reception of the divine love, the understanding of the divine wisdom. I am aware that, although the ancient metaphysicians universally adopted this general division, some of the moderns have doubted its correctness. . . . Respecting the understanding, there can be little dispute ; nor, I should think, respecting the will. . . . As to the will, a man assuredly *wills* whatever he *loves*. Thus every species of love that can have an abode in his mind, may be considered as belonging to a certain general faculty, which is most correctly denominated the will. The mistake seems to have arisen from confounding this general faculty, by which we are only *inclined* to certain actions, with the *determination to action*, which is the result of the operation of the will and understanding together."—*Noble on Inspiration*, p. 79. See the quotations from the Fathers on this subject below, pp. 53, 54.

[11] Chap. i. 29.

comes, the day of rest, without an evening; the day on which the creature is shewn in another form; when a garden is seen, with trees of life and knowledge; and God Himself walking in the midst of it, conversing with the man; and when for unquiet seas there are only sweet rivers. Who shall attempt to count the blessings here? When this comes, can anything be asked or added? A heart to praise only then is needed; nor is this wanting; for every faculty in the rest of the new creation praises God.[12]

VIII. — The Seventh Day

To this day of rest I now would pass, a stage attained by few, for few pursue it. For it is now, as of old: the Lord may work in many a house: He can find a rest in very few. So He works in many souls, and comes to give of His fulness; but few so entirely yield to Him, as to let Him indeed rest there. Foxes have holes, and birds of the air have nests in us, but few hearts give Christ a true resting-place. Yet this is the stage here drawn, the state of " full age," or " perfection," [1] when, instead of growth and change, and the varying life of faith, and the struggle between the old state and the work of God within us, we reach the life of vision and of rest, where the man through grace is drawn to live in a life of love above such strivings, not converted only, or even gifted, but at rest and full of peace, and, because at rest, reflecting God and heaven, like the deep still stream, which can give back each hue

---

[12] Bernard has a very beautiful passage, on the inward application of the work of the Six Days, beginning, " Sicut sex diebus, ita et sex virtutibus exercemur, ut post sacrarum vicissitudines actionum in tranquillo charitatis, quasi in vero mentis sabbato respiremus," &c. — *De Amore Dei*, l. iii. c. 14, § 52.

[1] Phil. iii. 15; Heb. v. 14.

and cloud of heaven, while the restless soul flows on, a brawling river, reflecting nothing, though the light has come, upon its troubled bosom. Such is this day of rest, when heaven is seen in the creature, and the "powers of the world to come" are already more than tasted.[2]

Its cause is first described. The rest is come, because through the Word of God His will is done perfectly.[3] No rest can come until His will is done. When it is so accomplished, whether for us or in us, for us or in us there may be rest. For us there is a rest, when we see the work perfect for us in Christ Jesus. In us there is the selfsame rest, when that work is perfected in us by the same Christ Jesus. He gives Himself for us, and thus by faith His rest is ours, so soon as our faith apprehends Him now in rest for us. But He also gives Himself to us, to work in us that which once through grace He wrought for us. Our faith, from the first day when it takes Christ for us, can rest in Him, for His work is perfect. But in us, as well as for us, in experience as in faith, the rest will come, when in us, as for us, His work and will is done. Thus the rest is in His, not in our own, will done. Our will can never give us rest. If His will rules, there will be a rest. Two wills struggling may prove life or growth, but no Sabbath. God will not, cannot rest, save where His will is done. Hence, at first, there cannot be this rest, for the flesh and the spirit strive together, and the man, who as yet is double, and lives in both, though "at peace with God by faith,"[4] cannot know "the peace of God which passeth all understanding;"[5] the law in his members warring against the law of his mind, even though God's true work is growing there. But in time the flesh

[2] Heb. vi. 1-5.   [3] Chap. ii. 2.   [4] Rom. v. 1.   [5] Phil. iv. 7.

is nailed to the cross, and now the man is no longer double, but single and simple. One life now rules him, and this is God's; and so the day of rest begins to dawn. For this is rest, to yield ourselves to God, to turn away the foot from doing our own pleasure; not doing our own ways, nor speaking our own words, nor seeking to find our own pleasure: then shall we delight ourselves in the Lord, and the creature find joy in God, and God joy in the creature.[6]

But to speak of the rest itself. Much is said descriptive of the nature of this true Sabbath.

And, first, it is " God's rest." It is not said, " the creature rested," but " God rested;"[7] not as though He could be weary, but to shew His satisfaction, and to teach that as the work was His and not the creature's, so the rest was His also. For God Himself has joy in seeing His work perfect. And if in the days of labour it is seen that all progress is because He works in us, much more is this felt when the day of rest is come, as it is written, " God rested from all His work which He created and made." For He works that He may rest in us. Let us not forget the complacency with which He surveys His own workmanship, and that each fresh act of submission to His Word leads to His, even as to our, rest.

Further, this rest is " blessed." We read, " God blessed the seventh day and sanctified it." He blessed the day.

---

[6] Isa. lviii. 13, 14. See also the connection of the well-known words in Matt. xi. 25-30. John, his witness, in bonds, seems to doubt, and asks, " Art thou He that should come, or look we for another?" Then that generation, whether mourned or piped to, mock; and the cities which have beheld His works reject Him. "*At that time* Jesus answered and said, I thank Thee, Father, for thus it pleaseth Thee." And then at once turning to those around, having shewn how He could find a rest in God's will, He says, " Come unto me, and I will give you rest. Take my yoke, and learn of me, and ye shall find rest."

[7] Chap. ii. 3.

In the six days of labour God had blessed certain gifts as the "living creatures," that is, certain powers or faculties divinely given. Now a day is blessed, that is, the creature's state, as well as some of its peculiar powers, obtains the Lord's blessing. And "God sanctified," that is, took it for Himself. In the days of labour God does not get His own. But the day or state of rest is wholly His. By it, in holy contemplation, far more than in action, is the creature perfected. God may get something from our works : He gets much more when we rest, and so pass out of self and its variableness wholly into His will.

On this day there is "no evening" seen.[8] In the days of labour, though the night is never once mentioned, from first to last the evening reappears. The evening and the morning make the day. But on the seventh day we read of no evening. And this omission, like those noticed of Melchisedek by St. Paul, is significant and full of deep teaching.[9] Evening is the state preceding and tending to night or darkness. Morning is the state succeeding it. Hence the evening suggests decline of light ; a relapse or tendency, however brief, to the creature's own darkness. All the days of labour have this evening, for they need it ;

---

[8] This is observed by nearly all the Fathers : by Augustine, *Serm.* ix. (vol. v. p. 53, ed. 1679,) and *De Gen. ad lit.* l. iv. c. 18, &c. : by Jerome, *Epist.* xxi. *De Celebratione Paschæ* : by Bernard, *De Amore Dei*, l. iii. c. 13, &c.

[9] In his Epistle to the Hebrews (chap. vii.) the Apostle points out how much is to be learnt from the simple fact that in the history of Melchisedek nothing is mentioned either of his birth or death : he is presented to us "without father or mother, having neither beginning of days nor end of life ;" an omission very unusual in Scripture with persons of note, but here with purpose, as the Apostle teaches. Other omissions in Scripture are as instructive. Those in St. Mark's Gospel, as compared with St. Matthew, are within the reach of most readers. The contrast between the books of Kings and Chronicles is as marked ; the omissions of the latter being, like the additions, full of meaning.

though even then each stage proceeds " from evening to morning;" with mornings which steadily grow into the day, unlike that fitful light from the cold north, that Northern Morning,[10] which without warmth at times shoots up at night, to go out and fade at midnight suddenly. Such northern lights are not the morning. But now the day of days has come without an evening. Now no darkness or shades return. And good as are the days when the work goes on from evening to morning, — yea, good as are the nights, while yet we need them, — far more blessed is the day of rest without an evening. For then is the dawn of heaven itself, when " at even time it shall be light," for the days " shall be as one day;"[11] when the soul is fit to bear unbroken day, and its very " darkness can be even as the noon day."[12] Then comes this day of days, when " the sun shall no more go down, neither shall the moon withdraw itself, for the Lord shall be our everlasting light, and the days and nights of mourning shall be ended;"[13] a day " as the days of heaven," whose " light is sevenfold, as the light of seven days;"[14] when " no night is there,"[15] nor toil, nor change, but God's rest, and our rest in Him for ever; as Enoch's life, who " walked with God, and was not, for God took him," whose life, the " seventh from Adam,"[16] being a true sabbath of rest, could know no evening. Such is this seventh day, a walk with God, uniting earth to heaven in blessedness. If we know it not, let us wait: to those who wait, it will surely come, it will not tarry.

And as to God Himself, the rest reveals Him to us in another character; for names denote character, and God

---

[10] Aurora borealis.
[11] Zech. xiv. 7.
[12] Isa. lviii. 10.
[13] Isa. lx. 20.
[14] Isa. xxx. 26.
[15] Rev. xxi. 25.
[16] Jude 14.

is known by another name upon the seventh day. Throughout the days of labour, He is " God." [17] Now on the Sabbath, He is the " Lord God." [18] The title " God " tells what He does. Elohim is One whose power and oath we may rely on. It speaks rather of His works than of Himself. " Lord " or Jehovah tells what He is, in His own perfections.[19] At first what God has done or will do, is far more to us than what He is; for we need His work; the names therefore which recall it will be those by which we best know Him. When the rest is come all this remains : His name as connected with His work cannot be forgotten : it is and ever will be precious; but we learn to add what *He is* to what *He does* for us. We all have felt how much Christ's work in the newly awakened soul takes the place of Christ's person; and how the questions which then arise are of the nature and extent of His work, more than of Himself. Then prayer and praise both speak His work. The earlier part of the Book of Psalms is full of such utterances. But we close the course by praising Him, not only " for his mighty acts," but " for His excellent greatness;" [20] on earth, with Paul, while God works in us, blessing Him as " the God and Father of our Lord Jesus Christ," for all that blessed work in Him, in that " He hath loved and raised us up in Him;" [21] in heaven to hear a higher strain, " resting not day nor night, saying, Holy, Holy, Holy, Lord God Almighty, which wast, and art, and art to come; for Thou art worthy; for Thou, O

---

[17] Chap. i. *passim.*

[18] Chap. ii. 4.

[19] " God," Heb. אלהים, from אלה, *to swear*, speaks of One who is pledged by oath and covenant; while the plural form of the name points us to the Three Persons in the Godhead, the Father, the Son, and the Holy Ghost, by whose agency the covenant is fulfilled. " Lord " is Jehovah, יהוה, the Self-existing, who is what He is, above our highest thoughts.

[20] Psalm cl. 2.

[21] Eph. i. 3, and ii. 4-6.

Lord, hast created all things, and for Thy pleasure they are and were created:" [22] a song praising Him for what He is, yet not forgetting what He has done; in His presence and His rest seeing Him above His works, Himself far more glorious.   Work indeed reveals the worker; but if somewhat of God is known in and by His work, how much more of Him is learnt in and by His rest, when His will can shine out perfectly!   Oh, to know that rest yet more, to know Him more; and to know Him more, to know yet more of rest.

Nor is it God alone who shines out more fully upon the seventh day: the creature itself on that day is changed, presented to us in another higher form.   For instead of " herb and tree," we have now " a garden drest," whose position is " eastward " and " in Eden;" [23] words full of meaning, and suggesting rising light, and pleasures at God's right hand for evermore.   For the " East " speaks plainly of advancing light and warmth; while " Eden " means *pleasure*, and is so translated in not a few versions. [24] The " garden " too speaks far more than we can bear of that Paradise into which some like Paul have been caught up; [25] a state not of faith but of vision, where the things within the veil, which " it is not lawful to utter " without the veil, are made manifest.   Such is this " garden," reached on the seventh day, far more glorious than the

---

[22] Rev. iv. 8, 11.

[23] Chap. ii. 8, 15.

[24] Heb. עֵדֶן, i. e. *delight*.   The LXX. and Vulgate both translate the word thus: the former rendering it τρυφῆς, the latter, *voluptatis*.   Augustine says, " Intelligamus nostra gaudia spiritalia significare omne lignum, formosum ad adspectum intelligentiæ, et bonum ad escam quæ non corrumpitur, quâ beatæ animæ pa-

scuntur; ' ad Orientem,' lucem sapientiæ; 'in Eden,' id est, in deliciis immortalibus et intelligibilibus. Nam deliciæ, vel voluptas, vel epulum hoc verbo significari dicitur, si ex Hebræo in Latinum vertitur," &c. — *De Gen. c. Manich.* l. ii, c. 9, § 12.   See also *Ambros. de Parad.* c. 3.   See more respecting " *the East*," below, on Gen. xi. 2.

[25] 2 Cor. xii. 4; Rev. ii. 7.

herbs and fruits upon the third day. Now instead of " seas," we have only sweet " rivers." [26] The man, too, instead of subduing every beast, is seen exercising toward them something like divine power. For before this day, in the first three days, names were bestowed on parts of the creation by the Creator : — " God called the dry land, Earth, and the waters, Seas, and the expanse He called, Heaven." But on the seventh day man is permitted to shew his likeness to his Maker by giving names to the living creatures, thus shewing his insight into God's work; —" the Lord God brought them unto Adam, to see what he would call them : and whatsoever Adam called every living creature, that was the name thereof." [27] Further, much is now shewn of the " woman," his help-mate, whose relation to the " man," as made out of him, is now discerned.[28] The apprehension, too, of the " trees of life and knowledge " is something quite peculiar to this seventh day.[29] All these things shew the creature in a form far higher and more removed from carnal conception than any hitherto presented to us. Whether we are fit even to look at such blessings, is a question for each to lay to heart. For surely not in vain was disobedient man shut out from that Paradise, the figure of which is here presented to us, — shut out in love, for all God does is love ; — shut out lest he should have a worse judgment. The disobedient cannot enter here. Such contemplations do not suit, and would not help them. But humble souls, at peace in Christ, may look and perhaps see some of those things

---

[26] Chap. ii. 10–14. It is to be observed, too, that whereas in the six days we only get אֶרֶץ, *earth*, on the seventh day we have the additional word אֲדָמָה, *ground*, which seems to intimate more care and cultivation. *Earth* might be uncultivated.

[27] Chap. ii. 19.

[28] Chap. ii. 20–25.

[29] Chap. ii. 9, 16, 17.

which belong to the seventh day, and learn thence what may be enjoyed when we rest in God's rest, because His will is done.

What, then, are these "rivers" of which we read, not here only, but in all the prophets; which are known on the day of rest and not before, and which now take the place once occupied by salt and tossing waters? In Eden the stream is one, but "from thence it is parted," and becomes four distinct rivers.[30] What is this, but that stream of living waters, which one and undivided for those who enter Paradise, — and without a name while it is there, for in its undivided flow the one stream is beyond all human description, — without the garden is parted into four streams, giving its waters to the world as Pison, Gihon, Euphrates, and Hiddekel? For divine truth, which is the living water, to those who can see it as it is within the veil, is one full stream, in undivided flow; but to us on earth it ever comes by four distinct channels. It may be said in general that there are four sources of truth, and but four, which are accessible to men, which are like rivers, in the fertility they produce upon their banks, and in the glorious power they all possess of reflecting heaven ; first, *intuition*, by which we get an acquaintance with moral or spiritual things, which are not objects of sense ; second, *perception*, through the senses, by which we only get an acquaintance with material things and their properties; third, *testimony*, by which we learn what others have found out through perception or intuition; fourth, *reasoning* or reflection, a process of the understanding, by which we unfold what is contained or implied or suggested by the perceptions, intuitions, or testimony. If I err not, the first of these is Pison; the

[30] Chap. ii. 10.

second is Gihon, or Nile,— since the fall the stream of
Egypt; [31] the third is Hiddekel, that is the Tigris; [32] and
the fourth river or channel of truth is Euphrates. Of the
first of these we know little after the fall, but " it compasseth the land of Havilah, where there is gold;" [33] the
land that is of much increase, where the waters produce
much fruit while they also roll down rich treasures. As
seen on the day of rest these are all good, like the birds
and beasts of the fifth and sixth days; yet like those
same creatures all capable of perversion, as the best
things may be perverted, by the fall. We know that
the fall has affected all gifts,— that some of the best
powers are become most devilish. So of these rivers
some are now the streams of Egypt and Babel, instead of
making glad the city and garden of the Lord. Euphrates,
the great head or stream of *reasoning*, has become the
channel of the strength and wealth of great Babylon;
while Gihon, or the Nile, the channel of knowledge
through *the senses*, is the river of Egypt, from which we
are redeemed. But here they are seen pouring out their
streams according to God's purpose and to God's glory.
And if we can but reach the seventh day of rest, then
again not only Pison and Hiddekel, but Gihon and
Euphrates also, reasoning and sense as well as faith and
intuition, all give their waters to the creature's joy and to
God's glory. Then, to use the prophet's words of a like
day, " Israel shall be the third with Egypt and Assyria,
whom the Lord of Hosts shall bless, saying, Blessed be

[31] In Jeremiah ii. 8, the LXX.
translate Gihon for Nile. Augustine, Ambrose, Jerome, Josephus,
Isidore, and I know not how many
more, tell us the same. They all
agree also in saying that Pison is
the Ganges.

[32] The LXX. here translate Hiddekel by Tigris. So, too, in Dan.
x. 4. It is easy to see how the one
name might change into the other,
Hiddekel, Digalto, Tigral, Tigris.

[33] Chap. ii. 11, 12. Havilah means
" *to bring forth.*"

Egypt my people, and Assyria the work of my hands, and Israel mine inheritance." [34]

On this day we learn much of the "woman." Till the sixth day we saw no man or woman. Fruits may bud on the third or resurrection day, and yet nothing be seen of the "man" in God's image; for he is not seen till the "dove" and "lamb" appear, that is, until the sixth day. Then we learn that the man is "male and female." Now on the day of rest we see her "taken out of him;" not from his thinking head or nervous arm, but from that region of the heart, where man is least man; where the heart's throbs are felt, and the fount of life wells up, the conceded dwelling place of love and the affections. Thence came forth woman, the type in her very nature, as in her birthplace, of those affections ; formed to yield to the man or understanding, as he to rule : the two, the understanding and will, making up the man created male and female. Now it is seen that there are two distinct lives in man, one of the intellect, the other of the affections, which, though now separate in the human mind, unite as far as may be, and by their union produce all those forms of life which grow in and out of man. By these do we

---

[34] Isa. xix. 24, 25. The Fathers, while holding the inward application of these four rivers, as representing certain powers or faculties of the soul, when it has reached the seventh day, (see *Aug. de Gen. c. Manich*, l. ii. c. 10, § 13 ; *Ambros. de Par.* c. 3, &c.) and connecting these with the fourfold sense of Scripture, i. e. its literal, inward, outward, and dispensational applications, which are apprehended by these faculties, (see *Gloss. Ordin. in loco*,) in a more outward application referred these four streams to the four Gospels, regarding each as one of the channels by which the living waters of Divine truth flowed forth into the world. (*Aug. de Civit.* l. xiii. c. 21.) In this application, if I err not, St. John is plainly Pison, "where there is gold, and the gold of that land is good." St. Luke, I think, is Gihon ; St. Mark, Hiddekel ; and St. Matthew, Euphrates. In the Epistles, also, we can trace these four rivers ; in Paul's arguments, Euphrates ; in James's moralising, Gihon ; in Peter, Hiddekel ; in John, Pison.

commune with God; the understanding, as it is the image of God's wisdom, being the vessel to receive His truth and wisdom; the will, as it reflects His love, to receive His goodness and love; the two together formed to bring forth spiritual fruit to God, and be the means of making known and working His mind and will in the lowest and outmost part of the creature. But the mysteries here cannot be spoken. This, however, is sure, that the divided life of the man and of the woman, full of blessing as it is, shall turn one day to a united life, which is "neither male nor female, but all one in Christ Jesus." These things are indeed unspeakable, but they are seen in measure when we reach the rest.[35]

[35] On this subject the Fathers have written much. Ambrose says, " Nam ante nos fuit qui per voluptatem et sensum prævaricationem ab homine memoraverit esse commissam, in specie serpentis figuram accipiens delectationis, in figurâ mulieris sensum animi mentisque constituens, quam αἴσθησιν vocant Græci: decepto autem sensu, prævaricatricem secundum historiam mentem adseruit, quam Græci νοῦν vocant. Rectè igitur in Græco νοῦς viri figuram accepit, αἴσθησις mulieris. Unde et quidam Adam νοῦν terrenum interpretati sunt . . . . Bestiæ autem agri, et volatilia cœli, quæ adducuntur ad Adam, nostri irrationabiles motus sunt, vel turbulentiores, vel etiam languidiores. Volatilia autem cœli quid aliud æstimamus nisi cogitationes quæ velut volatilium more nostram circumvolant mentem. Propterea nullus inventus est menti nostræ similis adjutor, nisi sensus, hoc est αἴσθησις. Similem solam νοῦς noster potuit invenire."—*De Parad.* c. 2, § 11, and c. 11, § 51. Augustine gives the same interpretation, only more fully, *De Gen. c. Manichæos,* l. ii. c. 11, § 15, &c. :—" Fœmina facta, dicitur, in adjutorium viri, ut copulatione spiritali spiritales fœtus ederet, id est bona opera divinæ laudis, dum ille regit, hæc obtemperat . . . . ideoque dicitur, 'Non est bonum solum hominem esse.' Ad hoc enim erat, quod fieret, ut non solum anima corpori dominaretur, quia corpus servilem locum obtinet, sed etiam virilis ratio subjugaret sibi animalem partem suam, per quod adjutarium imperaret corpori. Ad hujus rei exemplum fœmina facta est, quam rerum ordo subjugat viro; ut quod in duobus hominibus evidentius apparet, id est in masculo et fœminâ, etiam in uno homine considerari possit; ut appetitum animæ, per quem de membris corporis operamur, habeat mens interior tanquam virilis ratio subjugatum," &c. In c. 13 of the same book, he says the woman is " inferior animi pars, quam prudentia rationalis regit." Gregory the Great gives the same interpretation, *Moral. in Job,* l. xxx. c. 16, § 54 :—" Nos ipsos intuemur, ut

The " trees," too, as seen upon this day, are wondrous. Trees were formed and seen upon the third day. But the clear perception of their varied ends, and of God's will respecting them, is not discovered till this day. These trees, like all else wrought by God in the creature, represent some form or manifestation of the Divine Word or Wisdom, by the Word reproduced in us; their perishable nature,— for both grass and wood are perishable,— setting forth some gift or grace which is least enduring, as we know that both faith and knowledge shall vanish away.[36] Here, when through grace we reach the seventh day, we learn to distinguish between the tree of life and knowledge, and to understand how the last, through misuse and disobedience, may become a means of death to us. Knowledge is not evil. The tree itself was good, and only evil through man's weakness; like the law, (and indeed law is but knowledge,) which is " holy, just, and good," and yet " works condemnation." [37] But good as it is, let us take heed how we use it. Wisdom is the tree of life; — " She is a tree of life to them that lay hold upon her;" [38] and he

sciamus, in nobis aliud esse rationale quod regit, aliud animale quod regitur . . . . quod bene Adam dormiens figuravit, de cujus latere mulier processit. Qui enim ad interiora intelligenda rapitur, intelliget in seipso aliud esse quod regere debeat, tanquam vir; aliud quod regatur, tanquam fœmina." As to the final union of these in Christ, I subjoin the following very remarkable passage from Clement of Rome, or rather from the epistle which goes under his name :— Ἐπερωτηθεὶς γὰρ αὐτὸς ὁ Κύριος ὑπό τινος, πότε ἥξει αὐτοῦ ἡ βασιλεία, εἶπεν, Ὅταν ἔσται τὰ δύο ἕν, καὶ τὸ ἔξω ὡς τὸ ἔσω, καὶ τὸ ἄρσεν μετὰ τῆς θηλείας, οὔτε ἄρσεν οὔτε θῆλυ. — *Clem. Rom. 2 Ep. ad Co-*

rinth. ad fin. The same tradition Clement of Alexandria repeats, and thus explains : —Ὅτι θυμὸν μὲν ἄρρενα ὁρμὴν, θήλειαν δὲ τὴν ἐπιθυμίαν αἰνίττεται . . . ὅταν οὖν μήτε τις θυμῷ, μήτ' ἐπιθυμίᾳ χαρισάμενος, ἀλλ' ἀποδυσάμενος τὴν ἐκ τούτων ἀχλὺν, ἐκ μετανοίας καταισχυνθεὶς, πνεῦμα καὶ ψυχὴν ἑνώσει κατὰ τὴν τοῦ Λόγου ὑπακοήν· τότε, ὡς ὁ Παῦλός φησιν, οὐκ ἔνι ἐν ὑμῖν οὐκ ἄρρεν οὐ θῆλυ. Ἀποστᾶσα γὰρ τοῦδε τοῦ σχήματος, ᾧ διακρίνεται τὸ ἄρρεν καὶ τὸ θῆλυ, ψυχὴ μετατίθεται εἰς ἕνωσιν, οὔθ' ἕτερον οὖσα, κ. τ. λ.—*Strom.* l. iii. c. 13.

[36] 1 Cor. xiii. 8.
[37] Rom. vii. 7–13.
[38] Prov. iii. 18.

that eats of her shall live by her;[39] but knowledge, even of divine things, may but reveal our nakedness. The day of rest will shew, not only that good gifts of God need ruling, but that some may only judge us more, if by them we think to be as gods in independence.[40] For higher gifts involve a deeper judgment, if they are not used aright.

I say no more, therefore, on this day, though each word here involves a mystery. He who sees the " rivers," and the " trees of Eden," and the " East," and the " keeping of the garden," and the " naming of the creatures," and the " woman for the man," will see yet more to fill him with adoring praise and wonder. For truth is throughout so closely connected, that one truth cannot be opened without opening with it many others. Eye hath not seen, nor ear heard, the things which God hath prepared for them that love Him ; but God hath revealed them to us by His Spirit; for the Spirit searcheth all things, yea, the deep things of God.

Such is the Work and Rest of God, in a soul or world the same story. It is the self-same work which is only set forth more fully in the seven great lives recorded in Genesis; the order of which accords with the steps of the work and rest of God in creation. Thus, the first day revealed the creature's state, when light shone in, and shewed the earth's voidness. So Adam is the first great life in Genesis, discovering what the creature is, out of which and in which God purposes to work such great marvels. What he lacks is not yet known, nor is there

[39] John vi. 57.
[40] Irenæus (l. v. c. 20, *Contr. Hær.*) makes a very striking use of this against the Gnostics, whom he charges with preferring the tree of knowledge to the tree of life.

yet any understanding of what by grace can be brought forth out of him ; but the darkness which his fall has wrought is seen under the light of the promise, which, while it lessens the darkness, reveals its gross unsightliness. The second day then gives a heaven to earth, an expanse into which the breath of heaven may come, and which it may fill as its own proper dwelling place, dividing the waters from the waters, shewing that some are salt and earthy, and some heavenly. So Cain and Abel are something more than the " old man." Two lives, of the flesh and spirit, as unlike each other as heaven and earth, are shewn by nature or by grace growing out of the root of old Adam. Then, the third day revealed a rising earth, with herb and fruit-tree yielding fruit after his kind. And so the third great life, namely Noah's, sets forth regeneration, in which the creature is brought to know something of the power of resurrection; delivered out of that which hitherto had precluded fruit, into a state of purer and higher blessing, where, the flood of waters being already passed, vines may be planted, and become very fruitful. After this, the fourth day's work is lights; the sun and moon appear to rule the day, and still more to conquer darkness; as Abraham's life, which is the fourth great stage, shines out, not with mere light, but with the lights of faith and charity, emitting rays like sun and moon, by which the light, which we have already received, is governed, and the remaining darkness overcome. Till on the fifth day comes life in the air and sea, the eagle-eye and gentle dove are now visible ; answering to which is Isaac's heavenly life, the fifth great form of life divinely given, in whose spirit of meekness and understanding the very grace itself is shewn which the dove and eagle of the fifth day are formed to represent,— grace peculiar to the spirit of the Son, who is known as such when the Spirit "like a dove" descends and rests upon Him;[41] and whose portrait, as drawn by the beloved Apostle John, has ever been distinguished from other manifestations of the same Life by the form and "face of an eagle."[42] After which we reach the sixth day's stage, with beasts from the earth, the sheep and oxen strong to labour; a hint of Jacob and all his long service, toiling for others, sighing to rule, yet not ruling; till at the close of this stage the man appears, the image of God, the first who is called to rule all things, like to Joseph, the last great life, the crowning work, the one who after many struggles knows both rest and glory. I do not attempt to explain all this. But light shews many a link, where the darkness of a less instructed eye only beholds discord. And the tale which to some is but an endless and entangled skein, to those who possess the clue, is full of unity as well as deepest wisdom.

And I may add that as this work is fulfilled within, so is there also an accomplishment in the dispensations. In this application " one day is as a thousand years."[43] Six thousand years of labour precede the world's Sabbath. The parallel here has been often traced. Thus the first day gave light to the dark and fallen world. So the light of the promise of the woman's Seed is the great object which attracts us amid the deep gloom of the first thousand years. At this stage the waters (and in this view " the waters are peoples,"[44]) are not only unquiet, but undivided. But the second day divides the waters, as we know the sons of God and the sons of men became distinct and

---

[41] Luke iii. 22.

[42] The fourth cherubic face, "as of an eagle," by the consent of all ages has been applied to St. John's Gospel, as revealing Christ in the relationship of Son of God.

[43] 2 Pet. iii. 8.

[44] Rev. xvii. 15.

divided during the second thousand years.   After this, on
the third day, the earth appears; something firm and
fruitful now is seen above the waters; just as Abraham
and his seed were called out of the world to be as the
fruitful earth amid the restless and fruitless nations.   In
this day we see the righteous grow like the palm-tree,
and fruits of divers forms are borne to God's glory.   Then
come lights upon the fourth day, the sun and moon and
stars, divine gifts of government and prophecy, to be a
light to all nations; a sun indeed one day to be turned to
darkness, and the moon into blood.   After which, on the
fifth and sixth days, higher life appears, beasts, first in the
seas, then upon the dry land; as in the fifth and sixth
thousand years a form of life appeared on earth, unlike
all that went before it; first, the beast from the sea, which
St. John saw in his Revelation; and then, on the sixth
day, the beast from the earth; [45] and then the man to
rule, the image of God on earth, to spend the blessed
seventh day, the seventh thousand years, of rest in joy
and heavenly blessedness.[46]

Oh, the depth of the riches of the wisdom and knowledge of God!   Lo, these are a part of His ways; but
how little a portion is heard of Him.[47]

[45] Rev. xiii. 1, 11.

[46] Augustine, in his *First Book
against the Manichees*, goes very fully
into this dispensational application,
in chaps. xxii. and xxiii. §§ 33–41.
Any reader who wishes to see how
general this interpretation was in the
early Church, will find a mass of
quotations in Cotelerius' *Annotations
on the General Epistle of Barnabas*,
§ 15, and in the Commentary of
Corn. a Lapide, *On the Pentateuch*,
on Gen. ii. 1, p. 62.

[47] Job. xxvi. 6–14.

PART 1

ADAM, OR HUMAN NATURE

Chapter 3

" The first man is of the earth, earthy."—1 Cor. xv. 47.

" The old man, which is corrupt according to the deceitful lusts."—Eph. iv. 22.

ADAM, OR HUMAN NATURE

Chapter 3

GENESIS opens wondrously; first announcing a creation; then shewing it marred; then a restoration. "In the beginning God created the heavens and the earth." As for God, His work is perfect. If He created, His work must have been good. And yet the next thing is a darkened world. For "the earth was dark and without form and void." In some way, not revealed, God's work had been destroyed. God, then, in the six days, restores that earth, not made dark by Him, yet now in darkness; and on this ruined earth His work proceeds till His image is seen, and He can rest there.

This wonder, of a work of God soon self-destroyed, meets us again in the beginning. Scarcely is God's image seen in man, before that spiritual work is marred in Adam. The creature formed to bear God's image falls, and thus becomes a platform for another work. In each case mystery shrouds the fall. How the earth became "without form and void and dark," is not told us. And how the man, God's image, falls, is a great deep: for great is the mystery of godliness, and not less the mystery of iniquity. But the fact is here. We see man made by the Divine Word; and then man, as he makes himself by disobedience.

In this way the fall is shewn not to be man's normal state. Man, like Adam, may be far off from God, yet in his heart, as in Scripture, a witness will be heard, saying that this distance is through self-will. He may live in sin; but he knows that such a life is opposition to the will and purpose of his Maker. Sin is not the law of our being, but a struggle against it, as conscience tells every man. Therefore is God's work shewn before the fall, to confirm the voice which speaks in every heart, and which declares that though all men walk as Adam, sin is no part of God's work, but its opposite. Man's proper place is seen in Christ. Out of Christ we are not lost only, but rebellious. Man, through self, may be all that we see in disobedient Adam, debased and sunk from God and heaven into self, from joy and glory into misery; and yet in Christ man has been, and is, set in all that glory which God's work and rest typify; so that Paul can say, "God hath raised us up, and blessed us with all spiritual blessings in heavenly places in Christ."[1] Adam, ruling all creatures, is the type of man in Christ, as God makes him; fallen Adam, of man in self, as he makes or unmakes his own nature. The one, with glories more than eye can see, figured in the blessings bestowed in Paradise on the creature; the other, losing all through sin, with mind and will subject to, instead of ruling, lower creatures.

This latter sight, what man is in self,—how he falls and departs from his Creator,—how the understanding errs,—how the will is seduced,—how these highest powers yield to lower ones,—how the end is shame and distance from God,—how the Lover of men in grace meets and conquers this,—all this is shewn as in a glass, man's self being here presented to us. As Adam fell, we fall each one; for

·[1] Eph. i. 3

Adam lives yet in his progeny. And, fallen in him, we prove he is in us, by walking just as he walked. Adam yet re-lives old Adam's life, as Christ in us yet lives Christ's life. And just as things are true for us in Christ, which, if we are in Him, must in due time be true in us also, as death and resurrection; so, being fallen in Adam, we shall find his fall to be true also in our experience. Adam in us still lives old Adam's life. His life is the figure of our life when " we walk as men." [2]

I proceed, then, to trace his course; first within, then in its more outward application. We shall see how, in spite of every gift, man as man is prone to ruin all.

I.—ADAM, OR MAN

FIRST, to trace this path in that world of thought and will which is within; for, to this day, when we sin, nothing else is done but what is here set forth in the man, the woman, and the serpent.[1] In this view the man is the understanding, the woman the will,[2] the serpent some animal faculty or emotion in us—good, when in subjec-

[2] 1 Cor. iii. 3.

[1] " Etiam nunc in unoquoque nostrûm nihil aliud agitur, cùm ad peccatum quisque delabitur, quàm tunc actum est in illis tribus, serpente, muliere, et viro," &c.—*Augustin. de Gen. c. Manich.* l. ii. c. 14, § 21. " Serpens enim mulierem decepit, virum mulier ad prævaricationem de veritate deduxit. Serpentis typum accepit delectatio corporalis; mulier symbolum sensûs est nostri; vir, mentis. Delectatio itaque sensum movet, sensus menti transfundit passionem," &c.—*Ambros. de Par.* c. 15, § 73.

[2] I use the word "*will*" here for that general faculty of the mind by which we are *inclined* to certain actions, rather than for that *determination to action*, which is now generally called the "will," but which I believe to be the result of the united operation of the will and understanding. See note 10, p. 41. If the forms of language are any guide, (and surely they often utter the results of true and deep insight,) such words as θέλημα and *voluntas* may be quoted as witnesses that the old view of the will as the seat of love is in the main correct. Both θέλημα and *voluntas* describe the will as the organ of affection and desire, rather than of determination; and in this sense I here use the word.

tion, but which may be a means, under the influence of
the evil spirit, to tempt the will, and lead it to disobedience and independence, and so to misery.   For the will,
not the understanding, is that in us which is first assailed,
seduced by some lower sense or emotion, which seems to
promise more happiness.   But for the will, the emotions
would not be felt, but only thought about : but they are
felt : hence they are passions ; for we really suffer, though
we should command, them.   Only thus is man led away.
For our understanding,—that is, the man,—cannot be led
to consent to sin but by the will ; that is, that part of the
mind which loves, and which, as the woman to her
husband, is formed to be subject, and ought to be obedient.[3]   Here the will acts in independence.   If this will
stood firm, the temptation would be overcome.   But the
will yields, and becomes self-will, and then by it the man
or understanding is seduced.   The head goes wrong
because the heart is first seduced, while yet the
head or understanding is the man, whom the heart
or woman should obey.   But in every fall the heart per-
verts the head, the will tempts the understanding, as in
every restoration it is out of the heart or will that the new
life must come, "the woman's Seed," which is divinely
given to overcome the evil.   And yet what zeal is shewn
to enrich and deck the understanding, which, at the best,
is only half our nature, while those affections are unkept,
which, as being the spring and womb of every form of

---

[3] " Sed tamen per mulierem de-
cipit ; non enim etiam ratio nostra
(i. e. the man) deduci ad consensio-
nem peccati potest, nisi cùm delectatio mota fuerit in illâ parte animi,
quæ debet obtemperare rationi, tanquam rectori viro," &c.—*Aug. de
Gen. c. Manich.* l. ii. c. 14, § 20.
Again he says, — "Hic manifestè
ostenditur, non posse nos a diabolo
tentari, nisi per illam animalem
partem, quæquasi mulieris imaginem
vel exemplum in uno ipso homine
ostendit."—*Id. ibid.* c. 18, § 28.

future life, are ever the first and special object of the tempter. Alas! we learn all this too soon by falls, in which the promise of forbidden knowledge is yet the bait to draw us aside. To know is yet the snare; and the will, once set on this, is quickly overcome. Then, "when lust hath conceived, it bringeth forth sin; and sin, when it is finished, bringeth forth death." [4] Thus falls the will, throwing off dependence at the suggestion of a lower nature in us, which is very near it. [5]

The results I need not follow here; for it is the same story in the outward application. But I may note the sentence on the "woman,"—pain in bringing forth, and. subjection to her husband; as it is said, "And he shall rule over thee;" on the "man," bread by the sweat of his brow, with the earth cursed henceforth with thorns and briers. [6] For the fallen will, if it travails to bring forth other forms of life, produces them with pain and much difficulty: but, having done so, is more than ever subject to reason. [7] While the understanding,—that is the "man,"—finds the earth full of thorns: not easily does it gather truth, the bread of life; for, as the wise man says, "the corruptible body presseth down the soul, and the earthly tabernacle weigheth down the mind that museth upon many things." [8] On the one hand, there are

---

[4] James i. 14, 15.

[5] Augustine marks that this is done in the evening, "in the cool of the day," (chap. iii. 8,) when the sun of love and light is declining : — "Bene '*ad vesperam*,' id est cùm jam ab eis sol occideret, id est auferretur ab eis lux illa interior veritatis," &c.—*Aug. de Gen. c. Manich.* l. ii. c. 16, § 24.

[6] Chap. iii. 16–19.

[7] "'*In doloribus paries filios*,' ad-ditum est, '*et erit tibi conversio ad virum tuum, et ipse tui dominabitur*,' quia illa pars animæ, quæ carnalibus gaudiis tenetur, cùm aliquam malam consuetudinem volens vincere, passa fuerit difficultatem et dolorem, atque ita peperit consuetudinem bonam, cautiùs jam et diligentiùs rationi obtemperat tanquam viro," &c.— *Aug. de Gen. c. Manich.* l. ii. c. 19, § 29.

[8] Wisdom ix. 15.

the thorns and briers of perplexing questions, which, unless they are rooted out, will choke the good seed. On
the other, the understanding itself is weaker, and must
" sweat" for that, which once grew without labour. Thus
truth, like fruit, has to be sought and waited for ; the toil
to gain it being ordained to strengthen, even while it
corrects and humbles us.[9]   And if the man will not accept
this sentence, the ground is quickly filled with thorns and
thistles, so that he who will not eat by the sweat of his
brow here, will have to gather bitter things both here and
in another world.[10]

I cannot write what crowds upon me here, as to the
" woman," and her " Seed," who shall destroy and bruise
the serpent; or how Christ, if He be " formed within," [11]
is made of the woman in us, that is the human will ;
growing thence, out of the womb of human affections,
not by man, but by the Holy Ghost, who begets that new
life, to be in due time born amidst beasts, out of a pure
virgin affection, like Mary, in us; which is itself the
fruit of numberless other affections, some grievously
defiled as Rahab and Thamar, which have gone before.[12]
For from Adam to Christ are seventy-two generations, as
from Abraham to Christ are forty-two ; [13] that is, many a
form of life is produced, and many an inward travail and

[9]   " Pater ipse colendi
Haud facilem esse viam voluit," &c.
              Georg. i. 121.
[10] " Certè manifestum est quòd
nemo evadat istam sententiam, ' In
tristitiâ manducabis ex eâ omnibus
diebus vitæ tuæ ; spinas et tribulos
pariet tibi, et edes pabulum agri in
sudore vultûs tui,' &c. Hoc ipsum
enim, quòd in hâc vitâ quisque natus,
difficultatem inveniendæ veritatis habet ex corruptibili corpore, ipsi sunt
labores et tristitiæ quas habet homo
ex terrâ ; ac spinæ ac tribuli sunt
punctiones tortuosarum quæstionum,
quæ nisi exstirpentur, et de agro.
Dei projiciantur, suffocat ne fructi-
ficet in homine."— *Aug. de Gen. c.
Manich.* l. ii. c. 20, § 30.
[11] Gal. iv. 19.
[12] Rahab and Thamar are mentioned in the Lord's genealogy,
Matt. i.
[13] See Matt. i. and Luke iii.

death is known by us, before the will brings forth that life
of faith, of which Abraham is the appointed figure. And
after Abraham, or faith, more births will there yet be, in
which the energy of nature is more or less manifest, before that form of life appears, which is of the Holy Ghost,
and is the " perfect man." Some of these, as David and
Solomon, are like, but yet are not, the perfect man, but
only carnal forms or copies of Him; as we know that
before God's image comes in us, certain outward likenesses, and carnal prefigurings or preludings of it, in
different measures will appear in us. Many a form of
life grows, toils, withers, and dies, having produced
another to succeed it, which again dies out, and this many
times, before the image of God, the perfect man, the true
Seed, comes. But it comes at last, and the serpent's head
is bruised. She, by whom came death, brings forth the
Life-giver.[14]

And very wondrous is the woman's name; for " Adam
called his wife's name, Eve," or *Life*, not while she stood,
but after she had fallen, and by her fall had brought in
death.[15] So within, the fallen will is " Eve;" fallen, and
yet indeed the true " mother of all living." Only by the
will is another life produced. It is the opener of all evil
or good in the creature. As we love, we live. Therefore

---

[14] Any one who cares to see how
generally received this mystic application of Christ's genealogy was
among the Fathers, may do so by
consulting the *Catena Aurea* on the
Gospels, where the inward fulfilment is given *in loco*. See also
the extract from the *Ordinary Gloss*
further on upon the fifth chapter,
in note 13, p. 92. Augustine just
glances at this succession of forms
of life in us, in his *Confessions*,
(l. i. c. 6, § 9,) where he says, " Et
ecce infantia mea olim mortua est,
et ego vivo, &c." So Chrysostom
says, "Dost thou not see every day
a resurrection and a death taking
place in the periods of our life?"
Hom. on 1 Thess. iv. 15, page 410
of the Oxford Translation.

[15] Chap. iii. 20. Eve, Heb. חוה.
The LXX. here translate Ζωή for
Eve:—Καὶ ἐκάλεσεν Ἀδὰμ τὸ ὄνομα
τῆς γυναικὸς αὐτοῦ Ζωή.

must we " keep the heart with all diligence, for out of it are the issues of good or bad life." [16]   So the Lord teaches,— " From within, out of the heart, proceed evil thoughts," and every form of evil living; [17] and out of the affections grows that life which is life, and is eternal. [18]

And yet the man, and woman too, though she is the mother of all living, are shut out of Paradise. A flaming sword keeps the way, while at its gate are placed cherubim.   The fallen mind in mercy is shut out, because unfit to deal with heavenly things; while forms of truth (for these cherubim were such forms) reveal, as through a veil, some ray of glory such as the fallen mind and will can bear.   For now a coat of skin in mercy covers both.   Other things therefore in grace are made to agree thereto.

But all this may be more clear to some, if we trace its fulfilment in the outward kingdom.   The tale is one within or without, enacted before the face of the world, or carried on invisibly in the inmost soul of man.

Outwardly then we here have man as man.   Human nature in its ways and griefs and hopes is drawn for us, with the exactness of One who views it as it is, and who

---

[16] Prov. iv. 23.

[17] Mark vii. 21.

[18] " Quem autem non moveat, quòd post peccatum et sententiam Judicis Dei vocat Adam mulierem suam, Vitam, quia vivorum ipsa sit mater, posteaquam meruit mortem, et mortales fœtus parere destinata est, nisi quia illos fœtus adtendit Scriptura, de quibus superiùs dictum est. Nam vita quæ in peccatis est mors appellari in Scripturis solet. . . . . .

Quare ergo non illa pars nostra, quæ tanquam viro debet obtemperare rationi, cùm per ipsam rationem de verbo rectè vivendi sarcinam conceperit, appelletur, Vita, et vivorum mater ? " &c.—*Aug. de Gen. c. Man.* l. ii. c. 21, § 31. To the same effect is the well-known prayer in the Litany,—" to receive the word with pure affection, and (so) to bring forth the fruits of the Spirit."

presents the perfect figure of it in Adam to us, that, if we cannot look within, we may yet learn by Adam's ways to know our own tendencies. We are shewn here, first, the way of man; then, the consequences; then, the remedy.

II. — Man's Way

As to the way of man, as man, it is from God to self and independence ; a way not without its marked stages,— for there is first temptation, then sin, and disobedience,— and each of these has its own steps, but the steps and stages are all away from God. Such is the way of man. If he returns, that return is God's way for man, and not mere man's way.

First in this way comes the temptation. This at once touches a field of mystery, assuming the existence of an enemy of God and man ; though how he became such, or whence or what he was, or how he had power to reach this world, and to use its creatures, is not told us. What we know is this, that man is tempted, and that by some of the common creatures which surround him here ; the weaker vessel being ever first assailed, as being more likely to yield, and in yielding to draw the stronger with her. Christ was "tempted of the devil," and could say, " Get thee behind me, Satan," [1] for the New Man sees a spiritual world. But man as man sees but the creature, some outward thing, and not a spirit under it. Some paltry thing, the smallest, commonest creature, may be, and is often, used to ruin us. A tree or beast may stir our lusts, and a garden or fruit awaken passions and desires, which may prove too strong for us. For though

[1] Matt. iv. 1–10.

man, as Adam, sees but the creature, a world of spirits is working under it, by the creature tempting man to trust in self and creatures more than God.

Yet with this difference, that Adam saw only the creature, whilst Christ in His temptation recognised the devil as the direct agent in it, the two temptations varied not. The serpent's words in substance exactly answer to those recorded in the Gospel; first suggesting doubts as to God's love, then as to His truth, then openly attempting to put the creature into God's place. Such is the trial here : such was Christ's : and such is man's temptation yet. There is indeed no other.

First comes a suggestion questioning God's love ; and this is put with great subtlety, suggesting that the commandment was merely arbitrary, imposed by power, rather than ordained in love : — " Hath God said, Ye shall not eat ? "[2] As much as to say, He grudges ; He cannot really love you. Keeping out of sight what God has done, His unnumbered gifts and proofs of love everywhere, the serpent fixes on the one thing denied, and brings this forward in the way most likely to awaken hard and evil thoughts. Yet he only puts a question as to God. He questions what God does : thus he opens the temptation.

If we question what God does, we judge God ; we get out of our place, and put Him out of His. For simple as the question seemed, by it the serpent was drawing Eve to be God's judge, rather than His worshipper : — an awful place for men, yet one into which our adversary is

---

[2] Chap. iii. 1. It is noteworthy that the serpent always substitutes *Elohim* for *Jehovah*,—" Hath Elohim said," &c., vv. 1, 3, 5. This, compared with verses 1, 8, 9, 13, 14, &c., where in every instance we have Jehovah Elohim, is suggestive and significant.

ever drawing us; to lead ere long to make ourselves as gods, and to make God a liar. A really humble soul never judges God. It may not have peace or joy, but at least it will not judge God; submitting rather to His sovereign will; tempted to question, yet not questioning. Such a soul has broken through the snare. It is safe, for it will not entertain questions as to God's ways.

Eve, however, meets the question, as men yet meet it, with knowledge. She answers with the truth of God;[3] shewing how the serpent misrepresented God. And yet she fails. What was wrong here? This, that the woman was parleying with Satan instead of worshipping. Could Satan have gone on with success, if the woman, instead of arguing the point, had at once given God His place by worship and submission? Then God and the creature would both have had their place, and the serpent's subtlety would have been foiled. But Eve utters truth, while her soul drinks in the lie. Unconsciously she is taking the place of judging God.

And truth held away from God will not preserve: on the contrary, it may very readily be used against us. Balaam had the truth; but he walked not with God. Instead of helping him, therefore, the truth only judged him.[4] And we too may have some well-known text, when Satan, "that old serpent,"[5] suggests that God does not love us. Will it help us against the tempter's wile, if we are parleying with him, instead of worshipping? Alas! We all know how powerless truth is, if we are admitting questions suggesting doubts as to God's love.

Such is man's first trial; and thus, in doubts of God's love, comes in creature love. All the world is doing what

---

[3] Chap. iii. 2, 3.   [4] Numb. xxiv. 17, and xxxi. 8.   [5] Rev. xii. 9.

Eve did. They think God does not love them : they must therefore love themselves. So man turns to find his joy out of God, in 'things which cannot satisfy. This is the fundamental lie, — God does not love. Every other lie is possible after this. This it is which leads man away from God. Distance from Him is easy, if the poison of this lie is really rankling in us. Oh how deep this lie has gone ! Who likes to be at the mercy of God in everything ? Men will trust a strong box more than God, because they are not quite certain that He so loves, that at every step He will order what is best for them. God will stint them, they fear. God cannot make them happy now. This tree or that will give far more joy than God can; for love is joy, and, if God loves us not, we can but try self and creatures and creature love.

The next step is the denial of God's truth. " The serpent said, Ye shall not surely die." [6] Love being doubted, truth is next assailed. God now is treated as a liar. He said indeed, Ye shall die, if ye transgress. But fear not : ye shall not die.

Now here, as before, if God lose His place, something else must take it. If the truth is doubted, some lie will be believed. Where God is not trusted, Satan will be; and, indeed, the world's happiness consists in trusting him. To this day, wherever man is doubting God, he is building his happiness upon the devil's lie. Could men, if they believed God's word, go on happily in a course of disobedience and self-will ? But they believe a lie. Their happiness in sin rests on believing the devil. Carnal happiness apart from God could not live for a day under a faith that God is true, and will fulfil His word on those who disobey Him.

[6] Chap. iii. 4.

The truth is, man must trust some one. Boast as he may, he cannot stand alone. The man, therefore, who doubts the love and truth of God, having given up God, must trust the creature. If, therefore, creatures ask him to sin, he will obey them; for they are now in the place of God to him. If we believe God, we are free. If we will not trust Him, we are the tool and slave of any thing or any one who is stronger or cleverer than we are.

And now God's love and truth being denied, the next step is to take God's place openly. So the serpent says, "Ye shall be as gods." [7] He now can dare to say any thing; for if the poison of the first two lies has entered, God has quite lost His character in the heart of man. Self now may therefore seek to be "as God;" so entirely is spiritual perception gone when we begin to doubt God.

Some may not see the sin of this. Sin blinds us so that we do not know what is sin. Men see no harm in seeking to be gods, in setting themselves up to know or judge both good and evil.[8] Self-glorying therefore is thought to be no sin, till some wretched fruit of exalting self opens our eyes to see it; while judging good and evil seems almost to be our work, so readily do we pass sentence on everything, as though neither sin nor danger were connected with it. But both are sin, for they rob God. They take His place, to put self into it. God

---

[7] Chap. iii. 5.

[8] The expression, "knowing good and evil," may mean sitting in judgment on it, as in 2 Sam. xiv. 17, and 1 Kings iii. 9. Ambrose so takes it:—"Sciebat Deus te judicare non posse; ideo dixit, 'Nolite judicare, ut non judicemini.' Ergo quia scivit infirmum te esse ad judicandum, voluit obedientem esse mandato . . . Itaque quoniam judicare voluisti, ideo addidit, 'Ecce Adam factus est tanquam unus ex nobis, ut sciat bonum et malum.' Voluisti tibi arrogare judicium, ideo pœnam pravi judicii refutare non debes," &c.— *De Parad.* c. 11, § 52.

must be the centre where He is known. Let Him be dishonoured, self will be the centre; and each fair gift is turned into a curse, the creature exalting itself at the expense of God's glory; till, as in Nebuchadnezzar, loss of understanding is the result, and man becomes as a beast for his self-exaltation, " until seven times pass over him." [9] God does, indeed, call us to glory, but by glorifying Him, not by self-glorying. And in that day we too may judge, for man shall "judge the world," yea, "judge angels." [10] But the way thither is the way of Christ, who "grew in wisdom," while in subjection even to His earthly parents; in meekness and obedience offering Himself to God, taking man's place and giving to God His place. In such a path, blessing must be man's, for in it God is glorified. Let man arrogate the glory, blessing will depart, until God receives His own again. [11]

Still the serpent spoke some truth. They "became as gods." God Himself declares,—"The man is become as one of us." [12] And this is yet the tempter's way: he does not put forth a lie only, with the uncomeliness of a mere lie; but first a question full of plausibility, then a lie, and then a truth out of its place, working as a lie, and used to deceive us. For he can tell much attractive truth; but never for God against self, always to nourish self and self-will against the will of God. And there is a point where truth becomes the surest snare, aiding to fix us in the most awful self-deception; while held in sin, without conscience, to exalt self, it becomes our worst punishment. So a saint, when asked, "What was the most dangerous doctrine?" replied, "God's own truth held carnally and to

[9] Dan. iv. 30–32.
[10] 1 Cor. vi. 2, 3.
[11] Compare Mal. ii. 2, and Psalm
xxix. 1, 11, and xcvi. 7–10.
[12] Chap. iii. 22.

exalt self." For His light may blind, His ark destroy, His sanctuary smite, His table be damnation.[13] And a truth perverted may be the firmest chain to hold and bind and blind us for ever.

I might speak much here of other outward things, which had their weight in this temptation; such as the lust of the flesh, for "the tree was good for food;" the lust of the eye, for it "was pleasant to the eye, and fair to look upon;" and the lust of the mind, the pride of knowledge, for it was "a tree to be desired to make one wise."[14] All these concur, and thus falls man: thus grows the "evil heart of unbelief;" and God,— Father, Son, and Holy Ghost,— gives place to that other trinity, the world, the flesh, and the devil. The Father is superseded by the world: creature love serves now instead of God's Love. The Son, God's Truth, is doubted, and at once Christ's opposite, the devil, "who abode not in the truth," must be trusted. Then the Holy Ghost is grieved and assailed; and in His place the flesh or self is glorified.[15] In this order does the evil work, as then, so now, in every man; till man actually believes that sin is blessedness: not to sin and do as he will is now considered bondage. So deceived is he, that he thinks the evil good, and counts self-pleasing to be joy, though he finds no peace in it.[16]

[13] Lev. x. 1, 2 ; 1 Chron. xiii. 9, 10 ; 2 Chron. xxvi. 18-20 ; 1 Cor. xi. 29.

[14] Chap. iii. 3.

[15] The New Testament is full of these contrasts; the Father is ever set against the world, Christ against the devil, and the Spirit against the flesh. See 1 John ii. 15, 16 ; iii. 8 ; Gal. v. 17.

[16] For many of the best thoughts in this section, I am indebted to a paper, entitled "The Rejected Man," being No. 41 of the series, " *Words of Truth.*"

III.—The Fruit of Man's Way

But what are the real fruits of this way? The first is a bad conscience :—"Their eyes were opened, and they knew that they were naked."[1] Then under a sense of their shame, they seek to hide it. "They sewed fig-leaves together, and made themselves aprons."

Such a conscience, such an "opening of the eyes," though it may precede conversion to God, is not conversion. It is not even one of the good things which survived the fall. It was acquired in the fall, and in itself drives man away from God, and only proves that he now sees himself. Man cannot bear his condition, or change it; therefore he hides it. But hiding it is not repentance. Where there is true repentance, there is ever open and unreserved confession.

So they made for themselves "aprons," not coats. "God made them coats;"[2] but they were content to hide so much only of their nakedness as they saw before them. God covers all by that which has died. But as long as the shame alone of sin is upon us, we shall seek to hide it, rather than to find atonement. Some creature or gift of God will be used, to keep us from seeing what we are, and to hide us from our own eyes. This is the reason why men so love the world, because the utter loss of outward things would shew us what poor, naked, shameful, restless, aching souls we are; while the abundance of outward things in some measure hides this from us, and keeps us from the humiliating perception of what we are. Should not then our shame be hid? Surely. God would have it covered,

[1] Chap. iii. 7.   [2] Chap. iii. 21.

but with that which, while it covers, is also a witness of our true state,—which confesses what we are, and that sin has brought death, though almighty grace out of death brings forth righteousness.

This leads to a further fruit of sin. " They hid themselves from the presence of the Lord." [3]   God has now to call out to them, " Where art thou ? "   How comes it you are not with me ?   Oh, how much is there in these words !   God finds His creatures hiding from Him.   He would let them learn the position into which they have brought themselves by disobedience.   Does He do this by reproaches ?   He simply says,—Where art thou ?   How comes it you are not with me ?   Adam had his excuse at hand, and man's excuse is yet the same.

In this excuse of Adam's we may see a yet further fruit of disobedience.   Guilty man attempts to clear himself by throwing blame upon some other one. [4]   The righteous ever justify God ; the sinner's great mark is self-justification ; accusing God, or man, or Satan, without one word of self-renunciation.   And, observe, the excuses were all true, but no recognition of God's claims or open confession of guilt is to be found in them.   God asks,—How comes it you are not with me ?   We answer,—Because some creature has beguiled us ; which is true, but no fit answer for a sinner.   Nor does it spring from, nor produce a good conscience.   And truth without a good conscience will not help ; rather it may become a snare, serving to root us in the most awful self-deception.   Admitting sin is not confessing it.   Extorted concession is not confession.   But if God has not His place, all spiritual sense is gone.   That which has made us err in heart, makes us err in understanding also.

[3] Chap. iii. 8.   [4] Chap. iii. 12, 13.

But there are other fruits of sin more external, and having to do with man's body and his dwelling place. The earth is cursed, and henceforth sorrow and toil are to be man's due portion, until he return to the dust whence he was taken:[5] a lot which seems hard, and yet is mercy; by toil to draw man out of self, and then by death to destroy him that hath the power of death, that is the devil. But on this I need not enter here. This part of man's lot has ample illustration everywhere.

One consequence of sin remains, characteristic of the lot of man as man, namely, exclusion from paradise. Fallen man is driven out, lest as fallen he eat and live for ever.[6] This, too, is love. Old Adam is shut out, but the Seed can enter through the flaming sword and past the cherubim. The Head first passed, and then the members; and though man as man, that is the first Adam, without sore peril may not enter into that from whence God has excluded him, yet for man in Christ, the Second Man, the way is open, and we are invited thitherward.[7] Paul was caught up, how he could not tell, whether in the body or out of it, into paradise;[8] and John, and others too, have passed that sword, which turns every way to shut out old Adam. For saints the way is open yet. But for man as man to seek by magic arts, as many have sought, without God's truth and love, in selfhood to enter into paradise, to hold communion with the spirits there, from which as fallen God in mercy has excluded them, only tends to make men into devils; for fallen man deceived and now akin to evil, by laws he little knows of, will come into contact with his like, even with evil, and by it will be yet more deceived, even while he thinks an angel of light is

---

[5] Chap. iii. 16–19.
[6] Chap. iii. 22–24.

[7] Rev. ii. 7.
[8] 2 Cor. xii. 3, 4.

teaching him. To man, therefore, as man, the way is closed. Paradise suits him not; therefore he may not enter there. But, instead, at the gate are forms of the Divine, cherubim, veiling and yet revealing God's glory; "figures of the true," such as fallen man can bear, instead of purely spiritual communications, serving as a veil for heavenly things, and yet, like the veils of the tabernacle, which were covered with cherubims,[9] in and by the veil itself revealing heavenly things. Israel, therefore, is forbidden to hold any unlawful intercourse with the spiritual world by means of "enchanters, witches, charmers, consulters with familiar spirits, wizards, or necromancers," as the nations of Canaan had done, because the Lord would speak to them by a Man, a Prophet like unto Moses.[10] Such is God's provision for fallen man,—forms of truth for those unfit for spiritual things; not leaving the creature in the spiritual world to an intercourse with spirits, for which, as fallen, it is incompetent; but giving, instead, a human form, (the cherubim had "the likeness of a man,"[11]) by the mystery of the Incarnation in all its forms to teach us in the flesh such things as man can profit by, and yet ordained to shew us higher things, and to be the door to open, even while it shuts, paradise; by that very door

[9] Exod. xxvi. 31, and xxxvi. 25.

[10] See the context, Deut. xviii. 9-19.

[11] See Ezek. i. 5, and x. 15. The application of these cherubic forms, the lion, the ox, the man, and the eagle, to the four Gospels, or rather to the four views of Christ which they respectively set forth, is well known. Irenæus, in the second century, writes thus: "Qui est omnium artifex Verbum, qui sedet super cherubim, et continet omnia, declaratus hominibus, dedit nobis quadriforme evangelium, quod in uno Spiritu continetur. Quemadmodum et David postulans ejus adventum ait, 'Qui sedes super cherubim appare,' etenim cherubim quadriformia et formæ ipsorum imagines sunt dispositionis Filii Dei."—*Adv. Hær.* l. iii. c. 11. Ambrose says, "Plerique putant ipsum Dominum nostrum in quatuor evangelii libris quatuor formis animalium figurari, quod idem homo, idem leo, idem vitulus, idem aquila, esse comprobatur," &c. — *Prolog. in Luc.* § 8.

teaching man how to pass it, through the fiery sword and past the cherubim. For if we enter, we must yet pass the figures and the sword to that which is within. Any coming into heavenly places is through this narrow gate. If I do but die to my own righteousness, and seek to come into that rest and joy which is by faith, the flaming sword at once meets me. What pains has even this amount of dying and entering cost many! Much more, if faith turn to experience, shall we find how sharp that sword is. Mere flesh cannot pass it; but it may be passed, and must be passed, if we would enter paradise. And awful as it appears, by it is cut off much of that which is our sorrow here.

IV.—THE REMEDY FOR MAN

SUCH is man,—such is his way, such are its fruits. Now let us see the remedy. This too has stages, all of God; first a Call, then a Promise, then a Gift, from Him.

First comes a Call, a voice which will be heard, to convince man of his state, saying, " Where art thou ?"[1] A voice which may sound in different ways, but which in all is crying to draw man back again; at first only convicting of sin, yet by this very conviction làying the foundation for man's recovery; leading man to come to himself before it is too late, that he may come to his Father, and from Him receive another life; and asking, though man oft turns a deaf ear, why we are not with Him, who still loves and yearns over us.

Then comes a Promise, full of grace and truth, touching the woman's Seed;[2] a promise not to old Adam, for the old

---

[1] Chap. iii. 9.　　　　[2] Chap. iii. 15.

man is fallen, and must pay the penalty :— no reprieve is given to the flesh : the cross which saves us is Adam's condemnation :— but a promise to the Seed or New Man, who shall be born, in and by whom man shall regain paradise. And as the promise is not to Adam, so, strictly speaking, there is now no trial of him. What Adam is, has been already proved. Blessed with every gift, through self he spoils all. Man therefore must die, but in the Son of Man man's line is restored and raised up again. The fall of man, like the fall of the year, by God's almighty love and wisdom opens the door for broader and richer seed-times. The very grave becomes the cradle of life, and death the way to resurrection. The new man springs out of the old, and from its grave, as a fair flower in spring out of the dark earth. For the Son of Man is indeed true man, though every man is not a son of man.[3] In the Son or Seed the curse is overcome. All that rose up in man falls in and by the Son of Man ; and all that fell in man is raised again in the Son of Man, the Seed, the heavenly man. The promise cannot fail to this Seed. Unlike the first covenant, which, being of law, needed two

[3] Man and the Son of Man are not the same. Adam, for instance, was man, but not the son of man. The son of man is the new man, which grows by grace out of the old man. So David says : " What is man that thou art mindful of him, or the son of man that thou visitest him ? " Again, " Thou preservest man and beast, but the sons of men put their trust under the shadow of thy wings."—Psalm viii. 4, and xxxvi. 7. Augustine speaks much of this difference : " Omnis filius hominis homo : non omnis homo filius hominis possit intelligi. Adam quippe homo, sed non filius hominis. Quapropter hinc jam licet adtendere atque discernere, quid hoc in loco inter hominem et filium hominis distet : ut qui portant imaginem terreni hominis, qui non est filius hominis, hominum nomine significentur ; qui autem portant imaginem cœlestis hominis, filii hominum potius appellentur. Ille enim et vetus homo dicitur ; iste autem novus. Sed novus ex vetere nascitur, quoniam spiritalis regeneratio mutatione vitæ terrenæ inchoatur, et ideo iste filius hominis nuncupatur."—*Enar.* in Psalm. viii.

parties, the better covenant needs but one, for it is a promise, and is fulfilled by the Promiser. Henceforth blessing
stands not on a creature's will, but on deeper, safer ground,
even the Lord's will. "Thou shalt" now gives place to
"I will."   If we are heirs, it is "according to the promise." [4]

Nor is the promise all.   God adds a Gift:—"The Lord
God made them coats of skins and clothed them." [5] Again
He works, for sin had broken his rest; working, as ever,
to restore blessedness; to cover not with fig-leave screens
only that part of our nakedness which is before each of us;
but to give us, upon us, in token of our state,—for the
skins spoke of death, and so confessed trespass,—a covering which, while it puts us in our place, as sinful creatures,
yet shelters us.

Praise the Lord from the earth, ye dragons, and all
deeps; fire and hail; snow and vapours; stormy wind fulfilling His word; mountains, and all hills; fruitful trees,
and all cedars; beasts, and all cattle; creeping things, and
flying fowl; kings of the earth, and all people; princes,
and all judges of the earth; both young men, and maidens;
old men, and children; let them praise the name of the
Lord; for His name alone is excellent; His glory is above
the earth and heaven.

There is yet another view of man, which gives us the
dispensational fulfilment of the same history.   In this
view Christ and the Church appear. He is "the Man,"
who "left father and mother and was joined to His wife."
While He slept, she was made out of Him; and they two
became one flesh. [6]   This is "the woman, which is of the

[4] Gal. iii. 29.
[5] Chap. iii. 21.

[6] Eph. v. 31, 32. "Viro dormi-
ente, Eva facta est; moriente Christo,

Man," and this is "the Man who is also by the woman."[7] For Christ is both the woman's Seed and Lord: the "Man who was not deceived,"[8] but who by the woman and for her came under judgment. And in this view the expression here used as to the formation of the woman shadows forth a mystery. For we read "He *builded* a woman;"[9] and of the Church it is often said, that she is "builded." "All the building fitly framed together groweth unto a holy temple in the Lord; in whom ye also are builded together for an habitation of God through the Spirit."[10] So gifts are "for the building of the body of Christ;"[11] a building which grows without sound of axe or hammer. Without it the Man is not perfect: the woman is "the filling up of Him that filleth all in all."[12] Such is the Church in its relation to Christ: one flesh, one life, one spirit, with Him; bearing His upright form, made like to Him, to be an imitator of God, with a nature more than animal,—for "among the beasts there was no help-meet for Adam,"[13] nor can His Bride "bear the mark or number of the beast."[14] For she is one, pure, holy Church; a body of many members, not united by likeness of outward

---

ecclesia facta est: et illa de latere viri, cùm costa detracta est; et ista de latere viri, quando latus lanceâ percussum est, et sacramenta profluxerunt."—*Aug.* in Psalm. cxxvii. (*E. V.* 128,) § 11. "Quando dormivit in cruce signum gestabat, immo implebat quod significatum est in Adam: quia cùm dormiret Adam, costa illi detracta est, et Eva facta est. Sic et Domino cùm dormiret in cruce, latus ejus percussum est, et sacramenta profluxerunt, unde facta est ecclesia," &c. *Enar.* in Psalm. cxxvi. (*E. V.* 127,) § 7. This interpretation is common to all the Fathers.

[7] 1 Cor. xi. 12.
[8] 1 Tim. ii. 14.
[9] Chap. ii. 22. *Margin*, Heb. ‫בּי‬. "Non solum de costâ Adam in typum ecclesiæ semel ædificavit Evam, sed quotidiè credentes et membra corporis sui ædificat, et de terris ad cœlum levat."—*Hieron.* in Amos ix. 6.
[10] Eph. ii. 21, 22.
[11] Eph. iv. 12, εἰς οἰκοδομὴν, κ.τ.λ.
[12] Eph. i. 23.
[13] Chap. ii. 20.
[14] Rev. xiii. 17.

form,—for the eye is unlike the hand and foot, and some
are outward and seen, and some are unseen,—but linked
together by the bond of common life, each in its place
and measure completing the body, which is one Church,
one " Mother of all living," the Bride, all whose members
are encircled in the divine arms, and included in the
divine love, which, because it is divine and eternal and
almighty, has breadth and length and depth and height
enough to hold them all. This is the Church, the woman
whose "power is on her Head," and whose Head and
Lord is " the image and glory of God."[15] formed in the
earth to rule all beasts and creatures, and to have "all
things put in subjection under His feet."[16] This is indeed
"a great mystery," when seen as "concerning Christ and the
Church;"[17] and leads to depths where fallen creatures cannot follow, for " no man knoweth the Son but the Father."[18]
But this we know, that in Him we have life; and what we
know not now, we shall know hereafter.

[15] 1 Cor. xi. 7, 10.
[16] Heb. ii. 8.
[17] Eph. v. 32.
[18] Matt. xi. 27.

PART 2

CAIN AND ABEL,

OR

THE CARNAL AND SPIRITUAL MIND

Chapters 4, 5

"That is not first which is spiritual, but that which is natural; and afterwards that which is spiritual." — 1 Cor. xv. 46.

"The flesh lusteth against the spirit." — Gal. v. 17.

CAIN AND ABEL,

OR

THE CARNAL AND SPIRITUAL MIND

Chapters 4, 5

ADAM did not live very long, before two other forms of life might be perceived proceeding from him. In these, the sons of old Adam, we have the first and second births of human nature, those forms of life, both carnal and spiritual, which by nature or grace grow out of the old man in each of us. And very different are these forms, though, like chaff and wheat, they spring both out of one root. Their order never changes. That is not first which is spiritual, but that which is natural. Age after age it is the same, within, or without, or in the dispensations. The outcome of Adam varies not. Some forms of life there are, which are " of old ordained to condemnation."[1] These are the wild natural fruits; and, the root being known, its fruit is foreseen as surely as that brambles will only bear brambles. But besides these there are other forms of life, springing out of man, the fruits of " the engrafted word,"[2] which are predestined to glory. Each of these I would now trace, first within, and then more outwardly. The tale is one on

---

[1] Jude 4.   [2] James i. 21.

every platform. The outward fulfilments are but the manifestations that such or such a life prevails within.

I.—The First and Second Birth

WE have then here in Adam's sons, (that is, if we trace the story in its inward application,) the ways and works of the carnal and spiritual mind, which spring from the conjunction of the understanding and will, the inward man and woman.[1] That is not first which is spiritual, but that which is natural; and afterwards that which is spiritual.[2] What is first developed out of man is carnal,—that " carnal mind, ($\phi\rho\acute{o}\nu\eta\mu\alpha$ $\sigma\alpha\rho\kappa\grave{o}s$,) which is enmity against God ; which is not subject to the law of God, neither indeed can be."[3] This is Cain. But there is a second birth ; another life is born, which by grace springs out of the same old Adam ; and this second birth, this " spiritual mind," ($\phi\rho\acute{o}\nu\eta\mu\alpha$ $\pi\nu\epsilon\acute{v}\mu\alpha\tau\sigma s$,) is Abel, who so lives that he obtains witness of God that he is righteous. Long ere Adam dies,—and he must die in us, before the world of blessing rises beyond the flood of waters,—long ere we

---

[1] The *Ordinary Gloss* here is as follows : "Adam vero cognovit uxorem suam. Hic agitur de prolificatione, per quam intelligitur operatio humana, ad quam conveniunt vir et mulier, id est, ratio et pars sensitiva. Hæc operatio producitur a ratione et parte sensitivâ . . . . operatio mala, per Cain significata : Abel autem operatio bona. Abel enim Hebraicè dicitur הבל, quod est *vapor*, cujus proprium est ascendere sursum, sicut operatio bona tendit ad Deum. Cain autem a Deo maledicitur, quia malum opus a Deo punitur," &c.— *Gloss.*

Ordin. in loco. Ambrose adds : "Et sicut fœminis dedit vulvam natura, in quâ uniuscujusque animantis generatio formatur, ita est quædam virtus animæ, quæ velut quodam vulvæ genitalis secreto cogitationum nostrarum suscipere fœmina, conceptus fovere, partus solet edere. Neque enim aliter diceret Esaias, ' In utero accepimus, et parturivimus spiritum,' nisi vulvam animæ novisset," &c.— *De Cain et Abel,* l. i. c. 10, § 47.

[2] 1 Cor. xv. 46.

[3] Rom. viii. 7.

know the risen life, we may perceive the workings of these
two minds, the flesh and the spirit, striving together in us:
the carnal seed, the firstborn, lusting against the spirit;
while the spiritual mind, by its desires to please God,
seems but to raise the flesh to greater acts of carnal opposition.[4]

The workings of these two minds are shewn out here.
The carnal mind, like Cain, ignoring sin and the fall, is
busy to improve the fallen creature; offering the fruit and
cultivation of the cursed earth to God, as though such
things could please Him: while the other, that is the
spirit, confessing sin, by a sacrifice which involves, not the
improvement of the earth, but the death and suffering of
the creature, confesses death and yet looks for help in God,
trusting His love and truth to meet us in our helplessness.
To Cain it is quite natural to be out of paradise. The
world never strikes him as being anything but what it
should be. Abel's eye cannot but see that sin is in the
world, and his religion is an open confession of death,
though also of atonement through death. In both the
worship is offered "to the Lord;"[5] for the flesh can be sincere in its religion, and yet mistake grievously. Cain, as
much as Abel, sought acceptance; but his desire is witnessed in the form of his oblation. The flesh seeks to be
accepted as it is; not to be changed from what it is by
dying to its selfhood; but to be accepted, and yet remain

---

[4] " Illud igitur quod inter Cain et
Abel exortum est, inter duas civi-
tates, Dei et hominum, inimicitias
demonstravit. Et in uno quippe
homine 'caro concupiscit adversus
spiritum, et spiritus adversus carnem,'" &c.—*Aug. de Civitat.* l. xv.
c. 5. " Adjecit, inquit, parere Abel,
hoc est meliorem Eva ex se genera-
vit sententiam. . . . Et ideo in
nobis antè nascitur Cain, seipsum
præferens: postea Abel generatur,
in quo fit reverentia divinitatis. . .
Has duas sectas anima una parturit,"
&c.—*Ambros. de Cain et Abel*, l. i.
c. 1, § 4, and c. 3, § 10.
[5] Chap. iv. 3.

the same old Cain: and with a true and holy God this is impossible. Therefore the flesh is angry with the spirit, and rises, and overcomes, and for a season quenches it. But God raises it up again in Seth, that other seed, " which God appointed instead of Abel."[6] Thenceforth Cain, that is the flesh, is "cursed;"[7] a judgment which was not pronounced on old Adam; for man as man, though fallen under death, and with the earth cursed for his sake, is not directly cursed. But Cain is cursed:—"Cursed art thou from the earth:" even as the carnal mind is cursed which lusts against the spirit.

Then come the fruits of these two lives, for they too, each in their own way, must further develope themselves. Each bears its proper fruit in us, in an order and succession which is invariable. The names of the seed describe the progress of each, but their acts speak even more plainly. The one, the carnal mind, " goes out from the presence of the Lord,"[8] and busies itself with " cities," and with " works in brass and iron;" building on the earth, instructing artificers in varied works in brass and iron, establishing itself in what it is and has, instead of dying to what it is, that it may reach better things; while the other life, that of the spirit, finds its rest in God, and suffers and dies in hope of resurrection; one form of life after another passing away and dying out, to be replaced by still better thoughts and affections. " And he died," never noted throughout Cain's line, (for the flesh hates to think of such a change as is implied in dying,) is the understood portion of all Seth's line, save of him who was not, for God took him.[9] And the metals in which Cain's

---

[6] Chap. iv. 25.
[7] Chap. iv. 11.

[8] Chap. iv. 16.
[9] Chap. v. 8, 11, 14, 17, &c.

seed are workers, shew in figure the sort of truths with which the carnal mind is occupied. For the metals all figure truths; gold and silver, those which are more precious and spiritual; brass and iron, those of an inferior class, connected with the outward world, and merely natural things. In this hard world, iron is most useful. Cain's seed therefore prefer it to the gold or silver which may be used in God's tabernacle. Nevertheless, the Lord, foreseeing better days, has said, " For brass I will bring gold, and for iron silver, and for wood brass;"[10] foretelling an increase and advance of truth in the last days. It is noteworthy, too, that the lives before the flood in each of these lines are of a length never known after it. So the forms of life, which succeed each other in us before we have been brought to know regeneration, are much longer in coming to their end, than those which we know after we have passed the mystic waters. But long as these first lives are, they all die out, and of the fleshly seed not one survives the first world. The other seed is carried through the flood : the life which grows out of the spiritual mind, not only is not destroyed, but is much strengthened by that judgment. But the carnal mind never reaches the new earth, where the rainbow is set as a token of the covenant.

---

[10] Isa. lx. 17. Compare also the " nations ruled with a rod of iron," (Rev. xii. 5, xix. 15,) and the " golden mercy-seat" for redeemed Israel. (Heb. ix. 4, &c.) See, too, what is said of the "river Pison, which compasseth the land of Havilah, where there is gold, and the gold of that land is good." (Gen. ii. 11, 12.) Gregory the Great thus explains these figures : — "Quid vero aurum, nisi sapientiam appellat, de quâ dicitur, ' Thesaurus desiderabilis in ore sapientis est;' quæ et rectè auri appellatione signatur, quia sicut auro temporalia, ita sapientiâ bona æterna mercantur. . . . Quid etiam per argentum nisi divina eloquia figurantur, de quibus dicitur, ' Eloquia Domini argentum igne examinatum,' " &c. — *Moral. in Job,* l. iv. c. 31, § 61.

If we look further at the names in these two lines,—for the names in Scripture ever denote character,—we shall learn yet more of the different forms of life, which succeed each other in us, both in the flesh and in the spirit. For flesh and spirit, though in substance unchanged, take fresh forms at different stages. A life of faith, or of sonship, or service, are all at root the same elect spirit; but this one spirit shews itself in different forms, according to the varying degrees of its development; as the self-same tree or flower looks different at different stages of its growth. These different forms, which succeed each other, are here represented to us by different men, each of whom figures one stage or form of the inward life. Cain means *a possession*,[11] a name pointing, as his life, to hopes fixed on earthly things. Abel, that is *a vapour*,[12] speaks of soon passing hence, and of mounting up into another higher atmosphere. The names of this line, as raised up in Seth, tell all the different parts of the same mystery. We first have Seth, that is *replaced*; then Enos, that is *infirm man*; then Cainan, that is *lamentation*; then Mahalaleel, that is *praising God*. After this comes Jared, that is, *strong*, or *commanding*; then Enoch, that is *dedication*; then Methuselah, that is *the spoiling of death*; then Lamech, that is *humbled*; then Noah, *quietness*. Thus goes this life. Instead of Adam, there is a life *replaced* in a state to serve God. Then comes the sense of *wretched weakness*; then *lamentation* for this; then *praise* and thanksgiving; after which comes *strength* to command

---

[11] Heb. קִין.
[12] Heb. הבל, a *vapour*, or *vanity*. So the Preacher says in Ecclesiastes, "Vanity of vanities, all is vanity." הבל הבלים כל הבל ; and, again,

"Every man living is vanity," or Abel. Every living man is Abel. He who saves his life shall lose it; and he who loses, saves it. See note 1, p. 88.

and overcome; then a life of real *dedication*; then the *spoiling of death*; then true *humiliation*; and then a life of *rest*, which passes from the world of the curse to that beyond the deep waters.[13] Such was the course; such is it now. I need not trace Cain's line, though there too the names are significant. But I note that in Cain's seed we find an Enoch, though at a much earlier stage than in the other line; while in both, the last but one is Lamech, that is *the humbled one*, or humiliation. For the flesh professes soon to reach that dedication, (Enoch is *dedication*,) which the spiritual seed is long waiting for;[14] while the fact that in both seeds a stage is reached which

---

[13] The *Ordinary Gloss*, which is but a summing up of the comments of the Fathers, is as follows here:— "Interpretatio nominum hujus generationis mysterium signat. Adam interpretatur *homo* vel *rubra terra*; Seth, *positio* vel *resurrectio*; Enos, *homo*; Cainan, *lamentatio*; Mahalalel, *laudans Deum*; Jared, *roboratus*; Enoch, *dedicatio*; Mathusalam, *mortis emissio*; Lamech, *humiliatus*; Noe, *requies*. Procedens ergo, *homo* de terrâ, *resurgens* a peccatis, erit *homo deflens* peccata pristina, *et invocans Deum*; sicque laudans Deum, *roboratus* Spiritu Dei, *dedicatur* in vitam æternam. Atque *victor mortis*, Deo *subjectus*, requiem possidet sempiternam, quam significat Noe, qui *requies* interpretatur. Et notandum quia in generatione Seth nulla fœmina ponitur nominatim, sicut in generatione Cain: justorum enim est omnia viriliter agere, nihil fœmineum, nihil fragile usurpare. Procedit etiam hæc generatio per denarium usque ad Noe, in quo præceptorum significatur impletio, sicut per undenarium in generatione Cain transgressio. In generatione injustorum primus Enoch ponitur, qui *dedicatio* interpretatur, quia reprobi in præsente vitâ spei suæ radicem figunt. In generatione justorum Enoch ab Adam septimus ponitur, quia hìc manentem civitatem non quærunt, sed expectationem usque in finem temporis extendunt, quod septenariâ revolutione terminatur, cùm æternitas octava successerit; unde iste Enoch, qui ponitur septimus, translatus est,"&c.—*Gloss. Ord. in loco.* See also *Aug. de Civit.* xv. c. 17, 18.

[14] In the first line, Enoch is the son of Cain. (Çhap. iv. 17.) The elect Enoch comes in the seventh stage. (Chap. v. 21, and Jude 14.) "In stirpe Cain, Enoch, qui *dedicatio* interpretatur, primus nascitur: in electorum verò progenie Enoch septimus perhibetur. Quia videlicet reprobi in hâc vitâ, quæ ante est, semetipsos ædificando dedicant. Electi verò ædificationis suæ dedicationem in fine temporis, id est in septimo, exspectant," &c.—*Greg. M. Moral. in Job*, l. xvi. c. 10, § 15.

is, and is felt to be, indeed Lamech, only shews how the flesh, as well as the spirit, may be at length both *poor and humbled*; the one humiliation, like the care and sorrow of the world, only to bring forth a *worldly possession* which *runs or flows away*;[15] the other, like that godly sorrow, which brings forth a *rest* and repentance never to be repented of.[16]

But this inward view of the two seeds will not be seen by all. I turn, therefore, to the outward fulfilment of the same history.

II.—THE CARNAL AND THE SPIRITUAL

IN this view Adam's sons represent the two great classes of the sons of men, in whom respectively the flesh and spirit rule, and who, by the preponderance of the one or of the other, fall under one or other of those two great classes, the carnal and spiritual, which make up the human family; who, though born by nature from the same womb, and nursed at first by the same mother, in their ways and ends are most distinct, both worshipping indeed the same God, but very differently; the one, offering Him the improvement of the creature,—for carnal men must have a religion as well as spiritual men,—the other, accepting judgment for sin, pouring out a life to Him, in hope of resurrection : the one, ignoring the fact of the curse, and going out to fill the earth with crimes, and arts, and energies; the other, suffering as martyrs here, and departing

---

[15] Lamech's sons (Cain's Lamech) were Tubal-cain, Jubal, and Jabal. (Chap. iv. 22.) Tubal-cain means "*worldly possession.*" Jubal and Jabal mean "*that which runs or flows away.*" The other Lamech's son was Noah, or "*rest.*"

[16] 2 Cor. vii. 10.

to find, what they had not here, a home, in another world.
For " by faith Abel offered unto God." [1] He saw the
curse, and instead of hiding from himself that sin and
death are here, he makes this the base of his religion,
looking to God for better things to come. And his seed
offer still by faith. They see the curse, that they are sinful
creatures, for their sin cast out of paradise. But the death
of the Lamb, though it seals the judgment on sin, pledges
to them that there is a way through death out of it.
Therefore they are content to give up their lives. Others
may seek to improve self ; they will rather die to self.
Their acceptance is not in self improved, but in deliverance
out of self by the cross, through a Deliverer. Hence they
take willingly the sinner's place ; first by baptism confessing
death in them ; (for baptism is burial,[2] and we do not bury
live things, but dead things ;) and then living a life of
daily death in hope of resurrection.

Not so the other seed. Cain's line are all for cultivating
the ground, that is, improving the fallen creature. When
most religious, they yet spare the flesh. They like what
is beautiful in religion : they can appreciate good fruits.
But let there be the shedding of blood, a life poured out,
such self-mortification is with them rank superstition ;
while the judgment of the pride of reason and of sense
is treason against Him who suffered us to become such
creatures as we now are. They are not, they feel, in Eden,
but in a world where sin and sorrow reign on every hand.
Death is here : blink it they cannot. A curse is working
in that soil, on which they spend so much labour. But
they will approach God as though no sin were here ; as if
in soul and body all were right and normal. What have

---

[1] Heb. xi. 4.   [2] Rom. vi. 4; Col. ii. 12.

they to do with anything so horrid as the cross? No
bloodshedding—no "religion of the shambles"—for such
worshippers. Hence the efforts to seem other than they
really are. Hence the wrath, if anything open their eyes
to see their state in God's sight. Then these men, who
mock at the blood poured out, who say that crosses and
mortifications are brutal and brutalising, will not scruple
to hate a brother worshipper, if he be holier, or more
accepted, than they are; like their father Cain, who would
not offer the blood of the Lamb, but could stain his hands
in his own brother's blood. Surely "the way of Cain"[3]
remains; and the objectors to a worship by blood are yet
"murderers;"[4] though, like Cain, they profess not to be
conscious of it.

Is, then, the improvement of the creature wrong? Are
good fruits not acceptable? On the contrary, God accepts
them as a meat offering, where the blood ("for the blood
is the life,"[5]) has first been shed in a burnt offering. For
man's duty to his neighbour (and the meat offering is this)
is accepted, if God first has His portion.[6] But to think that
these fruits can alone satisfy God is just Cain's error, and
must meet with reprobation. God will accept anything He
can—anything which proceeds on real ground; but take a
place which does not belong to you, then God, because He

---

[3] Jude 11.

[4] "He that hateth his brother is
a murderer."—1 John iii. 15.

[5] Lev. xvii. 13, 14.

[6] The difference of the burnt offering and meat offering was this:—
a life was offered in the one, fruits
in the other. (See Lev. i. ii.) Life
is that which God claimed as His
portion in creation, (Gen. ix. 4;) as
an emblem, therefore, it represents
what the creature owes to God.
But the fruit of the herb and of
the tree was man's allotted portion,
(Gen. i. 29;) as such, it is the figure
of man's claim, or of what we owe
to man. What we owe to God or
to man is respectively our duty to
either. Thus, in the burnt offering,
the surrender of a life figured man's
duty to God; while fruits, in the
meat offering, represented man's
duty to his neighbour.

is true, cannot meet you there; for He deals with realities, and the course you pursue is not a reality. It does not confess your place as fallen; therefore He cannot meet it, though it may have cost you much. But only be true; and without attempting to meet God with the fruits which the cursed earth produces, only confess, by act and voice, that you are fallen, and that in this state, though sin be in the world, you yet give God credit for grace and power to meet it; then, as in Abel's case, so in yours, the faith that puts you on such ground must be accepted. Remember, Cain, because he got off true ground, lost the help of the true God. Abel, because confessing the truth of sin and death, found acceptance and all the help he needed.

III.—Their Lives

And the lives of these two seeds are as marked as their religions. As it was in Cain's day, so is it now. The seed, whose religion is to improve the fallen creature, "goes out from the presence of the Lord," and seeks to make a ruined world happy without God, by "building cities," and "inventing harps," and "instructing every artificer in brass and iron;"[1] in a word, by civilising the world with arts, striving to make life easy, and the world a safe dwelling place. The other are happy in God without the world; dying out of it, or rising to a better world. The one judge and slay their brother: the other do not judge even the murderer; but, inasmuch as the world is not purged from blood, they are as yet strangers and pilgrims in it. The one call lands after their own names,

[1] Chap. iv. 17, 21, 22.

and cities "after the names of their sons," to make the world their own, and not the Lord's, if possible.[2] The other "call themselves by the name of the Lord," and would make themselves the Lord's and not their own, with His name upon them.[3] So the one live,—for as I have already said, no death is recorded in any of Cain's seed; the other die, writing death as their portion; "And he died," is recorded of every one of them, save of him "who was not, for God took him;" while they count their years by days, as it is written of each, "All the days of such a one were so many years, and he died."[4] So run the seeds each in their course. The carnal line have by far the most to shew on earth; but the end of their cities and music is foreseen; Enoch warns of the day when the Lord shall come, and all His saints with Him; when the earthly city shall fall, and "the voice of harpers and musicians and trumpeters shall no more be heard in her; when no craftsman, of whatever craft he be, shall be found in her; because in her is found the blood of the saints, and of all that are slain upon the earth."[5]

Further distinctions are shewn in other points recorded here. There are, however, some similarities. The last generation but one in each line is Lamech; and as name denotes character, this sameness of name marks some resemblance. For the Church and world, the carnal and spiritual seed, in the long run, and just before the judgment, become too much alike. Still they differ. Lamech "dies" in Seth's line: he yet has faith of better things; while his speech (for the words of both are recorded) points out how deep a difference exists under the outward similarity. For Lamech in Cain's line boasts that

---

[2] Compare chap. iv. 17.
[3] Chap. iv. 26, *margin.*
[4] See chap. v. *passim.*
[5] Rev. xviii. 22-24.

Cain had been preserved spite of his sin, and argues from this that he may also sin with impunity:—"I have slain," he says, "a man to my wounding, and a young man to my hurt;" but since God has set a mark on Cain, lest he be destroyed, "if Cain shall be avenged seven-fold, surely Lamech seventy and seven-fold:"[6] that is, God has spared one who sinned like Cain; how much more will He preserve me, though I too am a murderer. So from grace this Lamech argues that sin may abound. The other Lamech also speaks, but it is of "the ground the Lord hath cursed," and of the "rest" out of it, which "shall comfort them:" —"This same shall comfort us concerning our toil, because of the ground which the Lord hath cursed."[7] The one says in effect, "Where is the God of judgment?" The other confesses sin, in hope of better things. All this is timely truth for us; for the days are near of the last judgment of the first creation. The time has come when the Church and world are both Lamech, that is "poor," with small difference to be seen anywhere. And yet under this, some misuse grace to sin, and some by grace look for a Deliverer; while a remnant escapes who see not death, and another is saved even through the judgment.

I add but a word on the dispensational fulfilment of this. In this view the two seeds, the elder and the younger, are the Jew and the Christian Church. That was not first which is spiritual, but that which is natural. First came the fleshly dispensation, and then the spiritual. The Jew seeking to improve the earth; Christ and the Church giving a life to God. The Jew slaying the righteous seed, which yet is raised up; the Church dying in hope of resurrection. Both of these are Adam's sons; both acknow-

[6] Chap. iv. 23, 24.   [7] Chap. v. 28, 29.

ledge the same one God, though in very different life and worship; the one, departing to be with Christ; the other, going out " from the presence of the Lord," as " fugitives and vagabonds in the earth;"[8] finding no ease or rest for the sole of their feet, and fearing, where no fear is, that every one that findeth them shall slay them;[9] but, like Cain, providentially preserved, for the Jew has a mark set upon him, lest he be slain. The Lord yet preserves him wondrously. But to the end his portion is of this earth, in the first, not in the new, creation.[10]

So the last shall be first, and the first last. The dead shall live, and earthly life shall pass away. And the souls under the altar shall be at rest, for they have washed their robes in the blood of the Lamb.

---

[8] Chap. iv. 16.

[9] Compare chap. iv. 14, and Deut. xxviii. 65, 66.

[10] Augustine (*Contr. Faust. Man.* l. xii. c. 9, and 13,) goes very fully into the dispensational application of all this history, dwelling particularly on the fact that the Jew, like Cain, was preserved, and had a mark set on him. So, too, Ambrose: " Figura Synagogæ et Ecclesiæ in his duobus fratribus ... Cain et Abel. Per Cain parricidialis populus intelligitur Judæorum, qui Domini sui et secundum Mariæ virginis partum Fratris, ut ita dicam, sanguinem persecutus est. Per Abel autem intelligitur Christianus adhærens Deo," &c.—*De Cain et Abel,* l. i. c. 2. See John viii. 44.

PART 3

NOAH, OR REGENERATION

Chapters 6-11

" The world that then was being overflowed with water perished."– 2 PET. iii. 6

" The like figure whereunto even baptism doth also now save us."—1 PET. iii. 21

NOAH, OR REGENERATION

Chapters 6-11

THE line of Seth has several generations before Noah
comes, in whom, through the judgment of the first creation, man is taken out of the sphere of fallen Adam, into a
world beyond the flood, where he is set in new blessedness.
So the spiritual mind goes through successive steps or
forms, before that form of life appears which passes the
waters, and thus knows regeneration.   For souls may be
quickened, and know that life in which the flesh lusteth
against the spirit: and in spirit, like Abel, offer spiritual
sacrifices, as many offered under the Jewish dispensation;
and as many yet offer, who in spirit are no further advanced than those righteous souls, " who through fear of
death were all their life-time subject to bondage;" [1] and
yet not know that way through the flood, which is fellowship in Christ's death and resurrection; a stage in which
the Word not only comes into our lot, and in union with
us here quickens and sanctifies us as in the first creation ;
but in which by that same Word we come into His lot,
and by Him find ourselves delivered out of this present
world, as baptism typifies; through the travail pains and

[1] Heb. ii. 15.

groans of this first creation, brought forth into another
sphere, where we are not begotten or quickened only, but
truly born.   Such a stage arrives in its season, and of it
Noah is the divinely appointed figure, in whom the whole
course of regeneration is set forth, every secret of this
great mystery being here drawn for us as God alone could
draw it.[2]

The subject is immense, whatever view we take of it,
whether inward, outward, or dispensational.   Its length,
and depth, and breadth cannot be told.   It has "wheels
within wheels, full of eyes, and looking every way."   Any
attempt therefore to know it must be "in part," and even
of that part still less can be expressed.   But if the excess
of light here dazzles as yet, let us rejoice that we may
possess these things with little or no knowledge of them.
To be born, it is not needful to know how we are born.
We must grow to manhood, or even age, ere we can think
on such things.   So with the new birth, we must be born
again, and grow up in Christ, ere these things open to us.
To apprehend therefore is well : but far better is it to be
apprehended for these things in Christ Jesus.[3]   Yet let
him that hath anointed eyes behold the wonders of the
work of God here shadowed forth for our learning.

We have then here Regeneration ; the way by which
man, already quickened and possessing spiritual life, is
borne, through the waters, to a world of light beyond.
The work is wrought within, as well as without us.   Yet it is
the self-same work and Worker everywhere, who, like
some musician in solo or in chorus repeating the same
sweet strain, repeats His work in a soul, or church, or age,
making each to echo back the same melody.

Noah then is the spiritual mind,—for he is only the

[2] 1 Pet. iii. 20, 21.   [3] Phil. iii. 12.

continuation of Seth's line, and figures the form of life which the spiritual mind takes at this stage in its development, when it has come so far as to know the judgment of the old creation, and the way through that judgment to a cleansed and better world. This stage, if we regard it closely, will be seen to embrace several distinct parts : for we may see Noah as in the world to be judged, still in the midst of its sins, though undefiled by them ; or as going through the waters, and tossed by them, separated from the old world, and yet not come to the cleansed world ; or, as on resurrection ground, coming out of the ark into that sphere where judgment is past, and he in joyful liberty. Each of these are stages of regeneration. There is, first, the discovery of the sin which is working in the first creation, upon the ground of the old man ; then the experience of the judgment of that old man, during which we are tossed about, and the waves and billows of God's judgments are inwardly passed through ; and lastly, the rest in resurrection life, when we feel and know ourselves in liberty and redemption beyond those dark waters. And each of these stages has its own parts, for in grace as in nature each general truth comprises many others. The outline may first be seen, then the particulars: first the dark cloud, then the countless rain-drops, full of beauties, if the sun shines. So is the truth, that heavenly rain, which, like its Maker, challenges our wonder the more we contemplate it.

I. — Noah on the Ground of the Old Man

Chapter 6

Noah first is seen as still in the old world, in the midst of the sins of Adam's sons, yet separate from them. Evil springing out of Adam had now become monstrous. "God looked upon the earth, and behold, it was corrupt, for all flesh had corrupted his way upon the earth." But in the midst of this, "Noah was a just man, and perfect in his generations, and Noah walked with God." [1] So while the flesh or carnal mind in us goes on from step to step bringing to light its own corruption, the spiritual mind within like Noah is true to God, and bears witness against the evil of the carnal mind, which is continually more and more displaying its enormity. The fruit and corruption of the carnal mind in man, like the seed of Cain, must shew itself before we fully know regeneration; for regeneration is not the improvement but the judgment of the old man, out of which the spirit is saved by a mystic death and resurrection. As an introduction therefore to this form of life we are first shewn the state into which both the lines of Cain and Seth are now fallen. Both flesh and spirit fail. But these very sins are through God's grace the occasion for lifting man, in Noah, into another world. For Noah, as I have said, is the spiritual mind, at the stage when it has come to know the utter corruption of the old creation, and that its deliverance must be through the death and judgment of the whole ground and works of the old man. Through sin and its judgment is man advanced. Noah is not brought out of the Adam world into the world of the rainbow beyond the deep waters, until Adam's seed are proved to be so corrupt, that they and their world must be condemned together. And just as Noah was not taken to a world of blessing through the waters, until the evil of man had fully shewn itself; and just as the doctrine of regeneration was not preached to men, till by their rejection of God's Son they had proved their utter fall and per-

[1] Chap. vi. 9, 12.

versity; so within, regeneration is not reached but through the discovery of the awful evil which is the legitimate fruit and development of the old man. Regeneration cannot be truly known till we have proved the corruptness and helplessness of all that springs from old Adam. For regeneration is no improvement of the old man, but a new birth out of its death and dissolution.

And indeed we shall find this law throughout, that the failure of one thing through grace brings in a better thing. Where sin abounds, grace yet more abounds. Thus that short-sighted wisdom which would prevent falling, would by so doing prevent all progress to higher things; for each advancing form of life, which God takes up, springs out of the failure of that which has preceded it. The seed falls into the ground, and dies, and becomes rotten; but the result is the resurrection of many seeds. So the juice of grapes or corn is put into the still; and thence, by decomposition and fermentation, (both forms of corruption,) is evolved a higher purity and spirituality. So is it here. The evil fruit of Adam becomes the occasion for God to lift the race in Noah to higher privileges. Now therefore is felt, what may have seemed like exaggeration till we reach this stage, that "every imagination of the thoughts of man's heart is only evil continually." [2] But the spiritual mind by all this is being led, it knows not how, to liberties and glories, which as yet it has not dreamt of. Meanwhile, like Noah in the world of old, it is a witness against all the evil which has sprung out of old Adam. Great are the confusions amongst which it dwells. Little may it be able to correct the evil. It seems, and is, part of the same creature. It may be tempted to think it will be destroyed with that sin which riots round it. But the Lord sees how

[2] Chap. vi. 5.

different this mind is from that in which it dwells, and in His time surely will deliver it.

The details in this view are most striking, as they are yet fulfilled in each regenerate soul, though, from our blindness as to the workings of our inward man, and our want of words to describe the processes of the inward life, it is difficult to express the spiritual reality; for the spiritual can only be uttered through the natural; and from the imperfection of the medium some darkness will come in. But the figure here is divinely complete, little as the mind of man as yet may be able to interpret it. The state of the creature is thus described:—" Men multiplied on the earth, and daughters were born to them." [3] " Men," as we have seen, are certain minds or thoughts; and a host of thoughts are now discerned to be alive within us; their "daughters" are the affections springing from them, which, by the words, " daughters of men," are shewn to be corrupt and carnal.[4] Then the " sons of God," that is, thoughts which are not of the earth, mix with " daughters of men," that is, impure affections.[5] If the world within

---

[3] Chap. vi. 1, 2.

[4] See what is said of the " man " and the " woman," above, pp. 41 and 53; and of Cain and Abel, p. 90. Ambrose, who in his book *De Noe et Arcâ*, has gone at great length into the inward sense of all this history, makes the " *sons*," " viriles quædam et fortiores disceptationes," and the " *daughters*," " molliores cogitationes," (c. 21, § 77.) Augustine is more exact in the passage cited above.

[5] It is generally assumed now that by the " sons of God " here, the children of Seth are meant. I doubt it, as the Old Testament usage of the words seems to point to angels. See Job i. 6; ii. 1; xxxviii. 7;

and compare Luke xx. 36. I am sure that in the inward fulfilment, the state described here is not only the corruption of the human spirit, but something worse, through fallen spirits. Justin M., (*Apol.* i. § 21, ii. § 6,) Irenæus, (*Adv. Hær.* l. iv. c. 36, § 4,) Clement of Alexandria, (*Strom.* l. iii. § 7,) Cyprian, (*De Hab. Virg.* c. 9,) Ambrose, (*De Noe,* c. 4, § 8,) Tertullian, (*De Hab. Mul.* c. 2,) and others, take the " sons of God " here to be angels. The words, τὸν ὅμοιον τούτοις τρόπον, in Jude 6, 7, declaring the similarity between the sin of Sodom and that of the angels who fell, are very remarkable.

could be seen, and the workings of spirit laid open, this is what would appear before regeneration. There is awful inward confusion, the result of the mixture of the flesh and of the spirit; the affections of the flesh seducing the higher thoughts of the spirit, and so producing "giants," that is, earthborn thoughts, which are full of crime and violence. Those who by grace have reached regeneration, know perhaps as little of the exact working of the evil in them, which they have groaned over, as Noah knew of the sin and corruption of the carnal seed; but they will remember the awful sense of inward confusion which preceded their deliverance, and how their spirit, though it sought to walk with God, was constantly grieved by the dreadful workings of the fleshly mind within them. Such as know most of this stage will best see the figure, as it is drawn for us in this history.

Meanwhile, in the midst of these confusions, which are the ripe and rotting fruits of old Adam, Noah, the spiritual mind, remains incorrupt, like the remnants which survive each fallen dispensation, not only bearing witness that judgment must come, but in act and deed passing sentence upon the old creation, laying the axe to the root of the trees,[6] in a work of faith, which is the divinely appointed way of safety. The ark, by which he goes through the judgment, formed by cutting down and judging the pride and strength of that soil in which the curse works, figures the cross by which we are severed from the world, by which it is crucified to us, and we unto the world. As that ark was made up of many beams, so is the cross which delivers us from the world composed of many parts; smaller crosses, all of which we need, add to its length and breadth, nor may we cut off any of them. A time will

[6] Matt. iii. 10.

come, if we reach the risen life, when we may go forth free; but while in the old world, or amid the waves, the cross, like the ark, is our safety: we dare not shorten it. In it is light, a " window " and a " door." [7] In it is food, " all food that may be eaten." [8] In it are " heights and depths." [9] By it alone can the flood be passed. Let us bear it, for it will bear us. [10]

In or by this ark the man is saved, and with him a remnant of all the beasts, both clean and unclean. This is a great mystery. Some speak as though in regeneration all the evil of the old nature were entirely left behind, so that nothing should remain of it. Hence they are surprised to see evil passions in regenerate souls. But a remnant of beasts goes through the flood of waters. These beasts, as we have seen, figure certain animal faculties or powers in the creature. Some are gentle and clean, as lambs and doves; some unclean and fierce, as wolves, or swine, or foxes. Yet even of the unclean a remnant lives. Regeneration does not wholly take away or abolish bad tempers. While man is conscious of the judgment, tossed with its waves, and so dying daily to the old nature, these evil powers or desires are so far checked as to cease for awhile to be hurtful to him. By providence and grace they are

---

[7] Chap. vi. 16. Some have supposed that this *"window,"* צֹהַר a word only occurring here, was an inward lamp or light; connecting the word with יִצְהָר or *"oil,"* and that again with the χρίσμα mentioned 1 John ii. 27, "the anointing," which makes the light or instruction of this world unnecessary. But the spiritual sense will be substantially the same, whichever view we take of this zohar or " window."

[8] Chap. vi. 21.

[9] Chap. vi. 15, 16.

[10] So Augustine says, "Mysterium commendabat . . . ut per lignum liberaretur figura orbis terrarum, quia in ligno figenda erat Vita orbis terrarum," &c.—*In Johan.* tract. ix. c. 11. He gives the same interpretation, *De Civitat.* l. xv. c. 26. So, too, Justin Martyr: Ὁ γὰρ Χριστὸς . . . . ἀρχὴ πάλιν ἄλλου γένους γέγονεν τοῦ ἀναγεννηθέντος ὑπ' αὐτοῦ δι' ὕδατος καὶ πίστεως καὶ ξύλου, τοῦ τὸ μυστήριον τοῦ σταυροῦ ἔχοντος· ὃν τρόπον καὶ ὁ Νῶε ἐν ξύλῳ διεσώθη, κ.τ.λ.—*Dial. c. Tryph.* c. 138.

so stilled, and by circumstances so modified and weakened in us, that for a season at least they are subject to the man; the Lord thus repairing in regeneration the loss which human nature had sustained in Adam's fall; for in Noah man recovers power over beasts: but they are not annihilated. And, indeed, just in measure as the man obeys God, are the beasts or lower powers subject to him; bears and lions and wolves, fierce and devilish spirits in us, being subject when our inward man is subject to the Lord. [11]

Such is the stage which issues in regeneration; first, a discovery of the monstrous evil which is working in the creature, in the midst of which the spiritual mind by the cross is prepared for deliverance out of the sphere of the old man, the beast-like powers meanwhile being by grace restrained. At this point comes the second stage, in which, though we have not reached the cleansed world, we are yet by the waves of judgment separated from the former

---

[11] Origen goes at some length into this inward fulfilment. He says:— " Si quis est, qui crescentibus malis, (these are the giants,) et inundantibus vitiis, convertere se potest a rebus fluxis et pereuntibus, et audire verba Dei, ac præcepta cœlestia, hic intra cor suum arcam salutis ædificat, et bibliothecam (ut ita dicam) intra se divini consecrat verbi." He then goes into the dimensions, and says that this inward ark is formed of truths of the cross, trees cut down, which are built together; not the truths of heathen authors, which are like leafy trees, uncut and unpruned, and under which Israel have often committed fornication, as the prophets say, and which are of no use to build this ark. He then speaks of the animals;—" Munda quidem animalia, memoria, intellectus, examinatio, &c.: immunda, ira, et concupiscentia," &c. — *Hom.* ii. *in Gen.* So also Cyril of Jerusalem:—"Ὥσπερ γὰρ ἐπ' ἐκείνου, διὰ ξύλου καὶ ὕδατος αὐτοῖς μὲν ἐγένετο ἡ σωτηρία, καινῆς δὲ γενέσεως ἀρχὴ, καὶ ἡ περιστερὰ ἀνέστρεψε πρὸς αὐτὸν, ... οὕτω καὶ τὸ πνεῦμα τὸ ἅγιον κατῆλθεν ἐπὶ τὸν ἀληθινὸν Νῶε, τὸν τῆς δευτέρας γενέσεως ποιητὴν, τῶν παντοίων γενῶν προαιρέσεις εἰς τὸ αὐτὸ συνάγοντα· ὧν τύπον ἔφερον αἱ διάφοραι τῶν ἐν τῇ κιβωτῷ ζώων καταστάσεις. κ. τ. λ.—*Catech.* xvii. § 10. So Ambrose : — " Justus habet in arcâ bestias graves. Nulla enim mens, nulla anima, quæ non recipiat etiam malarum motus agrestes cogitationum." — *De Noe,* c. 15, § 57.

world. After which comes the perfect deliverance into rest and liberty beyond the waters. To these later stages we will come in order. But first I would note the outward fulfilment of the scene, which we have already traced inwardly.

In this outward view, the world that then was, on which the threatened flood of waters was hastening, figures the world around, the home of the old man, on which judgment must come for men's wickedness. In this world two families of men are seen, both of which in different ways have shewn their own weakness. Everything is out of course. The sons of God and the daughters of men are mingled. The wickedness of man is great upon the earth, and the thoughts of his heart are proved to be evil continually. The crowning sin is the mixture of seeds. "The sons of God" contract ungodly alliances. If the "sons of God" here spoken of were angels, the fact foreshadowed is, that fallen spirits are allowed in some mysterious way to mix with mankind; whose monstrous fruit necessitates that flood of judgment which is threatened upon the last great form of evil, when the Antichrist shall be revealed, and men will be possessed by " him, whose coming is after the working of Satan, with all power and signs and lying wonders." [12] In a lower sense, this mixture of seeds is to be seen in that confusion between the carnal and spiritual which is so common everywhere. God's children mingle with the world. Oh, how different are the thoughts of God to the thoughts of His sons, except they walk with Him! "God saw the wickedness of men, that it was great:"—"the sons of God saw the daughters of men that they were fair." So "they took of all that they chose." [13]

[12] 2 Thess. ii. 9.   [13] Chap. vi. 2.

The world cannot always reach God's sons to entangle and defile them. But the sons of God can always reach the world, and sink down to act on worldly principles. We read, "They saw," and "they chose;" that is, men walked by sight and not by faith, and by self-will, not by God's will. And the result was, "giants, men of renown," and through them gigantic wickedness. Increased power brought increased crime : " the earth was corrupt, and full of violence." So is it now. The power and sin of Christendom are but the necessary result of this same mixture of the flesh and spirit; with just so much of truth as to enable men to trust each other, and just so much of worldly principles as to please and win the world; just so much of God's Spirit as to bring in power, and so much of the flesh as to abuse that power to maintain carnal principles. And yet there is a remnant witnessing against the corruption, whom God through this very confusion is leading to a full deliverance out of it — such souls at first, though quickened in spirit, like the believers in the Jewish dispensation, and though they " follow Christ in the regeneration," [14] do not yet fully know that perfect deliverance out of the sphere and judgment of the old man, to which they are called by " the washing of regeneration," [15] which is indeed participation in Christ's death and resurrection. But spite of their conflicts, God will bring them to this rest, and even the confusions amongst which they dwell serve God's saints, driving them from the ground of the old man into a purer and better world.

To this end the ark is the appointed means, figuring, in the outward as in the inward kingdom, the self-same cross of Jesus Christ, or more vaguely, the Church,

[14] Matt. xix. 28. [15] Titus iii. 5.

whose strength is the cross; which, safe in the covering of atonement,[16] bears those who trust it, through the waters. The elect are delivered, first mystically by baptism, that passage through the waters, which figures death and resurrection;[17] and then actually, through that dying to the world and nature, which is both the judgment of the old, and the way for God's children to the new, creation. In this ark are lower, second, and third stories;[18] for within the one same faith of the cross of Christ, very different is the attainment in the knowledge of that cross, even among those who by it pass through the one baptism. Few can enter into all the heights and depths opened to them; for few even of the saved here bear the image of their Head. Few are the sons of the Man of Rest, knowing the joys of sonship with Him, and with capacities to share all His experiences. For one such son are many who are as beasts, animal natures, rough, irrational creatures; who yet are saved, both the clean and the unclean, the Jew and Gentile, the fearful and the violent; and who are served and ruled by those in whom is seen more of the image of Him who is their Head and Lord. For it is not the spiritual only who are saved. In the one ark are found many carnal souls, living far more as beasts than as men, who yet being cleansed of God may not be cast off as common or unclean.[19] These cannot know the heights of the cross,[20] yet are they saved by

---

[16] The word here translated "*pitch*," (chap. vi. 14,) Heb. כפר, is the same word which is commonly used to express *atonement*, as in Exod. xxix. 36, xxx. 10; Lev. xxiii. 27, 28, &c. It means, primarily and simply, *a covering*. The word כפרת, *mercy-seat*, where the blood was sprinkled on the day of atonement, is from the same root. Our English word *cover* evidently comes from כפר.

[17] 1 Pet. iii. 20, 21.

[18] Chap. vi. 16. Compare with this the three stories of the Temple, 1 Kings vi. 4–8, which is but another view of the same mystery.

[19] Acts x. 15, 28.

[20] " Arca in summis angustatur,

grace, even as the spiritual; their evil natures being checked by that cross which is for them and for all the common deliverance. In one body are they saved together, all the members more or less comely;[21] and though with unequal, yet each with perfect joy, they shall, whether beasts, or creeping things, or flying fowls, whether young men or maidens, or old men or children, whether fathers or babes and sucklings in Christ, yea and the dragons also, all praise the Lord, in that cleansed earth which is beyond the waters.[22]

II. — NOAH IN THE WATERS

Chapter 7 and 8:1-14

LET us now pass on to that stage in Noah's life, to that point in regeneration, when by the cross our inner man is separated from the old world, and yet not come experimentally to the better world. This is a well-known stage, and as safe, if not as blissful, as that which follows it.

Seven distinct steps are marked in it, the order of which, like all the rest, is wonderful.

(i.) First (I trace it within) man is "shut in" by the Lord: he enters the ark, but "the Lord shuts him in,"[1]

---

usque ad unum cubitum, quià in Ecclesiâ, quanto sanctiores, tanto pauciores," &c.—*Greg. M. in Expos. sup. Evang. Hom.* xxxviii. § 8.

[21] 1 Cor. xii. 22-25.

[22] Psalm cxlviii. 7-13. The Fathers are full of references to this outward application of this history. Augustine (*Contr. Faust. Manich.* l. xii. c. 14-21,) goes into it at great length:—"Noe cum suis per aquam et lignum liberatur, sicut fa-

milia Christi per baptismum crucis passione signatum," &c. So too Ambrose, *De Noe et Arcâ*; Gregory the Great, *In Ezek. Hom.* xvi.; and *In Expos. Evang. Hom.* xxxviii. § 8; Origen, *Hom.* ii. *in Gen.*; Jerome, *Contr. Jovin.* l. i.; Cyprian, *Epist.* 69, and many others. Indeed, St. Peter's direct reference to this type, (1 Pet. iii. 20, 21,) gives the clue to the whole of it.

[1] Chap. vii. 16.

that is, secures him. So the soul which has embraced the cross, and has long waited by it to be saved and lifted up from Adam's world, comes to a point when that cross holds him as with nails, "shut in," so that now he could not, even if he would, turn from it. Thus "shut in," prisoners of hope, are we preserved; and dark and narrow as this lot appears, we would not change it for the freedom of those without, who may mock at our straitness, but who, if not so "shut in," must all perish. Thanks be unto Him who shuts us in,—who will not let us leave the narrow cross, which, to some a stumbling-block and to others foolishness, to them that are called is both the power and the wisdom of God; cutting us off from communication with what is without, restraining what is within, and yet saving us. Blessed are they who are thus "shut in."

(ii.) Then comes the flood:—"The flood was upon the earth; and the waters increased, and bare up the ark, and it was lifted up above the earth." [2] So is it within. The day arrives when the inward deep is moved mightily. The unquiet element in us is loosed. Now the floods of temptation and lust seem to break out everywhere, Oh, what fluctuations, tossings, and swellings are there! Such a flood has arisen within as Jonah passed, when he cried, "The waters compass me;" [3] or such as David knew, when he said, "Deep calleth unto deep, at the noise of thy waterspouts; all thy waves and thy billows are gone over me." [4] Now the fountains of the great deep seem broken up, and the windows of the heavens only pour down judgment. We are, as we say, "overwhelmed within us." A flood is out, destroying and changing the life of

[2] Chap. vii. 17.
[3] Jonah ii. 5.
[4] Psalm xlii. 7. See also lxix. 1, 2, 15.

man, crushing the life of nature out of us. But this, too, painful and awful as it is, and itself the judgment of the sin of the old man, and certain destruction if we do not know the cross, leads the spirit to greater joys and greater liberty. Thus is self and selfhood destroyed in us. We tremble and are astonished and cry out for fear, and yet by such a death the Lord frees us.[5]

There remains indeed another baptism. The creature cleansed by water must one day be purged by fire also. The old Adam world, the ground of the old man, being overflowed with water, perishes. But the heavens and the earth which are now beyond the water shall be baptised with fire, and that fire shall purge the floor, and crystallise the earth into transparent gold.[6] So within, there is first

---

[5] The experience of every age supplies illustrations of this stage; but the following letter of Terstegen is so beautiful and apposite, that I insert it here. It may comfort some : "My dear sister, — Notwithstanding the wretched state in which you describe yourself to be, I am still quite at ease regarding it, and am under no apprehension of evil consequences. Were I concerned for you after the manner of men, and were I glad to see your own life, the life of self, preserved, I might have reason to fear, because our Lord attacks it so forcibly and severely, and pursues it so warmly, that it must soon give up the ghost, which takes place and is accomplished by the complete and eternal resignation of yourself into the free hands of God. You see and feel nothing but sin and corruption within you. Whithersoever the mind turns and directs its view, everything is misery, grief, and sin; and the way to escape from it is closed, and appears as if it were always to continue so. Ah! thinks subtle self-love, could I only find a little nook to which I might retire, and take a little rest. Listen, O soul! cease thy turning: the more thou seekest to make matters the better, the worse thou makest them. Therefore as long as it pleases God to leave you miserable, corrupt, and without strength, let it also please you. You behold your real self at present, as you are in yourself. Thank God for having thus disclosed your inward wound to your view. Previously, when the dealings of grace with you were so gentle, nature and sense occasionally participated in it; but in the way in which you are at present, they are deprived of all support. It is impossible that nature and sense should acquiesce in this total destruction. But they must die. Commit yourself, therefore, wholly to God ; trust Him. and you shall be healed." —*Letter* xx.

[6] See 2 Pet. iii. 6, 7.

water, then fire; and by fire the heavens as well as the earth are purified. In both the Lord appoints the flood for good; and as when we pass through the waters, because He is with us they do not overflow us, so He says, " When thou walkest through the fire thou shalt not be burned; neither shall the flame kindle upon thee." [7]

(iii.) So the ark goes through the flood: we read, " The ark went upon the face of the waters." [8] It goes through them. We are not saved from death and judgment, but *through* it, and *out of* it. God does not save us from temptation. He Himself may loose the doors of the great deep within us. Even yet He leads His sons to be tempted; [9] for temptation is a necessary step to regeneration; that we, thus knowing how helpless we are in self, how lost on the ground and home of the old man, may resign all hope in self, and, knowing the worst, may yet triumph in deliverance out of it. The regenerate soul has known the worst, and through grace has come safe out of it. And just as the Lord uses our " clay," our very faults, when touched by virtue from His lips, to open blind eyes, [10] so does He use the great deep within us, which He has loosed in judgment because of abounding sin, to drive us from all hopes of creature help. Thus are we saved, not from, but through, the waters; and by death is he destroyed who has the power of death. [11]

(iv.) Then comes the wind from the Lord:—" God remembered Noah, and caused a wind to pass over the earth, and the waters assuaged." [12] Here is a wondrous change. " Shut in," " lifted up," or " passing through the waters," the spiritual mind is safe. But now come

---

[7] Isa. xliii. 2.
[8] Chap. vii. 18.
[9] Matt. iv. 1.

[10] John ix. 6.
[11] Heb. ii. 14.
[12] Chap. viii. 1.

gentle gales, the breathings of that Spirit which stills the floods and refreshes the weary voyager. The Spirit breathes, and the waters assuage. In other judgments a wind from the Lord was the agent of deliverance. The locusts of Egypt were thus destroyed: — "The Lord turned a strong east wind, which took away the locusts." [13] So the way through the Red Sea was made by the wind: — "The Lord caused the sea to go back by a strong east wind." [14] So again shall it be in the day "when the Lord with His mighty wind shall smite the tongue of the Egyptian sea, and make men go over dryshod." [15] And so within. God remembers His servant, and the breath of the Lord works for his deliverance. From this time forth the tossings decrease. The rest now is very nigh.

(v.) For the next step is the grounding of the ark. Now it rests firmly on the unseen world, though the waste of waters is still abroad, and no portion of that better land is yet visible. [16] The cross has brought us to another sphere. The fact is not cognisable by sight, nevertheless it is felt, for settledness is attained to. The future home is not yet seen. A veil of waters yet covers it. But the ark has brought us to "the everlasting hills;" and God, after that we have suffered awhile, now stablishes, strengthens, settles us. [17]

---

[13] Exod. x. 19.
[14] Exod. xiv. 21.
[15] Isa. xi. 15.
[16] Chap. viii. 4.
[17] 1 Pet. v. 10. The day of the ark's resting, if I err not, was the day of Christ's resurrection, viz., "the seventeenth day of the seventh month," which, after the redemption from Egypt, was called the first month. Here, as in all the allusions to time, are, I am assured, many mysteries; but I do not attempt to touch the subject. The Fathers, however, boldly enter on it. See Augustine, (*Contr. Faust. Manich.* l. xii. c. 15-18,) for his views on the times and numbers here; and for some very suggestive thoughts on the subject of numbers generally, see his work, *De lib. Arbitr.* l. ii, c. 11. Surely if all creation be a type, numbers and time must be significant.

(vi.) Soon more is reached. After the tossings cease, "the window is opened," and a new world appears. "The tops of the mountains are seen." Its light shines in.[18] What is seen at first appears isolated. The connexion is not seen between the points which we do see. The waters still only permit us glimpses, unconnected glimpses, of the coming world. Yet there it is — faith is turned to sight. These hill-tops are pledges of untold and unknown scenes of future joy. For many a day we have been shut up, and our way has been simply a path of faith ; but now the floods assuage, and light breaks in, and we can cry, "As we have heard, so have we seen." [19] For now we belong to the new creation, now that the old man and his monstrous progeny are destroyed and dead.

(vii.) After this, and just before the going forth to enjoy the better world in full liberty, "the dove and raven are sent forth," [20] figuring (for they are birds of heaven, and the heaven is the understanding,) certain powers or emotions of the understanding, both pure and impure.[21] In the actions of these is shewn the working of the good and evil which to the last remains with us. For of the impure a remnant still exists. The raven, finding its food in carrion, figures those inclinations which feed on dead things. The dove is that spirit of gentleness and peace, which, though with us before, appears more boldly now as heaven opens to us, to witness, like the dove which came down on Christ, that though the cross may yet remain, there is promise of better things. The ark does not change the raven. The cross may restrain,

---

[18] Chap. viii. 5, 6.
[19] Psalm xlviii. 8.
[20] Chap. viii. 7.

[21] See on the work of the fifth day, pp. 33, 34.

but does not alter impure desires. To the end the dead
things of the world are attractive to certain inclinations in
each of us. If, therefore, this raven can be free, it will
not return. But the inward man will not trust to such
guidance. He wants better proof, and this the dove supplies; when the time is come for the olive to bud she
brings a token. And the man understands, for now the
risen world is near. Then, but not till God plainly
directs it, the cross which has saved us is exchanged for
the enjoyment of that resurrection rest to which it has
carried us.[22]

Such is this stage within. Without, its accomplishment
is only the same workings on a larger scale. Shut up, safe
in the cross, the elect of God by judgments on the world
are lifted heavenward. Death buries one and then another
earthly hope. The highest hills, to which the world look
for succour, all are overflowed. But the Church by the
cross goes safe, though containing some, who, like the unclean raven, if they might, would leave it. Such shew
their nature ere the rest is reached.[23] After this the elect

---

[22] Ambrose, throughout his whole
comment, *De Noe et Arcâ*, gives the
inward sense of all this history. He
says, " Diluvii species typus est pur-
gationis animæ nostræ." (c. 13, § 46.)
Referring to " Noah, the just man,"
he asks, " Quis est 'justus' in nobis,
nisi mentis vigor, qui intra istam
arcam inclusit omne animantium genus,. . . omnes irrationabiles sensus,"
&c. (c. 9, § 30.) The flood is,
"Ebulliunt omnes fontes cupiditatum," (c. 9, § 30 :) " omnibus pariter
ingruentibus passionibus," &c. (c. 14,
§ 49 :) its cessation, " affluentia
erroris cessat." (c. 17, § 59.) The
raven is " impudentia et malitia,
quæ mortuis pascitur, sicut corvus :"

(c. 17, § 62 :) the dove is " simplicitas." (§ 64.) The raven, " malitia, diluvium amat." The dove
will not stay abroad while the flood
remains; " tardè enim inter sæcu-
larium fluctus cupiditatum portum
solet invenire simplicitas." (c. 18,
§ 64.)

[23] " Illas duas aves misit Noe. Habebat ibi corvum, habebat et columbam. . . Videtis utique quia necesse
est ut in isto diluvio sæculi utrum-
que genus contineat Ecclesia, et corvum, et columbam. Qui sunt corvi?
Qui sua quærunt. Qui columbæ?
Qui ea quæ Christi sunt quærunt."
Aug. in Johan. Tractat. vi. § 2.

also have another, larger, freer, fairer, dwelling-place. But this leads us to another stage, when Noah emerges into the world beyond the waters.

III. — NOAH ON THE EARTH BEYOND THE FLOOD

Chapter 8:15-22, and 9:1-17

THE scene here changes as from earth to heaven; from sin and floods to joy, and rest, and liberty.   Blessed had been the transition from the old world of sin to the safe but dark and narrow ark; for, with all its straitness, blessed is the cross: we are shut up indeed and tossed, yet safe and not forgotten.   But now comes a further wondrous change, from straitness to freedom, and from floods to quietness.   We have felt what it is to be in the old world, grieved by its confusions and corruptions, which we can‹ not remedy.   We have known the stage when we are separated thence by the cross, and yet have not reached the better world.   Now we reach that land of rest, and stand, as Noah here, on a new and purged creation, brought forth from that earth on which we were born, to a new world where death and judgment are behind us. Man in Christ has long since reached this.   Baptism is our profession of faith, that as Christ is risen, and we are in Him, we too are risen with Him.[1]   But now in experience our spirit comes there, from the things of the old man to a sphere where Adam and his carnal seed cannot enter.   In one aspect, as in Adam, we are still in the

---

[1] Col. ii. 12.   In baptism "we are buried and risen with Christ through faith;" but this is very different from "the power of Christ's resurrection," which Paul longed for. (Phil. iii. 10.) This latter is *experience* rather than *faith.*

old world, still on this side death, shut out from Paradise. In another, as Noah, as the spiritual mind which has experienced the judgment of the old creation, we are risen with Christ, consciously brought with Him into another world.

The blessings and responsibilities of this high calling are shewn in seven distinct particulars recorded here of Noah.

(i.) First, "They went forth." [2] This is true liberty, known in word perhaps, but not in power, save by the fellowship of Christ's sufferings and the power of His resurrection. Up to this point the elect is more or less in bondage, a "prisoner of hope," secure, yet still a prisoner. But when through grace we have so passed the judgment of the first creation, and have felt the tossings cease, and then have seen the hill-tops, and received the olive-leaf, the earnest of the inheritance, from the mouth of the gentle dove, which thus assures us of a world beyond the water-floods, then our freedom is near; all things are lawful, if all things are not expedient, for us. Many a conscientious doubt as to rules, or times, or places, now is resolved for us. To the pure all is pure. Henceforth we are free; we may "go in and out and find pasture." [3]

(ii.) But there is more than freedom here; for now "Noah builded an altar to the Lord, and offered burnt-offerings." [4] This is worship, in the main like that of Abel, though the burnt-offering testifies rather of obedience and acceptance than of sin and trespasses; in answer to which God opens all His heart, with secrets of love never fully told in Adam's world. Now beside the altar, those who have passed the flood understand God's heart,

[2] Chap. viii. 18.　　　[3] John x. 9.　　　[4] Chap. viii. 20.

saying, " I will not curse again." Yea, "though man's heart is still evil," God's heart speaks out, "I will not curse or smite again." [5] The risen man cannot say that in selfhood his imaginations even now are other than evil continually. But he knows that, spite of this, God is saving and has saved him. Here, too, he learns how the changes in the earth are all divinely regulated : — "While earth remains, seed-time and harvest, cold and heat, summer and winter, and day and night, shall not cease." [6] Before this, as darkness fell, he may have feared that the light was for ever leaving him, and that his fits of coldness would have no limit. Now he learns that these things are part of a divine plan. Darkness brings into light heavenly things unseen before. By the cold many a weed is nipped and withered, and many a hurtful worm perishes. "While earth remains" such changes are well. When earth is passed, we may be fit for changeless things. All this in its depth is learnt at this place, by the holy altar of burnt offering. Oh, how many things are only cleared up here! The same man who said, "Thy way is in the sea, and thy path in the great waters, and thy footsteps are unknown," says again, "Thy way is in the sanctuary : who is so great a God as our God ?" [7]

(iii.) Fruitfulness is another special blessing of this stage :—" God said, Be fruitful and multiply." [8] Just as in creation, when the third day rose, and the waters were restrained, the earth was made fruitful ; so now in Noah, the third great stage in man, the flood being passed, man increases wonderfully. " Except the corn of wheat fall into the ground and die, it abideth alone ; but if it die, it bringeth forth much fruit." [9] Now having died to the

---

[5] Chap. viii. 21.   [7] Psalm lxxvii. 13, 19.   [9] John xii. 24.
[6] Chap. viii. 22.   [8] Chap. ix. 1.

world by the cross, and the evil fruits which grow out of old Adam being judged by the overflowing waters, the new man within increases yet more. Being purged, he brings forth much fruit.[10]

(iv.) But the blessing goes further. Power is given over beasts:—"The fear and dread of you shall be upon every beast, and upon every fowl, and upon all the fishes of the sea: into thy hand are they delivered."[11] Animal faculties now are not only restrained by the ark or cross, but reduced to submission: the man or reason governs them. The ox strong to labour, the strength in us formed to serve, is not henceforth to spend its energies without direction. The lion and the bear, fierce thoughts, must be still. And if, when night comes down, these beasts will yet creep forth, and the young lions roar against their prey,— for in hours of darkness these beasts at times will still be heard,— when the sun ariseth they must lay them down in their dens, for then man goeth forth to his work and labour until the evening.[12] I know indeed that even after this, after man has passed the flood and is regenerate, lions may be loosed in judgment by the Lord: the man in us may be slain, and the beast may be seen standing by the carcase;[13] or, as in another case, the man may be blind, and the beast, which should be guided by the man,

---

[10] John xv. 2. "Non est igitur utile, cum vitiorum aliqua confusio est quæ mentem occupet, serere aliquas cogitationes, atque generare et parturire mentem. Cum autem compressæ fuerint cupiditates, et mens requieverit, tunc virtutes possunt et bona opera germinari . . . Sic justus multitudine virtutis augetur, et replet terram, quasi cor: . . ita nihil vacuum sapientiæ esse patitur."—*Ambros. de Noe*, c. 21, § 77, and c. 24, § 87.

[11] Chap. ix. 2.

[12] Psalm civ. 20-23. "Domitis igitur non solum terrenis omnibus passionibus, sed etiam sensibus corporalibus, bestias sibi quodam terrore subjicit et timore, in quibus species videtur inesse malitiæ atque feritatis. . . . . . Omnibus ergo his imperat justus, cupiditate, tristitiâ, timore," &c. — *Ambros. de Noe et Arcâ*, c. 24, § 87.

[13] 1 Kings xiii. 24, 25.

may see more than that inward man which was formed to govern it.[14] All this may be through sin. Yet our calling as regenerate is to rule the beasts, not to be ruled by them. If the animal in us is not subject to the mind, it is because the mind or man is not subject to the Lord.

(v.) Further, on this ground flesh is given to man for food. Before the flood man's food is " the green herb." He has " for meat every herb bearing seed, and every tree, in which is the fruit of a tree." [15] Now it is said, " Every moving thing that liveth shall be meat for you: even as the green herb have I given you all things." [16] Before the flood the bodies of beasts had been consumed by the fire of God: they had been His meat: their death had satisfied Him. Now, on resurrection ground, man too can eat, that is, find satisfaction in the same sacrifice. Before we know resurrection life, while we are yet in the world before the flood, in the home or sphere of the old man, we feed on the fruits of the earth, those fruits of righteousness, which, whether in Christ or in ourselves, naturally afford man some satisfaction. As yet the death of the creature is no satisfaction to the elect, though God is satisfied and we are clothed thereby. God's fire may fall and consume the offering: we give it up, but we do not really eat with Him. It is otherwise when this stage is reached. Then the death of what is animal is not only a witness, but it affords us food. We, too, can now be satisfied in the giving up of life, and great is the strength which the spiritual man derives from the meat which is thus given to him.[17]

[14] Numbers xxii. 23–31.

[15] Chap. i. 29.

[16] Chap. ix. 3.

[17] Ambrose says, "Significatur quòd irrationabiles passiones ita de-beant menti sapientis, ut olera rustico esse subjecta, atque ita his utamur ut agricola oleribus," &c. *De Noe*, &c. c. 25, § 91. Augustine adds, respecting the pouring out

(vi.) At this stage God gives authority to man to judge that which quenches the life which "was formed in God's image;" for God, having now by regeneration restored that image in man, would not have it again mutilated. At the hand of every man, therefore, He now requires the life of man, for in the image of God made He man.[18] Before the flood it was not so ; on the ground of the old man, Seth's line do not avenge the blood of Abel; just as before regeneration, while we yet abide in the sphere of the old man, the spiritual mind bears witness against the sins which in us grow out of old Adam, but has not power to correct or judge them ; for on that ground the evil cannot be remedied. The old man is corrupt, with his works. God's image cannot be seen in him. God will not therefore prune his branches ; for He is resolved to cut him down. But after the washing of regeneration, when the image of God is again brought forth through the judgment of the old man, when the spiritual mind has reached the risen life, and looks on Adam and his works as judged of God, with Him it judges any reviving remnant of them ; for, being regenerate, it has power to correct wickedness. All murder therefore now is judged ; and since " he that hateth his brother is a murderer," [19] for hate destroys the inward man, all such workings of the flesh must be sharply judged by the regenerate. Woe to us, if we use not the power committed to us, if the hateful works of the old man are suffered in us without self-condemnation.

(vii.) And now, to crown all the gifts peculiar to this stage, the covenant is re-made, and a heavenly token given

of the blood, which is commanded here (v. 4) — " Ejecto sanguine jubentur manducare, ne vita pristina quasi suffocata in conscientiâ teneatur, sed habeat tanquam effusionem," &c.—*Contr. Faust.* l. xii. c. 22.

[18] Chap. ix. 5.

[19] 1 John iii. 15.

of it:—"And I, behold, I, establish my covenant with you, and with your seed after you, and with every living creature that is with you. And this is the token of the covenant: I do set my bow in the cloud; and it shall come to pass, when I bring a cloud over the earth, that the bow shall be seen in the cloud. And I will remember my covenant which is between me and you and every living creature of all flesh; and the waters shall no more be a flood to destroy all flesh." This is the "new and better covenant," not "of law," with "Thou shalt," but "of grace," saying, "I will." "*I will* establish my covenant with you . . . and *I will* remember my covenant . . . and *I will* look on the bow in the cloud, and the waters *shall* no more destroy." For now man has learnt that all is of grace, resting not upon his own, but upon the Lord's, will.

Oh, that the force of this "new covenant," and all the difference between "*Thou shalt*" and "*I will*," were fully known by God's children; and that in every soul the "Thou shalt" of the old, had given place to the "I will" of the new and better, covenant! Let this be understood. The covenant of law, as given to the old man, first and last, is all "*Thou shalt.*" So God to Adam said, "*Thou shalt* not eat of it; in the day thou eatest, *thou shalt* surely die:" and by Moses repeating the same covenant of law, each command reiterates the same, "*Thou shalt:*"—"*Thou shalt* love the Lord with all thy heart;" "*Thou shalt* not steal;" "*Thou shalt* not covet." Such a covenant is all "of works." There is a command to be fulfilled by man, and therefore its validity depends on man's part as well as God's being performed perfectly. Such a covenant cannot stand, for man is always sure to fail in his part. Thus the covenant of law or works to man is and must be only condemnation. But, finding fault with this, the Lord will make " a new covenant;" and this new covenant or gospel says throughout, not "Thou shalt," but "I will." It is " the promise," as St. Paul says to the Galatians.[20] All that it requires is simple faith. " This is the covenant I will make in those days, saith the Lord; *I will* put my laws in their hearts ; and *I will* write them in their minds; and *I will* be merciful to their transgressions; and *I will* remember their sins no more; *I will* dwell in them ; and *I will* walk in them; and *I will* be unto them a God, and *they shall* be unto me a people." It is this "I will" which Noah now hears, and to which at this stage God adds " a token" set in heaven.

This token is " the bow set in the cloud." Before the flood, the elect, though not so fully instructed, yet had " the covenant."[21] But of its "token" nothing had been heard: for this is only learnt experimentally, when we have known and in spirit passed the deep waters. This token now appears " in the cloud." The cloud, brought over the earth, was not only a remembrance, but something like a remnant, of the judgment. We therefore sometimes " fear to enter the cloud."[22] If it might be so, we would have "tokens" of the covenant without the dark waters. But it cannot be. Only in dark and cloudy days can the bow of heaven be seen spanning the lower earth. Then, mid dark waters, when the sun breaks out, though the cloud may be dark, a bow appears amid the darkness; half a ring — half that ring with which the regenerate soul is now married to the Lord, and assured of endless rest with Him. The lower world yet hides the rest of the ring; but on high " a rainbow" shall be seen " *in a circle round* the throne."[23]

---

[20] Gal. iii. 16–18, 21, 22, 29.
[21] Chap. vi. 18.
[22] Luke ix. 34.
[23] So we read, ἶρις κυκλόθεν. Rev.

Such are the joys to which we are called by the power of Christ's resurrection and the fellowship of His sufferings.

And this, too, is fulfilled without. In this more outward view, Noah's blessings here are the joys of the Church as dead and risen with Christ. The Man of Rest and His sons are brought by the washing of regeneration to things which fallen Adam never heard of. Here freedom, and worship, and increase, and power,— power over those who are as beasts,— is freely given to them. Here the death of the flesh, in ourselves or others, is found to be, even as good fruits, the means of strengthening life. Here, too, sin is judged. In the world saints judge not:—"What have I to do to judge them that are without?"[24] In that sphere our work is to set forth grace, even while we witness that God's judgment is hastening. But in that Church which stands on risen ground, we must "put away from ourselves the wicked person."[25] Would to God that this were laid to heart. But too often judgment is exercised in the world, where grace should be manifested; while excuses are offered for want of discipline in that redeemed body, where all evil should be rooted out. Labour enough is spent to correct a ruined world: nothing is done to purge a failing Church. But this leads us to another stage, where the failure of the regenerate is fully revealed to us.

iv. 3. Ambros has another thought here :—" Iris, quasi arcus contentus, sed carens sagittâ, magis terrere nos vult, quàm ferire," &c.—*De Noe*, &c. c. 27.

[24] 1 Cor. v. 12.   [25] 1 Cor. v. 13.

IV.—Noah's Sons

Chapter 9:18-29, and 10

We are now to see what man brings forth, when grace has brought him through the judgment of the first creation into another sphere. Spite of all his gifts, nay by his gifts, Noah, that is, regenerate man, fails even as the unregenerate. His blessings ensnare him. Here we are shewn the agents and stages of this tragedy, from Noah's first error, and his children's crimes, down to all the confusions of Great Babylon. For Babylon the Great, with all her abominations, cannot precede, but follows regeneration.

First, we are shewn what springs out of Noah, that is all the forms of life which grow out of the regenerate. We may for a moment look at this, after which the different phases of failure will be manifest.

To speak then of these seeds as seen within. Noah is the spiritual mind, brought forth from the ground of the old man into a purer world. His sons represent those forms of life, which, produced by the spiritual mind in us before regeneration,— as Shem, Ham, and Japhet, were born before the flood, — develope themselves in us after we have known the judgment of the first creation. For regeneration bears in us more than one mind or form of life; and whichever of these is the master-life within, stamps us either as Shems, or Hams, or Japhets; just as he who lives in the animal or beast-like life may be designated as a fox, or wolf, or serpent, according to the form of life which most predominates. For there are in us many forms of life. Even the animal life (and in its place it is subservient to our blessedness) is full of variety. And no less does the higher life of the man or mind within, take, as we have seen in Adam's sons, many different forms at different stages of its development. In Adam's sons we saw the different forms of life which grow out of old Adam, that is the natural man. Now in Noah and his sons we are shewn all the forms which the regenerate mind may produce in each of us.

Now the forms of life which regeneration produces are as different as Shem, Ham, and Japhet; for man is composed of body, soul, and spirit, a wondrous compound of very different worlds; and of each a germ or seed buds out within, produced in man, as Noah's three sons, before regeneration, which after the flood shew whence and what they are, and their respective natures, whether of the body, or of the soul, or of the spirit; whether Ham, Japhet, or Shem, whose very names tell what they are, very different, yet all fruits of one common regeneration. There is, first and highest, the contemplative life, which delights in things unseen, in adoring love and holiness. There is again the active life, which is good, and does good, but deals more with external things. Besides these there is the doctrinal life, a mind occupied with truth, without the savour and power of it; a form of life, which, though growing out of the regenerate mind, is nigh to evil, and must be subdued and fought against. Shem is the first of these; Japhet, the second; the third is Ham, the father of Canaan, whom Israel have to overcome. For Shem, meaning *name*, represents that mind, which, knowing the Name which is above every name,— that God is a Spirit, and they who worship Him must worship Him in spirit and in truth,— is set, as names are set for things, to witness for His Name, and so reflect something of Him.[1]

---

[1] The word Shem, or *name*, is derived from the verb שׂם, to *place* or *put*, apparently for this reason, that a *name* is *placed* or substituted for a

Japhet, that is, *enlargement*, goes forth, in the sense of the freedom which is the portion of the regenerate soul, to spread abroad on the face of the earth something of that large blessing which God has given it.[2] Ham, signifying *burnt* or *black*, is the mind which is " seared as with a hot iron:"[3] knowing but not living in the truth; and thus producing Canaan, that accursed form of life, which is the inevitable fruit of a life of doctrine without love or communion. In point of honour Shem stands first, but in their development Japhet's and Ham's sons are given before Shem's; shewing, what indeed is proved by all experience, that the highest life in us is the last to develop itself.[4] " Of these was the whole earth overspread." And hence spring all the forms of regenerate life, good, bad, or indifferent.[5]

thing, as its sensible sign. The word is also closely connected with the שמים, or *heavens*. Indeed the latter word is but a masculine plural of the same word, Shem. These "heavens" are they who "declare the glory of God," and "in whom (as in Shem's family) God hath set a tabernacle for His sun."—Psalm xix. 1, 4.

[2] I may note how unchangeably to the present day the sons of Shem, even in the letter, that is the Asiatics, are men who love the contemplative life; while Japhet's sons, that is the European family, as much prefer the active life.

[3] 1 Tim. iv. 2.

[4] Compare the order in chap. ix. 18, and chap. x. 1, with that in chap. x. 2, 6, 22.

[5] Chap. ix. 19. Ambrose, as usual, thus gives the inward sense :—" Interior significatio demonstrat 'justum virum,' (he is speaking of Noah when come forth out of the ark,) tanquam arborem fructuosam, internecatis quæ escam ejus solebant arrodere, coartare processus ramorum, velut exsortem irrationabilium passionum, solum remansisse cum suis. ' Sui' autem sunt animi disceptationes." *De Noe*, &c. c. 15. § 55. He thus explains these " sons " more particularly :—"Huic verò tres filii nati, Sem, Cham, Japhet, quæ nomina significant bonum, et malum, et indifferens; ut et naturæ gratiâ bonitatem habuisse, et malorum tentamenta ei nequaquam defuisse, et indifferentibus, hoc est, velut supellectili virtutum abundâsse videatur."—*Id.* c. 2, § 3. " Sunt enim cogitationes mentis contrariæ," &c. — *Id.* c. 2, § 5. In the same chapter (§ 5) he explains Shem and Ham as " bonitas et malitia mentis ;" adding, " Cetèrùm non tàm hic homines quàm mores comprehenduntur, . . . nam Cham calor, Chanaan commotio est," &c.—*Id.* c. 32, § 121.

But this may be more plain to some in its outward
fulfilment as seen in the professing Church. Only, when
we look at evil without, let us not forget that the germ
of it all is within our own heart; and that evil men
around are only what they are by crushing in their souls
the seed of the divine life, and by sinking into some one
or other of those lower forms of life, which though working in us are not elect, that is, not our true life. This is
our trial, whether we will be beasts, or Cains, or Shems,
or Hams, or Japhets. Blessed are they, who, dying to
that in them which is opposed to God, forsaking self and
the fruits of that self, which stage after stage so perseveringly revives in us, step by step come back out of self to
God, to the life which is not of self, but of Him, and to
His glory.

To look then at this scene without. Noah and his sons
figure the regenerate Church, who with differing forms of
life have one root, brought through the one baptism from
the world of Adam, to new gifts and higher responsibilities.
Noah represents the Church generally: his sons, its com-
ponent parts and varieties; differing from one another as
Peter, Paul, and John,[6] and to differ yet more in their
development, but all part and fruit of one same tree,
whose produce shews its soil as well as its own distinct

---

[6] The thought, that Peter and John
are types of different forms of Christian life, is very common in the old
writers: John being taken as the
type of the life which is by vision of
Christ; Peter, of that which is by
faith and conflict. So Augustine:
"Duas itaque vitas sibi divinitus
prædicatas et commendatas novit
Ecclesia, quarum est una in fide, altera in specie, una in labore, altera
in requie, una in opere actionis,
altera in mercede contemplationis,
. . . . ista significata est per Apostolum Petrum, illa per Johannem."
Tractat. in Johan. cxxiv. Popery
and Protestantism shew for themselves that they are respectively
Peter's and Paul's children. John's
line of things is less capable of being
systematised and less corruptible,
and "will tarry till the Lord come."
John xxi. 22, 23.

vegetable life and constitution. As in the case of Jacob and his sons, each son or tribe figures the distinctive character of some part of the spiritual Israel, who are either Levis, addicted to service, or Naphtalis, satisfied with favour, or Judahs, possessing the gift of rule; so is it with Noah's sons: each presents one class of the regenerate: Shem, those who love the inner life; Japhet, the men of action; Ham, the men of mere doctrine; and Canaan, those unhappy souls, who, from being hearers only, have come, still self-deceived, to be deceivers also. These three, or if we count Canaan, (and he is named,) these four, represent the great distinguishing classes into which the Church may be divided. For as in the fourfold results of the Sower's work,[7] so here, we have three classes springing from the original seed, and a fourth class, which, though not actually from it, is yet mentioned in connection with it. There is true inward religion, and true outward religion; these are Shem and Japhet. There is also false inward religion, and false outward religion: these are Ham and Canaan. Every possible form of Christian life is the development sooner or later of one or other of these four great classes.

Let this solemn truth sink into our hearts. There is a form of life which grows out of the regenerate, which is accursed. For regeneration not only spares the beasts, though it gives us power to subdue and govern them, but it leaves in us a mind like Ham, which revives the ways of the old man in the regenerate soul. Hence the Church has had its Hams, and from them has grown up Great Babylon.[8] All history shews, not that it is likely, but certain, that in the Church's own bosom will be nursed its

[7] Matt. xiii. 18–23.   Ham. Chap. x. 6–10.
[8] Babel is the work of the seed of

worst enemies. Heresy cannot exist without the truth; and "*there must be* heresies, that they which are approved may be made manifest."[9] Then, and after the division in the days of Peleg, Eber's son,—for Great Babylon has then been built up,—the elect Hebrew is as distinct from the rest of Noah's sons, as Noah himself had been from the world before the judgment. Then the word is, " Get thee out from thy country, and from thy kindred, and from thy father's house, into a land which I will shew thee."[10]

It would be full of deepest interest to trace the course of these different families through their successive genera-tions. For in them is prefigured the parentage and birth of every sect and heresy which has sprung out of and troubled the bosom of the regenerate Church. Here, had we opened eyes, we might see how from the Apostolic Church has sprung, as from a common source, all that endless train of error which is around us in the different forms of Popery and Protestantism. Here we might trace the lineage of faith and love, and not less of false spirituality, fanaticism, ignorance, rationalism, and reli-gious formalism. These neglected genealogies give it all. Here we have the true " Theory of Development," given by One who cannot lie, and given " for our learning and instruction in righteousness."[11] Few, however, care to think on these things, or consider how surely certain forms of life gradually produce other forms most dissimilar; how the true spiritual seed, the men of holy contemplation, may beget a seed, as Shem begat Asshur, in whom the contemplative life is changed to one of mere reasoning, whence grows Assyria, with all its cities and its crimes.[12]

[9] 1 Cor. xi. 19.
[10] Chap. xii. 1.
[11] Rom. xv. 4, and 2 Tim. iii. 16.

[12] Asshur, the father of the Assy-rians, was Shem's son: chap. x. 22.

Few think how the Japhets, that is the men of active life, may produce sons who sink ere long into what is merely outward, and become as the nations; or how surely the men of mere doctrine, like Ham, will produce families in which their evil will increase, until Egypt, and Babel, and cursed Canaan are manifested; these last as truly sons of Noah as Shem, but like the chaff, though springing from the same root as the wheat, destined to be one day awfully separated.

Without pretending to go into details, a few general points in this development of the regenerate may be for profit here.

And first let us mark the respective proportions of the three great families which grew out of Noah. Seventy-two names in all are given us.[13] Of these, thirty-one are of Ham's, twenty-seven of Shem's, and fourteen of Japhet's line; so much more prolific is evil than good, even in regenerate man: reminding us of the lists of sins, so greatly outnumbering the catalogue of graces, enumerated by the Apostle;[14] and of the number of "the works of the flesh," as compared with "the fruits of the spirit."[15] So is it without, even as within. The evil seed, whose life is one of doctrine rather than of love to God and man, is that which under a variety of forms, for the present at least, most spreads and multiplies. "Broad is the way that leadeth to destruction, and many there be which go in thereat."[16]

---

[13] Chap. x. 1–32. The numbers here, I am assured, are all full of divine mysteries; as some of old have marked. Our version gives only twenty-six names here from Shem. The LXX. add one more, Cainan, between Arphaxad and Salah. St. Luke follows the LXX., chap. iii. 36.

[14] Rom. i. 25–31, and 2 Tim. iii. 2–5.

[15] Galatians v. 19–23. Seventeen "works of the flesh" are recorded, besides the comprehensive word, "and suchlike;" nine "fruits of the spirit."

[16] Matt. vii. 13.

Of these three lines, all whose outcome is shewn here, it may suffice to note a few particulars. I have not a doubt that every name recorded describes some distinct character. And though to a mere English reader any comment on names may seem fanciful, if not hazardous, yet to a thoughtful mind the names simply translated would, I believe, suggest many things. In reading Bunyan, when we meet with "Faithful," and "By-ends," and "Evangelist," and "Giant Despair," and others; or when we hear of places, such as "Slough of Despond," or "Vanity Fair," or "Mansoul," with its "Eyegate," and "Eargate," and "Mouthgate," the name suggests some mystery. But Bunyan, in writing thus, was only copying the style of Genesis, in which the names always express character; for I think no one can imagine that such names, as some here, would be given or recorded without some deep reason.

But I shall not attempt to trace all the line. This, however, I would repeat, that from Ham, that is the life of mere doctrine,— of truth without love,— proceeds a seed, which, being called Nimrod or *the rebel*, "becomes a mighty one;" in whom first the patriarchal life is changed into "a kingdom at Babel," a kingdom over brethren;[17] while another branch of the same stock of Ham is the renowned Mizraim or Egypt,[18] which as much as Babel, though in other ways, becomes a snare to God's elect. What these represent we may hereafter see; suffice it now to mark that Babel and Egypt both grow out of Ham; the greater number of whose sons bear names which are connected with, or descriptive of, war and strife and

[17] Chap. x. 8–10.
[18] Chap. x. 6. It is scarcely necessary, I suppose, to add, that Mizraim is the Hebrew name for Egypt.

bloodshedding.[19] Shem's line tell out yet more solemn truths. From him springs the Assyrian, as well as the true Israelite. Asshur no less than Eber is his son ;[20] so surely does the contemplative life, which produces true holiness, tend also to beget that spirit of mere reasoning, of which Asshur, or Assyria, is the appointed type. So near is the false to the true; so quick the descent from that which is, to that which is not, acceptable. I need not repeat what I have said of Japhet. Let us not forget how soon his seed, that is the fruit of active life, degenerates into that which God counts as the world, into a mere Gentile life which knows not God.[21]

Such are the seeds, whose fate is foretold in that prophecy of their father Noah, with the literal fulfilment of which we are so familiar; the spiritual sense of which no less reveals the course and end of those different forms of life which have been developed in the regenerate.

The fate of Ham comes first. In his seed Noah foresaw one who would be "cursed Canaan ;" who though called, as a son of this house, to liberty, would become " a servant of servants to his brethren."[22] These are they who, knowing much of the truth, "walk after the flesh in the lust of uncleanness, and despise government; presumptuous are they, self-willed; they are not afraid to speak evil of dignities."[23] Such, though they appear to have escaped the

---

[19] To trace only the names of the sons of Cush, Ham's firstborn: (chap. x. 7 :) " Seba " is *taking*, or *being taken* in battle: "Havilah," *labouring* or *bringing forth*: " Sabtah" (a word connected with besieging strong places) means *going round* or *compassing*: " Raamah " is *a voice of thunder*, as of an army shouting for the battle : " Sabtecha," *the cause of slaughter* :" " Dedan," *solitary*, or perhaps, *who judgeth* : names all akin to strife and misery.—Cf. *Hieron. Nom. Heb.*

[20] Chap. x. 21, 22.

[21] Chap. x. 2–5. " By these (*i. e.* Japhet's sons) were the isles of the Gentiles divided," &c.

[22] Chap. ix. 25.

[23] 2 Pet. ii. 10, 11.

pollutions of the world, through the knowledge of the Lord and Saviour Jesus Christ, again entangled therein and overcome, find their latter end worse than the beginning. But it is happened unto them according to the true proverb,—The dog is turned to his own vomit again, and the sow that was washed to her wallowing in the mire. That the Church has such a seed needs no proof: but that it "serves brethren,"—that it subserves a good end,—is not always seen sufficiently. Yet it must be so; for the Lord has said, "A servant of servants shall he be unto his brethren." Surely this is true within and without. And when we reach this stage of regeneration, like Noah, we see, that as dung upon the earth, or as the bitter bile which is secreted in the natural body, even so does the evil in the Church work for good, and the ungracious acts of false brethren serve to polish and bring out the grace in truer souls. "All things are ours, if we are Christ's."[24] Even sin and false brethren shall be our Gibeonites, "hewing wood" at least for us,[25] preparing to our hand something which we may use in self-sacrifice.

I need not dwell on Shem or Japhet's lot: each gets the blessing which is best suited to it; Shem to have "Jehovah for his God;" Japhet to be "enlarged by God, and to dwell in Shem's tabernacles."[26] But why of Shem is this alone pronounced? Is not Jehovah the God of all Noah's progeny? Is not the Name of the Lord known to all who are born and grow up in the house of the regenerate? Look for answer at the Church. Is God known there?

[24] 1 Cor. iii. 22, 23.

[25] Joshua ix. 27. These Gibeonites were Canaanites. "Cham porro, quod interpretatur calidus, . . . quod significat nisi hæreticorum genus calidum . . . Sed malus frater in filio suo, hoc est in opere suo, puer, id est servus, est fratrum bonorum, cùm vel ad exercitationem patientiæ, vel ad profectum sapientiæ scienter utuntur malis boni," &c.—*Aug. de Civit.* l. xvi. c. 2.

[26] Chap. ix. 26, 27.

Might not many, even true souls, almost as well be without God? Are they not doing all for Him, leaving Him nothing to do? Are they not thus like Japhet, with all their blessings tending to Gentilism? They may, indeed, load altars with gifts, but are not their altars inscribed, "*To the Unknown God?*" Is not this their thought:—There is a God—all we know of Him is, that we must offer to Him. "*To Him,*" not "*From Him,*" is their motto; and this, though He is shewing out on every hand, that He is not to be worshipped as though He needed anything, seeing He giveth to all life and breath and all things; and has not left Himself without witness, in that He does good, and gives us rain from heaven, and fruitful seasons, filling our hearts with food and gladness.[27] Shem has learnt the Name which tells all this. What God is in Himself is Shem's security. The Lord is what He is, and this is enough. He is Love, and because He is Love, He must go out of Himself in endless, countless kindnesses. Hence Shem's motto is, "*From the Lord, the known God.*" Shem has an altar "whereof he may eat,"[28] by grace spread for him. Shem can sing:—"He prepareth a table for me even in the presence of my enemies."[29] Whatever else Shem lacks, he has a God; and, having Him, in Him possesses all things. Japhet's blessing is the gift; Shem's is the Giver. Japhet rejoices in the blessing; Shem in Him who is the Blesser. If Japhet is blessed himself, it is enough for him; he knows not what it is to "thirst for God, even for the living God:" while Shem cannot rest in gifts short of God, sighing, "When shall I come and appear before God?"[30] But Japhet one day shall be "enlarged," and then "he too shall dwell in Shem's

---

[27] Acts xvii. 23–25, and xiv. 17.

[28] Heb. xiii. 10.

[29] Psalm xxiii. 5.

[30] Psalm xlii. 2.

tents." Then, wide as the sphere of the active life may seem, it shall find yet greater lengths and breadths in the realms of contemplation : when the name of the Lord, and what He is, appears ; and " according to His Name, so is His praise in all the earth." [31]

" These are the families of the sons of Noah, and by these were the nations divided in the earth after the flood." [32] These are the developments of regenerate man, and by these come all the divisions in that Church which professes " one baptism." The field here is one in which much gold lies hid. Blessed are they, who, finding it in humble prayer, use it in a still humbler walk on earth to God's glory.

V.— Noah's Failure

Chapter 9:18-29; 10; 11:1-9

It remains to note the peculiar forms of failure which are manifested in Noah and his sons, that is, in man regenerate. Sad is the contrast between Noah going forth with joy, and Noah drunken and exposing his nakedness; between "the whole earth of one lip and of one speech," and Great Babylon, with "tongues confounded," and its sons separated; between the first full joy of the regenerate soul, and the experience which follows of gifts misused and curses treasured up; or, to trace it without, between the Church as it was, when " the multitude which believed was of one heart and of one soul, neither said any that ought that he possessed was his own, and they had all things common," [1] and the Church as it is now, with

[31] Psalm xlviii. 10.   [1] Acts ii. 42-47; and iv. 32-34.
[32] Chap. x. 32.

"departures from the faith, men giving heed to seducing spirits and doctrines of devils, speaking lies in hypocrisy, with conscience seared, lovers of themselves, covetous boasters, proud, blasphemers, having withal a form of godliness without the power." [2] But such is the fruit and fall even of regenerate man.

Three chief forms of failure are described; first Noah's, then Nimrod's, then Great Babylon. Each differs in form, with a gradual advance in crime. In the first two, good things are misapplied. In Noah, we have blessings external to him misused, to his own hurt. In Nimrod, personal gifts are perverted to injure others. In Babel we have more open apostasy, and a systematic departure from the right position, with untrue and creature things substituted for true, and self-exaltation instead of God's glory.

In each regenerate soul all this may be. First, misuse of privileges leads to spiritual intoxication. The vine — some precious grace of Christ in us — tends, if misused, to make us forget ourselves, and to expose our nakedness; the failure of the ruling mind within giving an occasion to the other thoughts in us to shew themselves. Thus do our failings help to discover to us what different minds, after regeneration, yet remain in us, some of which we learn now must be judged, as being only subtle forms of the condemned old man. Shem, the mind which loves contemplation, and Japhet, that which purposes and performs true outward service, are each recognised; but Ham is cursed in his seed; the fruits of knowing and not doing are foreseen and reprobated. Nevertheless out of Ham the evil grows. Nimrod, a form of life the fruit of mere

[2] 1 Tim. iv. 1, 2; and 2 Tim. iii. 1–5.

intellect, aspires to rule and be the master-mind ; gifts of knowledge claim a place in us, which God cannot approve ; the result of which is a "kingdom at Babel," that is, some rule or rules which cannot sanctify. After which Babel itself grows up ; some form, which, though great and approved in man's eyes, in God's is simply confusion. We build up likenesses of truths within : we strengthen and fortify some opinion or imagination ; and we may call it edification ; but self is at work, usurping the Lord's place, and self-love, and thoughts of self-exaltation, "to make us a name," are indeed perverting everything. Thus a tower of pride springs up within, which we may hope will be a means to reach to heaven, (for in building this Babel we are self-deceived, and may be seeking right things in a wrong and self-invented way,) but which will only draw us from the true high ground of light, and leave us inwardly distracted and full of confusion. All this may be, and is, within, after we are through grace truly regenerate ; for no evil is without, the seed of which is not within : it may be hid, as the night is hid in the day, if the light of heaven rules us ; yet the root of self remains, and in it lies the germ of a Babel, a beast, an Antichrist, ready to make the temple of God his seat, if we depart from the cross of Jesus Christ. But the inward kingdom is not seen by all ; the outward manifestation of it, therefore, may be more useful here.

To trace it then without. Noah's fall comes first. This is the failure of the true elect through the abuse of good gifts. Noah's care in the cleansed earth is the vine.[3] In the sphere of old Adam, and before the flood, that is, before regeneration, Noah was no planter. There his work

---

[3] Chap. ix. 20.

was the ark : there, day and night, instead of planting the vine, he was cutting down the high trees; as the work of the elect in the world is to lay the axe to the root of men's pride; to lay them low, that by the experience of death they may reach a better life. But in the Church, regenerate man has other work. There the vine is to be trained, and pruned, and cultivated; there its precious juice, which gladdens God and man, is to be drunk with thankfulness and joy to God's glory. Yet this may be misused. Has the " cup of blessing " never been taken and perverted to men's own condemnation? Alas! not a few, like Noah, have profaned that wine which was given in love to " make us forget our poverty." [4] The truth of Christ's sufferings for us, carnally received, used as a reprieve to the flesh, has come back as a curse to those who have so regarded it; for, " the grace of God being turned into lasciviousness," [5] men have but " eaten and drunk their own damnation :" while even Christ's sufferings in us may be perverted if they minister to our pride or vain self-satisfaction. If, instead of walking in watchfulness and prayer, men put some gift in the place of meekness and humbleness, if they do not " watch and keep their garments," the result is always this, — " they have walked naked, and men have seen their shame."

Two things are brought out by this fall; sin in some, and grace in others, of the Church's children. Ham not only sees, but tells the shame abroad, without an attempt

[4] Prov. xxxi. 6, 7. Augustine (*De Civit.* l. xvi. c. 2,) and Cyprian (*Epist.* 63,) both refer this cup of Noah to Christ's blood and the Lord's Supper. But neither Augustine, nor any of the early Fathers, so far as I am aware, speak distinctly of the failure of Noah's sons, in its bearing upon the failure of the regenerate. The reason is clear; because in their days the evil, of which Nimrod and Babel were the figure, had not developed itself in the Church, as it has since then.

[5] Jude 4.

to place so much as a rag on that nakedness, which, as the sin of one so near to him, should have been his own shame. Shem and Japhet will not look upon it, but "walking backward,"— a path not taught by nature, but grace,— cover their father's nakedness.[6] So is it yet. We see what is akin to us. The evil have an eye for evil, while the good and loving are engaged in acts of charity. Thus He, whose work it is to bring to light the hidden things of darkness, by the failure of one, often reveals another's heart. The Church's fall, the misuse of gift in some, is made the occasion for stripping the self-deceiver bare. Men sit in judgment on the evil in the Church, full of impatience and self, laying all iniquity bare, not waiting for the righteous Judge; little thinking that, whilst they are judging evil, God by the evil may be trying and judging them; or that the spirit, which exposes others' sin, may be far more hateful to Him than some misuse of privileges. For Noah's fall was a misuse of blessings: Ham's exposure of it was want of love. God may, indeed, convince of sin, but never without ministering better things. We too, at times, must strip deceivers bare; but to see evil and accuse it, without a helping hand or pitying eye, is devilish. Shem and Japhet cannot do so. With such souls, the Church's failure only brings to view graces, which, were there no failure, could not be manifested. We mourn because the Church is fallen. But does not the Church's fall give larger opportunities for love and self-sacrifice? Every trying thing — every humbling and shameful thing — is but the occasion of shewing grace, if grace be there. Circumstances do but prove us. And that same trial, which shews the carnality of the carnal, only elicits grace in gracious souls; and that very infirmity,

[6] Chap. ix. 22, 23.

which is an occasion of falling to us, if we walk by nature, is an occasion of victory, if we walk by grace.

But a worse form of evil soon appears.[7] Noah misused blessings to injure and expose himself: Nimrod exalts himself to lord it over brethren; for of those over whom he ruled all had sprung, and this within a few generations, from one common father. Little is told us of this second form of apostasy; but that little is enough. And indeed the steps by which lordship over brethren is reached are not many.

The author of it is Nimrod, the son of Cush. Sprung from that seed, who, having been scorched by the truth, have "seared consciences," his very name, Nimrod or *rebel*,[8] points out the character of those actings, by which the family and patriarchal government instituted by God was changed into a kingdom ruled by violence.

The stages are these: "He began to be a mighty one;" this is the first step in the transition from "ensamples to the flock" to "lords over God's heritage;"[9] after which "a mighty hunter" follows, one who can first slay for us the wild beasts which threaten us; but who, having hunted them, will then hunt his brethren, till they too are ensnared and captivated. And all this shall be "before the Lord;" "even as Nimrod, the mighty hunter before the Lord." It was so in Israel, when faith in God and communion failed; a king was sought under whose shadow they might dwell safely, who might "fight their battles and go before them,"[10] and do for them what God had covenanted to do. In a word, a gift of God was sought for more than God; and the result, in Saul's case, as in

---

[7] Chap. x. 8 10.

[8] Heb., נמרד, from מרד, to *rebel*; reminding us of ὁ ἄνομος, "the lawless one," 2 Thess. ii. 8.

[9] 1 Pet. v. 3.

[10] 1 Sam. viii. 20.

Nimrod's, was that the "mighty one" became a "mighty hunter," pursuing those, who, like David, because they walked with God, could not be taken by all this mightiness.

It is well known how that which first was shewn in Nimrod again reappeared on resurrection ground, and was again enacted in that redeemed family, of which the Lord said, "Ye all are brethren." As it was foretold Antichrist should come, so did he come, and the success of the "rebel," or "lawless one," is but too well known. Men arose, with mighty gifts, used first to slay the lion and the bear, but soon to bring the congregation of the Lord into bondage. They stood in the Church for God and His Christ, as though God and His Christ were absent, rather than as witnesses that "the Lord God yet dwelt among them." [11] Thus did the best gifts become curses. Nimrod's course became a proverb:—"Wherefore it is said, Even as Nimrod, the mighty hunter before the Lord." Is it not a proverb, that spiritual dominion, or rather that which has claimed to be such, is too often a "mighty hunter," a spirit of domination, ever seeking to enslave, and to impose a yoke, not on the bodies only, but upon the minds of brethren? Christ's true rule aims to make all free: false rule to make all slaves, under the pretence of serving them. The Church of Rome, where "the rebel's" rule has been most seen, is proof enough; but it

---

[11] Psalm lxviii. 18; Eph. iv. 8. The connection is most noteworthy between God's "giving gifts to men," and the aim or end of this, "that the Lord God might dwell among them;" not that they should take His place. Augustine recognises the same truth in the Lord's words here respecting Babel:—"Quid sibi vult, '*Venite,* *et descendentes confundamus,*' (quod intelligitur angelis dictum,) nisi quia per angelos descendebat, qui in angelis descendentibus erat. Et bene non ait, Venite, et descendentes confundite; sed '*Confundamus ibi linguam eorum;*' ostendens ita se operari per ministros suos," &c. — *De Civit.* l. xvi. c. 5.

is not there alone that the works of the " mighty hunter" may be seen.

So Nimrod makes a " kingdom in the land of Shinar, whose beginning was Babel," that is, *confusion*. This leads to another form of evil : men's tongues are confounded, and then the one family splits and separates. But ere this is described, a fact is named, shewing the effect of Nimrod's course on Shem's purer seed.

We read : — " Out of that land went forth Asshur, and builded Nineveh, and the city Rehoboth and Calah." [12] Asshur is the son of Shem, [13] and here we have Asshur going forth from Nimrod's kingdom, to imitate him in building, if not a Babel, at least a Nineveh or a Calah. Nimrod's invention cannot be confined to Great Babylon. Other cities, " the cities of the nations," soon arise. Cities in type are systems or polities, very unlike those primitive pilgrim dwellings, " the tents of Shem." Here we have foreshewn the rise of those " cities of the nations," those national systems of religion, seen by the Apostle John, whose fate is connected, even as their birth, with Babylon the Great, and who, when she falls, fall with her. [14] Nor does the fact that these cities are the work of Asshur, the son of Shem, save them from the destruction that will one day overtake the works of Nimrod. What avails it for national churches to point to the elect seed who built them ? The question is not, What seed were they ? — but, What has been the building ? Whence got they their pattern ? Out of what land came they ? Have they built " cities," or were they content, like Paul, to be " tentmakers ?" [15] Alas, even Asshur finds pilgrimage

---

[12] Chap. x. 11.
[13] Chap. x. 22.
[14] Rev. xvi. 19.
[15] Origen, in commenting on the

Tabernacle in the wilderness, that movable tent, which, until Canaan was reached, was their place of assembly and worship and sacrifice,

hard travail : hence Asshur builds cities, and becomes almost as Babel. Asshur it is who carries Israel captive ; [16] Asshur it is who joins with Israel's foes ; [17] Asshur upholds the mart of nations ; [18] therefore Asshur and his company go down into the pit.[19] Wherefore let Israel say, " Asshur shall not save us," [20] though he is strong and buildeth mighty cities ; " for ships shall come from the coast of Chittim, and shall afflict Asshur, and he also shall perish for ever." [21]

The third form of failure among Noah's seed is the building of Babel, with the consequent scattering and confusion of the hitherto united family.[22] This form of evil, though allied to Nimrod's, is worse; for it is no good gift misapplied, but rather a systematic departure from the original position, with imitations of the true instead of truth, and self-exaltation instead of God's glory.

The course of this apostasy is soon traced ; and nothing can be more striking than the contrast here drawn between the primitive state of the redeemed family, and that which their sin brought upon them. Their original state is thus described : — " And the whole earth was of one language

thus connects that tent with Paul's vocation :—" Unde mihi videtur non fortuito contigisse ut Petrus quidem et Andreas et filii Zebedæi, arte piscatores invenirentur, Paulus vero faber tabernaculorum. Et quia illi vocati ab arte capiendorum piscium, mutantur et fiunt piscatores hominum, dicente Domino, ' Venite post me, et faciam vos piscatores hominum :' non dubium quin et Paulus, quia et ipse per Dominum nostrum Jesum Christum vocatus apostolus est, simili artis suæ transformatione mutatus sit : ut sicut illi ex piscatoribus piscium piscatores hominum facti sunt, ita et iste a faciendis ta-

bernaculis terrenis, ad cœlestia tabernacula construenda tralatus sit. . . . Facit tabernacula Paulus, et cum ab Hierusalem in circuitu usque ad Illyricum replet evangelium, Dei ecclesias construendo; et hoc modo facit et ipse tabernacula ad similitudinem tabernaculorum cœlestium, quæ ostendit Deus in montem Moysi."—*Hom.* xvii. *in Num.*

[16] Ezra iv. 2.
[17] Psalm lxxxiii. 8.
[18] Ezek. xxvii. 3–27.
[19] Ezek. xxxii. 22, 23.
[20] Hosea xiv. 3.
[21] Numb. xxiv. 24.
[22] Chap. xi. 1–9.

and of one speech." Difference of age we know there
was; difference, too, in character; some were Shems,
some Hams, some Japhets. But, spite of this, as yet
"they all spake the same thing;" as yet "there were no
divisions among them." As in the early Church, where
" the multitude of them that believed were of one
heart,"[23] there was but "one lip and one speech" among
them. Love enabled them, though not of one stature, to
be of one mind. As yet they could understand one
another and walk together.

Not long did this continue : soon apostasy begins. The
first step is, " They journeyed from the east." The day-
spring is in the east. There, to them that love the light,
" the Sun of Righteousness ariseth with healing on His
wings."[24] But now the company of resurrection pilgrims
are seen with their backs toward the east : their faces see
not this light; they are turned away from it.[25] Then
" they found a plain :" they leave their first high ground.
This plain, doubtless, like the plain of Sodom to Lot, had
its attractions; so "they dwelt there." And now, their
pilgrim character being at an end, their thoughts turn to
their own glory and establishment. Great Babel is the
result. "And they said one to another, Go to; let us
make brick, and burn them thoroughly. And they had
brick for stone, and slime for mortar. And they said, Go
to ; let us build us a city, and a tower, whose top may
reach to heaven; and let us make us a name, lest we be

---

[23] Acts iv. 22.

[24] Mal. iv. 2 ; Luke i. 78.

[25] " Per labium intelligitur prædi-
catio et doctrina. Istud autem labium ab ecclesiæ principio fuit unum
prædicando et docendo unum Deum,
unam fidem, unum baptisma, sicut
dicitur *Ephes.* iv. Sed in recessu
aliquorum ab Oriente, hoc est Christo,
(de quo dicitur *Zachar.* vi., ' Ecce
vir, Oriens nomen ejus,') turris superbiæ fabricata est, ex quâ secuta
est divisio linguarum, per doctrinam
et prædicationem hæresium diversa-
rum."—*Gloss. Ordin. in loco.*

scattered abroad upon the face of all the earth." Thus arose Great Babylon. Let us not pass from this scene till we understand it, for even yet Babylon is " mystery "— a thing unintelligible to not a few.

Its preparatory stages we have noticed. Men journey from the east; then they settle down; then they begin to build. At this stage, the scene presented is man taking counsel of man, and not of God. " They spake one to another ;" and the result of the deliberation is an attempt to imitate God; first in His words, then in His works. They said, " Let us make." God once had said " Let us make." [26] Here man takes upon him to speak as God. Then comes out their work: " They had brick for stone, and slime for mortar." Brick is stone artificially made,— man's imitation and substitute for God's creative work. Babylon is built of brick; so, too, Nineveh is built of brick. The prophet who foretells her downfall notes this, bidding her to " tread the clay, and make strong her brick-kilns; yet shall the fire devour them all." [27] In Egypt, too, brick-making is common. Egyptians like nothing better than to see captive Israelites toil in making brick.[28] Great Babel is built of brick, and for cement they have slime, as it is written, " And slime had they for mortar." This slime was that sulphureous compound, of which the region of the Dead Sea, and the plain of Babylon, are even now so full — a compound formed, as it is supposed, from the corruption of animal and vegetable substances. Well does it represent that dangerous cement — so ready to burst out into a blaze — that cement of self-love and lust of power, by which mystic Babylon is now held together. It is a " daubing of untempered mortar." Jerusalem is not so built, nor of her does man

---

[26] Gen. i. 26.　　　[27] Nahum iii. 14, 15.　　　[28] Exod. v. 7, 8.

say, "Let us make;" but the Lord Himself says, "I will." "Thus saith the Lord, Behold, I will lay thy stones with fair colours, and I will lay thy foundations with sapphires; and I will make thy windows of agates, and thy gates carbuncles, and all thy borders pleasant stones." [29] So another saith, "Ye also, as lively stones, are built up a spiritual house:" [30] and again, "Ye are God's building." [31]

Babel is built by other hands, and with other aims. Here man is working to ascend up to heaven. Self-elevation is the aim; self-energy the means: it is but consistent that self-glory, "to make us a name," should be the motive. And withal, (let not this be forgotten,) the reason assigned seemed good;— they wished for unity: their fear was, "lest they should be scattered;" therefore they built their high tower. We know too well how others also have builded, with the self-same aim, professing and perhaps really seeking catholic unity; and the result has only been greater scattering among those who were to be united. But when man builds for self-glory, and with imitations of the true instead of the true, the end may surely be foretold. When will men learn that catholic unity is not to be so attained? On such ground we may build, "lest we be scattered;" but the labour is in vain, and will only produce more scattering. The present state of Christendom, only more and more divided, the more carnal union is sought, should at last teach us by sight, even if we cannot walk by faith. The one remedy is Pentecostal grace,— that Spirit which can yet change carnal disciples into spiritual, and give them a message which their carnal brethren, dwellers in Mesopotamia, in Egypt, and in the parts of Libya about Cyrene, Parthians,

---

[29] Isa. liv. 11, 12.   [30] 1 Pet. ii. 5.   [31] 1 Cor. iii. 9.

Medes, and Elamites, Cretes and Arabians, who understand not each other, will yet all understand; [32] because it is not in the letter which divides, but in the One Spirit of Christ, which melts, and unites, and reconciles. Nothing else will heal the confusion: no outward form, however good, can ever accomplish it. Men at last will learn this in self-despair: till they learn it, each fresh effort can only produce confusion worse confounded.

It would exceed my limits to give examples of the " brick for stone," as it is to be seen this day in Great Babylon; but this I may say, the city is not only built up, but filled also with images of all God's truths and ordinances; yea, real vessels of the sanctuary may be there; true gold carried away with captive Israelites. On her outside is the likeness of a heavenly church, the likeness of priesthood and ministry, the likeness of the ordinances, duties, and ways of holiness. On her inside is the likeness of good knowledge, the likeness of repentance and conversion, the likeness of faith, the likeness of zeal for God, the likeness of love to God and His saints, the likeness of the Lamb's meekness and innocency, the likeness of justification, the likeness of sanctification, the likeness of mortification, the likeness of peace, joy, rest, and satisfaction; for as a fallen world is full of shadows of truth, so is the fallen Church rich in forms, which to the opened eye witness of a life which should be there; but the substance, the truth, the virtue of all these is wanting to her, and she herself is found persecuting that very thing, where it is found in truth, the image of which she cries up so boastfully. This is the woman that hath bewitched the whole earth, even as Jannes and Jambres withstood Moses, by imitating the works of God's elect. And of

[32] Acts ii. 7-11.

what truth shall we not find the likeness in Great Babel?
She has priesthood, and altars, and fine linen, and the
cross, and incense, and chrism, and rule, and discipline.
She has the form of every truth, to meet and seduce those
who ask for the reality. Do we "look for a city which
hath foundations?" Then Babel will forestall it, and be
a city too. As the Father of Lights will have His city, so
has the prince of darkness his, to tempt souls to rest short
of the city of the mystery of life, in the city of the
mystery of deceit and imitation.

Such are the failures on resurrection ground. Regeneration, so far from ending all man's wickedness, discovers
in man new forms of evil. So in the Revelation which
was manifested to the beloved John, he saw that red
horses, and earthquakes, and blood, and hail, and fire,
and beasts, and Great Babylon, were all part of the
"Revelation of Jesus Christ," [33] — a necessary result of
such a seed falling into such a soil. If He is to be revealed in the earth, it must be thus. The revelation
cannot, and in love may not, at once be perfected. In
my soul, too, I know that red horses, and beasts, and
earthquakes, and Babel, with her filthiness, must come in
me after regeneration, and after Christ's first coming to
my soul in grace has quickened it, before heaven opens,
and He comes the second time to rule all the creature, and
to make all things new. Then, when He who has come
in grace comes again in great power, the revelation of
Jesus Christ shall be perfected; but ere that is done,
much will intervene, and the very beasts are stages in the
way. The evil destroys and punishes itself throughout.
In its very nature it carries the seeds of its own dissolu-

[33] Rev. i. 1, and vi. 4, 12; viii. 7; xiii. 1; xvii. 4, 5.

tion; while grace, out of every fall, brings forth fresh blessings, proving that, if sin abound through man's weakness, grace shall yet much more abound. Thus it was with the fall of Noah's sons. The confusion of tongues issues in the call and life of Abraham, Isaac, and Jacob; in each of whom the development of man proceeds, with fresh discoveries of the riches of the God of all grace.

PART 4

ABRAHAM, OR THE SPIRIT OF FAITH

Chapters 12-20

" Abraham believed God."— ROM. iv. 3.

" He staggered not at the promise of God through unbelief, but was strong in faith, giving glory to God."— ROM. iv. 20.

ABRAHAM, OR THE SPIRIT OF FAITH

Chapters 12-20

THE progress and development of the natural life in man is, perhaps, the best figure of the progress of the spiritual life. In both One Hand is seen. Adam, Abel, and Noah, shew how in the spiritual, just as in the natural, there is first a stage, when we are begotten and yet not quickened; then a stage, when we are quickened and yet not born,—when we draw that nourishment which contributes to our growth through the medium of natural things, as the child in the womb receives strength through the mother; and a third stage, when, after we are quickened, we are born, out of that in which we were, into another sphere of greater liberty. Adam answers to the first; Abel, to the second; Noah, to the third of these. In Noah, man, already quickened, is brought, through the travail pains and groans of the first creation, into a sphere, where, like a new-born child, he is delivered out of the first world, into more perfect light and liberty. And this conscious exchange of one world for another,—this coming out of one sphere into another, is regeneration.

We are now to see how after we are thus born, in the spiritual just as in the natural world, we walk first by faith, implicitly trusting another. This life of faith is perfectly figured and set forth in Abraham. Then, as dear children, in the intelligent enjoyments of sonship, all the joys and experiences of which Isaac's life figures to us, we dwell awhile in peace by wells of water, till, fit for service, we go forth to toil like Jacob, and thence advance to suffering and glory, as is set forth in Joseph. No wonder, therefore, that Abraham's life in every age has suggested lessons of deepest import to thousands. It is the picture of that stage when life is strong; when the heaven-born child, in the energy of heavenly youth, is being exercised in all that may increase strength and skill and blessedness: when the Father of spirits is leading His child to know both himself and Him who has created and will not forsake him.[1]

In saying that Abraham is the life of faith, I do not mean that there has been no faith before this stage. There must have been faith at every stage, else there could have been no blessedness. Without faith Adam could have found no peace in the promise of the Seed: Abel offered

---

[1] The *Gloss*, in the *Catena Aurea*, on the Genealogy of Christ in St. Matthew,—while explaining Abraham, Isaac, and Jacob, as figuring certain successive forms of life in man, which end after many confusions in Christ, the image of God, wrought in us, — interprets Abraham, Isaac, and Jacob, as the lives of faith, hope, and charity, respectively. But this is only another way of expressing what I have said; for the spirit of sonship is hope, and true service is practical love or charity. The passage is as follows:— " Moraliter autem Abraham nobis virtutem fidei per exempla Christi significat, cùm de eo legatur, 'Abraham credidit Deo, et reputatum est ei ad justitiam.' Isaac significat spem, quia interpretatur *risus*; fuit enim gaudium parentum. Spes vero similiter est gaudium nostrum, dum æterna bona sperare facit, et de eis gaudere. Abraham ergo genuit Isaac, quia fides generat spem. (Cf. Rom. v. 3, 4, 5.) Jacob autem significat charitatem. Charitas enim amplectitur duas vitas, activam per dilectionem proximi. contemplativam per dilectionem Dei ; activa per Liam, contemplativa per Rachel, significatur. Lia enim *laborans* interpretatur, quia activa in labore est : Rachel, *visum principium*, quia per contemplativam principium, id est Deus, videtur."

by faith: Noah was saved by faith. But there may be, and are, such acts of faith, before we reach the stage which is a walk of faith distinctively. Just as Christ was begotten of the Holy Ghost, and yet had the Spirit given at His baptism, after which His life, already of the Holy Ghost, took another form in the manifestation of that same Spirit; so in us faith works from the first, but we go some way before we reach that stage in which the walk of faith is manifested. But this walk it is of which Abraham is the type, a form of life always following the full apprehension of regeneration.[2]

This stage is introduced by the description of the progress of regenerate man, before that life of faith appears which Abraham typifies. Therefore is the course of Shem's line given here, as the introduction to the life of Abraham.[3] For these ten generations prefixed to Abraham's life, shewing us all the steps from Shem to Terah, Abraham's father, give us all the phases or forms of the contemplative mind, after regeneration, till it produces Abraham, that is, the life of faith. Here, in the generations from Shem downwards, we are shewn how the contemplative mind, after regeneration, for a while degenerates. If the successive names are beyond us, this at least is clear, that Shem's line in Terah now worshipped idols.[4] Then

---

[2] Those who care to trace this further, will find some teaching in the difference between φρόνημα πνεύματος, (Rom. viii. 6,) and πνεῦμα πίστεως or πνεῦμα υἱοθεσίας, (2 Cor. iv. 13, and Rom. viii. 15,) as used by St. Paul. The φρόνημα πνεύματος is not exactly the same thing as πνεῦμα πίστεως. We get the φρόνημα πνεύματος, that is, *the minding of the spirit*, at the Abel stage, before we pass the mystic flood; but

after regeneration we get πνεῦμα πίστεως, or πνεῦμα υἱοθεσίας, that is, *the spirit of faith, or the spirit of adoption*. The marked distinction in these expressions of St. Paul may help some to see the reality of the difference between the Abel and the Abraham stage. And as this is true within, so is it in the dispensations.

[3] Chap. xi. 10-26.

[4] Joshua xxiv. 2. Those who wish to look further into the import

out of this bursts forth again the brighter stage set forth in the life and path of Abraham.

Here then, as in the previous steps, we see that this new form of life grows out of the discovery of failure in the former stage. Abel was not seen till Adam fell; nor Noah till the earth was full of violence. Each morning sprang out of a night; and so here, out of the decline of light in Noah's seed, a fresh day breaks forth again with greater light in Abraham. Just as in a tree, each new growth follows a winter; and the whole clothing of leaves, which had been put on in the former stage of growth, is put off preparatory to another great advance, which bursts forth out of the bonds of the winter, which has seemed to freeze and make the tree almost as dead; so is it in the soul of man: his development is a law of progress, but of progress through checks and conflicts; through winters which strip us, and leave us bare and apparently dead, without that clothing which has been thrown around us; yet not so dead but that the rays of heavenly light can again clothe, enlarge, and quicken us. Such is our life, progress through conflicts and apparent defeats; the harmonies of grace being as those of nature; night and day, cold and heat, in elemental strife, working out the appointed end through the balance of opposing forces everywhere. So we travel on: hindrances aiding our advance; castings down lifting us up; death bringing forth life; separation working a higher and purer unity; a wonder and a riddle even to ourselves.

And this darkness, out of which that walk of faith springs forth, of which Abraham is the appointed figure, is, I suppose, common experience. The liberty we have, as dead and

of the ten names, from Shem to Abram, will find a good deal on the subject in Parker's *Bibliotheca Biblica*, part i. pp. 286–289.

risen with Christ, may be and is perverted for a season; nor is the walk of faith reached till the soul has learnt some of the perversions which follow regeneration. The decline of Shem's seed shews this in type. Our souls, if we have ever reached to true Christian liberty, may witness the sad reality. As a Reformer said, " We prayed more in the days of our darkness than now." Thus practical antinomianism will more or less shew itself after regeneration. Then out of such a state comes the stage we are to trace, a walk of obedient faith with Him who says, " Get thee out of thy country to the land that I will shew thee." All the steps of this walk are here described, from Ur of the Chaldees, where Terah lingers, till we reach the better land beyond Jordan. There trial on trial comes in the way : there faith learns itself, and that its fruit is all of God : there at length another form of life appears, in which man is yet more advanced and perfected. It is an oft-told tale, but, like man's life, no less wondrous because it has been repeated on earth a hundred thousand times.

But to trace each step in order. We shall see that here, as ever, there is first a separating process, then a perfecting one.

I. — Abram's Separation from his Country and his Father's House

Chapter 12

" Now the Lord had said to Abram, Get thee out of thy country, and from thy kindred, and from thy father's house, unto a land that I will shew thee. And I will make of thee a great nation, and I will bless thee, and make thy name great, and thou shalt be a blessing. And

I will bless them that bless thee, and curse him that curseth thee; and in thee shall all the families of the earth be blessed."[1]

Thus begins the life of faith. As Noahs, that is, in regeneration, we come from the Adam world to a new world beyond the waters. As Abrams, that is, in the walk of faith, we start from Mesopotamia, the ground between the mystic Tigris and Euphrates, that is, tradition and reasoning.[2] This walk begins not of man, but of God. It is His call, wholly of grace, which leads at once to separation. For the called one was one of an apostate race, an idolater,[3] and the husband of a barren woman,[4] in Ur of the Chaldees, that is, not far from Great Babylon, the ground of false and perverted worship and self-exaltation. Still he was of Shem's line; for the spirit of faith grows up, though amid awful confusions, out of the contemplative mind. But the fine gold of Shem ere this has changed: the contemplative mind has fallen grievously. What hopes could one of such a fallen line have of being made very fruitful and blessed in a better land? Could such a dry tree look for fruit? Yet God speaks, and, as at creation, great results follow. By this Word of God fresh life flows in and shews itself, as the sun's heat penetrating a tree causes it to come up out of the dark earth and spread heavenward. So works the call of God, itself the spring and strength of all the faith that follows it. Babels may grow from men's words one to another, saying, " Go to, and let us make." The walk of faith begins not from man: the Word is its author and finisher.

As to the call, it was, and yet is, personal; addressed, not

[1] Chap. xii. 1–3.
[2] Respecting these rivers, see on chap. ii. pp. 50, 51.
[3] Joshua xxiv. 2.
[4] Chap. xi. 30.

to the outward man, but to Abram, the fallen inner man. To this God says, " Get *thee* out, and I will bless *thee*." The prophets mark this: speaking of this act, the Lord says, " I called *him alone,* and blessed *him*." [5] For the call of God, to be of any use, must be personally felt and realised by the inner man. The flesh may hear of it; yea, as with those who went with Paul, it may be struck to the ground by the glory of the revelation : the senses may witness some of the outward circumstances accompanying the call : but as Paul says, " They heard not the voice of Him that spoke *to me*." [6] For the outward man knows not the call of God, and will prove that it knows it not, by abiding to the last far off from Canaan, on the ground of sense rather than on that of promise; while the spirit of faith goes forth, it knows not where, to stand in the strength of the Lord on the high and heaven-watered hills of promise, which flow with milk and honey.

This call of God contains both grace and truth; grace in the promise, the New Covenant *" I will,"* which said, *" I will* shew thee a land, *I will* make thee fruitful, *I will* bless thee ;" truth in the separating word, *" Get thee out,"* obedience to which was the proof that Abram believed the *" I will."* This promise was the gospel. So St. Paul, alluding to it, says, that in it " the gospel was preached to Abram." [7] The gospel is—I must repeat it—a promise of God, a report concerning future glory and an inheritance ; which men may believe or disbelieve, but which is true, because it is God's word, and to meet which faith alone is needed. Men are slow to apprehend this. Feelings, or works, or something in us, is looked for as the ground of future blessing and salvation. But the Spirit and the Word

[5] Isa. li. 2.   [6] Acts xxii. 9.   [7] Gal. iii. 8.

with one voice testify that it is the Lord Himself who saves; and that to receive the salvation, faith, that is, taking God at His word, is the simple and blessed means. God is the Saviour; and faith takes God to be God, resting on Him in every fresh discovery of need and barrenness, and finding Him to be all He has promised, in His own unfailing "I will."

But there is more than promise in the call. Promise is its strength; but linked with this there is the separating word, "Get thee out," calling for prompt obedience. Grace saves. It is the promise which sets the heart at rest; which brings us from idolatry and distance to happy confidence. But the faith, which rests on God's "I will," hears God's purpose also to separate His saved ones unto Himself. There is to be, not only peace, but separation. So the word of truth comes, commanding sanctification. Man has often divided between grace and truth, preaching God's "*I will*," without the accompanying "*Get thee out*;" or attempting to separate men to God with a "*Get thee out*," without a full apprehension of God's "*I will*." The result has proved that this is not God's call. Where He calls, both grace and truth are ever found. So with the Apostles. Jesus, walking by the sea of Galilee, (Galilee of the Gentiles, the people that sat in gross darkness,) saw two brethren, Simon and Andrew, casting a net into the sea; and He called them and said, "Follow me:" — here is separation:—"and I will make you fishers of men:"—here is the never-failing "I will."[8] So again, "Come unto me, all ye that labour:" — here is separation, for He was "separate:"[9] then follows the promise, "I will give you rest."[10] So again, in the well-known words, "I will dwell in them, and walk in them, and I will be their God, and

[8] Matt. iv.   19.   [9] Heb. vii. 26.   [10] Matt. xi. 28.

they shall be my people: wherefore come out and be separate, saith the Lord, and touch not the unclean thing, and I will receive you." [11]

And these two points are yet in the Lord's call, nor can the spirit of faith afford to part with either. At times, indeed, for " the flesh is weak," even faith may shrink from all that the separating word claims from it. We are slow to believe that apostate things are to be forsaken, not improved. We would fain mend them, rather than leave them. How many, both in the world within and without, are attempting to put the evil to rights, when God's word respecting both is only, " Get thee out." But the Lord is faithful; and where He has appeared, the way of separation or sanctification will be trodden: and, indeed, " the spirit is willing," if the flesh is weak.

But this leads us to the way in which the call was obeyed. The word was,—" Get thee out of thy country, and from thy kindred, and from thy father's house." Abram gat him out from his country, and even from his kindred, but not from his father's house. He attempts to take his father, and his father's house, with him. [12] He obeys, but not wholly. So is it yet. The spirit of faith in us, when called to go forth from the outward things of Ur of the Chaldeans,—the ground of reasoning, where Babel is built up,—is called of God to leave, not only the more outward things, such as " thy country," but the more inward also, the " kindred and father's house." Some are more outward, as natural pleasures and affections; and some more inward, as " the old man," and " father's house." Of these the outward things are sooner left than the inward; for nature yet is strong, and the old life is still very near and dear to

[11] 2 Cor. vi. 17, 18.   [12] Chap. xi. 31.

us. So, like Abram of old, the spirit of faith in us endeavours to take with it into the land of promise the old man
of our corrupt mind which has never truly known the call
of God. But this old man, though ready to start for
Canaan, never reaches it. It cares not to go so far. Nay,
while it lives, even the elect, if he abides with it, cannot
reach his destination. Journeying thus, Abram gets half-
way to Canaan : so we read,—" They went forth to go into
the land of Canaan, and they came to Charran and dwelt
there." And there they stopped until this old man died.
Then Abram starts again : and now nothing stops him ;
for now, " they went forth to go into the land of Canaan,
and into the land of Canaan they came." [13] Stephen,
alluding to Abram's call, specially marks this:—" The God
of glory appeared to our father Abraham, when he was in
Mesopotamia, before he dwelt in Charran, and said, Get
thee out of thy country, and from thy kindred, and come
into the land which I will shew thee. Then came he out
of the land of the Chaldeans, and dwelt in Charran ; and
from thence, when his father was dead, he removed him
into this land, wherein ye now dwell." [14]

" So Abram departed." So starts the spirit of faith.
Great is the struggle to leave " country and kindred and

---

[13] Compare chap. xii. 5, and xi. 31.

[14] Acts vii. 2–4. Ambrose thus
gives the inward sense :—" Hoc enim
Legislator providè egit, ut quemadmodum lapsum mentis demonstravit,
(Adam enim mentem diximus, Evam
sensum esse significavimus,) ut illas
erroris caveremus semitas ; ita etiam
processum mentis et quemdam supe-
riorem reditum significaret. . . . Hæc
ergo mens erat in Charrâ, id est, in
cavernis, obnoxia variis passionibus.
Ideoque dicitur ei, ' *Exi de terrâ*

tuâ,' id est de corpore tuo. Exivit
de hâc terrâ ille, cujus conversatio
in cœlis est. ' *Et de cognatione*,'
inquit, ' *tuâ*.' Cognati sunt animæ
nostræ corporis sensus. . . . ' *Et de
domo tuâ*;' domus enim mentis pro-
lativum est verbum. . . . Ergo qui
vult perfectam purgationem conse-
qui disjungat se ab his tribus, a corpore, a sensibus corporalibus, a voce ;
in quibus sunt omnes circumscrip-
tiones sensuum, quibus decipimur,"
&c.—*Ambros. de Abr.* l. ii. c. 1.

father's house." To go forth "not knowing whither we go" is trial enough. To go forth from "father's house" at once seems impossible. Thus the old man of our fallen spiritual life, though it cannot really help us to Canaan, is still clung to. Indeed, at first it seems to help us. It is written, not Abram took Terah, but "Terah took Abram;"[15] for often some energy, which is really corrupt, is active, apparently in a good direction, when the elect is called. But Terah never passes Jordan; he can but reach Charran. Having got thus far, he has been pilgrim long enough; and so "he dwells there."[16]

We are slow to learn this lesson, but it must be learnt. Even faith cannot take the old man into the place of promise. Jordan is not really passed. Often has it been tried; but the old life cannot be brought into heavenly places beyond that "stream of judgment," with its deep waterfloods.[17] Thus we are in a strait. A new bond draws us heavenward, but the old one as yet has claims on us. So we start with both: we get "out of our country," and the old man for many stages bears us company; but at length he wearies of this path; Canaan is too far off: and so with him for a season faith too settles down. But in due time we are freed. The time must come at last,

---

[15] Chap. xi. 31.

[16] This place is mentioned as Laban's home, Gen. xxvii. 43; as a place easily conquered by the king of Assyria, 2 Kings xix. 12; and, lastly, as having an extensive trade with Tyre, Ezek. xxvii. 23. All this is significant.

[17] Jordan, (Heb. יַרְדֵּן) meaning "*the stream of judgment*,"—if with Jerome we derive it from יָרַד, (*Hieron. Comment. in Ezech.* xlvii. 18,) the stream which must be passed by Israel, if they would enter Canaan, is the well-known figure of that death by which we enter heavenly things. If, however, with Augustine, (*Enar. in Psalm.* xli. [*E. V.* 42,] 6,) and Gregory the Great, (*Moral. in Job*, l. xxxiii. c. 6, § 13,) we derive the word from רַד, *to come down*, and regard Jordan as the figure of that self-abasement, which is a death to self, through which every one must pass who would enter into rest, the lesson is, in substance, the same.

when we discover this much loved old man to be dead, and that he must be buried out of sight. Hitherto, spite of the call, we have acted as though the old man might be saved, or improved, or taken with us. But now the meaning of our baptism dawns upon us; the call is recollected, and we become once more pilgrims. This is no fable. Once, with the old man leading us, we went forth to go into the land of Canaan; but we only got to Charran, and dwelt there. But the old man was buried : then again we started to go into the land of Canaan, and into the land of Canaan we came.

But though Terah cannot enter Canaan, Lot, another form of life, closely allied to the old man of our former conversation, and from which Abram, or the spirit of faith, has at length to be separated, goes on some stages further with him.[18] Our blindness makes it hard to speak of this. Few perceive that the inward man, or mind, like the body, is not one member, but many, consisting of many faculties, both of the understanding and affections, the former of which are figured by men, the latter by women, throughout Scripture. But thus it is ; and Lot is one of these. As the son of Abram's elder brother, he is the continuation and fruit of what is first and natural, the same old life, only in another form; submitting awhile to be under the direction of true faith, to shew at last its true character. Lot is the natural upright mind in us, not spiritual, yet respecting truth, and, to a considerable degree, following it ; scarcely to be distinguished at first from the spirit of faith in us, but with undeveloped tendencies such as the spirit of faith never manifests; just,[19] yet loving what the spirit of faith loves not, and at length resting, or seeking to rest,

[18] Chap. xii. 4.   [19] 2 Pet. ii. 7.

where the spirit of faith cannot rest; till it bears sad fruits, which faith could not produce, and which at a further stage are, like Moab and Ammon,[20] in direct opposition to God's elect Israel. Such a mind still dwells with us, though our old man, like Terah, is confessed to be both dead and buried.[21] But this will not be clear to all; for souls, as bodies, live in happy unconsciousness of what is working in them. And indeed though the workings of nature and grace are a sight for some, they work on as well, perhaps even better, unperceived by us.

Having thus passed Jordan, let us mark the trials into which the spirit of faith at once is introduced. Many for lack of knowing this are stumbled, even when through grace they are in the right way, finding it so unlike that which flesh and blood would have chosen. We read here of pilgrimage and difficulty and want, yet of communion with God and happy worship. And these are still some of the chief marks of the position into which true faith brings the believer.

Pilgrimage is noticed first. "Abram passed through the land, to the place of Sichem, and to Moreh; and he removed from thence into a mountain, and pitched his tent, having Bethel on the west, and Hai on the east; and Abram journeyed, going and journeying still toward the south."[22] Nahor abides without change where his fathers dwelt before him, and builds a city, which he calls after his own name.[23] Abram dwells in tents to the end, possessing nothing abiding here, save a burial-place.

---

[20] Moab and Ammon are the children of Lot, chap. xix. 37, 38.

[21] Origen alludes to this inward Lot, in his comment on John viii. 39 :— Οἶμαι δὲ ὅτι ἐν ταῖς ἀρχαῖς καὶ ἐπίποσον ὁ Λὼτ ἕψεται ἡμῖν, κ. τ. λ.

Ambrose also, *De Abr.* l. ii. c. 2, and 6. In this view we should not forget that Lot's name signifies *a covering*. He is not the true inner man.

[22] Chap. xii. 6–9.

[23] Chap. xxiv. 10.

And the spirit in us which obeys God's call will even yet dwell in tents and be a pilgrim. The old man may rest in outward things and be settled, but the spirit of faith has here no certain dwelling-place. Its tent is often searched by rains and winds; yet by these very trials it grows strong and is kept from many snares. For the called one cannot be as Moab, " settled on his lees." " Moab hath been at ease even from his youth; he hath settled on his lees; he hath not been emptied from vessel to vessel, neither hath he gone into captivity; therefore his taste remaineth in him, his scent is not changed."[24] Abram, and David, and Israel, have all been emptied from vessel to vessel. Pilgrimage is their appointed lot, because true life is always progressing, moving. In the course of this discipline, trials befall them which others never meet with; failures, too, are seen, such as we never see in the prudent, worldly man. When did Nahor go down to Egypt, or deny his wife? When did Saul, like David, go down to Achish, and play the madman? But in this same course God is seen, and man is learnt. Man, indeed, is abased, but God is glorified. The pilgrim " learns what is in his heart." He cannot easily forget what his pilgrimage has taught him of his own weaknesses. Once he might, like Eve, have believed the word, " Ye shall be as gods." Pilgrimage has proved that even faith is not a god, but only a vessel to receive God. Thus by trial does faith learn God; and the true discovery of Him more than compensates for all the self-despair, which has been the means of making us acquainted with Him.

Thus Abram passed from place to place; from Ur to Haran, then to Sichem and Moreh, thence to Bethel and

[24] Jer. xlviii. 11.

Hai, and so on.[25] He was what some now call changeable. And further, he went " he knew not whither." This is yet the common charge against the walk of faith. How often have I heard it urged against those, who, in faith and obedience to the call of God, have made no small sacrifices, that they are changeful, here to-day, and there to-morrow; that it is difficult from year to year to know where we may find them. Others, if they are snugly housed in some " city of the nations," some great or small system or polity of man's making, may be reckoned on with some certainty. We can tell where to find them even to the end. They can boast, too, of their consistency. Where they were at first, there they are still. They have never altered a single view, because they have never taken a single step forward. But this faith, which talks of God's having called it, is unmanageable. Men in whom such a spirit rules, however comfortably they are settled to-day, may be off, we know not where, to-morrow. And what do they get by it? Plainly nothing. One thing only is plain: a man who talks of the call of God is not the man to be trusted with the care of this world's cities. He is a madman. So the world has judged long since : so it judges yet : nor indeed is it wholly in the wrong. A madman is one who

---

[25] On the mystic import of each of these places, the early Fathers have written much. Ambrose says, " Egressus perambulavit terram usque ad Sichem, quod interpretatione Latinâ dicitur *humerus* vel *cervix*, per quæ executionem præscripti operis intelligimus. . . . Unde per figuram locorum id expressum advertimus, quod devotionem suam sanctus Abram, non solum studio, sed etiam efficaciâ probaverit fructuosâ, qua ' ad quercum,' (*i.e.* Moreh,) usque pervenerit."—*De Abr.* l. i. c. 2. As to the " mountain on the east of Bethel," he adds,—" Recessit inde in montem contra orientem Bethel ; incrementum devotionis montis significat eminentia," &c.—*Ibid.* l. ii. c. 3. We may compare with this Augustine's spiritual interpretation of Sichem, on the words, " I will divide Sichem."—*Enar. in Psalm.* lix. (*E. V.* 60,) § 8. St. Paul's explanation of Salem is well known, Heb. vii. 2.

sees, or thinks he sees, what others see not; and seeing
such things, he walks accordingly.   The called of God has
seen what others see not, and he walks accordingly; and
those who see not what he has seen must think him mad;
and his failures and inconsistencies, the fruits of his unbelief
in the path of faith, only make him more unintelligible.
Nevertheless the Lord knoweth them that are His.   And,
much as there is for self-humiliation in the path of such,
there are eyes which can see how these very changes, and
even failures, only shew more clearly that the path trodden
is one, not of sight or nature, but of faith.   All this will
probably appear very absurd to those who think that a walk
of faith begins or is carried on from some calculations of its
effects on others, or of the credit it may bring.   That
inward man, which hears God's call and walks with Him,
is led often it knows not whither.   Scarce understanding
itself, often misunderstanding its appointed way, no wonder
if others misunderstand it.   But the Lord knoweth the
path of His elect; and when He hath tried them, they shall
come forth as gold.

But the spirit of faith is not a pilgrim only: Abram
has an " altar " as well as a tent; in worship receiving
fresh revelations.   " The Lord appeared to Abram, and
said, Unto thy seed will I give this land: and there he
builded an altar unto the Lord, and called upon the name
of the Lord." [26]   In Ur of the Chaldees God had said,—
" A land which I will *shew* thee:" now He says,—" A land
which I will *give* thee."   And let it be observed, that here
" the Lord appeared."   Before this He had " called," and
" spoken " to Adam, and Cain, and Noah, and Abram; but
we never hear of His " appearing" until now; for it is to

---

[26] Chap. xii. 7, 8.

the spirit of faith, above all others, that the Lord shews Himself; for faith brings man into trial, and trial needs special revelations, and these are not withheld. Angels' visits are only few and far between, because we so seldom are in the place really to require them.

The special trials of this stage are, first, "the Canaanite," and then "a grievous famine," in the land.[27] Canaan, the son of Ham, as we have seen, figures that mere outward religiousness which grows even out of the regenerate man.[28] This is felt by the spirit of faith, when it attempts to enter into heavenly things. The famine shews how the ground on which true faith must stand is indeed a "land of promise," not of present rest. The Canaanite holds it, and famine strips it, till the spirit of faith knows scarcely where to turn itself. And this is the walk with God, with the sense of sin and want sorely pressing us. We may once have hoped through obedience to be wholly freed from such. We may yet think it strange that such fiery trial should be needed, or that the rest so surely promised should yet be kept from us by others, and they the Lord's enemies. Yet such is the path; for the question is,— Can we be satisfied with God? And many a weary step is trodden before we have made this attainment.

In Abram's case the trial led to failure for a while. The Canaanite and the famine drove him down to Egypt. The faith which gets on to the ground of promise at first has not strength to be steadfast there. Indeed, it requires more grace to stand on the ground to which faith brings us, than to get upon it. Peter had faith to step out on the waters, but he had not faith to walk far when there: he had faith

---

[27] Chap. xii. 6, 10.   [28] See above, on chap. ix. and x.

to follow Jesus into the high priest's palace, but he lacked faith while there to witness faithfully. Every act of faith brings us into greater trials, where greater faith will be needed. Thus it is that many who walk by faith have failures, which those know not who do not attempt so much. So it was with Abram. Two stages are marked in his failure: first, trial leads him down to Egypt, and then Egypt leads him to deny his wife. The first step led to the second; for one wrong step, like one lie, if it be not immediately retraced, requires another. The first error was walking by circumstances. Then a step is taken to avoid trial, without asking the Lord's counsel. Then the Lord, and His counsel and care, being for the time forgotten, His promise respecting the seed is forgotten also; and the result is, Sarah is soon in Pharaoh's house; while failing Abram is well entreated for her sake:— " He had sheep, and oxen, and he-asses, and men-servants, and maid-servants, and she-asses, and camels." [29]

Egypt, meaning *straitness*, or *that straitens*,[30] is the ground of sense; outwardly, those who are living the life of sense, that is, in seen things; as Asshur or Assyria is the type of reasoning; outwardly, of those whose life being one of reasoning, by such reasonings pervert and

---

[29] Chap. xii. 15, 16.

[30] Heb. מצרים. This type is very generally understood. Ambrose, on this chapter, says,—" Caro nostra Ægyptus nostra est: in hanc descendit mens nostra, quando cogitat quæ carnalia sunt. Tunc autem adscendit, quando invisibilia desiderat. Ideo et Abram dicitur descendisse in Ægyptum. . . . Patitur hoc mens nostra interdum . . . propter colligationem animæ et corporis incli- natur ad carnales voluptates, quibus infirma subjicitur, fortior non tenetur," &c.—*De Abr.* l. ii. c. 4, § 13. Augustine says,—"Ægyptus autem, quoniam interpretatur *affligens* vel *comprimens*, sæpe in imagine ponitur hujus sæculi, a quo spiritaliter recedendum est, ne simus jugum ducentes cum infidelibus," &c.—*Enar. in Psalm.* cxiii. (*E. V.* 114,) § 3. So too Gregory the Great, *Moral. in Job,* l. xxvi. c. 13, § 21.

darken truth.[31] These both are snares on the right and left for Israel; though both at length to be used and blessed, as the Lord distinctly promises.[32] For when " the Egyptian serves with the Assyrian " both are " blessed." But here Abram, the spirit of faith, tried by the difficulties on the ground of promise, goes down to seek rest in Egypt, that is, the ground of sense; rightly called *straitness*, for it is indeed a narrow land, not watered as Canaan with the rain of heaven,[33] but by its river, which one day threatens to destroy the sons of Israel. Yet not to Egyptians only is Egypt an enchanting land; it has charms which are felt even by God's elect, treasures gathered up through years of proud empire, and a wisdom which left no room for faith. Here comes the elect, thinking to find some refuge; and here Sarah is at once denied with an equivocation. Women, in this inward view, are certain affections. Sarah is the affection or principle of spiritual truth.[34] In Egypt Sarah is denied: those affections which the spirit of faith ought to defend and cherish most carefully, (for from them must spring the promised fruit,) are brought into danger of defilement from earthly things. For Pharaoh at once desires to have Sarah, and is only kept from violating her by the Lord's immediate judgments. So does sense now seek to enter into the things of faith, and, could it do so, it would at once violate them. But the Lord saves them : Sarah is not defiled ; and Abram, being reproved, turns again, and so departs from Egypt.

But this will be clearer to some as seen without. In this view Abram is the type of those in whom faith is the

---

[31] Asshur, אשור, means *steps.* Reasoning is a series of *steps.*

[32] Isa. xix. 23—25.

[33] Deut. xi. 10 ; Zech. xiv. 18.

[34] See below on chap. xvi. p. 210.

ruling life, that is, the men of true faith. Such are found
by God, when members of a fallen Church, serving idols,
and barren, and nigh to Great Babylon.   There the Lord's
voice is heard, and they who hear it start at once, leaving
kindred and country, to go they know not whither. These
are the works of Abraham, which must be done, if indeed
and in truth we would be Abraham's children: for the
Truth has said, " If ye were Abraham's seed, ye would do
the works of Abraham;"[35] and his first work was to go
forth with God, not knowing whither he went. So walk
the men of faith, whose faith is believing in God, not in
what others believe about God.   Nevertheless, for awhile
they seek to take some with them, who, never having personally heard the inward call of God, though ready to begin
the course, will never be willing or able to cross over
Jordan.   With such even believers can only go half-way.
But in due time the Terahs are found to be dead; when,
leaving them, not without tears, the elect gird up their
loins and go on over Jordan.   Then come the first trials
of the promised land, Canaanites and famine, which drive
us down to Egypt.   There, while seeking a little rest,
Sarah is denied, that is, the spiritual principles of the New
Covenant.   Believers hope, by denying their true relation
to this, to gain greater safety and liberty.   Who knows not
how common this is?   Sarah, the principle of grace, is
denied, that failing Abrams may have, as they say, greater
liberty, a wider field of usefulness. Take an example. Circumstances of trial have brought believers off their true
ground of promise into worldly things.   Such love Sarah.
Nothing is dearer to them than the covenant of grace. Yet

[35] John viii. 39.   Origen's comment on this verse contains many
very striking thoughts.   See *Com.
in Johan.* tom. xxi.

Sarah is again and again denied. And as of old, so now, the thing is done with an equivocation : — " Say thou art my sister." Words are used to Egyptians, which, though true in a sense, are not true in the sense in which Egyptians take them. So now, men called of God, who believe we are saved by grace, and that neither ordinances nor flesh can make a Christian, will so far practically give up Sarah as to lead the world to think that, as the world, the New Covenant can yet be theirs. This may be done in many ways. Meanwhile the men who know the truth and love it, and yet act thus, have an equivocation which they think clears them. They do not mean by certain words what others naturally gather from them. And though they see they are misunderstood, they still persist. According to these men, the equivocation, " Say thou art my sister," is all right. It is no harm running the risk of mixing or defiling the holy seed. According to these men, Sarah may be a mother of Egyptians; and no thanks to such if God's grace prevents it. The consequence is, even an Egyptian can rebuke Abram. So far from a greater sphere of usefulness, the equivocation deprives the elect of all power over the other's conscience. But Sarah cannot be a mother of Egyptians. The Lord appears to vindicate Himself and free His failing servant. " The Lord plagued Pharaoh and his house with great plagues, because of Sarai, Abram's wife. And Pharaoh called Abram, and said, What is this that thou hast done unto me ? Why didst thou not tell me that she was thy wife ? Why saidst thou, She is my sister ? So I might have taken her to me for wife. Now therefore behold thy wife : take her and go thy way. And Pharaoh commanded his men concerning him, and they sent him away, and his wife, and all that he had."[36]

[36] Chap. xii. 17—20.

Thus was Abram delivered: thus even now are individuals freed: thus shall the poor captive Church escape at last. The world will not have us among them, because our principles judge them: and God will not have us there. In this one thing God and the world agree. Both, at last, say to us, "Behold thy wife: take her and go thy way." [37]

Such was and is the path of faith. To not a few now living, these first stages are well known, and familiar as household words. I knew a man in Christ, above fourteen years ago,—no question is it, whether he was in the body, —who being called by grace, when he was serving other gods, obeyed in part, seeking to take the uncalled with him into the promised land. And I knew such a man, that, though he went forth to go into the land, yet he only got half way, and dwelt there; the old man, whom he took with him, hindering his advance, until, as days passed on, he found the old man dead; when, having buried him, he became what the men of that country called "unsettled," seeking to go further. So he went forth again to go into the land of Canaan, and into the land of Canaan now he came. Heavenly things and places, once heard of, were seen; but withal, there was trial, and ere long famine. Then Egypt was turned to, and Sarah was denied, till grace restored the wandering pilgrim. And that grace is yet as near as of old. None can look for it far off or near, and look in vain. Is a ruined world around us, with monstrous births, gigantic evils, the fruit of strange unions between the sons of God and men?—then an ark is pre-

---

[37] Augustine, (*Contr. Faust. Man.* l. xxii. c. 38,) traces at considerable length the dispensational fulfilment of this history. In this view Sarah is the Church, or New Covenant body, which, in its way to the land of rest, gets into the world's house for awhile, but is not suffered to be defiled there.

pared, to admit not only the Noahs, but even for unclean and creeping things, if they will enter it; which shall take them from the world of the curse, and of the thorn, to the world of the covenant and the rainbow, beyond the waters. Is the ruin deeper still, a ruined Church, which, brought through the waters, has misused its blessings and exposed its shame; which has bred fierce hunters, or built great Babels?—God yet remains; and His grace, if sought, is yet enough for every failure, in the world, in the Church, in our flesh, or in our ways. He cannot fail. He grudges nothing. He has freely given His Only Son. In Him are hid for us eternal countless gifts. In Him, the true Restorer of all things, we are accepted; and He waits that those things, which are hid in Him for us, may by Him be wrought in us through His Spirit. And if, to know His fulness, we need to know our emptiness,—if our ruin is the complement of His sufficient grace,—most gladly let us glory in our infirmities, that the power of Christ may rest upon us.

But it is time to pass on to another stage in this path.

II.—Abram's Separation from Lot

Chapter 13

We saw in creation a separating process, before a perfecting one: we shall see it again and again in man's development. Abram separated from Ur, and from Terah, and from Egypt, has further to be separated from Lot also, before he can be perfected; for it is only "after that Lot was separated from him, that the Lord said unto him, Lift up now thine eyes, for all the land which thou seest, to thee will I give it." The particulars of this separation are fully given; and painful as it is, happy are they in whom it is accomplished.

Abram and Lot, as we have seen, within, represent the spiritual and the upright natural mind respectively, which seem at first so closely united, that for awhile we are scarcely conscious of any distinction or difference between them; so unitedly do they move and act together, like the shell and kernel of a nut, which in its unripe state are scarcely to be distinguished, still less to be separated, but which, in proportion as they ripen, acquire and manifest a distinct separateness. So Lot, our upright natural mind, for a season, takes step for step with the spirit of faith in our advance to good things; but as we proceed we see they are not one, for nature at its best desires and longs for that which faith has given up. From the first God sees they are distinct; for Abram "walks with God," but Lot, (again and again is it noticed,) "walks with Abram."[1] Nevertheless, long after faith perceives the old man to be dead, it yet strives, if possible, to bring the natural mind into unity with itself; toiling that the outward should be as the inward, the natural as the spiritual, for it feels the bond of kindred to this outward man, saying as Abram to Lot, "We are brethren."[2] It seeks, therefore, first by grace to take it heavenward; yet the giving of it up may be the real way to greater perfection

---

[1] See chap. xii. 4, xiii. 1, 5, &c.

[2] Chap. xiii. 8. Ambrose, after giving the outward application of these words, "Homines nos fratres sumus, ... omnes enim homines unius naturæ partus sunt," adds, "Multo autem verius ad unam refertur animam, cujus rationabile, (*i.e.* Abram,) cognatos habet, ut supra diximus, sensus irrationabiles: quod autem rationabile, virtutum habet copulam. Unde fraternâ quâdam sibi copulantur necessitudine vitia virtutesque hominis; quia illa carnalis, istæ rationabilis animæ sunt," &c.—*De Abr.* l. ii. c. 6, § 28. Origen (*Hom.* vi. *in Gen.*) gives in substance the same interpretation, part of which is quoted below, on chap. xix.

in the inner man : for the outward man being thus allowed
to go his way, the spirit of faith may be freer and have
less distraction. So Paul, while praising a single life, and
the higher privilege of an entire victory over natural affections and the natural man, writes to the Corinthians, that
if they cannot at once restrain those affections, which though
lawful are merely natural, they may yield to them.[3] What
is this but letting Lot, the outward man, have his way, for
the greater peace and freedom of the inner man. So the
spirit of faith in us, finding this outer man to be, like Lot,
though "righteous," yet earthy, gives it its way ; and thus
gradually learns both to be and to feel itself more distinct
and really separated from it ; though for stages after this,
faith yet sighs over it, and makes more than one effort to
save it from the judgments which it brings upon itself.[4]

Such is the general import of this scene, as wrought
within ; but the particulars are, for such as can read them
in this light, no less instructive. For instance, the ground
where this takes place is not in Egypt, but when Abram
has come back again to the place whence trial had driven
him ; for, be it observed, Abram is brought back to that
very point from which he had swerved to go down to
Egypt, even "to the place where his tent was at the first."[5]
Places figure certain states ; indeed, the word "state"

[3] 1 Cor. vii. 7—9.
[4] The inward fulfilment of each
particular here is traced at considerable length by Ambrose :—"Ergo
mens viri sapientis ejusdem animæ
irrationabiles motus studet corrigere,
sibique conjungere.   Potest enim
fieri ut quæ interdum displicent,
emendentur gratiâ . . . quod si emen-
dare non potest, non exasperet in-
temperantiâ.   Deprehendit ardorem
libidinis quam conjugio coerceat ; ne

dum quæritur continentia, obrepat
impudicitia.   Ideoque bonorum ma-
gister, "Dico," inquit, "non nuptis
et viduis, bonum est illis si sic permaneant, sicut et ego ; quod si non
contineant, nubant : melius est enim
nubere, quàm uri." . . . . Rectè igitur
Abram cum bonâ veniâ voluit nepo-
tem dimittere," &c.—*De Abr.* l. ii.
c. 6, § 31.
[5] Chap. xiii. 3.

simply means a "standing place."[6]   So the soul comes
back to the ground it once held, with increased apprehension of its value, after the experiences of Egypt.   And
here, on the ground of promise, it is that Lot finds an
occasion to depart from Abram; here, while the spirit of
faith would stand on the promise, the outward man makes
some gift the occasion of going his own way.   Thus does
the advance of our spirit ever bring out and test the old
man.   None have so proved what the natural man is as
those who have come into the light of heavenly things.
For heavenly things and places, if they do not excite, at
least expose, the flesh.   The natural man, which can be
quiet in natural things, cannot rest when we approach to
what is spiritual; so true is it that what is good for the
pure is evil to the impure, so that heaven is hell to some,
and darkness and blindness are mercy to those who do not
love the light.   Thus Abram's advance brought out what
was in Lot; but Lot's gifts or riches helped to bring about
the separation, being not the cause, indeed, but the occasion
of strife.   Abram and Lot were both rich, although in
different ways.   "Lot had flocks, and herds, and tents."
Abram had these, but was "very rich in silver and in
gold" also.[7]   The outward man can and does possess much;
but the gold and the silver, that is, the higher forms of
truth, are not those which he obtains, or even wishes for.[8]

[6] Status, from *stare*, to stand.

[7] Chap. xiii. 2, 5.

[8] See above, respecting the metals,
on chap. iv. p. 93.   Ambrose, on the
different riches of Abram and Lot,
says, "Erat autem dives (Abram)
pecoribus, argento, et auro.   In pecoribus corporales sensus intelligo,
quia et ipsi irrationabiles sunt; in
argento sermonem, in auro mentem.
Dives erat Abram, quia regebat
sensus irrationabiles, ... habebat
sermonem fidei colore splendidum,
purgatum spiritalis gratiâ disciplinæ:
habebat mentem plenam prudentiæ.
. . . . . Lot quoque dives erat, sed
Scriptura eum pecoris tantum abun-
dantem adserit; . . . . non habebat
argentum, ... etenim argentum ig-
nitum lingua justi: non habebat
aurum, quod habebat ille qui vidit
Christi posteriora," &c.— *De Abr.*
l. ii. c. 5, § 20 and 24.

The "flocks" lead to the strife. What are these but those animal emotions which, as they belong to Abram or Lot, are under the power either of the spirit of faith or of the outward man ; and the thoughts which direct these, and keep them from wandering, are their "herdsmen," who strive together for mastery.[9] And faith, not yet possessing, but waiting for, power, yields for a season, receiving in the place of Lot greater revelations of the loving will of God. For " the Lord said unto Abram, after that Lot was separated from him, Lift up now thine eyes, and look from the place where thou art, northward, and southward, and eastward, and westward : for all the land thou seest, to thee will I give it. Arise, walk through the land in the length of it and in the breadth of it ; for I will give it unto thee."[10] And so when we reach this stage, and Lot departs,—when the spirit of faith is made to feel its difference even from the upright outward mind,—we find that there are lengths and breadths, toward the north and south, toward the sun-setting, and toward the sun-rising, in

---

[9] I am almost afraid to speak of this, though saints of old have done so ; but the following extract from the comment of Ambrose on this chapter, will prove that the interpretation in the text is at least no novelty:—" *Non capiebat eos terra,* hoc est, una anima motus diversos non recipiebat naturaliter sibi repugnantes. . . . . Qui igitur ' pastores' sint, et quorum animantium, et quæ rixa inter pastores Abræ et inter pastores Lot consideremus . . . . Pastores hos definire possumus. Pastores, inquit, jumentorum. Jumenta autem sensus corporis irrationabiles significari accipimus. Qui sunt ergo pastores sensuum, nisi . . . . mentis nostræ cogitationes, qui, si pastoralis disciplinæ gnari et tenaces sunt, non permittunt longius sensuum gregem vagari, et inutilibus aut noxiis inhærere pabulis ; . . . . mali autem inutilis disceptationis permittunt eos impetu suo ferri. . . . Hinc ergo cogitationum nostrarum discordia ; cum caro repugnat adversus spiritum, et spiritus adversus carnem, non mediocris pugna est."— *De Abr.* l. ii. c. 6, § 27.

[10] Chap. xiii. 14—17. " Sequitur locus, quo evidenter docemur quantum mens superfluis portionis irrationabilis exhaustis proficiat ; non enim otiose Scriptura posuit, ' Et dixit Deus ad Abram, postquam recessit Lot ab eo, Respice oculis,'" &c.— *Ambros. de Abr.* l. ii. c. 7, § 37.

directions toward coldness and warmth, toward light and darkness, of which as yet we have not so much as heard; and all this again and again secured by the unfailing " I will." So faith goes on. Having already reached Bethel, it now comes on as far as Hebron. Bethel is " the house of God;" Hebron is " fellowship." [11] Having known worship, faith now apprehends communion. In due time it gets still further, but at present it rests at Hebron.

Such is this scene within. Its fulfilment in the world without may to some be more intelligible. In this view Abram is the man of faith, who, having already left the ground of nature, after some declension is again escaping from the world. Such men of faith, coming up out of Egypt, have to come back to the very point whence trial had driven them.[12] They " come up," [13] for Egypt is low ground, and the ground of promise, on which they would again stand, needs some patient climbing if we would pos-

---

[11] Chap. xiii. 18. The import of the name Bethel (ביתאל) is well known. Hebron (חברון, from חבר, *to be joined together*,) means *fellowship*. Hebron is also called Mamre, see chap. xxxv. 27, meaning *vision*. See on chap. xviii. 1.

[12] Chap. xiii. 4.

[13] Chap. xiii. 1. In Scripture, going into Egypt is always "*going down*," and coming out of it is always "*coming up*." Within the borders of the land also, when the elect goes further into its interior, it always is "*going up*." See chap. xxxi. 1; Joshua vii. 2, 3, 4. So too from the interior to Jerusalem is "*going up*." —1 Kings xii. 27, 28; 2 Kings xx. 5, 8; Matt. xx. 18; Mark x. 33. The reason for this lies, first, in the form of the country, and yet more

in the spiritual reality of which Canaan and Egypt were formed to be types. Origen goes at great length into this: " Observandum est nobis scripturas sanctas legentibus, quomodo in singulis quibusdam locis ascendere commemoratur et descendere. Si enim diligentius consideremus, inveniemus quia nusquam fere in sanctum quis locum dicitur descendisse; neque ad vituperabilem conscendisse memoratur; quæ observationes ostendunt Scripturam divinam non (ut plurimis videtur) inerudito et agresti sermone compositam, sed secundum disciplinam divinæ eruditionis aptatam; neque tantum historicis narrationibus, quantum rebus et sensibus mysticis servientem invenies," &c.—*Hom.* xv. *in Gen.* xlv. *ad init.*

sess it. They come, step by step, " from Egypt to the South," then " from the South," then " to Bethel," and so on ;[14] for not by a single step can a believer get right when his failure in faith has taken him out of the way. But having reached Bethel, worship begins again :—" Abram called upon the name of the Lord." In Egypt Abram had no altar, for communion with the world mars communion with the Lord ; but as soon as the pilgrimage is renewed, the altar again has its appointed feast and offering.

This is a point on which some have much to learn. They hope for communion with the Lord while still in worldliness, as if the Lord's altar could stand yet in Egypt, and attendance at it be the common privilege of believers and unbelievers ; so little difference do they see between Pharaoh's kingdom and the promised land, between this world and heavenly places. But such things cannot be as yet. Israel may indeed " sigh and cry," even in the house of bondage ; but worship and communion belong to higher ground. So when Pharaoh said to Moses, " Go and sacrifice to God in this land," Moses said, " It is not meet to do so ; for we shall sacrifice the abomination of the Egyptians : lo, shall we sacrifice the abomination of the Egyptians before their eyes, and will they not stone us ?"[15] Here is the reason why the elect cannot worship with Egyptians. Because the worship of the Church and world are so opposed, that the one is " an abomination " to the other. Israel slays and sacrifices what Egyptians worship. Israel sees that the ox and lamb must shed their blood. Israel knows why this is, and does not grudge it. Egyptians cannot understand it. The ox is their god. Hence the Church, if bound by the world, ceases to worship, or else,

[14] Chap. xiii. 1—3. Augustine, (*Annot. in Job*, vol. iii. p. 669,) refers to the mystic sense of " the South."
[15] Exod. viii. 26, 27.

like the unfaithful remnant in Jeremiah's days, worships as Egyptians do.[16]   But here the man of faith is come to Bethel, " to the place of the altar," and there " he calls upon the Lord."

But this high ground has its own trials.   Those who, like Lot, until now have walked with men of faith, when they come to this point find reasons for going back ; and this, though trying to the elect, is good, for as outward men drop away from us, the Lord more and more reveals Himself.

What Lot is we have already seen.   Inwardly, he represents that upright outward mind, which goes some steps with faith towards heavenly things.   Outwardly, he represents those in whom this outward mind is the ruling life, whose souls live in religious outward things.   Of this class some ever start with men of faith.   The Abrams " walk with God ;" the Lots " go with Abram."[17]   These last are the men who take right steps because others take them, who make sacrifices because others do so, rather than because a present God calls for such a step or such a sacrifice.   Such, sooner or later, will shew what they are, righteous souls, but wholly unable to walk where the men of faith walk, leaving them as soon as they resolutely press on to the best things, and destined to beget a seed, like Moab and Ammon, to be a thorn in the side of the seed of the men of faith.

And gift ever helps on this division : to this day " flocks and herds" are an occasion for manifesting the tastes, and thus of separating the inward and spiritual from the righteous outward man ; while the cause lies in this, that one seeks heaven, the other is still in measure hankering

---

[16] Jer. xliv. 15—17.   [17] Chap. xii. 4, and xiii. 1, 5.

after this world. Yet the gifts are only the occasion: the cause was this, that one had an eye turned to the plain of Jordan, while the other looked onward into the hills of promise. For we read, that " Lot lifted up his eyes, and saw the plain of Jordan, that it was like the land of Egypt."[18] In this to him lay its attractiveness. Hence, as soon as the "herds" and "flocks" gave an excuse, he at once separates himself, and goes down Jordan-ward. These " flocks," in this view, are those lower natures, those animal souls, who are ruled and led, some by outward, some by spiritual men,—for each have their own flocks,—and the strifes of the herdsmen, who lead these respective flocks, are the occasion for the Lots to leave the Abrams. Oh! what strife has there been about flocks! It is not numbers, nor an abundance of gift, which can make brethren dwell together in unity. Rather will gifts be an occasion for strife; for schism is the growth, not of spiritual poverty, but of spiritual wealth. Hence, at Corinth, where "they lacked no gift," there was strife among the herdsmen, the more because the gifts abounded, while they were " yet carnal."[19]

And this happens not in Egypt, but as soon as the men of faith seek unflinchingly to go up to the higher ground the Lord has promised them. Lot does not depart from Abram in Egypt. While Christians are in the world, its habits and institutions, and the barriers which these raise between man and man, are enough to preclude strifes between brethren. Besides, the outward man has enough while in the world to satisfy his outward tastes. But when Egypt is left, brethren are thrown together in a way hitherto all unknown. Now comes the test to prove their

[18] Chap. xiii. 10.   [19] Compare 1 Cor. i. 7, with 1 Cor. iii. 1.

grace, for few things search us more than collision with our brethren.[20]　Then the lack of outward things stirs up the outward man.　Well do worldly-minded Christians know this, and wisely do they choose the lower ground, where their natural tastes find more that is in accordance with them ; where outward things keep them from coming to themselves, and what they are remains undiscovered by them ; where thus their weakness may be mistaken for strength, and circumstances take the place of grace.　For, indeed, till we are stript of things around, we little know what spirit dwells in us ; so much do the things of time and sense without keep us from discovering what really we are within.　Hence, some never know what restless selfish souls they have, until the things which have kept them from themselves are for ever taken from them.　Others, who by trials get glimpses of themselves, instead of going on to search out the evil hidden in them, that they may overcome it, seek rather to hide it from themselves and others, and, to do this, continually seek more and more of outward things.　But faith is content to learn itself, if it may learn God.　It would rather be weak with Him than strong without Him.

Thus, for awhile, is the path of faith more lonely.　The true believer is more than ever cast on God.　The Lots " choose" according to the sight of their eyes ; and so, by degrees, get from communion with the godly to communion with the godless.　Unlike souls, sooner or later, must separate.　If there be not one spirit, no bond or arrangement can keep men long together.　Each is gravitating to his own place by a law which none can gainsay,—dust to

---

[20] So Thomas à Kempis says, "It is no small matter to dwell in a religious community or congregation, to converse therein without complaint, and to persevere therein faithfully unto death."—Book i. chap. 17.

dust, and the spirit to God, who is a spirit. Let us not forget the steps of Lot. First " he saw ;" then " he chose;" then " he journeyed from the east," like some before him ; then " he pitched towards Sodom ;" then " he dwelt there." [21] In a word, he walked by sight, then by self-will, then away from the light, then towards the unclean world, at last to make his home in it. This is the path of Lots in every age. And such, though " righteous" and "saved," are only " saved so as by fire." [22]

The separation accomplished, the Lord appears, not to the righteous one who goes towards Sodom, but to him who still abides in the path of faith. To souls left by brethren, the Lord draws near, to tell us that if, by standing on the ground of promise, we lose brethren, we do not lose Him. " The Lord said unto Abram, after that Lot was separated from him, Lift up now thine eyes." As if to say, Lot hath of his own will lifted up his eyes : he hath seen what he can from his stand-point. Now lift up thine eyes, and see from my stand-point. " Look from the place where thou art, northward, southward, eastward, westward." Fear not to look whence the cold cometh, and towards the place of heat, towards the light, and towards darkness. As yet little knowest thou of all these. But " all that thou seest, to thee will I give it." And mark the advance in the revelation here. First, the promise respecting the land was, " A land which I will *shew* thee :" then, when come into the land, the promise ran, " To thy seed will I *give* it:" now it is, " To thee will I give it, and to thy seed *for*

---

[21] Chap. xiii. 10—12. In our version, the words מקדם, in verse 11, which, in chap. xi. 2, are translated "*from the east*," are here simply translated "*east*." The LXX. in both places render it ἀπὸ ἀνατολῶν. The Vulgate also gives, "*ab oriente*," which the Douay Version follows, translating, "*from the east*."

[22] 1 Cor. iii. 15.

ever." [23] Then follows the exhortation, " Arise, walk through the land,"—learn by experience what it is,—" in the length of it and in the breadth of it, for I will give it thee."

Such is another stage of faith's way; and trying as the separation here described is, both in the inward and outward world, it is one we must know, if we would know the best things. Surely he who thus loses brethren or children or lands receives a hundredfold.

III.—ABRAM'S CONFLICTS TO DELIVER LOT

Chapter 14

WE come now to the conflicts into which the spirit of faith is drawn, in its endeavours to deliver and save the outward man, which yet is dear to it. The letter tells of the part which Abram took in the wars which the seed of Shem carry on against the seed of Ham ; for of the kings whose contests are here described, four are of Shem's, and five of Ham's seed.[1] In spirit we see here the conflicts into which our faith is drawn, through the workings of certain powers springing from the Shem and Ham within us, in hopes of freeing and saving that outward man, of which Lot is the appointed figure.

First, to mark it within. To understand this we must remember what Shem and Ham represent respectively. They are certain minds growing out of the regenerate soul, which as years roll on produce many varying forms of life.[2] Now we read that before Lot left Abram, and before Abram entered into this conflict, the kings of the line

[23] Compare chap. xii. 1, 7, and xiii. 15.   [1] Chap. xiv. 1—16.
[2] See on chap. x.

of Shem,—Shinar, Elam, and the rest,—had been engaged in overcoming certain giants and others of the line of Ham, that is, certain reasoning powers springing from the contemplative mind in us, though much debased and fallen, as Shinar and Elam were, yet strive to overcome those open and gigantic evils, which, like the Rephaim, spring out of Ham, that is, the darkened and rebellious mind. These gigantic evils are put down by Shem's seed; but another branch of Ham's race, namely, the kings of Sodom and Gomorrha, rise in rebellion; when again Shem's seed strive to restrain them, and after sore conflict do overcome them. At this point the conflict of these two seeds touches Abram, that is, the spirit of faith; for Lot, the outward mind, having departed from Abram or faith, is taken captive by the kings of Shinar and Elam, those reasoning powers which grow out of the contemplative mind, and is only delivered by an effort of faith, and even so only delivered for a season, for Lot again returns to dwell in Sodom.[3]

---

[3] Ambrose thus traces the inward fulfilment here:—" Quinque reges quinque sensus corporis nostri sunt, visus, odoratus, gustus, tactus, auditus. Quatuor reges illecebræ corporales atque mundanæ sunt, quoniam et caro hominis et mundus e quatuor constat elementis. Meritò reges dicuntur, quia habet suum culpa dominatum, unde Apostolus ait, ' Non regnet peccatum in vestro mortali corpore.' Sensus igitur nostri facilè delectationibus sæcularibus cedunt, et quadam earum potestate capiuntur. Corporales enim delectationes et illecebras hujus sæculi non vincet, nisi mens quæ fuerit spiritalis, adhærens Deo, et se totam a terrenis separans. Deflexio, (*i. e.* Lot,) omnis his capitur; unde Johannes ait, 'Væ habitantibus in terrâ.'"—*De Abr.* l. ii. c. 7, § 41. As to the numbers here, viz. five and four, Augustine says, that *five* always refers to something connected with the senses.—*Enar. in Ps.* xlix. (*E. V.* 50,) § 9; *Tract. in Johan.* xv. § 21, and xxiv. § 5. He instances the five barley loaves, the five husbands of the woman of Samaria, the five brothers of the rich man, and other fives, as all connected with the five senses; while *four* is always connected with the world.— *Serm.* cclii. c. 10; *De diebus Pasch.* The mystical serpent of the Hindoos is generally represented with five heads, which are said to signify the five senses. See

But all this effort on Lot's behalf, fruitless as it seems,
—for Lot returns to Sodom, and settles down where he is
only saved so as by fire,—brings into view the mind of faith
in its relations to those powers which are figured by the
contending kings. Abram stands apart from all. From
such powers faith receives no help, waiting for its portion
from the Lord Himself, and when it pleases Him; and
while thus refusing to be enriched on earth, suddenly receiving gifts from One, whom as yet it knows but little of.
For now the Prince of Peace comes in and makes a feast;
and faith strengthened by such food is proof against all the
seductions of the king of Sodom, that is, the defiled and
self-loving fleshly mind.[4]

Such is the conflict figured here, true in thousands who
cannot yet unravel it. They know that before faith comes
their reasoning mind has striven to overcome certain
gigantic evils in them, that some of these have been overcome, and that after this the evil apparently subdued has
again burst out in them, and that again their reason has
sought to master it. All this conflict they have known,
and further that at a certain point, faith, which has now
come, takes part in these struggles, seeking to bring the
outward man to walk with the inner man. But the conflict, though felt, is not understood; and hence the picture
of it here, as set forth in type, is unintelligible.

Payne Knight's *Inquiry into the Symbolical Language of Mythology*, p. 56.

[4] "Denique ubi se vicisse putat, tentatur. . . . Quid enim est quod ait, 'Rex Sodomorum exivit obviam Abræ,' nisi quod post has luxuriæ victorias, vis quædam libidinis potest rationabili menti subrepere, ut infundat ei irrationabiles passiones. Sed perfectæ mentis est, nihil de terrenis illecebris adsumere. Ideo Abram dicit, 'Nihil sumam de omnibus tuis.' Quasi contagium declinat intemperantiæ, quasi labem refugit corporalium sensuum, delectationes mundi rejicit, quærens quæ supra mundum sunt, hoc est, extendere manus ad Dominum," &c.— *Ambros. de Abr.* l. ii. c. 8, § 45.

I therefore turn to trace it without, as it is fulfilled in the outward kingdom of the professing Church. The self-same minds are there at work, but, the field being wider and more outward, their works are more visible.

In this view Abram's effort to save Lot figures the conflict into which true men of faith come in their attempts to deliver those of their brethren, who, like Lot, though righteous, yet cling to outward things,—fightings in which true believers would have no part, were it not for the declension of their brothers, who go down Sodom-ward.

Here incidentally much light is thrown on the state of that world, from which by grace the man of faith is separated.

We read that the kings of Sodom and Shinar, with their respective allies, have long opposed each other bitterly; but all their wars have ended the same way: the king of Sodom is always conquered by Shinar or Babylon.[5] The story is told at length. The king of Shinar first masters the king of Sodom. For a certain period, "twelve years," the king of Sodom pays tribute. At the expiration of this time he rebels. Then comes the king of Babylon with his allies, and smites first the Emims and other giants, and then all the country of the Amalekite; after which he routs the king of Sodom, who loses all his goods, but is not slain.[6]

The import of this is most plain. Shem's sons here strive with Ham's sons; shewing what bitter strife and keen controversy there is between the religious and the irreligious world, subsequent to regeneration. For the kings of Shinar and Elam are of Shem's seed, sons of him

[5] See chap. x. 10, and xi. 2. In Joshua vii. 21, אדרת שנער, "the garment of Shinar," is translated the "goodly Babylonish garment." See also Dan. i. 2, and Zech. v. 11.

[6] Chap. xiv. 1–10.

who passed the flood, but who have fallen from contemplation into mere reasonings, and so have perverted the best things. Sodom is the seed of cursed Ham, closely allied to Mizraim or Egypt, and in a land "like the land of Egypt," [7] the figure of those who turn from the truth, and live in open ungodliness and shameless self-love. [8] Now these two seeds, Shinar and Sodom, have at times great conflict and controversy. But always with one result; Sodom is no match for Babylon. The religious reasoning world can always master the irreligious world. Yea, though at times Sodom throws off the yoke, Babylon can always reimpose it. In these conflicts, too, Babylon (as a sword of God, for even "the wicked are His sword," [9]) is used to rid the world of certain gigantic evils : for the king of Babylon "smote the Rephaims, (or giants,) in Ashteroth Karnaim, and the Emims, (who were also giants,) in Kiriathaim." [10] The religious world, in its conflicts with open irreligion, has plainly destroyed some gigantic and crying

[7] Chap. xiii. 10.

[8] In the Apocalypse, the three great forms of the world set before us are Sodom, and Egypt, and Babylon. In Rev. xi. 8, the great city is seen as "*Sodom and Egypt,* where also our Lord was crucified." This is the sensual and ignorant world. In chapters xvii. and xviii., the same great city is seen as *Babylon* : this is the religious world. In chap. xvi., which foretells the "seven last plagues," we find the plagues of each of these cities. The "noisome sore," (v. 2,) the "waters turned to blood," (v. 4,) the "kingdom full of darkness," (v. 10,)—these are the plagues of Egypt.—Exod. ix. 8—11, vii. 17 —20, x. 21—23. The "drying up of the Euphrates, and the invasion of the kings of the East," (v. 12,)—this is the judgment of Babylon.—Jer. li. 13, 36, and l. 38 ; Isa. xliv. 27, 28. The "voices, and thunderings, and lightnings, and great hail," (v. 18,) —this is the destruction of Sodom. —Gen. xix. 24, 25.

[9] Psalm xvii. 13.

[10] See Deut. ii. 10, 11. I may add here, for it is significant, the rest of the history of these Rephaim. They were first smitten by Babylon : a remnant, however, was left till Joshua's days.—Josh. xii. 4, xiii. 12, xvii. 15. The last of these giants seem to have been slain in the time of the kingdom under David.—1 Chron. xx. 4, 6, 8. They are never heard of when we get to Solomon's reign.

evils. But Babylonians are not therefore Israel: the religious world, though religious, is still the world. Babylonians may destroy Rephaim; at times it suits their purpose to do so, for there are evils in the world which stink even in the world's nostrils; nay, they may even "lay waste the field of the Amalekite and Mount Seir," for the flesh in some of its forms is hated by the religious world.[11] They can do all this, but they cannot walk with God. Nevertheless, they can overcome Sodom, though its king escapes them, to meet ere long his destruction from another hand.

Now "Lot dwelt in Sodom."[12] This fact links the strifes of the religious and irreligious world with the walk of the man of faith. Abram at Hebron, a stranger with his tent, though he may hear these "rumours of wars," has no personal interest in them. Very different is it with those, who, like Lot, live in the world. To such the strifes of the religious or irreligious world must be of deepest moment. Thus many questions, with which we should have nothing to do, touch us simply because we are not where we ought to be; and thus the faithful too, who are in their place, are involved in conflicts through the captivity of their unfaithful brethren.

But this is not the doctrine of the world, for Sodom and Babylon both agree that the believer should not stand aloof from such controversies. Often have I heard the

[11] Chap. xiv. 7. The Amalekite was one of Esau's sons.—Gen. xxxvi. 1, &c. As such, as the offspring of him, who, as the rejected firstborn, has ever been one chief type of the flesh, Amalek, even as his father Esau, stands a type of the same flesh, though in rather a different aspect, and at a further stage. See more on this under chap. xxxvi. Mount Seir was Esau's dwelling.—Chap. xxxii. 3; Deut. ii. 5. It is "the field of the Amalekite," not the Amalekite, which the king of Shinar now lays waste. This is significant.

[12] Chap. xiv. 12.

grounds on which both sides claim the pilgrim. Babylon, the religious world, cannot understand how persons claiming to be the called of God can hesitate to join them in opposing open evils. Gigantic evils, such as Emims and Rephaims,—the sphere of the flesh's dominion, " the field of the Amalekite,"— and above all, "Sodom," the wicked world, with its many crimes, seem to Babylonians reason enough for the believer to join them in subduing such adversaries. On the other hand, there are some in Sodom, righteous souls living in too great contact with the irreligious world, who, having by experience known Babylonian bondage, are content, like Lot, to make common cause even with the godless and unclean, if only they can break the yoke of the king of Babylon. And such would like to see true believers with them; but from both is Abram separate, till his brother Lot is led away captive towards Babylon. Then does he come down from the quiet hills of promise to the strifes in which his brother is, giving up his ease to rescue a brother out of Babylonian captivity.

Thus is Abram brought into collision with Babylon, that is, the religious world. We never hear of his fighting with Sodom. His place is separation from and intercession for, not war against, it. But as respects the religious world, the believer at times, to free brethren, is forced to contend with it. And strange as it appears, that believers will not join in the strifes of Sodom or Babylon, it seems yet stranger that, if either are assailed, the religious world should be that which is fought against. But so it has been from Christ's days to these: Pharisees are judged, while open sinners are pitied. The motives of the men of faith are not seen or understood, and "though he discerneth all things, yet is he discerned of no man." [13]

[13] 1 Cor. ii. 13.

The result is, Lot is freed by Abram. The pilgrim brother [14] is the means through whom deliverance comes. The man who has been alone with God is the man who can break the chains of Babylon for his unfaithful brethren. And many a gift yet comes to failing souls through brethren with whom they hold no communion, whom they judge as extreme in their views, and to whom they practically prefer the company of such as know not God. Sooner or later, however, God vindicates His own. The pilgrim brother is the helper in time of need.

This leads to trial of another sort. Abram, victor over the kings of Shinar and Elam, is tempted by the other king; for " the king of Sodom came out to meet him after his return from the slaughter of Chedorlaomer ; " but Abram, strengthened by Melchisedek's bread and wine, and blessed by him, refuses the king of Sodom's proffered fellowship.[15]

Such a trial meets believers yet; the rulers of the darkness of this world [16], successfully opposed in one form, meet us in another. The hour of victory is the chosen time. Opposition to one form of evil brings us sometimes very near to other evil ; and he who has been in collision with the religious world will surely be met by another spirit from the irreligious world. If the king of Shinar be slain or put to flight, the king of Sodom is at hand, though humbled, seeking the man of faith. And without God's grace, it would be natural enough for the man who had opposed Babylon to make a league with Sodom. Many have been thus ensnared ; but men of faith, in the hour of

---

[14] Here, only (chap. xiv. 13), Abram is called "the Hebrew," העברי, rendered by the LXX., ὁ περάτης, or *the passenger*.

[15] Chap. xiv. 17–24.

[16] Eph. vi. 12 ; 1 Cor. ii. 8.

temptation, are met by other help. Thank God, there is a
" Priest of the Most High," who is also " King of Righteousness and Peace," who in times of danger draws nigh to
the elect, and, by His gifts of " bread and wine," strengthens
them. I need not tell what " bread and wine," or what
" King and Priest," is represented here,[17] who has said, " Lo,
I am ever with you," but who peculiarly reveals Himself
when we seem to be tempted above that which we are able,
and by foretastes of the good things of Salem leads us to
refuse " from a thread to a shoe-latchet" from Sodom's
wicked rulers. For the fainting soul, even of a saint, if
empty, might thirst after the dross which the king of Sodom
offers us. Well does the tempter know his time, and that
when the man is " an hungered," then is his opportunity.[18]
Israel learnt this in the desert. Water failed them ; then
thoughts came in of " the vines and pomegranates of
Egypt." Then the Lord gave water ; and he that drank
thereof thirsted no more for Egypt, but was satisfied. Then
" they sent to Edom, saying, Let us pass, we pray thee,
through thy land ; we will not pass through thy fields or
through thy vineyards, neither will we drink of the water
of thy wells ; we will go by the king's highway ; we will
not turn to the right hand nor to the left until we have
passed thy borders." [19] So it is ever. The soul must be
filled. If it have not the Lord's comforts, the vines of
Egypt will be thought of. If it be full, and the living
waters are tasted, the pilgrim can say, " I want not thy
goods, only let me go onward along the king's highway."

[17] See Heb. vii. 1–28. Having
the comment of an Apostle here, we
need no others ; but the following
passages in the Fathers may interest
some : — Clem. Alex. *Strom.* l. iv.
p. 637 ; Cyprian, *Ep.* 63 ; Isid. Pelus.
l. i. *Ep.* 431 ; Augustine, *De Civit.*
l. xvi. c. 22.

[18] Matt. iv. 2, 3.

[19] See Numbers xx. 5, 17, and xxi.
5, 16–22.

And so when men of faith after conflict are faint, the
rulers of the darkness of this world meet them, and might
entrap them, did not the bread and wine of the King of
Salem make them proof against all other blandishments.
And " Melchisedek blessed Abram and said, Blessed be
Abram of the Most High God, Possessor of heaven and
earth ; and blessed be the Most High God, who hath delivered thine enemies into thine hand." He blesses the
believer, and blesses the Most High ; and, foreseeing
faith's long trial, reveals God's character under that name,
—" Possessor of heaven and earth,"—which Abram at that
moment most needed; as if to say, If He is thy God, if
thus He meets thee by His Priest, in an hour of weakness
feasting thee with bread and wine, for which others have
laboured, and which cost thee nothing, then thou needest
not the gifts of Sodom's fallen king. And Abram feeling
this, not only refuses to be enriched by Sodom, but
becomes a giver : " He gave Melchisedek tithes of all."
For gifts call forth gifts ; and of that which God hath
given it, faith gives a portion with gladness to the Lord's
Anointed.

And withal, Abram, while prescribing this high path for
himself, can see how vain it is to expect it from those who
do not know God. If there is a mark of pretended grace,
it is the zeal to make our walk the rule, to raise or cut
down all to our standard. Where there is real grace, its
possessor knows how He who came down here for men
meets them where they really are, and not where they are
not ; and that as grace is a gift, if others lack it, no end is
gained by laying on them burdens which without grace
they cannot bear. So Abram says of those who went with
him,—Aner, Eschol, and Mamre,—" Let them take their
portion : I have lifted up my hand to the Lord that I will

take nothing." [20]　But these may not know Him.　He therefore requires none others to walk as he does.　If example avails, there is his example ; but life is a reality, not to be copied without power.　The true believer, therefore, would rather that men should be true according to their measure and where they are, than false by pretending to be what they have not attained to.　If he gloried in their flesh, it might be otherwise ; but such an one glories, not in disciples, but in the cross of Christ.

The King of Salem yet lives, " a Priest for ever after the order of Melchisedek ; " and the believer who has striven with the rulers of the darkness of this world, will yet meet Him with His bread and wine in the pilgrimage. " As we have heard, so have we seen, in the city of the Lord of Hosts, in the city of our God." [21]

IV.—Abram's Trials through the Word of God and Prayer

Chapter 15

But conflict, though it ends in triumph, produces weariness.　After great efforts and great success the spirit of faith is often suddenly, and, as it thinks, unaccountably, depressed.　A reaction is felt, when dryness succeeds to that life and energy which has carried us on hitherto.　At such an hour our very blessings try us.　That our trials are blessings has been already learnt.　Now we learn that blessings are trials too.　And though in measure the elect must have proved this before,—for God's call, and Sarah, and Lot, and the flocks and herds, all of which were bless-

---

[20] Chap. xiv. 22, 23.　　　　　[21] Psalm xlviii. 8.

ings, had all been trials also,—the lesson now is learnt in reference to a class of blessings from which till now we expected nothing but peace. God's own promise and worship are found to try Abram more deeply perhaps than anything which had as yet befallen him.

First, the promise tries him. We read, " After these things the word of the Lord came unto Abram, in a vision, saying, Fear not, Abram, I am thy shield, and thy exceeding great reward. And Abram said, Lord God, what wilt thou give me, seeing I go childless ?" [1]

Now this answer expresses deep soul-trial, the time of which is specially noted — " after these things." This is not faith's first experience. When the word first calls us, though it costs us outward grief, the joy it gives, not to say the excitement it occasions, keeps us from dwelling on our want of fruit. The Lord has promised a land and a seed. On this we can leave our country and kindred, not knowing what the promise will cost us, or how much is to be endured before we obtain the fulfilment of it. We eat the words, and in our mouths they are sweet as honey : we know not that they may be bitter in the belly.[2] Even Terah, the old man, is stirred by the call, little knowing what its results may be. So we start with joy ; but years on years pass away : mercies by the way are given, but we have as yet neither the promised fruit nor the inheritance. At last an hour comes when we have counted all things but dross and dung for Christ. The world has come, only to be rejected. Faith, bold to rely on God alone, will not take from it " even a shoe-latchet." At such a moment the Lord speaks again. The old promise is heard. Still we are barren. And the soul, feeling that it is apparently

[1] Chap. xv. 1, 2.　　　　　　　　[2] Rev. x. 9.

as far from the fulfilment as when it first started,—further, in one sense, for there was then some energy in the flesh, which the trials of the way and weary years have now well-nigh quenched,—answers with something between a sigh and a prayer, saying, " Ah, Lord God, what wilt thou give me? " I have no seed, no fruit : as yet my only heir is this steward born in my house, this " Eliezer of Damascus." Shall he, this spirit of bondage, be the seed? Can this be the promised blessing? Surely there must be something better? So argues faith, even in its depression ; and the Lord at once answers, that this steward, this spirit of bondage, is not the promised seed: " This shall not be thine heir; but he that shall come forth out of thine own bowels, he shall be thine heir." [3] Precious words, but no less a trial to the spirit of faith, which against hope believes in hope.

A " seed " and a " land " are still the hope which tries the believer. Fruit does not indeed at first much press or exercise us. We look forward to it, because God has named it ; but other things surround and occupy us, and its absence for a while does not disquiet us. At such a stage we have enough to do with the old man who goes with us, or with Egyptians, or famine, or strifes with brethren, to think much of the promised fruit. It is far otherwise when the old man has been buried, and we are left alone ; when all having been forsaken, and the tempting world denied, we yet are fruitless and strangers without our inheritance. Earnestly then the soul begins to long for that which God has promised it. Fain would it see " the seed," Christ formed within us. Hitherto Christ *for us* has been enough, the word of God pledged on our behalf. Now

---

[3] Chap. xv. 4.

Christ *in us* is longed for daily, the image of God, the spirit of sonship, to live and grow in us. And God replies that such too is His will; that if we go without this, we lack what He has promised us. " He brought him forth abroad, and said, Look towards heaven, and tell the stars, if thou be able to number them. And he said, So shall thy seed be." " He brought him forth " out of his narrow tabernacle; faith is led beyond those limits which flesh and blood throw around it, into that expanse where the breath of heaven may touch it, and the countless lights of heaven shine on it, and in this freer air God Himself speaks again, saying to faith, " So shall thy seed be."[4] And although the words, " Lord, what wilt thou give me ? " and, " Lord, whereby shall I know that I shall inherit it ?" shew fear as well as faith, yet " Abram believed, and it was counted unto him for righteousness." [5]

So ends the trial through the word, while out of the trial faith reaps fresh blessing, even righteousness. Faith takes God to be God, and thus honours Him far more than by many works. And therefore God honours faith, " counting it for righteousness," more precious to Him than gold, yea, than much fine gold. Surely in a world where nearly all doubt God, the sight of a poor barren creature in utter helplessness resting on God's promise must be a spectacle even to heavenly angels. Even the eyes of the Lord run to and fro through the whole earth, seeking it, and where He finds it, He makes Himself strong in behalf of it.[6]

---

[4] " Quid est autem quod ait, 'Eduxit eum foras'? Tanquam foras educitur, ut exeat fores corporis et angustias carnis operientis, ac Spiritus sancti infusionem, et velut quamdam descensionem videat," &c.—*Ambros. de Abr.* l. ii. c. 8, § 48.

[5] Chap. xv. 6. Rom. iv. 3, 6.

[6] 2 Chron. xvi. 9.

Faith, however, still must be tried; and the very worship to which the reception of the word now leads, though the door to fresh blessings, opens through fresh disquietudes.

The steps are these: the soul believes that it shall be even as the Lord has promised; but though it believes, it does not understand how or through what experience the blessing is to come to it. In answer, therefore, to the promise, it says, " Whereby shall I know that I shall inherit it?" The Lord replies by a command to sacrifice, and in this worship and sacrifice His way is manifested.[7] Beside the altar light breaks in. Faith may be strong and grow while yet in outward things; but light comes, while we stand before the Lord, by the holy altar of burntoffering. At every stage we prove this truth. Noah is taught much beside his offering.[8] So, too, is David in later days.[9] Abram no less by the altar learns the reasons for the delay in the possession of the inheritance. There is opened the experience of his seed: there again the covenant is renewed and added to. The seed, it is declared, shall be a stranger here, but in God's time it shall come with great substance to its inheritance.

To look for a moment at this worship; for the spirit of faith yet worships in no other way. " The Lord said, Take me a heifer, and a she-goat, and a ram, and a turtle-dove, and a young pigeon. And he took unto him all these, and divided them, but the birds divided he not." This was in substance Abel's offering, the figure of the sacrifice of Christ, both for us, and in us; though at this stage we have far more detail and greater insight into

---

[7] Chap. xv. 9–18.　　　　　[8] Chap. viii. 20–22.
[9] Psalm lxxiii. 16, 17.

particulars. Here all the forms, "bullock, goat, and turtle-dove," that is, service, sin-bearing, and innocence, if we take the outward view, — inwardly, all those powers which must die in us, when in and through Christ we present our bodies a living sacrifice,—are each discerned; the different parts too are marked; the head, and legs, and inwards, all being discriminated; that is, the thoughts, the walk, and the affections, no longer overlooked in the general thought of offering, now claim our notice as we give them to God, a willing sacrifice to His holiness.[10] Faith will not offer less than these, and in thus offering it learns the Lord's purpose.

And to this day sacrifice is the key to the secrets of the Lord's heart. Many a word tries us until the sacrifice for us and in us is apprehended. Then the word is understood; then the oath is heard; then the reasons, why our God acts as He does, open upon us. To how many low and doubting thoughts is the apprehension of Christ's sacrifice for us an answer. To how many struggles is Christ's sacrifice in us the one reply. We wonder we must wait for our inheritance. We wonder we must prove what flesh is; that it is barren, dead, worthless. The slain Lamb is seen; that life and death witness that to meet God the creature must first suffer; that we must die to have God's life exhibited. If we have presented our bodies a living sacrifice, this truth will be yet more manifest. For the

---

[10] On this subject I have spoken at length in "*The Law of the Offerings,*" pp. 77–83. Lira, in his comment on the text, says, " Prædicta animalia repræsentabant humanitatem Christi, in quantum fuit instrumentum nostræ redemptionis ; quia ovis repræsentat ejus innocentiam, capra similitudinem carnis peccati, bos fortitudinem Christi ad sustinendum laborem, maximè in passione. Turtur etiam castitatem Christi significat : columba vero, quæ sine felle est, ejus mititatem."—*In loco.*

veil, (and " the veil is His flesh,"—that flesh in which He yet walks, for He hath said, " I will walk in them," [11]) when rent by the cross, opens to view the great mystery. Now we can see why we must suffer here : faith is almost turned to sight beside the sacrifice. And though even after such communion an hour may come when the soul again is faint because of the way, the remembrance and savour of such hours do not soon leave us : we go on in the strength of it many days.

Sweet, however, as are the ultimate results of such experience, the apprehension of the cross, in our intercourse with God, at the time costs us not a little. One distraction after another presses the spirit of faith, while it is occupied with the appointed sacrifice.

First, " the fowls come down on the carcasses." [12]   No sooner are the bodies of the beasts offered, and the parts laid open before the eye of God and the worshipper, than the fowls come down, to mar the offering if they can. So when the believer has set before him the sacrifice, and in the contemplation of it would fain learn to see and feel with God, the fowls, " evil spirits in heavenly places," [13] powers within or without subject to the wicked one, messengers of " the prince of the power of the air," [14] come to distract our

---

[11] Heb. x. 20 ; 2 Cor. vi. 16.

[12] Chap. xv. 11.

[13] Eph. vi. 12.

[14] Eph. ii. 12. The "birds" stole away "the good seed." Our Lord explains this by, "Then cometh the devil, and catcheth away that which was sown in their hearts." Matt. xiii. 4, 19. Compare also Deut. xxviii. 26 ; Jer. v. 27 ; Rev. xviii. 2. Gregory the Great thus beautifully comments here :—" Sæpe enim etiam corda justorum subortæ cogitationes polluunt, terrenarumque rerum de-

lectationibus tangunt ; sed dum citius manu sanctæ discretionis abiguntur, festinè agitur, ne cordis faciem caligo operiat, quæ hanc jam ex illicitâ delectatione tangebat.   Nam sæpe in ipso orationis sacrificio importunè se cogitationes ingerunt, quæ hoc rapere, vel maculare valeant, quod in nobis Deo flentes immolamus. Unde Abram cùm ad occasum solis sacrificium offerret, insistentes aves pertulit, quas studiosè, ne oblatum sacrificium raperent, abegit.   Sic nos cùm in arâ cordis holocaustum

communion, as far as may be. He that has stood beside his offering knows what distractions these winged messengers cause, while we rise up like Abram to "drive them away."

Then comes "darkness:"—"when the sun went down, a deep sleep fell on Abram; and, lo, a horror of great darkness fell upon him." [15] While on earth, our appointed life of faith is one of alternate light and darkness. We would watch while we are beside the altar, though such darkness cover the earth that our very spirit feels it. But it is hard to watch at such times, when nature sleeps. A horror of great darkness, however, is not overcome by slumbering. We must go through the trial with our God: in it we shall learn what purposes He has in trying us.

Here the hour of trial proves an hour of light; the darkness which shuts out the world does but reveal heavenly things. Abram learns through the darkness more of God's will. Before this, he had the promise of a seed. Now he learns some details of the appointed cross, and that only "through much tribulation" the kingdom will be won. The "smoking furnace" is seen, ready to purge away the dross; but beside it appears the "burning lamp." [16]

Thus in light ends this trial. The spirit of faith, awaking to its own barrenness, not only with the heart

---

Deo offerimus, ab immundis hoc volucribus custodiamus, ne maligni spiritus, et perversæ cogitationes rapiant, quod mens nostra offerre Domino utiliter sperat," *Moral. in Job*, l. xvi. c. 42, § 53.

[15] Chap. xv. 12.

[16] Isa. lxii. 1. "Solis occasu excessus cecidit super eum, ... desinit enim videre sæcularia, qui incipit audire divina. Unde Abræ tenebras mirari non debes. .... Con-

tinuo autem dictum habes, 'quod peregrinum erit semen tuum, et servitio opprimentur.' .... Diversi enim domini in servitute nos volunt tenere, ... passiones, · motusque corporis, (these are the Egyptians,) velut hostes inquietant, ... donec Deus diabolum judicet, passiones restinguat, ac subjiciat menti sedulæ," &c. *Ambros. de Abr.* l. ii. c. 9, §§ 61, 62.

believes unto righteousness, but receives in worship enlarged promises. It may yet err in its efforts to bear fruit, but henceforth there is no more anxious disquietude.

V.—Abram's Efforts to be Fruitful by Hagar

Chapter 16

Now comes a well-known scene. True faith, though it justifies, does not therefore prevent us (while the Lord yet waits till self-will be dead) from trying our own strength. Here these efforts and their results are shewn, proving that, even of the fruits of faith, " that is not first which is spiritual, but that which is natural." Here the means which the spirit of faith adopts to be fruitful,—how it comes to use such means,—and the result,—all are represented perfectly.

The means are these. Abram takes Hagar, hoping by her to obtain the promised fruit.[1] Women are always the affections of the will. Hagar is the natural self-will, Sarai, the submissive spiritual will: the former the type of that in us which affects law ; the latter, of that purer and truer will which affects spiritual truth ; so that, generally speaking, we may say Hagar is law, and Sarai grace ;[2] our

---

[1] Chap. xvi. 3.

[2] Gal. iv. 22-25. Origen speaks at great length on this : " Profectus etenim sanctorum Scriptura figuraliter per conjugia designat." Then after speaking of the elect's embracing scriptural truths, and the consequent fruits, he says, " Si etiam ex his eruditionibus, quæ extrinsecus videntur esse in sæculo aliquas contingimus, (verbi causâ) ut est eruditio literarum vel artis grammaticæ, vel etiam dialectica disciplina; et hæc omnia extrinsecus quæsita ad nostra instituta producimus, tunc videbimur vel alienigenas in matrimonium sumpsisse, vel etiam concubinas." . . . . He instances Solomon as a typical example of this, and adds, " Et si de hujuscemodi conjugiis, disputando, contradicentesve redarguendo, convertere aliquos poterimus ad fidem Christi, . . . tunc ex dialecticâ vel rhetoricâ videbimur,

principles ever being what our affections are. Here
we see both these wills working in connection with the
spirit of faith; and faith, having so long looked in vain to
Sarai, now turns to Hagar, hoping by the energy of the
flesh or by works to aid, if not to accomplish, God's promise.
God's purpose is, out of the death of self, by His own
power to bring forth a heavenly life; for He knows, if we
know not, that the flesh profiteth nothing, and He would
in our ruin shew His resources. But without exception,
though we are elect,—though through faith righteous,—
though we have stood beside the sacrifice,—though we talk
about the cross, and profess to believe it,—yet have we not
learnt to distrust sense, and put away all fleshly hopes.
The truth is on our lips, that by strength no man prevails,
—that when we are weak, then are we strong,—that except
a corn of wheat fall into the ground and die, it abideth
alone; but that, if it die, it bringeth forth much fruit. As
to our acceptance we may have learnt this: but as to our
service, as to our fruitfulness, as to our obtaining Christ's
image, how few live in it! We cannot think that the death
of our own strength, and of our own will, even when that
will is to serve and please God,—that weakness, disappointment, failure, in self,—that this can indeed be the
right way,—this seems impossible. So we seek to live
rather than to die, and strive to call forth our own energies
rather than to be patient at their dissolution. It is not till
we have got the fruits of such a course,—till we have
personally experienced the consequences of having seed by
Hagar,—till we have tried all we can do, and having tried
it have heard God say, that this fruit which we get by
Hagar, that is by the energy of the flesh, is " a wild-ass

quasi ex alienigenâ quâdam vel
concubinâ, filios genuisse." The
whole passage is well worth turning
to. *Hom.* xi. *in Gen.*

man,"[3] and cannot be the heir, " for in Isaac shall the seed be called," that is, in the son or fruit of the long-barren freewoman ; — it is not till we have expressed our regrets for Hagar's son, and have sighed, " Oh, that Ishmael might live before thee," and have seen all his behaviour to the true seed, and his mockery of him when at last he is given to us ; — it is not till we have gone through all this, and much more, and are worn out, and "as good as dead," that we can give up the flesh with all its hopes, and giving them up find that the death of self, which we have so struggled against, is but the appointed way to gain the promise. So, till we are content to be dead, we take Hagar, and with various experiences of her, and with her, we keep her, till Isaac, the spirit of sonship, being weaned, the bond-maid is no longer wanted, and we learn to say, though not without a struggle even to the end, " Cast out the bond-woman and her son."

But this is anticipating. We are now to see what woman, spiritually, what principles, the spirit of faith embraces here, as a means to gain the seed.

She was " a bond-maid,"—" Sarai's maid." [4] And self-will is yet a "bond-woman," and "gendereth to bondage."[5] All the elect learn this. With each a time comes, when fruit is sought " as it were by the deeds of the law," and in our own strength. We long to " bear the image of the heavenly," and we look for it through our own energy. Some fruit is borne : Hagar is not barren : but the spirit of sonship is not obtained in this way. The proof is, a

---

[3] Chap. xvi.· 12. In our autho-rised version, Ishmael is called here "_A wild man._" Heb. פרא אדם, that is, literally, " _A wild-ass man._" So in Ezek. xxxvi. 38, the elect are in the Hebrew called " _Sheep-men_ ;" צאן אדם, rendered in the common version, " _Flocks of men._"

[4] Chap. xvi. 1.

[5] Gal. iv. 22–25.

bond-maid yet is in the house, and her fruit, the spirit of bondage, is not cast out.

Further, this maid was " an Egyptian." Egypt is the ground of sense, that is the outer world. To this Hagar belongs. In her we lay hold of that which in its very nature is of this world. For " the law is not made for the righteous, but for sinners ; " [6] in seeking help from it, faith is using a worldly principle.

But how comes faith to use such means ? Several circumstances combine to lead to this.

First, " Sarai was barren ; she bare no children."[7] Sarai is the principle of grace, the affection of spiritual truth. From this the spirit of faith looks for seed ; but years pass, and there is still barrenness. Faith does not therefore cast out Sarai ; for she is ever loved and regarded as the true wife ; but because she is barren, we look elsewhere, not yet knowing that these inner affections must be fruitless, till the self which yet cleaves to the spirit of faith be " as good as dead." When at last in self-despair we are thus dead, then, and not till then, Sarai will bear fruit. Indeed, if at first we could have had our way, Sarai, even as Hagar, would have been made fruitful through our energy. The principle of grace would have been as another law, requiring strength in us to make it productive ; whereas the truth is, that while we are thus strong the Lord cannot let us have fruit by Sarai. From Hagar, or law, God may grant some fruit, such as it is, through the elect's own energy. But from Sarai no seed shall be so obtained : she is, and must be fruitless, till our own strength is put away. But this is learnt only by long experience. Here faith has not learnt it : therefore, seeing Sarai barren, it is tempted to have recourse to other means.

[6] 1 Tim. i. 9.   [7] Chap. xvi. 1.

Then Hagar is at hand: — "Sarai had a handmaid." Abram had not to seek her: there she was, already serving him. How she came to be there is hinted in the fact, incidentally noticed, that Hagar was "an Egyptian;" telling that Abram had been in Egypt, and possibly had received this woman as a reward of his unfaithfulness there respecting Sarai. Be this as it may, Hagar now is there, already occupying a position in attendance on the true wife; and being there, and useful in her place, through the impatience of the elect ere long she usurps another's place. Just so the inner affection of spiritual truth has the principle of law waiting upon it as a servant. And, as a handmaid, law is in its place in Abram's house; a place whence it should not be expelled, at least until the spirit of sonship has obtained a certain growth. The evil is, that this service of law, though useful in itself, and needed for a season, through the impatience of the elect, becomes the occasion for that further trial of the flesh, which like all such trials is doomed to end in disappointment.

But Sarai's barrenness and Hagar's being at hand are not Abram's only inducements to turn to the bond-maid. The free-woman herself stirs up Abram to this: — "Sarai said unto Abram, Behold the Lord hath restrained me from bearing. I pray thee, go in unto my maid. It may be that I may obtain seed by her."[8] There is a stage when grace itself, and the promise of fruitfulness which is connected with it, by acting on our impatience, may so excite, as to lead the spirit of faith to try carnal means, even though for ends which God has promised. Indeed impatience, a zeal for God, without a corresponding faith in the zeal of the Lord of hosts, is ever leading to this. Even to faith it is hard to wait on God, and let Him do

[8] Chap. xvi. 2.

His own work in His own way. With right principles exciting us, we may be marring His work, by our haste in attempting to do it for Him. So even Sarai may, and does, mislead us, if, instead of patiently awaiting the Lord's time, that inward affection stirs us up, in connection with other means, to try our own strength. Thus did Abram hearken to Sarai; and thus excited even by the truth, and with right ends, does the elect yet try his own resources. The present age gives countless proofs of this. Christ, the true seed, is by many longed for ardently. Both in Church and world we wait for His appearing. But He tarries. Then Sarai speaks to those, who, though men of faith, are so far from " being as dead," that they are still full of self-will. The result is one scheme after another, all aiming to obtain the promised seed, by doing rather than by dying. Vain hope ! Ishmaels enough may be thus gotten. Isaacs are not so born.

But to trace the results, as figured here.

The first is, Abram gets a son: Hagar is fruitful;[9] but her son is not the promised heir. For to Abram and his seed were promises made; " He saith not, And to seeds, as of many; but as of one, And to Thy seed; which is Christ."[10] For Abram or faith has many seeds; but that form of life, which, though of faith, is produced by self-will, (and the first fruit of faith is ever such,) is not elect, and cannot be the true heir. Hagar's son is but " a wild-ass man." The spirit of faith has indeed thus produced another form of life, and thus something at first appears to have been gained. The end proves, that, as far as the true heir is concerned, all this effort has availed nothing. Faith by self-will has only got " a spirit of bondage again

---

[9] Chap. xvi. 4. [10] Gal. iii. 16.

to fear." The "spirit of adoption" is not thus begotten.[11]

The next result is as unsatisfactory. "When Hagar saw that she had conceived, her mistress was despised." If carnal strength succeeds in bearing any fruit, the immediate result is contempt of better things. For the flesh can achieve nothing without being exalted. Sarai, therefore, instead of being "built up," as she hoped, by Hagar, reaps through her fresh humiliation.

Nor is this all. For this contempt, Sarai deals hardly with the bondmaid, who therefore flees out of the elect house.[12] If through faith's impatience the principle of law is exalted out of its place, and thus dishonour is done to grace, that is the free-woman, a re-action follows, for grace or Sarai is best loved, and though barren never loses her rightful empire over the believing heart. The principle of law is harshly judged, and so, being abused, for awhile departs and is lost sight of. Who that knows this path but has seen how the affection of law, when contempt has through it been poured upon a higher principle, is

[11] Jerome here thus gives the inward sense, that while our faith deals with the law and the letter, Isaac is not come, but Ishmael only is born in us; whereas Isaac is come, if we enjoy spiritual things:—" Nunc breviter ad altiora tendendum est, ut dicamus unumquemque nostrum primùm non juxta repromissionem nasci, quamdiu Scripturarum verbis simplicibus instruitur, et Judaicis adhuc expositionibus delectatur: quando vero ad sublimiora transcenderit, et legem intellexerit spiritalem, tunc eum de repromissione generari." Then, after giving the dispensational fulfilment, he adds:—" Melius esse ut non solum de his qui in Ecclesiâ sunt intellectum, alios servos, alios liberos, arbitremur; sed etiam de uno eodemque homine; quamdiu sequatur historiam, ancillæ eum esse filium: cùm autem, aperiente Jesus scripturas, incensum cor ejus, et in fractione panis inspexerit eum, quem antea non videbat, tunc et ipsum Saræ filium nominari," &c.—*Hieron. in Epist. ad Galat.* l. ii. c. 4. Ambrose too, after tracing the outward, gives in substance the same inward application, here:—" Sed etiam in singulis Sara est, et in singulis Agar. Sara vera sapientia est: Agar autem est versutia, tanquam ancilla perfectioris virtutis. Alia enim sapientia spiritalis, alia sapientia hujus mundi," &c.—*De Abr.* l. ii. c. 10, § 73.

[12] Chap. xvi. 6.

ejected even from that place, where as hand-maid it might be most useful. So does legality lead to antinomianism, and this when law as yet cannot be dispensed with. The time comes, indeed, after Abram is circumcised and Isaac is born, when there is no further need for the bond-maid, and she is cast out for ever. But this is not yet. At present the bond-maid is needed. She is therefore sent back by the Lord to her true place as "Sarai's maid."[13] For "the law is good, if it be used lawfully."[14] The sorrow comes from exalting it out of its proper place.

Thus goes the life of faith. And here exercises begin in reference to law, which only end in the final dismissal of the bond-maid. At the point where this chapter ends, this conclusion is not foreseen; for after this the elect yet beseeches that the fruit of the flesh may be his heir.[15] But exercises of soul here begin which only end in the perfect discovery of God's mind upon the subject.

I need not shew how here, as throughout, this history has had its fulfilment upon every platform where God has worked in man. We are familiar with its accomplishment in the dispensations. In the history of God's dealings with mankind, before the death of the flesh is known, and before Sarai conceives, that is, before the Gospel times, the actings of the spirit of faith are found in connection with Hagar or law throughout a whole dispensation ; thus on the broadest scale developing the results of dealing with the flesh to gain the seed. We know how when the fulness of time was come, and the true Isaac was born, Ishmael, the seed according to the flesh, mocked and rejected Him ; and we know how since that hour the bond-maid and her seed have been cast out, though for that seed in its time a

[13] Chap. xvi. 8, 9.   [14] 1 Tim. i. 8.   [15] Chap. xvii. 18.

suited blessing tarries. This fulfilment in the dispensations is so well known, that I need but allude to it.[16] But there is also the fulfilment in the outward kingdom now. Here, men of faith, because the gospel is so long unfruitful, turn to law, by law and human energy to raise up a seed to fill the elect house.   In the Church, because Sarai is barren till the flesh in the elect is dead, the impatience of believers, as yet not dead, by the flesh has sought and obtained a seed. But it is " a wild-ass man," with the " mark of the beast " upon it. The true seed now, as of old, only comes out of death and barrenness through resurrection power.[17]

Thus are we shewn here, outwardly, what men, — inwardly, what in man, — shall inherit the kingdom. The inward fulfilment is that which first concerns us. May we there apprehend what we are apprehended for !

VI.—THE TRUE WAY FOR ABRAM TO BE FRUITFUL

Chapter 17

THE last scene shewed the efforts of faith to be fruitful by its own energy, and in connection with self-will. The results having proved that this is not God's way, the elect comes now to a point where the way of fruitfulness according to God is fully opened to it. The mind of God is

[16] Jerome says, speaking for others as well as himself, " Pæne cunctorum super hoc loco ista est explanatio; ut Agar ancillam interpretentur in lege et in populo Judæorum; Saram autem liberam, in Ecclesiâ, quæ de gentibus congregata est, quæ est mater omnium nostrum. Hæc diu non peperit, antequam Christus de virgine nasceretur," &c.—*Comment. in Ep. ad Gal.* l. ii. c. 4. Ambrose enlarges on the same view, *De Abr.* l. ii. c. 10, § 72 and 74. Augustine also, *Enar. in Psalm.* cxix. (*E. V.* 120,) § 7.

[17] Augustine often expounds this view; see *Enar. in Psalm* cxix. (*E. V.* 120), § 7, and elsewhere.

now revealed, that the promised seed comes after the circumcision of the flesh, not by its energy, but by its mortification, and by means of a change wrought in faith itself by the inbreathing of Him who now makes Himself known to us as " God Almighty." This is the lesson of this stage, that faith's true fruitfulness is only in God's strength and through self-renunciation. Where we are more, God to us is less. God will be more, yea everything, to us, when we are nothing. Grace even as nature abhors a vacuum. Only let us be empty, and the breath of heaven will fill us abundantly. The revelation by which Abram learns this, and his submission, figure that instruction which faith yet receives from God, and to which it yet yields the same implicit and prompt obedience.

We have here, first, the revelation by which Abram learns the true way of fruitfulness. It comes after many weary days,—" when Abram was ninety years old and nine;"[1] and even then is given by degrees, first briefly and generally, then in fuller detail, when Abram bows to welcome it. It comes not till Abram is hopeless in himself. Then, as the first brief announcement is met by worship and submissiveness,—for " he fell on his face,"— while in this posture the fuller revelation of God's mind is granted to him. How much is here! We are quick to be up, and while up and doing like Abram we do nothing to any purpose. We are slow to be " on our faces," yet it is here God's mind is learnt, while in the sense and confession of our weakness we lie low before Him.

But to speak of these communications. The first is this,—" I am God Almighty: walk before me, and be perfect, and I will make my covenant with thee, and I will multiply thee exceedingly."[2]

---

[1] Chap. xvii. 1.   [2] Chap. xvii. 1, 2.

Now this, though brief, contains the germ of all that follows, declaring that the seed depends upon God's " I will," because He is " God Almighty ; " while as to the means, singleness of eye and heart towards God,—" Walk before me, and be thou perfect," [3] — is the great requisite. Here, as ever, there is the " I will " of God, pledging the result, and also the sanctifying word, " Walk before me," shewing the path in which the elect will find the blessing.

All this, however, is only more perfectly developed in the second and fuller revelation which God vouchsafes to His servant, when he falls down and worships. Many particulars are here revealed, as to the source and channel of the blessing, and as to the means both on God's and man's part.

For the source, it is not in the creature, but in God. Jehovah, revealed as " God Almighty," here to barren Abram, seven times repeats His " I will : "—"*I will* make my covenant with thee, and *I will* multiply thee, and *I will* make thee exceeding fruitful; and *I will* make nations of thee, and *I will* establish my covenant with thy seed after thee ; and *I will* give to thy seed the land wherein thou art a stranger, and *I will* be their God." [4] As if He had said, Thou child of grace, hast thou not yet learnt that my word, my " I will," is that which makes thee fruitful ? Now hear again my covenant,—I will make thee fruitful : not from thyself, but from me is thy fruit found. Not by thy energy out of Hagar,— not by blood, nor of the will of the flesh, nor of the will of man, — but because " I will," shalt thou have the seed. And so of the inheritance : thou hast not earned or deserved it, nor can

---

[3] " Perfect : " Heb. תמים, *sincere* or *unmixed*; the same word as that used of Noah, chap. vi. 9. See also Deut. xviii. 13. [4] Chap. xvii. 2–8.

thy strength win it thee ; but this also is assured to thee, because " I will give it thee."

The channel, too, by which the seed should come is declared. Faith now learns that Sarai, the barren free woman, that is, the spiritual will, is to bear the desired fruit.[5] Long has this will been fruitless in us : most dear to us, we have yet turned from it, to be built up through Hagar or self-will. But faith now learns God's way of fruitfulness, that He will " make the barren woman within us to keep house, and to be a joyful mother of children."

As to the means God uses for this, He first changes Abram and Sarai's names, adding to each a letter which is most significant. Abram now is changed to Abraham. A name ever implies quality. Here the Lord takes something of His own name, (for the added H is a special part of the Divine name,) and adds it to the elect, thus in a new name giving him a new character.[6] What He adds

---

[5] Chap. xvii. 15–19.

[6] Chap. xvii. 5, 15. In Numb. xiii. 16, we find a somewhat similar change : Oshea's name is changed to Jehoshua, with the same spiritual reason. Jerome says on this, — "Dicunt autem Hebræi quod ex nomine suo, Deus, quod apud illos Tetragrammaton est, ‏ה‎ (*He*) literam Abræ et Saræ addiderit," &c. — *Quæst. Hebr. in Gen.* Others have observed respecting the name Jehovah, that it is formed simply of the five vowels, I, E, O, U, A, with a twice-repeated H. The vowels, or vocals, are so called, because they are sounds by themselves ; unlike the consonants, which can only be sounded with a conjoined vowel. It is remarkable that the name Jehovah, the Self-Existing-One, is composed of those sounds, (and it contains all of them,) which can and do exist by themselves, and which give life and breath to the rest, if we may so speak ; with the double addition of the H, the letter of out-breathing, in the middle and end of the name. Luther, in his *Comment on the First XXII. Psalms,* (on Psalm v. 11,) after tracing a mystic sense in the letters and form of the name, Jehovah, in which he sees a figure of the Trinity, —the proportions of the Name (as he says) figuring the procession of the Son and of the Holy Ghost,— says of the letter H, " The first syllable terminates in the letter *He,* which is a soft breathing, indicating that the proceeding in the Divine Persons is not carnal but spiritual, and all-sweet, and all-gentle. For if the aspirate letter be extended in sound, it is nothing more than a certain soft *proceeding* of wind or

is the mystic letter *He*, (ה) that sound which is only formed by an out-breathing; the addition of which, making Abram into Abraham, shewed how the elect should be made fruitful, even by the Lord's out-breath, that is the Holy Spirit.

And to bear good fruit the spirit of faith even yet must be breathed on by the Lord, and by that breath be changed from Abram to Abraham. Until we are so breathed upon, though beloved and elect, faith in us is, and will be, barren. To bear fruit we must obtain the "new name;" a new character must be in-wrought, the result of the gift of the Spirit or breath of Him, who by communications of Himself moulds us to His pleasure. Surely we are His, beloved and called, long before we know the baptism of the Spirit. Like those of old we follow the Lord, at first knowing Him after the flesh, before we reach to Pentecost and know him spiritually. We may like Peter on the Mount even see the glory of the living Word, and the law and the prophets testifying to Him, and yet after this deny Him. But the time arrives when we, who have followed Christ in the flesh, come to be tried by His cross, and to see His resurrection. Then,—when the cross is no more a puzzle, — when we see it is the way to life, and that the flesh verily profiteth nothing,—when we have tarried until we are endued with power, and the Holy Ghost has come on us, the out-breathing of God,

gentle blast; so that it most appropriately figures forth the proceeding of the Son. And in like manner the whole name is terminated in the same letter of a soft breathing; so that we are to understand that the second *proceeding* is also spiritual, and not at all differing from the former, except its being the second, and proceeding from the first," &c. —Vol. i. p. 277, *of the Translation by Cole*. If in the laws of number and of sound nothing is by chance, He who has been pleased to reveal Himself as Jehovah surely has a reason for the very form of this name, as indeed for all else.

making us who have once followed Christ carnally, sparing ourselves, now willing to follow Him even to the death of self, — then are we from Abram changed to Abraham. The Lord hath breathed on us: we can go and bring forth much fruit. Till this change is wrought, we shall be barren. When, by the Lord's revelation of Himself to us, it is accomplished, the fruit we long for is not far off.

One thing, however, yet remains to be done or suffered by the elect. Abraham, as a pledge of his entire dependance, must submit to certain appointed suffering, before he can obtain the seed. Because the Lord has covenanted with him, and has breathed on him, and so changed him, therefore Abraham must on his part suffer in his flesh, so testifying that his hope is not in the flesh or its energies, but only in Jehovah, God Almighty. So God, after His sevenfold promise, and after His gift of a new name, says, " Thou shalt therefore keep my covenant : and this is my covenant, which ye shall keep ; ye shall circumcise the flesh of your foreskin, and it shall be a token of the covenant betwixt me and you." [7]

Now this circumcision signified the mortification of that fleshliness which yet cleaves to the elect spirit. Even the spirit needs to be judged, and " true circumcision is that of the heart, in the spirit and not in the letter." [8] In circumcision a part of the flesh was cut off: " the filth of the flesh was put away." [9] So faith must judge whatever of the flesh is in it, " laying aside all filthiness and superfluity of naughtiness, to receive with meekness the engrafted word," [10] — that measure of the Divine which is

---

[7] Chap. xvii. 9–11.
[8] Rom. ii. 29. Compare Deut. x. 16, and Jer. iv. 4.
[9] 1 Pet. iii. 21. I am assured that the words, σαρκὸς ἀπόθεσις ῥύπου, allude to circumcision.
[10] James i. 21.

communicated to it,—that so in the strength of the Lord, and not in self, but rather in self-judgment, it may indeed be fruitful. And this spiritual circumcision, like that which was its type, is not a figure only, but an actual seal, an enduring mark impressed upon us; for as it declares that we have given up all fleshly confidence, so it shews itself in counting all things but loss for the excellency of the knowledge of Christ Jesus; reckoning all that the flesh can achieve but as dung, if only the fellowship of Christ's sufferings and the power of His resurrection may be apprehended. So Paul says, "We are the circumcision, who worship God in the spirit, and rejoice in Christ Jesus, and have no confidence in the flesh."[11] To the eye of sense such an operation seemed not only dangerous to life, but one which, when performed in years, even if the patient survived, would probably preclude all fruitfulness. The offering of Isaac was not a severer trial of faith, or one more apparently opposed to the fulfilment of the promise. Such a trial to the believer is self-mortification. Yet faith triumphs. We are "circumcised with the circumcision made without hands, in putting off the body of the sins of the flesh:"[12] "by the spirit we mortify the deeds of the body,"[13] and so "bear in our bodies the marks of the Lord Jesus."[14]

That this practical judgment of self must precede the fruit of promise is not understood, nor is it required, when we begin our pilgrimage.[15] At this stage it is revealed to faith. Need I say that this mortification is not our righteousness;—that is of faith, as it is written, "Abraham

---

[11] Phil. iii. 3, 8, 9, 10.
[12] Col. ii. 13.
[13] Rom. viii. 13.
[14] Gal. vi. 17.
[15] " Et primum quidem, ante immutationem nominis, nihil de circumcisione præcipitur. Non enim poterat, cum adhuc esset Abram, suscipere circumcisionis insigne," &c.—*Origen, Hom.* iii. *in Gen.*

believed God, and it was counted to him for righteousness;" — but this self-judgment comes to seal that righteousness, " as the seal of the righteousness of the faith which a believer has, being yet uncircumcised."[16] Long before self is mortified, the elect is righteous; nor are we circumcised thereby to win the promise. On the contrary, God first and freely promises. He says, " I will multiply." Then He adds, " *Therefore* thou shalt circumcise." God does indeed look for self-judgment, but not as the ground, rather as the result, of promise. So the Spirit ever speaks : — " I will be their God : *therefore* come out from among them, and be ye separate :"[17] so again, " Ye are bought with a price; *therefore* glorify God :"[18] and again, " Ye are risen, and your life is hid with Christ in God; mortify *therefore* your members which are upon the earth."[19]

Would to God that this lesson were learnt; but, alas, mortification is well nigh out of date. Instead of judging the flesh, on all sides we see attempts to perfect it, and this in the hope of thus seeing the seed of promise. But some by the blood of Christ, shed first at His circumcision, have better learnt God's mind. Only let them be faithful to it. Only let the Church's creed,—" He died and rose," — be her life. Then, as with the Head, so with herself, the dying of the corn of wheat shall result in the bringing forth of much fruit.

As to the time and subjects of this rite, much is here for such as can receive it. For the time, the "eighth day" is appointed.[20] Seven days in type include the stages or periods proper to the first creation. The eighth day, as it

---

[16] Rom. iv. 11.
[17] 2 Cor. vi. 17.
[18] 1 Cor. vi. 20.

[19] Col. iii. 3, 5.
[20] Chap. xvii. 12.

takes us beyond and out of these, brings us mystically into a new order of things and times, in a word into the new creation or resurrection. Those even in Abraham's family, who are yet in the first seven days, that is, in the first creation, are not to be circumcised.[21] Inwardly, the men of Abraham's house are all the thoughts which are connected with and subject to the spirit of faith. Some of these were strangers, some home-born. All were now by faith and with faith to be circumcised: for now we must " bring every thought into subjection to the obedience of Christ."[22] Outwardly, Abraham's house is the Church, and its inmates the varying natures which fill the house of faith. Of these all who have grown out of the seven days must be circumcised. Practical mortification of the flesh is not to be pressed on babes in Christ, till the eighth day is apprehended by them ; but on all the rest the seal must come, not to make them barren, but that they may be yet more fruitful.

---

[21] With the same import all creatures newly born were counted in their blood, or unclean, for seven days, and might not, before the expiration of this period, be offered to God. Neither calf, lamb, nor kid, could be presented as an oblation before it was eight days old.—Lev. xxii. 27. Of the mystic import of the eighth day, and its connection with circumcision, Augustine says, " Hujus rei signum circumcisio data erat patribus, ut octavo die circumcideretur omnis masculus. Circumcisio fiebat in cultellis petrinis, quia petra erat Christus. In istâ circumcisione significabatur exspoliatio carnalis vitæ octavo die per Christi resurrectionem," &c.—*Serm.* ccxxxi. § 2. Again he says, " Quapropter ante resurrectionem Domini, quam-

vis sacros patres plenos prophetico spiritu octavi sacramentum nequaquam lateret, quo significatur resurrectio : (nam et pro octavo Psalmus inscribitur, et octavo die circumcidebantur infantes, et in Ecclesiaste ad duorum Testamentorum significationem dicitur, ' *Da illis septem, et illis octo ;* ') reservatum est tamen et occultatum," &c.—*Epistol.* l. ii. lv. c. 13.

[22] 2 Cor. x. 5. Ambrose thus gives the inward sense here :—" Circumcide tuum non solum vernaculum, sed etiam pretio emptum. Vernaculi sunt motus naturales (mentis ;) pretio empti, ratione et doctrinâ acquisiti. Egent autem et illi et hi purgatione et incisione luxuriæ," &c. —*De Abr.* l. ii. c. 11, § 79.

Now see how the spirit of faith meets this word. Abraham receives it with something not unlike questioning:—
" He fell on his face and laughed, and said in his heart, Shall a child be born to him that is an hundred years old, and shall Sarah, that is ninety years old, bear ?" But this soon changes to prayer. At first the prayer is lacking in intelligence; for he said, " Oh ! that Ishmael might live before thee." [23] Nevertheless, he prays and bows himself, even while pleading for his own will. This struggle too passes. God speaks to his heart, telling him that though the fruit of his own energy cannot be the heir of promise, it shall receive a suited blessing; and the elect, though his soul heaves like the sea after a storm, pleads no more for his own will, but obeys promptly and explicitly. " In the self-same day was Abraham circumcised, and all the men of his house with him, as the Lord had said unto him." [24]

How exactly all this is yet fulfilled, those know who from Abram have been made Abraham. The struggle of doubt and hope within, — of our own wishes against the Lord's will,— the desire for the abiding of that which is of self, even when God himself promises better things,— how all this, which so much savours of the will of the flesh, ends in prompt obedience and willing self-renunciation, is experience which not a few have learnt. Happy they who have thus mortified the flesh with its affections and lusts. Painful as the discipline may be, apparently contrary to that which we desire, the end will shew how good it is for us that we have been thus afflicted. Till we are so afflicted we shall lack the promised seed.

A few words will suffice for the dispensational fulfilment here. Perfection and self-mortification were not required

[23] Chap. xvii. 17, 18.   [24] Chap. xvii. 23–27.

from men of faith until the time came for Sarah to be fruitful, that is, till Gospel days. But when the time was come for a new and wider revelation,— when God would shew himself as El Shaddai, the Almighty, who could bring fruit even out of death and barrenness,— when His outbreath was given in a way unknown before, making His elect partakers of the Divine Nature, and possessors of His spirit,— then with this grace was a judgment of self demanded, which before this had not been asked of men. How truly did the elect then cry as Abraham here,— " Oh, that Ishmael might live before thee." How earnestly did Paul long for Hagar's son, when he said, " My heart's desire and prayer to God for Israel is, that they might be saved." [25] But the fruit of the flesh could not be the heir, though even to them a suited blessing is covenanted. Well might Paul, as he thought upon it, break forth in wonder, " Oh, the depth of the riches, both of the wisdom and knowledge of God ! "

VII.—The End of Lot

Chapter 18 and 19

Now comes the end of Lot, which must be known before Isaac, the spirit of sonship, is given to us. Thus, one after another of the things once walked with drop off from around Abraham as he advances. For the path of the spirit of faith is one of ever increasing separateness to God ; until, being stripped of all external aids, it is without any other hope cast wholly and for everything upon the Lord alone. Terah, the old man, is first left. Then, when we escape from Egypt, Lot separates himself. After

[25] Rom. x. 1.

this, great efforts are made to reclaim him, shewing how much the outward man is yet clung to and yearned over. But a time comes when Lot is seen no more. This stage here begins to open to us.

What Lot is we have already seen. Inwardly, he is that mind in us, which, though righteous, leans to outward things; which, therefore, though moved for a while to go with faith, departs from it after Egypt is left, and goes down Sodom-ward.[1] Such a mind is in us at this stage. But the time comes in the life of faith, when Sodom, the work of Ham's seed, must be judged in us; when divine judgment is seen to consume and overthrow all the plain of Sodom, that is, the ground of self-love. For Sodom is not judged at first. There is a time when self-love is not consumed in us. Now its doom is seen; and by this is brought out the full difference between the spirit of faith and the upright outward mind. To each the Lord now speaks. The spirit of faith, having judged itself by circumcision, receives the Lord in a way unknown before, with fresh promises, and an enlarged apprehension of God's will; while the outward mind, still vexed with self-love, and able to receive only an inferior revelation, is rescued thence to produce a shameful fruit, which is destined to become a thorn in the way of Abraham's true seed. After which Lot is seen no more. Having shewn what it is, the outward mind no more affects the path of faith. For a time it tries us, but a day arrives when its full unlikeness to the spirit of faith is seen in a light never to be forgotten. Thenceforth, whatever trials we may have, we know the difference between these, and knowing it walk more simply and intelligently.[2]

---

[1] See on chapters xii. and xiii.

[2] Origen at some length traces the inward fulfilment here:—"Loth, qui non respexit post se, rationabilis

This outline of the inward sense here may suffice for those who can pursue it inwardly. The outward fulfilment will be better known. In this view, Abraham is the type of those in whom the spirit of faith is the ruling life: Lot, of those who, though righteous and saved, are rather outward than inward men, who hold the truth, but never seem to apprehend the inward spirit of it. As if to shew the contrast between these, Lot's path is drawn here beside Abraham's. Both are seen entertaining heavenly visitors; both gladly welcome such a visit; this is common to both: but beyond this how different the circumstances, and the results to each, of this intercourse!

There is first a difference in the form of the Divine manifestation. In Abraham's case we read, "The Lord appeared to him at midday, and lo, three men stood by him:" in Lot's, "There came two angels to Sodom at even."[3] In the first case, the Lord appears in human form, and three persons are apprehended. In the other, only two are seen. By the obedient soul, from Abram changed to Abraham, the promise, "If any man keep my word, *we* will come unto him, and make our abode with him,"[4] is fully realised. Three persons, Father, Son, and Spirit, will be known, stooping in a form we can bear to come under our roof, not in darkness, but in the light, as guests to commune with us. While those who yet are in the world, like Lot, receiving their heavenly guests "at

sensus est; uxor autem hic carnis imaginem teneat.   Caro est enim, quæ respicit semper ad vitia, quæ cùm animus tendit ad salutem, illa retrorsum respicit, et voluptates requirit. . . . . Vide ne tibi, cùm effugies flammas sæculi, . . . insidientur duæ filiæ istæ, quæ a te non discedunt, sed sequuntur te etiam cùm ascendis in montem, id est vana gloria et major soror ejus superbia. Vide ne te istæ filiæ sopitum ac dormientem, dum tibi nec sentire nec intelligere videris, complexibus suis instringant. . . . Vigila ergo et observa ne de his generes filios."— *Orig. Hom.* vi. *in Gen.*

[3] Cf. chap. xviii. 1, and xix. 1.

[4] John xiv. 23.

even," that is, in declining light, be their faith what it may, will in experience lose one person, and have less perfect communion.[5]

The ground they stand on is as distinct. Abraham is " in the plains of Mamre, in his tent-door ; " Lot is " sitting in the gate of Sodom." True men of faith, as pilgrims with their tent, in obedient self-judgment rest at Mamre or Hebron, that is in vision or communion. Others, righteous but not self-judged, seek to judge " in the gate of Sodom," the defiled world-loving world.[6] The one not only give up the world, but are content to be given up by it, which is far harder. The other take a place of power here, hoping, unjudged as they are, to correct the faults of others who are living in self-love. But can the Lots correct or reform the world ? Rather they themselves are

[5] This is the common exposition of the Fathers. Gregory Nyssen says, —" Apparuit enim, inquit, ei Deus, ... et ecce, tres viri astabant supra eum. Et ecce, accurrit et adoravit pronus in terram, et dixit, Domine, si nactus sum gratiam coram te, ne prætereas puerum tuum. . . . . Ecce igitur dicit quòd Deus quidem apparuit ei, sed quòd tres tamen viri essent, qui conspecti fuissent : ipsum autem rursus non quasi tribus dixisse, Domini, si inveni gratiam coram vobis ; sed Dominum singulariter ternos, nominasse, et tanquam unum invitasse ad divertendum."—*Test. c. Jud.* p. 152 ; Ed. Par. 1638. So too Cyril of Alexandria :—Ὀφθῆναι δὲ καὶ ποτέ φησι τῷ ᾿Αβραὰμ, καθημένῳ ἐπὶ τῇ δρυὶ τῇ Μαμβρῇ, τρεῖς ἀνθρώπους, τῆς ἁγίας καὶ ὁμοουσίου Τριάδος ἐπέχοντας τύπον. Εἶτα πρὸς αὐτοὺς εἰπεῖν τὸν θεσπέσιον ᾿Αβραὰμ, οὐχὶ μάλλον Κύριοι, Κύριε δὲ μοναδικῶς, κ. τ. λ.— *Contra Julian,* l. viii. p. 268. So too Ambrose, *De Abr.* l. i.

c. 5, § 33. Origen dwells much on this manifestation being vouchsafed " *at mid-day :*"—" Quod si credimus hæc per Spiritum Sanctum scripta, non puto frustra placuisse Divino Spiritui ut etiam tempus et hora visionis Scripturæ paginis mandaretur, nisi et horæ istius et temporis ratio aliquid conferret ad scientiam filiis Abrahæ, quibus utique sicut opera Abrahæ, facienda, ita et visitationes istæ sperandæ sunt. . . . . Si enim lux quæ in ipso est mentis, et puritas cordis clara fuerit, iste meridianum tempus in semetipso habere videbitur, et per hanc puritatem cordis quasi in meridie positus Deum videbit. sedens ad quercum Mambre, quod *ad visionem* interpretatur."— *Hom.* ii. *in Cantica.*

[6] To " *sit in the gate* " was to take the place of authority. See Deut. xxi. 19 ; Ruth iv. 1 ; Lam. v. 14 ; Psalm lxix. 12 ; Prov. xxii. 22 ; Isa. xxix. 21 ; Amos v. 10, 12, 15 ; Prov. xxxi. 23.

only "saved so as by fire."[7] A stage is, indeed, to be
reached by grace, when the elect not only "gets him out,"
as Abram, from the ground of the old man, but when he
can go down thither again, as Jacob, to win flocks thence,
which he may bring back to Canaan. There is yet a
higher stage, when, as Joseph, he can even in Egypt have
it all bowed down before him, while he is its deliverer.
But at the Abraham stage this cannot be. To Abram the
word is, "Get thee out into a land which I will shew thee."
The path of faith as such is not to cleanse the world, but
to lift man out of it to dwell in heavenly things. Further
on, the elect may be fit for more. As a believer, his place
is the ground of promise, in marked separation from outward things. True believers, therefore, dwell apart with
God, while the Lots, unjudged, and unfit to judge others,
dwelling in Sodom, strive by efforts to improve it, to justify to themselves a position which they feel at least questionable. For few have known the true walk of faith,
even in the measure Lot knew it when he walked with
Abram, but have some misgivings when they compare their
position as professed improvers of the world, which yet is
not improved, with that of those who in separation from
it are bearing witness of a better. So they labour in the
fire, comforting themselves, that, while the Abrahams are
useless to the world, they are doing something for it. What
they really achieve may teach them at last that Sodom
cannot even be helped, much less saved, by unchastened
outward men. But Lot has not yet learnt this : while
therefore Abraham is at Mamre, Lot is in the gate of
Sodom, calling its sinners, "brethren."[8]

Another contrast between these men may be seen in

their reception of their guests, and the circumstances attending it. In both there is the same desire for communion; but while in the one case this at once is granted, in the other at first it is denied: with the one, communion is undisturbed; with the other, when at last obtained, it is marred by the intrusion of the men of Sodom. To Abraham's request, " Pass not away, my Lord, but let me fetch a morsel of bread," the answer at once is, " So do as thou hast said." To Lot's petition, " Turn in, my lords, I pray you, into your servant's house," the reply is, " Nay, but we will abide in the street all night."[9] Eventually, indeed, they yield to his importunity, and he sups with them, and they with him. But whereas in Abraham's case communion is reached, as it were, naturally without an effort, in Lot's there is a struggle of prayer before his desire is granted. By the self-mortified pilgrim communion is easily obtained. Those who live in the world, judging it rather than themselves, though they would gladly welcome the Lord or His servants, find that, before communion can be enjoyed, a temporary denial and a spiritual struggle must be experienced. Further, in Abraham's case, the communion is unbroken. No rude alarms from without disturb his quiet intercourse. In Lot's, " the men of Sodom compass the house," and Lot, distracted, " went out at the door to them, and shut the door after him."[10] Abraham, having but One Master to serve, can stand before Him in peace. Lot with two masters, the Lord and the world, can satisfy neither, nor is himself satisfied. Forced away from his guests by those among whom he dwells, the communion of saints, if known at all, is known with many interruptions.

---

[9] Cf. chap. xviii. 5, and xix. 2.   [10] Cf. chap. xviii. 8, and xix. 5, 6.

Other contrasts abound throughout this scene. Of Abraham it is said, " He ran to meet them : " of Lot only that " he rose up." [11] The one, as soon as the Lord appears, instinctively draws nearer to Him : the other, though welcoming Him, does not shew the same alacrity. In the feast prepared, too, a difference may be seen. By Abraham " a calf " is slain, — there is the pouring out of a life, — and " fine meal " is added : in the other we find only " unleavened bread and wine," an acceptable service, yet not so costly as the former. [12] And there is yet this difference in the communion of saints. Some can grasp the highest aspects of Christ's death, apprehending Him as the " ox," and the " fine flour," in which was no unevenness : others have a lower view of the same offering, seeing it only as " unleavened bread and wine." Happy is it to see Christ in any form, but happiest he, who, walking with the Lord, and giving to Him without grudging, in such acts has the fullest views of Him who has even " given Himself " to us.

A further contrast is to be seen in the state of the respective families of Lot and Abraham. Abraham, to the question, " Where is thy wife," can reply, in words he could not have used in Egypt, " She is in the tent." In Lot's case, the women of his house are in jeopardy, offered to the men of Sodom, in hope of staying worse abomination. [13] Women, in this outward view, are principles. [14] If

[11] Cf. chap. xviii. 2, 6, 7, and xix. 1. Origen, (*Hom.* iv. *in Gen.*) dwells at considerable length on this, and on the difference between the feasts prepared by Lot and Abraham.

[12] In the authorised version we read, " Lot made *a feast,* and did bake unleavened bread." The word משתה, here translated "*feast,*" is elsewhere more correctly rendered " *a banquet of wine,*" as in Esther v. 6, and vii. 7. See also Isa. xxv. 6. The LXX. here render it by πότον, " *a drinking.*"

[13] Cf. chap. xviii. 9, and xix. 8.

[14] See what is said of Eve, on chap. iii. ; also respecting "the daughters of men," on chap. vi. ; also of Sarah and Hagar, on chaps. xii. and xvi.

we walk with God, we are in no danger of having our principles defiled by the world's rough handling. Not so if our home is the world : there our purest principles are in danger of being abused, nay, often they are abused, for the world, if it touches, cannot but dishonour them. I know, indeed, that in every age men like Lot have been found, who, tempted or forced by their position, prostitute their principles to the use of the ungodly. I know, too, that in so doing they hope to improve the world, and to keep it from worse abominations. So have liberty and peace, and other fruits of righteousness, been pressed upon the world, in the hope that in embracing these it may, as the world, be somewhat bettered. And what is the result? The principles are perilled or defiled, the world meanwhile being not a whit the better. But the Lots do not believe this, until bitter experience proves it. Is then nothing to be done for the ungodly world? Much surely. Do what Abraham did for Sodom,— pray for it : nay, if you are sent, do what God's messengers did,— testify of coming judgment, and shew the way of safety. Bring those you can out of it. But think not that as a Lot you can reform or change it by your principles. It may defile you and them ; you cannot change it. Were you a Joseph, you might do something. Being only a Lot, or outward man, though righteous, you are powerless.

Further, Abraham waiting on his guests " stood by them " in calm communion. Lot " went out," anxious for his children. Not one word is recorded addressed by him to the heavenly strangers while they are in his house.[15] Men of faith can speak to the Lord, and in communion receive fresh promises. The Lots can but speak to their

[15] Cf. chap. xviii. 8, 9, and xix. 14.

children or the world, and receive warnings, that, if they flee not, they must be destroyed. Lot's words here are very characteristic. He goes out to direct others, but his preaching is, first, not in exact accordance with the word of the Lord, and then, not in accordance with his own conduct. The Lord had said, " Hast thou any here? Bring them out." Lot only says, " Get you out."[16] It is all the difference between " Come," and " Go:" and alike as these may seem, the difference is by no means trifling. Again, his preaching is not in accordance with his walk. Lot preaches, " Get you out of this place, for the Lord will destroy it;" but he himself " lingers."[17] Here we see his reason for altering the Lord's words. He could not " bring " others out if he tarried there: he must say, " Get you out." How many righteous Lots in Sodom are yet attempting thus to bear the Lord's message. Even while they say, This world is condemned, they linger in it, and are at last only separated from it by force, against their own will. Yet they hope such preaching will move others. But the truth from such lips is paralysed. Its preachers are its greatest hindrance: they may like Lot be " saved by fire," but " their works shall be burnt up, and they shall suffer loss."[18]

Very different too are the words addressed to Abraham out of Sodom, and to Lot yet lingering there. To both the Lord declares that city's fate, but how unlike to each the terms of the communication. To the one He speaks as to a friend, saying, " Shall I hide from Abraham the thing that I will do? " To Lot He says, " We will destroy this place: escape for thy life, lest thou also be consumed."[19] Such as walk with God can in quiet learn of Him. Such

---

[16] Chap. xix. 12, 14.
[17] Chap. xix. 14, 16.
[18] 1 Cor. iii. 15. Compare John

xv. 6, and 1 Cor. ix. 27.
[19] Cf. chap. xviii. 17-21, and xix. 13-17.

as walk with the world must, even as the world, be alarmed to " flee for their life, lest they be consumed." A carnal Christian cannot bear spiritual words. Paul, though he might speak wisdom among them that were perfect, could not speak to the Corinthians as unto spiritual.[20] Even the Holy Ghost, whose office it is " to take of the things of Christ " to shew them to faithful souls, to the world speaks only " of sin, and righteousness, and judgment." [21] Worldly Christians therefore, though they talk for ever of assurance and election, so long as they are in the world will hear God's voice warning and alarming them. Out of Sodom they shall hear of peace; in it, the word, and it is in love, must be a warning, lest they also be consumed.

Even more unlike are the prayers of these men. Abraham, with confessions that he is " but dust and ashes," waiting on God in Christ-like intercession, yields his will to God's will. Lot, full of self, styling himself God's " servant," prays only for self, in a prayer which through-out is a struggle to obtain his own will.[22] The Lord had said, " Stay not in all the plain : " and Lot answered, " Oh ! not so, my Lord ; " that is, not thy will but mine be done : (is there not too much of such prayer ?) to justify which he speaks of grace ; " Not so, my Lord, for thy servant hath found grace in thy sight." This is ever so : Christians in the world plead grace as a reason for self-indulgence and for obtaining their own will. Then, again, what confusion is in the prayer. He speaks of the " mercy shewn in saving his life," and yet of " some evil (he knows not what) taking him ; " not saying, " I will not," but " I cannot :"— " I cannot escape to the mountain, lest I die." Thus he

[20] 1 Cor. ii. 6, and iii. 1. Compare Heb. v. 11-14.

[21] Compare John xvi. 8, and 13, 14.

[22] Cf. chap. xviii. 23-33, and xix. 18, 19.

pleads for his own way to the end, his last request being for Zoar, a little matter,— " Is it not a little one ? "—the gracious answer to which is one of the unnumbered proofs, that as the heavens are high above the earth, so great is the Lord's mercy to all them that fear Him.

But one fact more is known of Lot. Sodom is judged : the condemnation of this world is clearly seen. Then Abraham gets up early to the place where he stood before the Lord, as though yet waiting on Him. Lot, unsatisfied with his self-chosen refuge, gets up to the mountain, without a command, only to fall there grievously.[23] Wine first, and then his daughters, cast him down. So when outward men, through mere alarm of judgment, attempt without command to walk where faith walks, their very gifts will cause their fall. The higher the ground, the harder for them to occupy it. There the cup of blessing, misused by Lot's daughters, that is, by the evil working of those principles which have been produced and are most cherished by outward men, will give occasion for those very principles first to corrupt, and then to be themselves corrupted by, those who cherished them. Thus will righteous Lots unintentionally produce out of their own self-defiled principles a seed to their own shame and the grief of God's elect ; a seed which Israel may be forbidden to dispossess,[24] but which cannot come into the congregation of the Lord,[25] to the end dwelling nigh to the wilderness, short of the land beyond Jordan.

Such is the end of Lot. Henceforth he is no longer a snare to the man of faith. Within, when once the outward

---

[23] Compare the Lord's command to Israel, to go up into the land, which they disobeyed, with the result of the self-will of the same men, who afterwards chose to go up presump- tuously, without a divine command. —Deut. i. 26–44.

[24] Deut. ii. 9–12, and 19–21.

[25] Deut. xxiii. 3, 4.

mind has shewn its full unlikeness to that spirit of faith, with which for a while it seemed so closely linked, it ceases to be a hindrance: it may live, but henceforth it does not trouble faith. So without, the fall of outward men may grieve, but it will not stumble the men of faith. It may even help them, as the removal of dead wood serves the vine no less than the purging and pruning of the fruitful branch. " All things are yours." " In all these things we are more than conquerors through Him that loved us."

VIII. — ABRAHAM IN THE PHILISTINES' LAND

Chapter 20

ONE trial more remains for faith before Isaac, the spirit of sonship, is manifested. Terah and Egypt have long since been left; Sodom is judged; Lot too is gone, no more to trouble us. In other words, the old man, and sense, and self-love, and the outward man, have all been given up or overcome. At this point another trial meets us. Abraham, saved from Egypt, and Sodom, and Lot, comes into the Philistines' land; and there, through fear lest he should be killed for his wife's sake, is tempted to deny his true relation to her. " Abraham said of Sarah, She is my sister: and Abimelech, king of Gerar, sent and took her." But God interferes, making known to the Philistine, that, because she belongs to another, he may not touch her. Sarah, therefore, is restored untouched to Abraham, who with her receives considerable presents from Abimelech.[1]

Thrice does the elect fail thus. In Egypt Abraham has already once given up his wife. Now with the Philistines

[1] Chap. xx. 1–16.

he repeats the same act. Isaac, too, at a later date fails in like manner.[2] There must be, therefore, some peculiar tendency in the elect to that form of failure or error, which for our instruction is recorded here. What is it? Can we be guilty of it? Or may we say that Abraham's sons do not fail here as there father did?

Throughout this book every man or woman, sprung from Adam, figures (if we take the inward application) some mind or affection which by nature or grace springs out of human nature. Abraham is the spirit of faith. Sarah, speaking broadly, is the principle of the New Covenant. What is Abimelech? He was a Philistine. On turning to the chapter[3] which gives us the development of the seeds which multiplied on resurrection-ground, we read that the Philistines were the children of Mizraim or Egypt. Egypt is sense;[4] outwardly, those who live the life of sense, that is, in seen things. The Philistine is only the same spirit, in rather a different aspect, and at a further stage. Thus, if Egypt figures worldly wisdom, that knowledge through the senses which cannot really know God, the Philistine represents the further attainments of the same, when it is seen attempting to enter into heavenly things. For the Philistine stretches out toward the land of Canaan;[5] but he would enter that land without circumcision,[6] without

---

[2] Chap. xxvi. 6-11. David also "changed his behaviour before Abimelech."—See Psalm xxxiv. *title*; and 1 Sam. xxi. 13.

[3] Chap. x. 13, 14.

[4] See on chap. xii.

[5] A glance at any map, shewing the relative position of the Philistines, and Egypt, and Canaan, will make this clearer to those who are not familiar with the localities of the countries named here.

[6] The Philistines are continually mentioned as "uncircumcised."—See 1 Sam. xvii. 26, 36, xxxi. 4; 2 Sam. i. 20, &c. Those who can trace the mystic significance of numbers will observe that there were "five lords of the Philistines."—Joshua xiii. 3; Judges iii. 3; 1 Sam. vi. 4, 16, 18. *Five* always refers to something connected with the senses. —See note above, p. 193.

passing the wilderness, and without crossing Jordan or the Red Sea. Such is the Philistine, knowledge derived from sense, which seeks to enter into heavenly things without death and resurrection. It is a race famed for giants,[7] but with all their might they cannot possess the promised land. Knowledge derived from sense is not elect: it cannot inherit, though it may seek to intrude into, heavenly things.[8]

What is figured here then is this. The spirit of faith, delivered from outward hindrances, discovers that even the knowledge which aims at heavenly things may be a snare to it. An attempt is made by knowledge to take the things of faith, and hereby faith's best things are seriously imperilled. For knowledge may not take the things of faith. Nevertheless, when faith fails to hold its proper truth, knowledge attempts to lay hold on that which as exclusively belongs to faith as Sarah did to Abraham. But this is not allowed, and cannot be. The New Covenant or spiritual truth belongs only to the spirit of faith. On the other hand, if faith owns this relationship, then knowledge may strengthen faith, and give it many gifts, which may serve for the veiling or adorning of the truth. For even as Abimelech gave gifts to Abraham, after that he confessed the true relationship in which he stood to Sarah, so may knowledge enrich faith with many useful things, if only the true relationship between

---

[7] 1 Sam. xvii. 4-7; 2 Sam. xxi. 15, 16, 18, 20.

[8] Origen gives the same interpretation, taking the Philistine to represent *worldly knowledge* or *philosophy*: —"Sed et hoc non puto otiosè Spiritui Sancto, qui hæc scribit, curæ fuerit comprehendere, quod duo alii cum Abimelech venerint; (alluding to "Ahuzzath, his friend, and Phicol, his chief-captain;" see chap. xxvi. 26;) qui tres, ut ego arbitror imaginem totius philosophiæ tenent, quæ in tres partes dividitur, logicam, physicam, ethicam, id est, rationalem, naturalem, moralem. Rationalis est illa quæ Deum patrem omnium confitetur, ut est Abimelech," &c.— *Hom.* xiv. *in Gen.* xxvi.

faith and the covenant of grace is not denied. It is not lawful by knowledge to take hold of the things of faith, but some of the things of knowledge may be received by faith, and of these a covering may be made for the protection of the things of faith. Faith, holding the truth, can possess the things which knowledge gives, but mere knowledge cannot enter into spiritual truth.

For example, take the truth of the cross. Mere earthly knowledge never embraces it. But faith, firmly holding this truth, may be confirmed and enriched by many considerations, which properly belong to the province of mere worldly knowledge, that is, the Philistine. For even nature says, that the ground must be pierced by spade and plough before it will yield its best fruits, — that thorns may grow without a chastened earth, but that corn-fields only smile after the ploughers have ploughed upon its back and made long furrows. Every creature slain to support our life, the threshing needed to separate the wheat from the chaff which covers it, the crushing of the grape to produce the precious wine,—these " voices in the world "[9] all preach the cross, and that life and joy are through death and sorrow everywhere. Thus can faith in us receive from knowledge many things which serve to enrich and strengthen it, while knowledge on its part cannot possess spiritual truth. On the other hand, faith freed from outward things now finds that even knowledge may be a snare to it; for knowledge attempts to take the things of faith, and faith failing to hold them firmly thereby imperils the promised seed. Had the Lord not interposed, it might have been doubtful whether Isaac were Abraham's seed or Abimelech's. But God interferes : the things of faith are preserved inviolate. Faith may fail : God never fails.

[9] 1 Cor. xiv. 10.

Outwardly too the scene here is fulfilled, when, through the failure of believers to avow their special privileges, men of mere worldly knowledge are deceived so as to think that as worldlings they can possess the things of faith. That believers fail thus is a fact, shameful and humbling, but as certainly a fact as that Abraham denied Sarah in the Philistines' land. In this outward view, the Philistine represents those in whom the spirit of worldly knowledge is the ruling life, who, like the Philistine, stretch out to enter holy things without spiritual circumcision, without death and resurrection.[10] In the presence of such, through fear of man, the believer is often tempted practically to deny Sarah, by giving worldlings reason to think that as the world, that is, by mere knowledge, without faith, the New Covenant can properly belong to them. The result is that worldlings, knowing no better, think that the New Covenant is something which they may know carnally, and accordingly they so attempt to know it. For this the elect are to blame. Words are used, which, though true in a sense, are not true in the sense in which they are taken by worldly men, and by these the world is deceived. Had Abraham avowed Sarah's relation to him, that she was his wife, Abimelech would in all probability not have attempted to meddle with her. And if believers would but say that certain truths belong to certain men, the world would not so often attempt to grasp what is not theirs. But this is shrunk from. And from fear of giving offence,

[10] Of this outward view Origen says,—"Videtur mihi quod hic Abimelech formam teneat studiosorum et sapientium sæculi, qui philosophiæ operam dantes, licet non integram et perfectam pietatis regulam, attigerint, tamen senserint Deum patrem et regem esse omnium," &c. —*Hom.* vi. *in Gen.* xx. Augustine traces a yet more general application, seeing in Abimelech the rulers of this world, who seek to take the Church, not knowing its true relationships, but are not permitted to violate it.—*Contra Faustum,* l. xxii. c. 38.

by suggesting that there is anything which worldly men cannot comprehend, they are by the Church's culpable equivocation brought into real danger. Not knowing that Sarah belongs to men of faith, they attempt to lay hold of her by knowledge, that is, as Philistines. The soul which believes is not a Philistine. Such a one may freely take Sarah, for such a one is an Abraham, though perhaps only just commencing his path from Ur of the Chaldees. But for others without faith this is not allowed. Sarah cannot be wife or mother of Philistines.

This is important truth. In our poor pride we cannot believe that anything can be too high or pure for us, or that through our earthliness heavenly things may be a curse, or that as the air of heaven is death to the fish of the sea raised into it, so the things of the Spirit of God may only destroy and ruin us. And yet when we think of the way in which He who is Love has given, and still gives, the light of truth to a world which lies in darkness, — how He gave it by degrees, under thick veils and shadows, for the space of many hundred years; not surely because He grudged the light, but because mankind could only bear little; — when we think how, even when the Light Himself appeared, after so many thousand years of thick darkness, He yet came under a veil of flesh and blood, allowing only a few who loved Him, and just in proportion as they loved Him, to see His true brightness, when His raiment did shine as the sun, and He was transfigured before them; — when we think of the heathen world, why, with a God of love, they are so left; and of the many Christians, who are God's beloved children, whom yet He leaves in dimness all their days, seeming even at times providentially to keep them from more light, though light is all around; — when we remember that He who acts thus is the only wise and loving God, we may be sure that the light of truth is awful as well as blessed, and that there are good reasons for giving it little and little, and for leaving man for a season " in the lowest parts of the earth."

The truth is, things in earth or heaven are good or otherwise to us, not according to their own intrinsic goodness, but according to our fitness to deal with them. Being what we are, God's best things would consume us. Therefore in love (for indeed God's judgments are love) is fallen man shut out from open vision of heavenly things. Therefore is the Incarnation the way the Lord has met us, a veil covered with cherubic forms, hiding yet revealing heavenly things. Therefore are carnal men kept back from spiritual things, because carnally received they would increase their condemnation. And great as are the sins and judgment of the world, far greater would they be, did not God sometimes interfere to check them in their advance on holy things. Carnal knowledge of grace would not improve them. In mercy therefore are they withheld from it. But men of faith have failed to declare this as they should, so that worldly men like Abimelech can reprove the Abrahams. And however believers may justify to themselves the equivocations, by which the world are deceived to think that as the world they may have part or lot in the New Covenant, neither God nor man will hold them guiltless. The Lord may indeed forgive the sin, but Abraham must confess it, so that henceforth, if he cannot help, at least he may not by his blessings be a snare to others.

This lesson learnt, the believer is not far from the attainment of that fruitfulness which he has so long waited for. Being so far purged, he is fit to bear good fruit; and the fruit is borne, not to his own joy only, but like Isaac to the joy of many others. For when Isaac comes, a covenant is made with Philistines.[11] If they cannot be Sarah's sons, they shall in their place at least receive some blessing through Abraham. We shall see this when we come to Isaac's life. Would to God that all through grace had reached it. Then the Lord shall hear the heavens, and the heavens hear the earth, and the earth shall hear the corn and wine and oil, and they shall hear Jezreel. For He will sow her unto Himself in the earth, and will say to them that were not His people, Ye are my people, and they shall say, The Lord is our God.

[11] Chap. xxi. 27–34.

PART 5

ISAAC, OR THE SPIRIT OF SONSHIP

Chapter 21-26

" Now we, as Isaac was, are the children of promise."—GAL. iv. 28.

" We have received the spirit of adoption, whereby we cry, Abba, Father."—ROM. viii. 15.

ISAAC, OR THE SPIRIT OF SONSHIP

Chapters 21-26

AT this stage, when Adam, and Cain and Abel, and Noah, and Abraham and Lot, have already shewn themselves; when in the inward life we have known the old man, and the strivings of flesh and spirit, and regeneration; and the spirit of faith has been freed from much that impeded it in the earlier stages of its pilgrimage; — at this stage appears another form of life, rightly called Isaac or laughter,[1] because it brings great joy with it, the spirit of sonship, the fruit of Abraham or faith, another development of the elect spirit, another shade of the light of life in man. For not only do many forms of life grow out of the old man, before the true spirit of sonship or adoption is born in us; but even the elect spirit, which in due time is to produce this, (though from the first it contains it as the root holds the flower, and as Levi was in the loins of Abraham when Melchisedek met him,) does not bring it forth until other forms of life have first been produced and manifested. The stem must bud and grow before the fruit comes forth. So Adam, and Abel, and Noah, and Abraham, that is, the old man, and flesh and spirit, and regeneration, and the life of faith, must precede in our

---

[1] Heb. יִצְחָק, from צָחַק, *to laugh.*

souls (as the root and stalk precede the fruit) that spirit of sonship which Isaac represents, as Isaac or sonship must again precede that evangelic service which Jacob typifies. Abraham, Isaac, and Jacob are types of the divine life in man, manifesting itself in the spirit, in the understanding, and in the body respectively; — for this is only another way of saying that they are the spirit of faith, of sonship, and of service: for sonship is the bringing of the divine life into our understanding, and service is bringing it into our outward and bodily acts; — and this cannot be done at once, but by degrees and successively. Sonship is come, when the things which are in the spirit are in the understanding also. Service is come, when the things which have been in the understanding are seen in the body and wrought outwardly. The subject, like all which is of God, is infinite. We only make it definite by not touching the infinite.[2]

Each of these then is the same elect spirit, only seen at different stages of its development, and taking at each stage a different form, by which the same One Spirit may shew itself in its sevenfold variety. The Holy Ghost in all supplies the common light-power; but the creature gives to the colourless light a medium by which it may variously reflect itself. For as the same one light of the sun

---

[2] It may interest some to mark how Abraham, Isaac, and Jacob, as they figure the divine life in man, also figure something of the life of God Himself. That they have been so regarded by some is well known. The Fathers hesitate not to say, that in Abraham, Isaac, and Jacob, they see types of the ways and works of the Father, the Son, and the Holy Ghost. The quotations given below, on the dispensational view of chapters xxii. xxiv. &c., are examples of this. Blind leaders of the blind may urge this exposition as opposed to that which I have given here. But the one is the very reason and ground of the other. Our life as saints is but the result of our being made partakers of the divine nature. If He lives and walks in us, our ways must resemble His ways, and hence the life of the elect will be a reflection of His life.

appears to us different, through the reflecting medium of the atmosphere of the planet which intercepts it, by which, according to the peculiar fitness of each for reflection, one star differeth from another star in glory; so in us the one same Spirit of God shews variously through the different mental atmospheres which are furnished by the successive stages of man's development. Fair indeed is the form of life now reached in Isaac, in whom to faith is added knowledge, — for the spirit of sonship is a spirit of understanding also, — an Isaac indeed, that is, joy, to all who possess it, and bringing gladness not to Abraham's house alone, but to many afar off.

Let us note some of the features of this much longed-for child, the circumstances of his birth, and the treatment which he at once meets with.

I. — The Birth of Isaac, and its Results

Chapter 21

THREE facts are recorded : — Isaac is born contrary to nature ; then, while yet he is a babe, his blood is shed in circumcision ; then at his weaning he is mocked by Hagar's son. Such is and must be every Isaac's history.

First, he is born out of the common course of nature, when Abraham and Sarah are both " as good as dead ; " for Abraham was now " a hundred years old," and Sarah was " barren " and " past age."[1] Then the Lord visited Sarah as He had said, and the Lord did unto Sarah as He had spoken. So comes this form of life in us, through despair of self, " not of blood, nor of the will of the flesh, nor of the will of man, but of God." [2] It springs indeed

---

[1] Chap. xxi. 5, 7, and Heb. xi. 11, 12.　　　[2] John i. 13.

from faith, but not till faith itself by long fruitlessness has learnt its own nothingness, that it is but the channel, not the spring. While therefore the strength of the flesh remains, though other fruit is borne, Isaac is not given us. But Abraham's fleshly strength is now all gone: self-will is no longer looked to as the means of bearing fruit: the true relationship to Sarah is confessed: then out of that long-barren womb comes the promised seed. Isaac is conceived. A new life grows within, soon to shew itself to the joy of faith and of the inward spiritual will.

Then, whilst yet a babe, Isaac's blood is shed in circumcision. "Abraham circumcised Isaac, being eight days old, as God had commanded him."[3] Abraham was ninety years old and nine, when he received this seal:[4] for the spirit of faith, when it first starts, and even when it has crossed Jordan, may be without self-judgment, unchastened, unmortified. How many, in whom faith lives, are yet unjudged, and have not reached to "the putting away of the filth of the flesh" by inward circumcision. But with the spirit of sonship or adoption this cannot be; from the very first this pure life is truly circumcised; and that uncleanness, which faith may carry with it many days, is cut off at once from the new form of life which now is given to us.

Other trials follow, first "weaning," then "mocking." While he is a babe, Sarah herself "gives her son suck." Pure milk at first is Isaac's food. But "the child grew and was weaned, and Abraham made a great feast the same day that Isaac was weaned." Then "the son of the bond-maid mocks" the heir. "He that was born after the flesh persecuted him that was born after the spirit."[5]

---

[3] Chap. xxi. 4.   [4] Chap. xvii. 24.
[5] Chap. xxi. 7-9, and Gal. iv. 29.

So is it now. While this new life is young, it needs milk. At such a stage the carnal seed of faith does not trouble it. But it grows and is weaned. Then a feast indeed is spread, and then the bond-maid's son at once rises up in mockery. If we have reached to sonship, and are in spirit "weaned children," and the milk of our mother can be exchanged for strong meat, then will faith perceive how the fruits of Hagar rise against the purer fruit which Sarah now has brought forth.[6] Then begin fresh trials to faith; for faith now sees that its own first fruits are opposed to the purer spiritual life. How many men of faith have not yet a glimpse of this. We go far before we know that the life which faith first produces in us, a seed loved by us, the fruit of our own efforts, and to get which even Sarah has stirred us up, is at heart a mocker and a persecutor. While it is alone, the real mind of this son of the bond-maid is undetected, save by the eye of God. But when the true fruit of grace is come, faith itself perceives the mockings of Hagar's son. Thus is sonship opposed from the first, not least by that which Abraham himself, that is the spirit of faith, has brought forth and nourished up; by a mind in us, which though of faith is carnal, the fruit of union with Hagar or law, and rather natural than spiritual. But Isaac though mocked, is the heir; and his coming casts out that which had hitherto occupied the house of faith.

Let us mark the results of the coming in of this new life, both in and out of Abraham's house.

[6] "Merito quæritur, cur Abraham nec die quo natus est ei filius, nec die quo circumcisus est, sed die quo ablactatus est, epulum fecerit. Quod nisi ad aliquem spiritalem significationem referatur, nulla solutio quæstionis est, tunc scilicet esse debere magnum gaudium spiritalis ætatis, quando fuerit factus homo novus spiritalis, id est non talis qualibus dicit Apostolus, 'Lac vobis potum dedi,'" &c.—*Augustin. Quæst. in Gen.* l. i. n. 50. Origen notices the same thing.—*Hom.* vii. *in Gen.*

Within the house of faith, Isaac's birth soon leads to the final dismissal of Hagar, with whom her son is sent away. While the new life is yet a sucking babe, Ishmael remains; but when he begins to mock, because "a great feast" is made for the child, who now can bear strong meat, then Sarah says, "Cast out this bond-maid and her son, for the son of this bond-woman shall not be heir with my son, even with Isaac."[7] Sarah yet speaks so, when her son is weaned. While she is barren, while the promise tarries, while as yet the spirit of sonship is not come or only a sucking babe, she endures the presence of the bond-maid and her seed. But when Isaac is mocked, the bond-maid is cast out. Both bondage and law are now dismissed. For a time they have had their place and use with faith. But their work is done when the spirit of sonship is come. They depart now to return no more.

But this casting out "was very grievous to Abraham," not so much on Hagar's as on her son's account.[8] At this stage the giving up of self-will or law is not so trying to faith as the giving up of that form of life which faith has produced out of self-will. But to give up this life, which we ourselves have produced, is "very grievous" even to men of faith. We cling to what we have or are, and are slow to believe that there can be a something better than that we now rejoice in. We cannot think that a life which springs from faith can be cast out, not yet seeing that faith's first fruit is carnal. Faith would, therefore, if it might, keep Ishmael; but the fruit of law and bondage must be given up. Up and onward is the path for evermore. One after another of the things of childhood must be put away.[9] "God said unto Abraham, Let it not be

---

[7] Chap. xxi. 10; Gal. iv. 30.   [8] Chap. xxi. 11.   [9] 1 Cor. xiii. 11.

grievous in thy sight because of the lad: in all that Sarah hath said unto thee, hearken to her voice." [10]   Trying, therefore, as it is to cast out the bond-maid, let us hearken to all that Sarah saith unto us; for "in Isaac only shall the seed be called:" yet also upon the son of the bond-maid will the Lord bestow a suited blessing; for he shall live and beget a mighty seed, because he also, though carnal, is the fruit of faith. [11]

Isaac's birth has results also out of Abraham's house. The Philistine, seeing a son born contrary to nature, comes to Abraham, and seeks peace.   "It came to pass at that time that Abimelech spake to Abraham, saying, God is with thee in all that thou doest.   Now, therefore, swear unto me that thou wilt not deal falsely with me.   And Abraham said, I will swear." [12]   No sooner does the spirit of sonship come, than worldly knowledge in us feels and confesses that God is with faith.   Thenceforth, therefore, it submits.   And the spirit of faith shews kindness to the strange land in which it dwells.   Worldly knowledge is put into its place, but not destroyed.   It even receives good things from faith. [13]   It is not allowed to think that the wells are its work.   The offered lamb is witness that the waters have been drawn by faith's energy. [14]   But withal no unkindness is shewn towards the Philistine.   Worldly knowledge still lives, and faith yet sojourns many days in near contact to it. [15]

Such is this scene within.   Without, in substance it is the same thing.   In this view Sarah and Hagar are the two covenants.   True men of faith beget a double seed.

[10] Chap. xxi. 12.
[11] Chap. xxi. 13.
[12] Chap. xxi. 22, 23.

[13] Chap. xxi. 27.
[14] Chap. xxi. 30.
[15] Chap. xxi. 34.

Some are Hagar's and some are Sarah's children. Those begotten through law are yet the bond-maid's sons. Those whose life is of grace are children of the free-woman. Every church or house of faith will produce both of these. As long as the Isaacs are unweaned, the Ishmaels live with them. But the feast of fat things, provided when Sarah's son are weaned, ever calls forth the hatred and mockery of the children of the bond-woman. Then comes a separation, painful indeed to men of faith, which yet God sanctions, saying, "Hearken to all that Sarah saith unto thee." So the Ishmaels go forth into a dry land, with some portion of the bread of men of faith; but the water for them is only in bottles,[16] — doctrine for them is only in certain forms, — and this is soon spent, and though a well is at hand, and they are faint, their eyes see it not. For they are not accustomed to draw for themselves. And so, when the water in the bottles is spent, because they have only a bottle, they almost perish. Isaac lives by wells, and digs them often, and has strifes for them with Philistines. The bond-maid's sons look not for such streams, and see them not, even though a well is close to them; till God, who yet loves them, sends them help, to point out the well, and give them drink out of it. So they live and grow and dwell in a thirsty land. There with worldly principles, that is "an Egyptian wife,"[17] like Nimrod and Esau, they are "archers,"[18] quick to hunt, ready for controversy and to judge evil; blessed nevertheless for Abraham's sake, and forming a great nation and a mighty people.[19]

---

[16] Chap. xxi. 14–19.

[17] Chap. xxi. 21.

[18] Chap. xxi. 20. Compare Gen. xlix. 22, 23; Judges v. 10, 11; Psalm xi. 2, and xci. 4, 5.

[19] Origen goes into this outward fulfilment at considerable length:—
"Duo sunt ergo filii Abrahæ, unus de ancillâ, et unus de liberâ; uterque tamen filius Abrahæ, licet non uterque de liberâ. . . . Omnes ergo quidem qui per fidem veniunt ad agni-

The fulfilment of all this in the dispensations is well known. When in the course of ages the New Covenant out of the death of the flesh brought forth the promised seed, and sons indeed were born in the Church, then the fleshly seed, because it mocked, was cast out. St. Paul himself expounds this view: — " Neither because they are the seed of Abraham are they all children, but, In Isaac shall thy seed be called ; that is, They which are the children of the flesh, these are not the children of God, but the children of the promise are counted for the seed." [20] In the Acts of the Apostles we may see how the spirit of faith seems to yearn over Hagar's rejected sons, feeling it " very grievous " to give them up. Nevertheless they were dismissed. And then, like Ishmael, though the well of water was nigh at hand, they could not see it ; " for blindness in part was come upon Israel, until the fulness of the Gentiles should come in." [21] The fleshly Jew was cast out ; and then the Gentile, seeing the blessings so richly poured on faith, confessed its power and sought peace. I cannot doubt that the facts of this chapter have a bearing also on the coming age. In this yet future view, Isaac is " the sons

---

tionem Dei possunt filii Abrahæ dici, Sed in his sunt aliqui pro charitate adhærentes Deo, alii pro metu et timore futuri judicii. . . . . Super his cum depelluntur a lacte fit convivium magnum : super illis autem non potest exhiberi convivium, nec haberi lætitia. . . . Dat ancillæ utrem aquæ, non habebat enim puteum aquæ vivæ, nec poterat puer haurire de puteo aquam. Isaac habebat puteos. . . . . Ismahel autem de utre bibit aquam. . . . . Uter legis est litera, de quâ carnalis populus bibit. . . . . bibit de puteis qui profundiora quæque haurit," &c.—*Orig. Hom.* vii. *in Gen.*

[20] Rom. ix. 7, 8. Origen gives this dispensational fulfilment also : —" Populus qui secundum carnem est abjectus tam diu jacet in fame et siti, donec aperiantur oculi synagogæ. Hoc est quod Apostolus dicit esse mysterium, quia cæcitas contigit ex parte in Israel. Ista est ergo cæcitas in Agar. . . . Nunc enim jacent Judæi circa ipsum puteum, sed oculi eorum clausi sunt."—*Orig. Hom.* vii. *in Gen.* The same interpretation is given by Gregory Nyssen, *In Baptism. Christi*, tom. ii. pp. 805, 806. *Ed. Paris*, 1615.

[21] Rom. xi. 25.

of God." The whole creation groaneth and travaileth, waiting for the manifestation of these heavenly children.[22] When they are born from that long dead and barren womb, whence they shall issue when their time is come, then indeed shall be a day of laughter, then shall the bond-maid truly be cast out, then shall the world be glad, and the Lord be known by a new name, " the Everlasting God."[23]

Such a day has in spirit already dawned on some. Oh, may its rising hasten over all the earth.

II.—The Offering up of Isaac

Chapter 22

We have seen what were Isaac's first trials, — spiritually, the earliest experiences which the spirit of sonship or adoption meets here; first, judgment in the flesh, then weaning, then mocking: we are now to see its trials, when, being weaned, it has grown to somewhat of maturity. This much longed-for life, our Isaac or joy, though an heir of grace and promise, is born to be a sacrifice, not that it may perish, but that greater blessings may be reached by it through this self-sacrifice. This too is yet a stage in the way, for the way is the same yesterday, to-day, and for ever.

We read, " It came to pass that after these things God

---

[22] Rom. viii. 19–23.

[23] Chap. xxi. 33. Never before Isaac's birth, is the Lord called by this name, אֵל עוֹלָם, *the Everlasting God.*" By this name He is revealed, not so much the God of a particular family or people, as of an age or dispensation. It asks, "Is He the God of the Jews only? Is He not of the Gentiles also?" Ainsworth translates here, " *Deus æternitatis vel mundi.*"

did tempt Abraham, and said unto him, Abraham, Take now thy son, thine only son Isaac, whom thou lovest, and get thee unto the land of Moriah, and offer him there for a burnt-offering upon one of the mountains which I will tell thee of."[1] Ishmael is not offered, but cast out. Isaac is to be offered up as a sacrifice. This is indeed that cross of Christ, whereby the world is crucified unto us, and we unto the world ; the surrender of that meek life in us, which has been formed by divine power out of faith's nothingness, the special offering of those in whom this Son is come, and who, " if sons, are heirs, if so be that they suffer with Him, that they may also be glorified together ; "[2] a view of the cross much more inward than any known before, so much deeper and nearer to us than Abel's lamb, or Noah's tree which takes us through the waters, that to some it seems to be almost another thing, while yet it is the self-same cross, only now apprehended far more inwardly.

And first to mark Abraham's part in this scene, that is, the part which the spirit of faith takes in this sacrifice. Isaac yields himself, but it is of Abraham God asks him. Abraham it is who girds the ass, and cleaves the wood, and gives up his Isaac, when the Lord requires the sacrifice. For it is faith which gives up the life it has produced to Him by whose strength it has produced it. The Lord would shew how He can fill the heart; how after the flesh and world are left, faith can, if only He remains to it, give up His gifts also, and again be nothing that God may be all, assured that in being nothing it shall obtain all things.

This is the trial here. Can faith give up that much loved life, that son so long waited for, of whom it had been

---

[1] Chap. xxii. 1, 2.   [2] Rom. viii. 17.

said, " In Isaac shall thy seed be called." It is not to leave
this or that outward thing ;—this was done long ago, when
we came out of Ur of the Chaldees;—it is not the trial of
weary pilgrimage, wandering from day to day without a
certain dwelling place; it is not even the giving up of
Hagar's son, the fruit of our own energy, to which our
God now summons us. It is nothing less than to give up
that life, to which all God's promises have so long directed
us, — which He has given to be our joy, and from which
He Himself has bid us expect such blessings, not to ourselves only, but to others, — in the assurance that as He
gave it at the first, He will, though now He seems to take
it from us, give it back again. Faith therefore shrinks
not even here, but binds its own fruit, and gives it back to
God, accounting that He, who can raise up the dead, will
restore the precious life which He first quickened out of
our barrenness.

To do this, Abraham leaves his servants and the ass,[3]
even as faith, when it is tried, leaves behind it all those
thoughts, which, like the servants, by their presence, might
oppose the sacrifice.[4] Thus it travels on to Mount Moriah,
that is to ground chosen of God,[5] for faith dares not choose
its own crosses, or where or when it will endure suffering.

[3] Chap. xxii. 5.

[4] Chrysostom thus comments on
this :—" Suffer not aught of worldly
thoughts to occupy thy soul then.
Bethink thee that Abraham also,
when offering this sacrifice, suffered
nor wife, nor servant, nor any other
to be present. Neither then do thou
suffer any of thy slavish and ignoble
passions to be present with thee;
but go up alone into the mountain
where he went up; and should any
such thoughts attempt to go up with

thee, command them with authority,
and say, ' Sit ye here, and I and the
lad will worship and return to you.'
And leaving the ass and the servants
below, and whatever is void of reason and sense, go up, taking with
thee what is reasonable," &c. *Hom.*
v. on 2 Cor. ii. 17, p. 74 of the
Oxford Translation.

[5] Moriah means "chosen of God."
Heb. מריה, a contraction for מראהיה.
It was in after times the site of the
temple. 2 Chron. iii. 1.

But if in the journey of life trial is appointed, so grievous as to threaten to crush that inward life which is so precious to us, — be the trial what it may, pain, contempt, or misrepresentation, or, what is far more trying to the elect, confusion of soul, inward distraction, desolation, darkness, —whatever it be, if it be God-appointed, let us go onward, the spirit of sonship shall not perish. But let us take heed that we are not on self-chosen ground. Self-chosen penances, self-inflicted pains, are not the sacrifice faith offers upon Mount Moriah ; rather do they savour of horrid Moloch, to whom even Solomon may bow, but whose worship is abomination. Great as those sacrifices may seem which are imposed by self-will, much more precious are those which God calls us to. One day in which we yield our will to Him is of more value than years of toiling self-will. Such yieldings of our will are safe. The life which has sprung from faith cannot perish thus.

For Isaac does not perish here. Being lifted up, he is, as Paul says, " received back again." [6] The spirit of sonship does not die : having been bound upon the altar, it is brought back again, as from the dead, with greatly increased blessedness. This is that inward death and resurrection, which all who possess the spirit of sonship must know in due time ; to be offered up, and yet to live ; to lose our life, and yet to keep it. Thus are we crucified with Christ, nevertheless we live, yet not we, but Christ liveth in us. We bear about in the body the dying of the Lord, that the life also of Jesus may be made manifest in our mortal bodies. We come back to walk awhile with them who tarry with the ass, and have never reached to Mount Moriah, in the knowledge of that, of which those who have

[6] Chap. xxii. 12, and Heb. xi. 19.

so tarried may indeed hear, and even speak about, but have never realised; as men who have endured a real death, and who by it have learned to judge all things here in the light of heaven.

Isaac, though offered, does not die; but something does die there on Mount Moriah. A ram is caught and offered there, and Abraham calls the name of the place Jehovah Jireh.[7] These beasts figure, as we have already seen, the different animal faculties and powers, which are implanted in the creature; against some of which the inward man has to fight, while others may be in measure tamed and made subservient; either, as the ass, to bear the man upon his way, or, as the ox or lamb, to pour out their blood in sacrifice. Of those whose blood is accepted of God, there are some which at times we find it hard to capture. Many a mere animal desire, which we would fain catch and bind, escapes us, even though we pursue it, till, having laid our Isaac on the altar of the Lord, the animal hitherto uncaught is suddenly placed within our reach. Then is it caught and bound by faith; then is it slain, and with joy we say, Jehovah Jireh. "In the mount of the Lord it shall be seen." Now we know that the sacrifice of our Isaac shall not destroy this meek life. What is animal only dies. The man, God's image in us, is not only unhurt, but receives yet more blessing.

And what blessing! "Our light affliction, which is but for a moment, worketh out for us a far more exceeding and eternal weight of glory."[8] For "the angel of the Lord called unto Abraham out of heaven the second time, and said, By myself have I sworn, saith the Lord, for because thou hast done this, and hast not withheld thy son, thine

---

[7] Chap. xxii. 13, 14.   [8] 2 Cor. iv. 17.

only son, that in blessing I will bless thee, and in multi-plying I will multiply thy seed as the stars of heaven and as the sand which is on the sea-shore, and thy seed shall possess the gate of his enemies." [9] Oh, what a gate there is within, held long by our adversary! But the seed of faith shall henceforth keep it, and the enemy be driven out. "And in thy seed shall all nations be blessed." The whole creature shall be a gainer by Isaac's sacrifice. His birth brought blessing to the Philistines' land. His offering shall be felt even beyond Jordan. For the promise is that many far off shall be blessed in him; and lo! at once others are fruitful and blessed in him. So we read, "It came to pass that after these things it was told Abraham, Behold, Milcah, she also hath borne children to thy brother Nahor." [10] I do not doubt that this increase of Nahor's line is recorded here as the commencing fulfil-ment of the Lord's promise. For I know that faith can-not offer thus without great blessing coming through it on the other and lower faculties of the regenerate soul. Not even the beasts shall be barren, for God hath said, "If ye hearken to these judgments, there shall not be male or female barren among you, or among your cattle." [11] The inward life shall radiate to that which is without, and even the outward man be a gainer through the grace of the spirit.

Such is the scene within. The other fulfilments of it are well known. In the outward kingdom of the visible Church, the sons of God have laid down their lives, not to perish, but to live a higher life. Not only have God's sons lived in spite of sacrifice, but great fruit has thence been

[9] Chap. xxii. 15–17.
[10] Chap. xxii. 20–24.

[11] Deut. vii. 14; Exod. xxiii. 26.

found, even among those who before this were barren and scarcely knew God. Need I trace the same act in a higher sphere as fulfilled in Him, who above all others was the well-beloved Son.[12] This view, as indeed the dispensational fulfilment throughout all Genesis, leads us to considerations full of deepest mystery, when we see that God Himself has sacrificed, and that not a mere creature, but His Only-begotten Son. How the sacrifice of Christ in us, when we reach to know the spirit of sonship and its offering, is but the reflection and result of the same thing in God,—how the path of saints is therefore God's own path, and their ways a feeble shadow of His ways,—how every good thing in us is but His work, who, being the living and unchanging God, repeats His ways and works of love on every platform, and who, because He is love, cannot but sacrifice, for love involves sacrifice in its very nature, and God is love,—in a word, how the patriarchal lives, figuring the divine life in man, figure the life of God Himself, Father, Son, and Holy Ghost,—may be seen in the sanctuary, but cannot well be spoken of in an evil world and by such poor tongues as ours. Blessed be His glorious name for ever. We can at least fall down and adore Him for His unutterable love, assured that the whole earth shall be filled with His glory. Amen, and Amen.

And may He give unto us to know yet more the power of Christ's resurrection through fellowship of His sufferings.

---

[12] This view of Isaac's sacrifice is common to nearly all the Fathers. Augustine continually alludes to it: "Nam et Isaac filius Abrahæ, quid erat in figurâ nisi Christus, quando sicut ovis ad immolandum ductus est, et quando sicut Dominus crucem suam, ita et ipsa sibi quibus fuerat imponendus ligna portabat," &c.— *Contra Maximin. Arian.* l. ii. c. 26, § 7, and *De Civit.* l. xvi. c. 32. So too Tertullian, *Adv. Jud.* c. 11; Origen, *Hom.* viii. *in Gen.*; Ambrose, *De Abr.* l. i. c. 8, § 71 and 72; and others.

Then shall these things be seen in us also. The world indeed will not know us, "for it knew Him not;" yet shall it be blessed and made fruitful by our sacrifice. Like the sun, then, far greater than we seem to men, let us shine on, though others here, deceived in us as in the light of heaven, know not our true greatness.

III.—SARAH'S DEATH AND ISAAC'S UNION WITH REBEKAH

Chapters 23 and 24

THE stage now reached, though fulfilled in the inward life of all in whom the spirit of sonship has been offered as a sacrifice, is one hard to describe, partly because of our very imperfect apprehension of what is wrought within, but more because we lack words to express even what we see and feel of these mysteries. Even in the outward world every day we are discovering our need of new words to describe what we apprehend of its powers and agencies, and are slowly labelling as best we can its phenomena, of which after all we know next to nothing. In our outward birth and growth too there are countless things, not only unknown, but unspeakable. How much more, therefore, must we expect to find ourselves unable to describe what is done in the inward world and in the development of the spiritual man. For we want not only heavenly eyes and ears, but a heavenly language for heavenly facts. Nevertheless some things may be said "in part," respecting the fact so fully figured here; for "we know in part, and prophesy in part;" but even this part will shew some of the depths and lengths of the work of our sanctification.

To trace it then within. We have here the death of one

woman and the introduction of another into the elect
house. Sarah dies, and Rebekah is sought and brought
into Sarah's tent, and becomes Isaac's wife.[1] Men are
always certain minds: the women, the affections, more
vaguely the principles, with which they are allied;[2] for
our principles are what our affections are; hence we are not
wrong, as we see in Hagar and Sarah, in saying that the
women figure certain truths. Now Isaac is the spirit of
sonship in us: Rebekah, that affection or principle by
embracing which this spirit in us becomes fruitful. This
scene therefore represents those experiences and exercises
of soul which precede and lead to the union of the spirit of
sonship with that inward affection or principle of truth
by which it bears fruit. The figure here perhaps will be best
expressed, if in these brief and imperfect notes I speak of the
women simply as certain truths. Truth comes successively
or by degrees; in forms, and in successive forms, suited to the
form of that elect spirit to which it is to be united. Thus
new principles, or rather fresh forms embodying the same
principles, are taken into union by the various forms of the
elect spirit, at the successive stages of its development.
The form of truth answers to the spirit which receives it;
and thus truth substantially the same continually puts on
fresh appearances. Truth cannot differ from itself; but
as the same elect spirit at different stages takes different
forms, so the truth which is embraced by that elect at
different stages is seen in different forms also. It dies
out in one form and lives in another, and yet all the forms
may live to God. For as He is the God of Abraham, and

---

[1] Chap. xxiii. 2, and xxiv. 67.

[2] To avoid repetition, I refer to
what has been already said respecting
the typical force of "the woman."

I feel how much our present imperfect terminology hinders the
exact expression of the full meaning
here.

Isaac, and Jacob, and not the God of the dead, but of the living, so is He the God of Sarah and Rebekah and Rachel also, for all in spirit live to Him. Sarah's outward form may die, and as an outward form the truth she figures may die also, but death only gives to the spirit greater liberty, so that her death sets forth the greater spiritualising, even through the destruction of its outward form, of that truth or affection which she represents.[3] And then another form of truth is found, suited to the advancing development of the elect spirit, that is, to Isaac. And thus the elect who as the spirit of faith is joined to truth under the Sarah form, when Abraham is old, when faith is matured, at the next stage as the spirit of sonship is united to Rebekah, not another truth, but another form of it.

In this scene we are shewn how this truth is brought into union with that spirit which is already waiting for it. It is not done without much inward exercise. For every truth is at first more in connection with the natural than with the spiritual man; just as Rebekah was in Laban's house in Mesopotamia, midway between the Tigris and Euphrates. Thus at first each truth is in the memory, in the land between Euphrates and Tigris, that is, between the channels of reasoning and of testimony;[4] and while there it dwells in Laban's house, in the sphere of our outward and natural man. Here it cannot be fruitful with Isaac. Truth therefore needs to be carried hence, and

---

[3] Gregory the Great thus alludes to this: — "Quid nobis per Abrahæ duplex sepulchrum innuitur, ('duplex' referring to the name Machpelah, or 'the double cave,' where Sarah was buried,) nisi quod perfectus quisque extinctam a præsentis vitæ desideriis animam suam, sub bonæ operationis tegmine et contemplationis abscondit,"&c.—*Moral. in Job*, l. vi. c. 37, § 56.

[4] Respecting these rivers, see on chap. ii. pp. 50, 51, above.

conveyed more towards the interior or inward spiritual man; where, united to the true life in us, it may become fruitful and produce fresh forms of life. All that hinders this,—how Laban strives to prevent Rebekah's departure out of Mesopotamia,—how the outward man in various ways holds truths, and would hinder their passing from the sphere of the outward into that of the inward man,—cannot be told, though it is fulfilled every day. The spiritual man may discern within him something of the process; but words are wanting to tell it aright, and not less hearers who could profit by it.

I therefore turn to trace this scene, as it is fulfilled on the wider platform of an age or dispensation. The work is one; but some will see it without, whose eyes are not opened to understand it as it is fulfilled within them.

In this view Isaac is that Son who was born contrary to nature, and mocked, and offered up: who yet was brought back as from the dead, at whose coming the bond-maid's seed were cast out, and a covenant of peace made with the Gentiles. This is the Heir for whom the Bride is sought by Abraham's servant out of a far country.

In this servant who is sent to seek the Bride, we have the figure of the faithful ministers of the house of faith.[5] His commission is to go into that land whence Abraham had been called, and thence to bring a bride. This is one

---

[5] This outward fulfilment is much enlarged on by the Fathers. Gregory the Great says:—"Quis est puer, qui ad deducendam uxorem mittitur, nisi prophetarum ordo, atque apostolorum, omniumque doctorum, qui dum verbum prædicationis bonis mentibus faciunt, ad unamquamque animam unigenito Filio conjungendam, quasi provisores fiunt," &c.—

Apud Paterium, super Gen. l. i. c. 53. So too Origen at great length:— " Puer iste sermo propheticus est, quem nisi susceperis, nubere Christo non poteris. Scito tamen quia nemo inexcitatus sermonem propheticum suscipit, sed qui scit haurire aquam," &c.—*Hom.* x. *in Gen.* So Augustine, *Serm. de Temp.* 75. (al. *App.* 8.)

end of service here, not only to serve within the house of
faith, but at the Master's command to go down among
those who are afar off, to gain some of them. But the
servant doubts and declares his fears,—"Peradventure the
woman will not be willing to follow me;"[6] even as faithful
servants yet at times will question whether their service
will effect anything. To which the Master answers again
foretelling both the company His servants shall have on
their journey, and the result also, saying, "The Lord God
of heaven, even He shall send His angel before thee, and
thou shalt take a wife unto my Son from thence;" and
then, lest the servant shrink from the responsibility,
bidding him only to go and deliver his message;—"then
shalt thou be clear." And surely many a servant's heart
might fail, did he not know that obedience, not success, is
that for which the Master holds him answerable.

The servant's equipment is then described. "He took
ten camels of his master, and of all the goods of his
master in his hand he took something."[7] He does not start
unprovided with means, or lacking precious credentials to
witness of his master's wealth; nor does he take the jewels
of the house of faith alone, but rough things also, suited to
the desert land through which he is to pass, to bear these
good things safely. These camels within, as we have seen,
figure certain animal powers or emotions; outwardly,
therefore, they are that form which is the expression of
these emotions; just as the bride, who within represents

---

[6] Chap. xxiv. 5.

[7] Chap. xxiv. 10. I follow the
rendering of the LXX. and Vulgate
here, which seems to be the most
correct. "Pergens secum de bonis
omnibus domini sui detulit, quia
(doctores) in his quæ de Domino
loquuntur in semetipsis virtutum
divitias ostendunt; et tanto citiùs
ad sequendum Deum pertrahunt,
quanto auditoribus suis in semetipsis
monstrant, quod enarrant." — *Greg.
M. apud Pater. in Gen.* l. i. c. 53.

certain principles, outwardly is that form which embodies these principles, that is, the Church. Thus do faithful servants yet go forth, taking of the things of Christ, to shew them to those who are afar off; content to use rough means, like the unclean camels here, to come to those, who, because they are yet in outward things, could not be reached otherwise.[8]   Some vain servants will not use camels, shewing that they are not wise, even if they are faithful; for without these they do not reach outward men; unlike to Abraham's servant here, unlike to Paul, who was " all things to all men to gain some of them,"[9] who used all he had, rough things as well as smooth, sometimes speaking "as a fool,"[10] and sometimes spiritually, because he really yearned for souls, and was full of true knowledge of the love of the Master's heart.   To him " nothing was common or unclean;"[11] for " to the pure all things are pure."[12]

Thus equipped, the servant goes to that land, between Tigris and Euphrates, whence the elect had come forth.

---

[8] The camel was one of the " unclean " beasts. Lev. xi. 4. Gregory the Great goes at length into the import of this: —" Possunt per camelos, qui ungulam nequaquam findunt, sed tamen ruminant, terrenarum rerum bonæ dispensationes intelligi; quæ quia habent aliquid sæculi, et aliquid Dei, per commune (that is, one partly like the clean, partly like the unclean,) eas necesse est animal designari.   Neque enim terrena dispensatio, quamvis æternæ utilitati serviat, sine perturbatione mentis valet exhiberi.   Quia igitur per hanc et ad præsens mens confunditur, et in perpetuum merces paratur, quasi commune animal, et aliquid de lege habet, et aliquid non habet.   Ungulam namque non findit, quia non se penitus anima ab omni terreno opere disjungit; sed tamen ruminat, quia benè dispensando temporalia, per certitudinis fiduciam cœlestia sperat.   Terrenæ igitur dispensationes, quasi camelorum more, capite legi concordant, pede discrepant; quia et cœli sunt illa, quæ justè viventes appetunt, et hujus mundi sunt ea, in quibus opere versantur." — *Moral. in Job,* l. i. c. 28, § 40.

[9] 1 Cor. x. 20–23.

[10] 1 Cor. iii. 3, and 2 Cor. xi. 21, 23.

[11] Acts x. 15, 28.

[12] Titus i. 15, 16.

We read that "he arose and went," — brief words, marking the zeal and promptness of his obedience. Then, having reached the city of Nahor, he prepares to fulfil his work and deliver the message, with which he is entrusted. First he prays: — "And he said, O Lord God of my master, I pray Thee send me good speed to-day, and shew kindness unto my master Abraham."[13] Whilst he is praying, one comes out of the city to the place where he is standing. To her he speaks words, on which he has already asked God's blessing. Then finding such a response from the damsel as he had asked for, he again worships, bowing his head, and blessing his master's God. Then, when he comes to the house of the desired bride, he will not eat till he tells his tale:—"There was set meat before him, but he said, I will not eat, till I have told my errand." So he opens his mouth, and tells of his master, his glory and greatness, and how he seeks a wife out of this distant land.[14] Who cannot see true service here, beginning with prayer, not for its own so much as for its master's sake, that kindness may be shewn to the absent lord, and not resting till its work is done, and it has uttered something of all his glory; how "He is become great, and has flocks, and herds, and silver, and gold, and men-servants, and maid-servants, and camels, and asses." Thus of old did faithful servants toil, and verily blessed are such servants.

And now to look at the Bride who is thus sought. She is one of Abraham's natural kindred, not a Canaanite, but of the same family as Isaac has sprung from ; only that she is yet in Mesopotamia, and he in the land beyond Jordan.[15] Further, she is an "appointed" person. Twice is it repeated that the woman is not chosen of man, but "the

[13] Chap. xxiv. 12.
[14] Chap. xxiv. 33–49.
[15] Chap. xxiv. 3, 4.

one whom the Lord hath appointed out for his servant Isaac." [16]

All this is true of the true Bride elect. Is she not of the same family as Isaac, and also elect according to God's foreknowledge for Him? " Forasmuch as the children were partakers of flesh and blood, He also Himself took part of the same; for verily He took not on Him the nature of angels, but He took on Him the seed of Abraham." [17] And as such, He seeks His bride not from angels, the spirits beyond Jordan, but from among the dwellers here. Though Himself brought nigh, He forgets not those far off; and out of them His bride is chosen for Him.

The servant finds her at a well. [18] It is while drawing water that she first hears of Isaac. So with many others. Jacob finds his bride, Moses also, by a well, where they had come to draw water. [19] Rebekah not only first hears of Isaac, she also first sees him, by a well, " by the well Lahai-roi." [20] By no chance are the wives found by wells of water. By no chance did Christ " sit thus upon a well." [21] Surely if we have been " betrothed in righteousness," [22] it was by wells of water that the Lord's servant met us. For " understanding is a well of life to him that hath it," [23] and what are means of grace but wells also. We may indeed sit by these wells in vain. Like mocking Ishmael, we may lie close beside them, and yet see no water. But the soul which daily comes to draw, which comes empty, saying, " My soul is athirst," and is exercised to draw and carry home a full vessel, which desires

---

[16] Chap. xxiv. 14, 44.
[17] Heb. ii. 14, 16.
[18] Chap. xxiv. 13.
[19] Chap. xxix. 2–10, and Exod. ii. 15, 16.

[20] Chap. xxiv. 62.
[21] John iv. 6.
[22] Hos. ii. 19.
[23] Prov. xvi. 22.

unasked to make others around who seem in need partakers of the same, and freely gives it them,— such a one, like Rebekah, will find by the waters a guide to lead her to purer and better lands; while those who draw not will scarcely meet him who comes to tell of a lord who waits to receive a stranger.

And indeed it is by her use of this well, that the servant recognises the person whom he is in search of. For the mark, by which he was to know the bride elect, was, that when he asked for drink, she should give it, and then shew her interest in him by caring for his camels.[24] True servants, even as their Lord, who said, "Give me to drink,"[25] like Him, asking something only to give back better things, yet appear at first to come to ask more than to give. We do not see when first they speak that they are givers. But souls who will respond to the claim of love made on them, and are prompt in their attention to the rough and outward things of Abraham's servant, (for all are busy with the "camels" before they see the "jewels,") shall ere long see the ear-rings and bracelets also, and be decked, though yet in the far country, with some of the precious things of Abraham's house.

So we read, "Then the man took a golden ear-ring, and two bracelets, and he put the ear-ring on her face, and the bracelets on her hands."[26] What are these but the precious things of faith, "more precious than of gold which perisheth," brighter than outward pearls or costly array, "the ornament of a meek and quiet spirit, which is of

---

[24] Chap. xxiv. 14, 18, 19. "Puer juxta fontem stetit, atque ex præfixâ sententiâ, quæ puella eligenda esset, proposuit; quia prædicatores sancti, sacri eloquii fluenta considerant, atque ex ipsis colligunt è quibus auditoribus fiduciam certitudinis sumant," &c.— *Greg. M. apud Pater. in Gen.* l. i. c. 53.

[25] John iv. 7, 10.

[26] Chap. xxiv. 22, 47.

great price." [27]   And this is " put upon the hands," as well as " in the ears."   True ministry does not leave the hands of the elect without some fit ornament.   Not content only to fill the ears, it seeks to occupy the hands also with something not less valuable.[28]   At this stage the bride receives but one ear-ring and two bracelets.   After this, when the damsel is already given to him, the servant puts, not one jewel only, but many " precious things of silver and of gold and of fine raiment" upon her.[29]   For there is growth in grace, and " to him that hath shall be given," and she that hath received an ear-ring by the well shall, if she will follow towards Canaan, receive yet more an hundredfold.

This done, she is led to confess who she is.   When Isaac's jewels are on her, she says, " I am the daughter of Bethuel, the son of Milcah, which she bare unto Nahor."[30] Not before she is adorned does she utter this.   So now. A confession there must be from us, — the servant looks for it, — that the bride acknowledge she is one of a fallen people, from whom the seed for God has been separated. But this is not drawn from her until she has received pledges that she is an object of love, and possesses earnests of that to which she is appointed.

After which she declares that she and her house are able and willing to receive the messenger.   He said, " Tell me, I pray thee, is there room for us ?   And she said, We have room enough for thee to lodge in."[31]   How many, if

---

[27] 1 Pet. i. 7, and iii. 4.

[28] " Inaures Rebeccæ pii auditûs insignia, et viriæ ornamenta factorum sunt." — *Ambros. de Abr.* l. i. c. 9, § 89.   So too *Greg. M. ubi supra.*

[29] Chap. xxiv. 53.

[30] Chap. xxiv. 24.

[31] Chap. xxiv. 23, 25.   " Ecclesia

. . . . prædicationis verba in amplo caritatis gremio suscepit.   Doctori enim spatiosus ad manendum locus est in auditoris corde, ... unde et quibusdam dicitur, ' Capite nos, neminem læsimus, neminem corrupimus,' " &c. — *Greg. M. ubi supra.*

questioned, " Is there room enough ? " must confess, if they spake truly, " We have no room ; my father's house, the outward man, is filled up with other things." Like that church at whose door the Master stands, which, thinking itself rich and increased with goods, cares not to open to Him, how many, filled up with self, have no room to receive Him who seeks to lead them heavenward. Not so the soul which has Isaac's bracelets upon her. She has received the gift ; she cannot reject him by whom the gift has come.

Then " she runs and tells them of her mother's house, saying, Thus and thus spake the man unto me."[32] Not content to have received some good thing herself, she tells others, nay, she " runs " to .tell them. Those who have received of the Lord's good things cannot keep silence. They must run and tell others among whom they dwell the good tidings. There may indeed be a speaking about the Lord without grace. Not only are there hearers, but talkers also, who are not doers. But where the heart is full, it must unburden itself, and make others partakers with it, " for out of the abundance of the heart the mouth speaketh."

And now the bride is yet more adorned, not as at first with a single ear-ring or a single bracelet for each hand. Now the servant puts much more on her, " jewels of silver and gold," and (what has not yet been mentioned) " fine raiment " also.[33]   " To her was granted to be arrayed in fine linen ; for the fine linen is the righteousness of saints." [34]   So again it is said, " Hearken, O daughter, and consider ; forget also thine own people and thy father's house : so shall the King greatly desire thy beauty ; for

[32] Chap. xxiv. 28, 30.   [33] Chap. xxiv. 53.   [34] Rev. xix. 8.

He is thy Lord, and worship thou Him. She shall be brought unto the King in raiment of needle-work; the virgins, her companions that follow her, shall be brought unto thee." [35] Raiment, as being that which first meets the eye, and also a sign of our station and employments, represents our habits here. Indeed "habit" is but dress. Here the dress is one marked by great costliness, — "clothing of gold, with raiment of needle-work." And the "fine linen" yet is "raiment of needle-work," wrought "on both sides," with countless stitches, each in itself almost invisible, by which, stitch on stitch, the work is wrought out, until it displays that pattern which pleases the master's eye. This now is put upon the bride, while "her brother and mother also receive precious things," [36] for the world too profit by the Church's call, though they will not leave their Mesopotamia to find a better land.

One thing yet remains to be done. The bride must leave her kindred and father's house. The servant came, not to make his home there, but to take some from that far country to share in Isaac's lot. But the bride has friends who would delay her going, saying, "Let her abide with us, at least a few days," —brothers, who, though they welcomed the messenger, would yet keep him in that land where they will continue to live, and where they die.[37] But the servant cannot stay. Then they say, "We will call the damsel, and inquire at her mouth. And they

[35] Psalm xlv. 10, 11, 14.

[36] "Quæ enim priùs inaures et armillas recepit, jam nunc vasa aurea et argentea ac vestes accepit, quia sancta Ecclesia quæ antè per fidem, obedientiam, et operationem percepit, excrescens postmodum etiam ad spiritalia dona convalescit, ut prophetiæ spiritu et virtutum gratiâ repleta, ampliatis jam muneribus ditescat. Puer verò matri ejus ac fratribus dona obtulit, quia gentilitas ex quâ Ecclesia ad fidem venit, post conversionem ejus in gloriâ temporali convaluit," &c.— *Greg. M. ubi supra.*

[37] Chap. xxiv. 54–58.

said unto her, Wilt thou go with this man? And she said, I will go." By the well she could not have said all this. She did not say it even when the first jewels were put upon her. But now she has heard of the glory of her lord, and that he waits for her, and, spite of flesh and blood and its hindrances, she says, "I will go."

Nor are these vain words. "She arose, and her damsels, and they rode upon the camels,"—for she too must use a camel yet, though she shall surely "light off it when she beholds Isaac." [38] Thus "she followed the man." But the rough things which bear her shall soon be changed for the heart of Isaac and the secret of his tabernacle. O blessed day! Then indeed all the tears, and sufferings, and labours, which must be travelled through, shall seem as a dream, not worthy to be compared with the glory that shall be revealed in us. O Lord, Thou hast called us to this end. Keep us as Thine own, unspotted from the world, till we are for ever with Thee. Amen.

IV.—KETURAH, AND ISAAC AT LAHAI-ROI

Chapter 25:1-11

AT this point Abraham takes another wife. Here, as throughout, every fact and word presents the exactest figure of that which is wrought within at this stage of man's development. But before we come to this, let us recall one peculiarity of that development.

I allude to this, that as our inward life changes its form at every fresh stage,—from Adam to Abel, then from Seth to Noah, then to Abraham, and from him to Isaac and

---

[38] Chap. xxiv. 61, 64.

other sons,—so the truth embraced at each successive stage differs in form according to the varying form of the elect spirit which embraces it. Sarah is Abraham's wife; in other words, the spirit of faith lays hold of truth under the Sarah form, that is, the promise; but the spirit of sonship loves another form of the same, as we read, "Isaac took Rebekah, and brought her into Sarah's tent, and she became his wife, and he loved her." [1]

But there is more than this; for faith not only embraces truth under a form somewhat different from that which the spirit of sonship apprehends; but the spirit of faith itself, as it fulfils its course, lays hold of several different principles. Isaac has but one wife; as in us the spirit of sonship never embraces any but the one true principle of the New Covenant. But Abraham and Jacob each have more. For faith at first takes law, hoping thereby to be fruitful in its own strength;[2] while Jacob or service, as we shall see, though wishing only to have the spiritual, finds that it has unintentionally embraced that which is first and natural.[3]

The stage we now have reached is marked by Abraham taking another wife. We read, "Then again Abraham took a wife, and her name was Keturah; and she bare him Zimran, and Jokshan, and Medan, and Midian, and Ishbak, and Shuah." [4] Now, after Sarah's death, that is, after the form in which we have first embraced the New Covenant as a form is dead, for it yet lives in spirit;—when we see that forms of truth, even the best, are given to serve us for a season, and then as forms to pass away;—when this is not only believed but known, and a new form of truth,

---

[1] Chap. xxiv. 67. See above what has been said on this subject, on chap. xxiii.

[2] See above, on chap. xv.

[3] See below, on chap. xxix.

[4] Chap. xxv. 1, 2.

suited to the growing spirit of sonship, is found and loved by it ; — at this point Abraham takes another wife : that spirit of faith, so long without fruit, which in its haste tried law, and " when as good as dead " begot the seed of promise out of the barren free-woman, now takes another form of truth, by which it rapidly produces many sons. The question is, What form of truth ? What principle is it that Keturah represents ?

Now, though we have not an Apostle's word to tell us, as in the case of Hagar and Sarah, the spiritual import of this third wife, we have or may have, if we will wait, that same Teacher, even the Spirit, which was in saints of old ; for the Light of their light remains undimmed, nearer to us than its most faithful witnesses, soon to shine, (Is not the morn already breaking ?) not upon a few, but over the whole earth. Of course, if a soul though elect has reached only to the Noah stage, this scene will not be understood. Even though Abram lives in us, if we are only now leaving Ur of the Chaldees, — if Terah is with us, — if the bond-maid is not gone, — nay more, if Sarah yet is in the flesh, — Keturah cannot be known, for she only comes when Sarah as an outward form has passed away. But if this is done, then Keturah will come, and indeed has come in thousands who are fruitful by her in spirit, though in their understanding they do not know her name.

For Keturah is that practical truth, which, neither law nor promise, neither bond-maid nor free-woman, succeeds to both at this stage of faith's life, when the truth which Sarah represents has passed from an outward form into a higher state. St. Paul's epistles are full of Keturah. All those exhortations which are not mere law, and which as clearly are not the promise, though they are meant to follow it, are this third wife, given to be embraced by those

in whom Sarah or the New Covenant has already borne
fruit. But this sort of truth does not attract the believer,
until Sarah passes into a higher sphere. Then we take
Keturah to wife. She is, as her name imports, " a savour
of a sweet smell."[5] And her fruits are sweet to God and
man, though, like Midian; they may soon be corrupted and
even oppose the chosen line. How many lovely fruits
have there been borne, the offspring of faith, and that not
by law, but by the precious truth which Keturah represents,
— fruits of ascetic life, which have proved in the event to
be prejudicial, or at least opposed, to the highest inward
life. Indeed the word " ascetic " means in itself simply
practical.[6] Its conventional sense declares the common
end of such efforts, answering exactly to the course and
destiny of Keturah's sons.[7] Such fruits, sweet as they are,
one and all are liable to rapid deterioration. They possess
indeed some of the good things of faith,[8] but from the first
they are distinguished by faith from the spirit of sonship,

---

[5] Heb. קטורה, *incense.* Compare
this with what St. Paul says of practical truth, Phil. iv. 18, and Heb.
xiii. 16.   Origen, having argued
that some mystery must be hid
under this union of Abraham with
Keturah,—first, from the fact, that he
who was " as good as dead " in his
hundredth year, now at a hundred
and thirty-seven begets many sons ;
secondly, from the analogy of the
other two wives, both of whom, according to St. Paul, were certain
principles ; thirdly, because he who
marries truth, though it may die out
in one form, will always hold it in
another ; in which sort of marriage
the older we are the more fruit we
may bear, as Abraham here did, —
thus defines what principles Keturah
represents : — " Denique Cethura,

quam nunc senex Abraham sortitur
in matrimonium, θυμίαμα interpretatur, quod est incensum vel bonus
odor. . . Si quis ergo vestrûm est in
quo suavitas misericordiæ, si quis
sine intermissione orando offert Domino semper incensum, et dicit,
' Dirigatur oratio mea sicut incensum
in conspectu tuo, elevatio manuum
mearum sacrificium vespertinum,'
hic Cethuram duxit uxorem. . . .
Profectus etenim sanctorum Scriptura figuraliter per conjugia designat," &c.—*Hom.* xi. *in Gen.*

[6] 'Ασκητικός.

[7] See Numb. xxv. 16, 17, and
Judges vi. 1, 2, for examples of the
way in which Midian, one of Keturah's sons, may injure and oppress
the elect seed.

[8] Chap. xxv. 6.

which is the true heir.   Isaac is not Keturah's son.   Sonship is not of law, nor of that practical truth, which, though
not law, is somewhat akin to it.   Sonship will no more
come of these than figs will grow from slips of myrtle, or
vines from planting acorns.   Yet Keturah's sons, like oaks
and myrtles, are lovely too, and pleasant in their season,
though they cannot inherit all Abraham's good things.

"Then Abraham gave up the ghost and died." [9]   The
spirit of faith, like that truth which it has so long been
united to, now passes away as an outward form from forms,
to live as a spirit with God who is a Spirit.   Isaac now
succeeds to Abraham's place.   The form, in which the elect
life henceforth shews itself, is not faith so much as understanding, for the spirit of sonship is also a spirit of understanding.   He, in whom it lives, not only believes, but to
faith has added knowledge and intelligence, even "the
mind of Christ."   For when Isaac is come, we are no more
under the schoolmaster, as servants or children not knowing a father's will; but as sons, and because we are sons,
are led in the spirit of sonship into all knowledge and
spiritual understanding, even to the full assurance of understanding in the acknowledgment of the mystery of God the
Father and of Christ. [10]   Up to this point, though the
spirit of sonship has come, it has been comparatively
feeble, and faith has been the ruling life.   But now faith
is no more in the flesh, but is changed from an earthly
form into a spirit.   Isaac therefore takes Abraham's place ;
that is, faith is succeeded in our souls by spiritual understanding, which like Isaac inherits all Abraham's wealth,
and is his heir, possessing all the riches of true faith. [11]   I
feel how little words can express the spiritual reality repre-

[9] Chap. xxv. 8.   [10] Col. ii. 2.   [11] Chap. xxv. 5.

sented here. Those only who know the blessed fact within
will be able really to see the force of Abraham's death and
Isaac's succession to all his goods; faith now lost in sight,
while in its place the spirit of understanding, which is the
spirit of sonship, inherits the things of faith.[12]

Soon Isaac has even more. "It came to pass after the
death of Abraham, that God blessed his son Isaac." If we
ask, How? we are told only this, that "he dwelt by the well
Lahai-roi:"[13] this was his blessing. And this is a blessing
yet. To us few blessings would be greater than a spiritual
dwelling by this same living well. Lahai-roi means "the
life of vision."[14] It was the place where life and vision
were preserved after the angel of the Lord had spoken and
revealed himself. It figures that depth of the word, into
which we drink, when "the well of the living and seeing,"
that is the spiritual sense, is really opened to us.[15] Nature

---

[12] Saints of old spoke much of
this. They may seem at times to
have drawn the line too widely
between πίστις and γνῶσις, and πι-
στικός and γνωστικός; but there is
important truth in the distinction.
That we know so little of faith
changing to knowledge, shews where
we are. See John viii. 31, 32, where
our Lord promises to "those who
believed on Him," that " if they
would continue in His word, they
should *know* the truth, and the truth
should make them free." Compare
also St. Paul's *faith* in Christ dead
and risen again, 1 Cor. xv. 3, 4,
with his longing desire " to *know*
Him, and the power of His resurrection," Phil. iii. 10 ; and his prayer
for those of whose "*faith* he had
heard," that " the Father of glory
would give them the spirit of wisdom
and revelation in the *knowledge* of
Him," &c. Eph. i. 15, 17, 18. See

also 1 Cor. ii. 5, 6. Those who wish
to consult the Fathers will find some
striking thoughts on this subject,
Clem. Alex. Strom. l. vi. c. 9, and
l. vii. c. 10, and *Origen. in Job*, t.
xix. pp. 263, 264. Ed. Huet.

[13] Chap. xxv. 11.

[14] So Gesenius and others translate the name. The LXX. render
it τὸ φρέαρ τῆς ὁράσεως, " *the well of
vision*." I may add that, in chap.
xvi. 13, 14, where the name first
occurs, the true translation in verse
13 seems to be,—" Have I even seen,
(*i. e.* have I my sight preserved,)
after my vision?" Therefore the
well was called Beer-Lahai-roi, " *the
well of the life of vision* ;" because
here life was preserved after seeing
the angel of the Lord.

[15] " Puteus viventis et videntis,
(*i. e.* Lahai-roi,) est sacræ Scripturæ
profunditas, quam nobis ad irriga-
tionem mentis præbuit omnipotens

cares not to drink of such a spring. The waters are too deep for the carnal, who, if they see them, only wonder and pass on. But Isaac loves the well. In his eyes it is not his least blessing, that he may dwell and drink here. Blessed it is, like Abraham, to dwell at Bethel and Hebron, by faith to rest in worship and happy fellowship. Blessed is it to see Salem and her king; in peace to eat the holy bread and wine. Blessed is it to know Beer-sheba, the well of the oath; to drink the refreshing streams which the word of the covenant makes to flow around us. But more blessed far is Beer-Lahai-roi, the well of the life of vision, where we learn to live among and see unseen things. None dwell here but the pure in heart. None else see God, or the hidden things of God. Others will see the world, or themselves, or their own or others' sins, or even certain doctrines. But the " pure in heart see God;" [16] and there, beholding His glory, are changed step by step into His image, to see as He sees things which eye hath not seen, even the things which the Spirit reveals to them who walk with God. O Lord, give unto me thus to dwell at Lahai-roi; to know yet more and more of this blessed life of vision; not only to visit the well, and depart, but, like Isaac, to abide and learn there, until in Thy presence, still blessed in Thee, this " life of vision " shall be mine for evermore.

Such is this scene within. Like all the rest it has its

Deus." — *Greg. M. apud Paterium*, l. i. *supr. Gen.* c. 53. "Hæc est benedictio, quâ benedixit Dominus Isaac, ut habitaret ad puteum visionis. Intelligentibus grandis est ista benedictio. Utinam et Dominus mihi donet hanc benedictionem, ut habitare merear ad puteum visionis. . . . Si non solùm secundùm literam sed aliquid et secundùm spiritum attingere potuero, videbor apud puteum visionis," &c. — *Orig. Hom.* xi. *in Gen.*

[16] Matt. v. 8.

fulfilments in the outward world, and in the dispensations also.

Outwardly, Abraham here represents men of faith, now matured and richly blessed : Keturah's sons, those children of faith whose spiritual life has sprung out of the affection of practical truth, rather than out of either law or promise. Such souls, the distinctive mark of whose life is a peculiar reverence for religious practices tending to asceticism, will in the next generation shew marks of deterioration, in a greater zeal for what is outward than for what is truly spiritual ; and become, like Midian, snares to Israel,[17] though a Moses may find a wife there,[18] and a Jethro of this seed be " for eyes " to the elect, when they come into the wilderness.[19]   But they are not the chosen heirs.   Sarah's sons, the children of promise, are the seed which shall inherit all things.

In the dispensations also this scene is fulfilled.   When Sarah, that is, the Gospel dispensation, has, even as Hagar or law, run its full course; when the marriage of the Bride is come ; then appears not only one seed or son in Abraham's house, but many seeds.   So shall it be when the Son obtains His rights; when faith is changed to sight, and the children of the promise are blessed, and know the life of vision; while others, born after the marriage of the Bride, are witnesses that in Abraham all nations shall be blessed.   Then not only shall the favoured " vine and fig-tree " be glad, but " the field shall be joyful, and all that is therein : then shall all the trees of the wood rejoice before the Lord ; " (though the vine still differ from the oak, and the fig and olive from the pine-tree;) " for He cometh,

---

[17] Numb. xxv. 17, 18.
[18] Exod. ii. 15, 16, 21.

[19] Exod. xviii. 1, 24, and Numb. x. 29–32.

for He cometh to judge the earth : He shall judge the world with righteousness, and the people with His truth." [20]

When that day dawns, may we be with that Son, whom the Father hath appointed Heir of all things, to share His joys, blessed not only by Him, but with Him, drinking of the water of life, "the life of vision," for ever. Amen.

V. — The Trials of Isaac respecting Seed

Chapter 25 : 12-23

The stage now reached is one of high blessing. Abraham no longer lives in earthly form. Faith henceforward is no more in the flesh, but is changed from an outward form into a spirit which sees God ; while Isaac takes Abraham's place : that is, faith is succeeded in our souls by spiritual understanding, which, like Isaac, dwells at Lahai-roi, and is Abraham's heir, possessing all the riches of true faith. Yet even here the elect must still be tried. He desires fruit, but for long years Rebekah is barren.[1] Infinite love ordains it thus for good. With such rich gifts the soul requires some check to keep it healthy. Thus delays, which try our patience, are needful for us, as the shade and cool of evening, which seems to stay their growth, is needful to the plants as much as warmth and sunshine. Such delays are really rests ; for unbroken joy, like constant sunshine, would parch the spirit ; while in these rests our God and Father teaches His elect their own insufficiency, and that all their fresh springs are in Him alone.

The trial here then is again respecting fruit, and it touches Isaac both directly and indirectly. At the very

---

[20] Psalm xcvi. 12, 13.　　　　　　　　[1] Chap. xxv. 21.

time he is lamenting his own barrenness, Ishmael, the seed
of Hagar, is seen to increase rapidly.   Thus there is grief,
first, from the elect's own weakness, and then, from the
rapid growth of the carnal seed; to find the fruit of the
spirit so late in manifesting itself, and the fruit of the
flesh so early, strong, and numerous.

The spread of Ishmael's seed comes first; that carnal
spirit, which springs from the union of faith with law
within us, begets many forms of life.   " These are the
generations of Ishmael, whom Hagar, Sarah's handmaid,
bare unto Abraham: these are their names, according to
their generations; Nebajoth, and Kedar, and Adbeel, and
Mibsam, and Mishma, and Dumah, and Massa, Hadar,
and Tema, Jetur, Naphish, and Kedemah, twelve princes
according to their nations." [2]   Thus spreads the carnal seed.
The elect, the spirit of sonship and understanding in us,
may be at Lahai-roi.   Grace may have bestowed a well of
vision.   Instead of naked Adam, there may be the spirit
which like Isaac has offered itself to God, which is beloved
and blessed of Him.   Yet all this checks not the growth
of the flesh, and that even while the elect spirit in us is
mourning its own barrenness.   For the fleshly seed breaks
forth as it will: it has " children at its desire ; " [3] it " is not
in trouble like other men, neither is it plagued like other
men; therefore pride compasseth it as with a chain, violence covereth it as a garment." [4]   The sons of God must
often say, " My time is not yet, but your time is always
ready: " [5] "we are weak, but ye are strong ; we are despised,
but ye are honourable." [6]   The flesh has no such delays.
It brings forth its fruits of wrath and envy and emula-

---

[2] Chap. xxv. 13–16.   [5] John vii. 6, 8.
[3] Psalm xvii. 14.   [6] 1 Cor. iv. 10.
[4] Psalm lxxiii. 5, 10.

tion, even though the spirit dwells at Lahai-roi. And the very grace bestowed upon the inner man seems at times only to excite the flesh to greater activity and open opposition.

Meanwhile the spirit waits from year to year, sighing for, yet not seeing, the seed the Lord has promised it. Isaac is sorely tried. For twenty years Rebekah, the beloved of his heart, is " barren," and produces no fruit.[7] Then, having conceived, she feels two different lives, opposing each other within, even before they shew themselves. Thus barrenness first causes grief. That is removed. Then fruitfulness brings with it fresh disquietude. A cross there must be, to keep us low, and to shew the unfailing resources of God our Saviour.

Rebekah is spiritual truth.[8] Such truth should not only be a living and active principle in us, but should produce other forms of life. For this end is it given. Nevertheless, for years after sonship is mature in us, it brings forth no fruit. It rests in peace at Lahai-roi, but the new life of service, which it should produce, is not yet manifested. Nor does Isaac feel this at first. But Hagar's seed increase. Rebekah still has no child. Then he cries to the Lord for help, and is heard. " The Lord was entreated of him, and Rebekah conceived seed."

So is it yet. That form of truth, which the spirit of sonship has embraced as a living principle by which to be fruitful, lives within us for awhile before it bears fruit. But the elect still waits on God. Faith may try carnal means, may take a Hagar: the spirit of sonship cannot do

[7] Chap. xxv. 21. Compare verse 20, — "Isaac was forty years old when he took Rebekah to wife," with verse 26, — "Isaac was threescore years old when she bare Esau and Jacob."

[8] See on chap. xxiv.

so. It may be fruitless, but it will not embrace law. It is in itself a proof of God's almighty power. To Him therefore it cries for strength, and Rebekah is no more barren; in God's strength she bears fruit.

But this fruitfulness has its pains also. Rebekah no sooner conceives, than she is sorely disquieted. "The children struggled within her, and she said, If it be so, why am I thus?"[9] And so the truth which the spirit loves, when at length it labours to bring forth another life, is felt to contain two distinct elements. Till it conceives, we do not perceive this. Nevertheless, it is so. We say of that truth which Rebekah figures, that it is spiritual; and so it is. But we are deceived if we think that therefore, as apprehended by us, it is unmixed and wholly free from outward things. Our understanding can only possess forms of truth, and to these certain fallacies connected with the senses invariably connect themselves. Hence, when at this stage the spirit in us by the truth has begotten a new life, the inherent difference of the elements which go to form the truth makes itself felt, even before these differing elements are distinctly developed into separate forms of outward life. At the faith stage this is not known. But now, when the spirit of understanding is come, it is first felt, and then its cause is understood. Happy should we be, could we bear only Jacobs; but formed as we are, if our principles are fruitful, the seed will to the end be diverse, and inward struggling must be the result.

Here then we learn the reason of that inward strife or conflict, which so often re-appears in the progress of the elect spirit. The Lord Himself teaches us why it must be; at the same time promising that the first and natural shall in the end give place to the spiritual:—"Two nations

[9] Chap. xxv. 22.

are in thy womb, and two manners of people shall be separated from thy bowels, and the one people shall be stronger than the other people, and the elder shall serve the younger."[10] Thus even Isaac begets him whom God hateth,[11] and thus, though sonship is come, do we feel the same old contest which was waged from the beginning,— "the flesh lusting against the spirit, and the spirit against the flesh, so that we cannot do the things that we would;" and this not from Hagar's seed alone, but even in the fruit of Isaac, the true and beloved heir. So it must be while we are in this tabernacle. A seed cast into the earth draws into union with its life the nature of the soil wherein it shoots forth. According to its soil the selfsame plant varies its hue and form. In it is both the vegetable life, and the life's clothing, which is of the earth earthy. So the wind, which breathes from the south, comes mixed with odours, testifying over what it has passed, and what it bears with it. So with the spiritual seed. The womb it grows in is of the earth. Hence with the heavenly in us the earthy grows also. We forget this, and therefore are troubled. But He, who hath loved us, " knoweth our frame, and remembereth that we are dust," and will work His pleasure in us spite of that flesh, the deformity of which His indwelling makes even more apparent.[12]

---

[10] Chap. xxv. 23.

[11] "Esau have I hated." — Mal. i. 23 ; Rom. ix. 12, 13.

[12] After alluding to the outward fulfilment of this scene, as one which needed no comment, Origen thus gives the inward application : — "Et de singulis nobis hoc dici potest, quia duæ gentes, et duo populi intra nos sunt. Nam et virtutum populus, et vitiorum, intra nos est. De corde enim procedunt cogitationes malæ, adulteria, furta, et his similia. Vides quantus malorum populus intra nos est. Si vero mereamur illam vocem dicere Sancto Spiritui, 'A timore tuo, Domine, in utero concepimus,' . . . tunc et alius intra nos populus invenitur in spiritu generatus. Fructus enim spiritus est charitas, gaudium, pax," &c. — *Orig. Hom.* xii. *in Gen.* So too *Augustin. in Psalm.* cxxxvi. (*E. V.* 137,) § 18.

Such is the scene within. In the world without, Rebekah is that body which is formed by the truth, that is, the true Church, whose barrenness oft-times afflicts God's sons, while Ishmael's seed, the children of law, increase and multiply. But the true Church is fruitful through prayer. Then comes fresh grief, to find in the same one mother a double and conflicting seed, who, like the chaff and the wheat, though from one root and stalk, are destined to a very different end, the one to be gathered safely into the garner, the other to be rejected and burnt up.[13] But the very nature of the Church, even as of truth, whilst upon earth, involves the presence of an outer as well as an inner element; and this, though we may not see it in the Church's constitution, (though it is there,) will surely come out and shew itself in her double seed.[14] What son of God has ever loved and preached the truth, without discovering ere long that from the self-same seed, within the same household of God, proceed two diverse families; one, akin to that part of the truth which is outward; the other, to that which is more inward and spiritual. Thus, in the one Church two seeds grow and strive, causing no little pain to their perplexed mother. If hereby she is led to the Lord, though perplexed, in His presence she is taught His purpose and learns to trust in Him.

[13] Matt. iii. 12.

[14] Augustine often refers to this outward fulfilment. Commenting on the words, in Psalm cxxvi. (*E. V.* 127,) 3, "the fruit of the womb is His reward," he says, "Cujus ventris? Ecclesiæ; in cujus ventre, quia ejus typum Rebecca gestabat, duo illi gemini tamquam duo populi luctabantur. Una mater in visceribus suis dissentientes fratres nondum natos continebat: pulsabant materna viscera discordiis internis. Sic et modo, quamdiu gemitus datus est ecclesiæ, quamdiu, parturit ecclesia, ipsi sunt intus et boni et mali. . . . Jacob dilexi, dicit Deus, Esau autem odio habui. Ambo de uno utero processerunt: unus amari meruit, alius reprobari." See also *Serm.* 4, *Class.* i. *De Jac. et Esau;* and *Tract.* xi. § 10, *in Johan.* iii. 3, 4.

VI. — ISAAC'S TWOFOLD SEED, THE ELDER AND THE YOUNGER

Chapter 25:24-34

Two new forms of life now appear. Those minds, the legitimate fruit of the spirit of sonship in us, whose mutual opposition has been felt ere they were seen, now manifestly shew themselves. There is still a double seed,— "two sons," — "the elder and the younger," who shew through life their essential unlikeness to each other, until at last the younger overcomes. These "two" at each stage are always flesh and spirit: "that is not first which is spiritual, but that which is natural."[1] But as we advance, and man is more and more developed, both flesh and spirit are apprehended and shew themselves in different forms. We have seen how man becomes regenerate man, and how regenerate man is developed into the man of faith, and again how the man of faith through many trials is developed into man possessing the spirit of sonship and understanding. So the flesh at each stage re-appears in some new form. Cain, Ishmael, and Esau, all are "that which is first and natural." But in Cain we have the fleshly mind as it grows out of Adam, that is, the mere natural man. Ishmael is the same carnal mind, as it springs, through intercourse with law, out of a true man of faith. Esau is this same flesh, as it grows out of one in whom the spirit of sonship lives and walks with God. So strong is this root in us, so quick stage after stage to shew itself, not only in that which is of the flesh, but in connection also with that which is elect and spiritual; a

[1] 1 Cor. xv. 46.

sad witness of the rock whence we are hewn, and the hole of the pit whence we are digged.

In Isaac's sons, then, we see the flesh and spirit, as they grow out of one in whom the spirit of sonship is the ruling life. Here we have the flesh at the best. Esau is in many respects lovely and lovable; outwardly, a great advance on Cain, yet at heart still carnal, sensual, devilish. Jacob on the other hand does not shew so well as some of the earlier forms of the elect life. For the spirit here is not the spirit of faith or sonship, but of service, instinctively "laying hold with its hands," to bring the natural man, or so much of it as it can win, into subjection to a higher life. In this attempt the spirit goes through much toil, which, though in its result it advances the elect, in the performance brings to light weaknesses which we have not seen hitherto. We do not at first know what may be brought, not out of our flesh only, but out of our spirits, by trying circumstances. But if we labour as Jacobs to see "the elder serve the younger," our attempts will open a page within, humbling indeed, but not less profitable.

These sons, the different forms of life, which at this stage of sonship are produced by the elect soul, are now manifested. They are thus described at their birth:— "The first came out red, all over like a hairy garment, and they called his name Esau: and after that came his brother out, and his hand took hold on Esau's heel, and his name was called Jacob."[2]

To look at the elder first. He was "red," or ruddy, as the word is rendered by our translators in the only two other places where we find it.[3] It describes natural health

---

[2] Chap. xxv. 24–26.

[3] 1 Sam. xvi. 12, and xvii. 42, Heb. אדמני, from the same root as Edom. The LXX. translate it πυρράκης.

and strength, in contrast to that weakness out of which Abraham and all the elect are made strong. So fair is the flesh at this stage. Some think that the carnal mind, because " it profiteth nothing," [4] and " cannot please God," [5] must therefore be without attractions, an unsightly deformed thing. In some forms it is vile indeed; but in others, and especially as Esau, it is for a season beautiful. But its beauty soon corrupts. Ere long Esau is Edom, that is, the red one; [6] his hue, like the " red horse," and " scarlet beast," [7] bespeaking that fierce life within, which will come out through all its coverings. Then we see that Edom is little else than Adam; slightly altered, but at bottom the same old man, which is of the earth, earthy. [8] Such is the flesh, at its best; fair at first, but degenerating as it grows, until it shews all its inbred violence.

Esau's other mark was " hair." He was " all over like a hairy garment." [9] This too figures grace and strength. The Lord, describing the growth and comeliness of Jerusalem, says, " Thy hair was grown;" [10] while "well-set hair " is set in contrast to " baldness," as strength to weakness, and beauty to burning. [11] Esau has all this strength; but it avails as nothing in obtaining heavenly things. Therefore the priests at consecration had to " shave all their flesh." [12] Therefore the leper, before he could be cleansed must " cut off all his hair, his beard, his eye-brows, even all his hair." [13] For, in consecration or cleansing, the

---

[4] John vi. 63.
[5] Rom. viii. 8.
[6] Chap. xxv. 30, and xxxvi. 1, 8.
[7] Rev. vi. 4, and xvii. 3.
[8] In the Hebrew, the difference between Edom and Adam, אֱדֹם and אָדָם, is only in the vowel points, both names being most closely connected with אֲדָמָה, or *earth*.

[9] Chap. xxv. 25. The name Esau is by some translated " hairy." See Gesenius on the word. Jerome however (*Nom. Heb.*) renders it by "*operans*," from another root.
[10] Ezek. xvi. 7.
[11] Isa. iii. 24.
[12] Numb. viii. 7.
[13] Lev. xiv. 8, 9.

strength of the flesh is to be put away, because, while that strength lasts, God cannot be fully known. Besides hair, from marking strength, if excessive, shews wildness; as the growth of Nebuchadnezzar's hair, until "it was like eagle's feathers," indicated his thorough brutality.[14] So does strength in the flesh tend, if it increase, to make us like to beasts, rough, brutal, wild, and unclean. The flesh, as Esau, becomes all this; so nearly akin is even its beauty to that which is wild and animal.

Of the younger less is said. We only read that "his hand took hold of Esau's heel," whence "his name was called Jacob."[15] This name, in its very form and composition, figures that which Jacob represents, namely, the divine working in the natural,[16] and his unconscious act reveals what Jacob is, as the hair and colour mark what Esau signifies. Jacob is that life which "takes hold with the hand," that is, the spirit of service, in contradistinction to the earlier forms of the elect spirit. This is the form which the spiritual mind assumes, when Isaac or sonship produces its legitimate fruit. Jacob is worker throughout,

---

[14] Dan. iv. 33. "Pili carnis sunt vitæ veteris cogitationes ; . . . . bene autem per Moysem dicitur, 'Levitæ radant omnes pilos carnis suæ'. . . . quia is qui in obsequiis divinis assumitur, debet ante Dei oculos a cunctis carnis cogitationibus mundus apparere, ne illicitas cogitationes mens proferat, et pulchram animæ speciem quasi pilis fruticantibus deformem reddat."—*Greg. M. Moral. in Job.* l. v. c. 33, § 59.

[15] Chap. xxv. 26.

[16] The word is formed from עָקַב, *the heel*, (that part of Adam which was to be bruised, that is, his fleshly part,) with the addition of יִ, a letter, which, like הִ, in Hebrew is symbolic

of the divine; as we see in its addition to the name Oshea, changing it to Jehoshua.— Numb. xiii. 8, 16. This idea, of the divine working in the natural, is exactly that set forth in Jacob. Augustine says, "Supplantatio enim vocatur Jacob. Et nec ipsa supplantatio inanis est, quia in figurâ accipitur, quomodo dolus. Non enim jam erat tanta malitia in fratre, ut vellet supplantare fratrem suum. Tunc enim dictus est supplantator, quando manu fratris sui nascentis pedem tenuit . . . . Supplantatio autem carnalium, vita spiritalium est," &c.— *Serm.* iv. *Class.* i. § 28.

busy with his hand, not so much a life of faith or sonship as of untiring service; toiling to win and bring into subjection things which till now had been given up as altogether beyond the elect's reach. In all this much of earthly craft is seen; and Jacob, because of his haste, is lovingly disciplined, until he learns the folly of many of his schemes to bring about what God had promised. And yet throughout he is blessed in his work. First one and then another of the things once subject to Laban or the outward man are brought to serve Jacob. This of course is not seen yet. But the first act, the " laying hold with his hand," shews in what new form the younger or spiritual life is now to be manifested.

Such are these sons at birth. As they grow, their characteristic unlikeness yet more shews itself. Esau is " a cunning hunter, a man of the field; " Jacob, " a plain man, dwelling in tents."[17] The one is the revival of the same wild life, which we have already known at an earlier stage and coarser form in Nimrod and Ishmael. The other continues that pilgrim life, which Abraham's tent and altar have so long exhibited. Their acts shew what each is, and place the real difference of these two minds in a light never to be forgotten.

For " Esau came from the field, and was faint; and he said unto Jacob, Feed me with that red pottage, for I am faint. And Jacob said, Sell me thy birth-right. And Esau said, Lo, I am at the point to die, and what profit shall this birth-right do me? So Esau sold his birth-right to Jacob. Then Jacob gave Esau food, even pottage of lentiles, and he did eat and drink, and rose up, and went his way.

[17] Chap. xxv. 27.

Thus Esau despised his birth-right."[18]   These "lentiles"
were the food of beasts more than of men; and the
"famine" mentioned here [19] may explain how Jacob
came to be seething such pottage.   It is elsewhere named
as being used in a time of dearth, and there was "death in
the pot," until the prophet healed it by casting in "fine
flour." [20] For corn and wine, not lentiles, are the bread we
should possess; as Isaac says, "With corn and wine have
I sustained him." [21]   Not for such meat however, but for
lentile pottage, fit rather for swine than men, Esau sells
his inheritance.   Whoever else may gain it, he cares not
to keep it.   And having done this, without one expression
of regret, he "rises and goes his way," as if satisfied.   Such
is the flesh in every age.   For a momentary gratification
it will give up the hope of heavenly glory.   Promises,
because they tarry, are counted less than vanity, while
the husks which the swine eat are esteemed a fit blessing.

Circumstances however as usual give the occasion for
this :—"Esau came from the field, and he was faint;"
his pursuits there, though exciting, do not satisfy him.   At
such a moment the pottage is seen, and becomes through
his emptiness the occasion of bringing out the true value
he puts on spiritual things.   So the flesh, spending its
strength in worldly pursuits, following this or that natural
emotion or creature faculty, till it is quite wearied, and
feeling at times that the field thus used does not satisfy,

---

[18] Chap. xxv. 29—34. In the
authorised version the 34th verse is
rendered, " Jacob gave Esau *bread
and* pottage of lentiles." But the
more correct translation seems to be
that which I have given above, viz.
"*food, even* pottage," &c. The same
word, לחם, is used of the offerings,
where they are called "the *food* of
God," Lev. xxi. 17; and of "the
tree with its fruit" or "with its
food," in Jer. xi. 19 : עץ בלחמו.

[19] Chap. xxvi. 1.

[20] 2 Kings iv. 38–41.

[21] Chap. xxvii. 37.

instead of turning to cast itself upon a present God, too often by its very sense of emptiness is drawn to some passing bait, for which at such moments it will give up the birth-right. For spite of its excitements, nay, through them, the flesh is often faint, and feels that its field, if it is to afford solid satisfaction, needs the sower's seed and patient culture. Could it at such a time turn to the Lord, all would be well; but instead of this, the faintness is made the occasion for self to choose its own remedy. The result is the mess of pottage is seized, and the birth-right thus for ever lost to it.

But this, though the occasion, was not the cause. That lay far deeper : —" Esau despised his birth-right." [22] His own words betray him,—" What profit shall this birth-right do me ? " He says, " *This* birth-right," as Joseph's brethren, when they would mock him, say,— " *This* dreamer cometh; " [23] or again as Israel, when they turned away from Moses,—" As for *this* Moses, we know not what has become of him." [24] It is not mere pressure of circumstances, but real contempt of the blessing, which in every age makes the flesh so ready to give up the hope of coming glory. Ignorant of God and the joy of His love, but loving the things of time and sense which this world offers, the flesh prefers the barley to the gem: no wonder therefore that it so lightly parts with what it does not value. Talk to the flesh of the " comfort of love," of " fellowship of spirit," of that " kingdom which is righteousness and peace and joy in the Holy Ghost," of " the inheritance which is reserved in heaven for us, incorruptible, undefiled, and which fadeth not away,"—such themes will touch no answering chord, or raise a single wish or aspiration ?

---

[22] Chap. xxv. 34.   [23] Chap. xxxvii. 19.   [24] Exod. xxxii. 1.

Rather it shrinks from such as from a burden, and turns to earth, to its dust and dross, or its morsels of meat such as the flesh loveth. In these is its heaven, in these it would rest, and eat and drink and go its way.

Still the flesh will have its excuse. Grovelling as it is, it cannot give up heaven without an attempt at self-justification. Like Esau it says, " I am at the point to die." [25] I cannot live unless I act thus. I cannot exist on so vague a thing as the promise. I may be losing the birth-right, but of what use is it, if I cannot live here? Necessity compels me. I cannot help it. Thus argues the flesh; but the excuse is not held good. In all such reasonings God is shut out. Esau is in the Lord's eyes " a profane person." [26]

Of Jacob less is seen here; but his acts shew a mind as unlike to Esau as may be, and set on other things; the one giving up his birth-right for meat; the other giving up his meat, if by any means he may obtain the inheritance. Jacob may fail in the way he seeks the blessing; he may trust too much to his schemes, not yet disciplined to wait on God to receive of Him what He has promised. But there cannot be a question whether he values the birth-right. His very errors shew that it is more to him than all other things. Such is the spirit of service in us, striving to overcome the flesh, without God, and in its own energy; but ready at all times to give up the world, parting with present good to obtain better things. Many a weary step does this attempt cost Jacob. Even after years of travail, Esau is yet to him " my lord Esau; " [27] so hardly does the elder serve the younger, so slowly even at this stage is the flesh overcome.

---

[25] Chap. xxv. 32. [26] Heb. xii. 16. [27] Chap. xxxii. 4, 18.

And yet " Isaac loves Esau," [28] and would if possible bless the first-born. For though sonship is come, and we live in the spirit, we love the flesh, and cling to the fruits of nature which yet grow in us. This occurs at every stage. The spirit of faith prays " that Ishmael might live before God." [29] Even when Isaac is weaned, the rejection of the bond-maid's son is to Abraham " very grievous." [30] And now when these natural fruits are Esau, when the flesh is seen in the comeliness it possesses after the spirit of sonship rules the elect house, it is hard to give up what seems so fair. The day comes when Esau is known ; even then, spite of his ways and the grief which his Hittite wives cause,—spite of our knowledge that he is rejected,—that flesh and blood cannot inherit the kingdom, and that though attractive it must be cast out,—we yet love Esau, and would make him the heir, and bless him, even though we know it cannot be.

But enough of this inward view. Without, Isaac's sons are those in whom respectively the flesh or spirit is the ruling life ; who, though born in the house of the Son, and from one womb, after many struggles are for ever separated. The one, pursuing the rough things of the world, (for in this view " the field is the world," [31]) faint

---

[28] Chap. xxv. 28.

[29] Chap. xvii. 18.

[30] Chap. xxi. 11.

[31] Matt. xiii. 38. " Quid enim per venationem Esau, nisi eorum vita figuratur, qui in exterioribus voluptatibus fusi carnem sequuntur. Qui etiam agricola esse describitur, quia amatores hujus sæculi tanto magis exteriora colunt, quanto interiora sua inculta derelinquunt. Jacob verò vir simplex in tabernaculis vel in domo habitare perhibetur ; quia nimirum omnes, qui in curis exterioribus spargi refugiunt, simplices in cogitatione atque in conscientiæ suæ habitatione consistunt. In tabernaculis enim aut in domo habitare, est se intra mentis secreta restringere, et nequaquam exteriùs per desideria dissipare ; ne dum ad multa foras inhiant, a semetipsis

with such pursuits, sell their hope of glory for the meat which perisheth': while the younger or spiritual seed give up such meat, if by any means they may obtain better things. From the same Church spring both these seeds. For awhile one house is able to contain both. But a few years see them widely apart; the one with a kingdom and kingly sons in Mount Seir, the other with flocks won out of Laban's hand, returning as pilgrims to dwell in the promised land.

Soon shall the toil and grief be done. Jacob shall rejoice, and Israel shall be glad.[32] Then one shall say, I am the Lord's, and another shall call himself by the name of Jacob, and another shall subscribe with his hand unto the Lord, and surname himself by the name of Israel.[33] Fear not therefore, O my servant Jacob, saith the Lord, and be not dismayed, O Israel ; for, behold, I will save thee from afar off, and thy seed from the land of their captivity ; and Jacob shall return, and be in rest, and at ease, and none shall make him afraid.[34]

In the dispensations too this is fulfilled. The two sons, the natural and the spiritual seed, the Jew and Christian Church, are both the fruit of that Word of God, who is the Son and Heir, the true Isaac. All through the Jewish dispensation, born with it, was there a younger seed, not carnal but spiritual. All the holy prophets were of this line. In due time the younger or spiritual gained the birth-right openly. But before this, the younger was in the house, and in him God's covenant was fulfilled, though the elder was cast out. So St. Paul quotes Esau as a proof

---

alienatis cogitationibus recedunt."— *Greg. M. Moral.* l. v. c. 11, § 20. Augustine often refers to the same outward fulfilment. See *Serm.* iv. *Class.* i. *De Jacob & Esau*; *Enar.*

in Psalm. xlvi. § 6.; and elsewhere.

[32] Psalm xiv. 7.
[33] Isa. xliv. 5.
[34] Jer. xlvi. 27.

of Israel's fall.[35]   He at least in Rebekah's sons could see a figure of the dispensations.

VII.—ISAAC IN THE PHILISTINES' LAND

Chapter 26

HERE Isaac comes into collision with the Philistine, and the result is something like a repetition of Abraham's conduct under the same circumstances.   In the main the two scenes are alike, shewing the dangers which await the elect spirit when it leaves its own high ground to go down towards Egypt.   The difference is that in Abraham we see the trial, as it meets us at the faith stage of our spiritual life.   Isaac shews the same, when instead of faith the spirit of sonship and understanding is come and rules within us.

Now the Philistine, as we have already seen, represents that spirit which seeks by knowledge to enter into heavenly things.[1]   Unknown before the flood, such a mind too surely grows out of the evil nature which still lives in us after we are regenerate.   This mind is the Philistine in us, who is left to prove, and does more than once severely prove, the true elect.[2]   For the ground of promise often tries us: most truly is it the " land of promise," not of attainment, or of perfect rest.   If, then, in addition to the common trials of the way, extraordinary pressure comes, and the

---

[35] Rom. ix. 10. This dispensational fulfilment is continually alluded to or expounded by the Fathers ; by Augustine, *De Civit.* l. xvi. c. 35 ; *Id. Quæst. in Gen.* 73 ; by Ambrose, *De Cain et Abel,* l. i. c. 2, and *In Psalm.* cxviii. *Serm.* 20 ; by Irenæus, *Contr. Hær.* l. iv. c. 38 ; by Cyprian, *Adv. Jud.* l. i. § 19 ; by Origen, *Hom.* xii. *in Gen.,* and by many others.

[1] See on chap. **xx.** and the notes there.

[2] Judges iii. 1–4.

springs fail, and the fields wither, the temptation is strong
to leave the ground of promise, to find on the ground of
sense or worldly knowledge that which for a season the
promise does not minister to us. Egypt holds out strong
inducements to go there ; and this not only in the days of
Abraham, that is, at the stage when faith is our ruling life ;
but also in Isaac's days, that is, when the spirit of sonship
is come and is even fruitful in us.

Now "there was a famine in the land, beside the first
famine that was in the days of Abraham."[3] Pressed by this,
Isaac moves towards Egypt, but stops or is stopped at
Gerar in the Philistines' land. "The Lord appeared, and
said, Go not down into Egypt; dwell in the land which I
shall tell thee of : and I will be with thee, and I will bless
thee, and to thee and to thy seed I will give all these countries ; and I will perform the oath which I sware unto Abraham, and I will make thy seed to multiply as the stars of
heaven ; and I will give unto thy seed all these countries,
and in thy seed shall all the nations of the earth be blessed."
But "Isaac dwells in Gerar" for awhile ; and here each of
his peculiar blessings is seriously imperilled through the
Philistines ; till pushed by them from place to place he
returns again to Beersheba, where the Lord again appears
to him, saying, "Fear not, for I am with thee." On this
ground the Philistine takes his proper place, submitting
to the elect's superiority; after which Isaac finds fresh
wells of water, beside which again he dwells in peace.[4]

All this is yet fulfilled in those who by grace have
reached this stage of man's development. After long enjoyment of Beer-Lahai-roi, and the good things of Canaan,
comes a time of dearth and dryness. The soul is parched :

---

[3] Chap. xxvi. 1.   [4] Chap. xxvi. 2–33.

the usual blessing is withheld. The ground of promise seems to yield us nothing. Then we think of the good things of sense, not dependent like the hills of promise upon the dews and rain of heaven, but, like Egypt, ever rich in itself, in its own abundant and apparently un-failing river. So we turn to go down thither. Once turned, a few steps bring us into the Philistines' land, that is, the ground of worldly knowledge,—a descent which can be effected only too easily.[5] Here the elect's best blessings, first, intercourse with God, then possession of Rebekah, and lastly, provision sufficient for him, are each and all more or less affected, though spite of all failure Isaac by grace is not only sustained but even enriched here.[6] For the elect can gather much from science or knowledge, though mere knowledge cannot enter into spiritual things. The whole experience on this ground is here described, fulfilled in spirit in thousands who in their understanding are all but unconscious of it.

Intercourse with God is Isaac's first blessing. "The Lord appeared to him, and said, Sojourn in this land, and I will be with thee."[7] This was the presence of the Lord, better than all His gifts. But this belongs to certain ground. In Egypt, nay among the Philistines, half way to Egypt, the elect cannot enjoy this. If Isaac walks with God, the Lord appears. Walking with Philistines, the Lord's presence is unperceived by him. But no sooner does he come back to the old ground of promise, than heavenly revelations are at once again restored to him. So we read, "Isaac went up from thence to Beersheba, and the Lord appeared to him the same night; and Isaac builded an altar there, and called upon the name of the Lord."[8]

---

[5] See on chap. xx.
[6] Chap. xxvi. 12.
[7] Chap. xxvi. 3.
[8] Chap. xxvi. 23-25.

It is so still. The ground of promise often tries us, but conscious intercourse with the Lord is here abundantly enjoyed by us. Driven by trial we get off this ground, turning to sense; and we find, that though this or the other trial ceases, God's revelations cease also. On the ground of promise, God is needed. To stand there, did not God interfere, would be far beyond our spirit's powers. Our very need therefore calls out for God, and in the need He reveals Himself as He could not otherwise. But if, instead of this, trial is an excuse to leave the ground of promise, to take refuge either in sense or knowledge, though we reap the good things such ground can give us, for a season we lose the Lord's better manifestations.

Isaac's next blessing was Rebekah. In Gerar "Isaac said, She is my sister."[9] He shrinks from owning his true relation to her, while the ground he takes subjects her to the risk of dreadful profanation. Very strange it seems that men like Abraham or Isaac should so lightly have imperilled what must have been most dear to them. Could we see into the world within, we should perceive how that truth, which is to us what Rebekah was to Isaac, is imperilled by us with just as little thought, with no more apparent remorse or inward self-condemnation. Our inward man, when pressed by dryness and dearth, forsakes the ground of promise, and seeks relief in mere knowledge. Then the truth we love, our Rebekah, is risked, through the mind in us, which by knowledge would enter heavenly things. But the truth may not be so known or embraced. The spirit of sonship, is that which alone may lay hold of spiritual truth. Mere knowledge would only pervert it. God therefore interferes to prevent such adulteration.

[9] Chap. xxvi. 7.

We have already seen this at the faith stage. Here we learn that even when the spirit of sonship is come, we are still liable to the very same temptation. Grace, indeed, again averts a fall, but the elect cannot but be humbled as he reviews such stages of his pilgrimage.

Further, upon this ground Isaac's more outward blessings, his " bread and his water," are the occasion of strife and envying. He sows, and the Philistines envy his fruits: he digs wells, and they labour to stop and fill them up.[10] Then he removes and digs again, but the herdsmen of Gerar still strive. He digs yet again, and the Philistines yet more strive with him. On the ground of knowledge the elect can never rest. He may reap much there; he may open living wells, " for the earth is the Lord's, and the fulness thereof;"[11] the fields of knowledge, therefore, the Philistines' land, may be subdued, and much may be obtained thence; but on this ground there are disturbing thoughts withal, which can only be escaped by returning to the true ground of promise, where the Lord's oath again comforts us. There Philistine herdsmen cannot come:[12] there the restlessness of mere knowledge cannot trouble us. Beside "the well of the oath," we rest in peace. Here the Philistine in us submits himself, and takes his proper place. So we read, "Then Abimelech came to him, and said, We saw the Lord was with thee: let there now be an oath between us and thee, that thou wilt do us no hurt. And Isaac made them a feast, and they sware one to another, and they rose up and departed from him."[13] Knowledge is rebuked, but no violence is offered to it. For the elect is

---

[10] Chap. xxvi. 12–15.
[11] Psalm. xxiv. 1.

[12] As to these " herdsmen," see on chap. xiii.
[13] Chap. xxvi. 23–31.

now on ground where "the oppositions of knowledge, falsely so-called," [14] cannot disquiet him.

I have thus briefly traced this scene within. But the same thing is continually being re-enacted in the outward Church. Sons of God through trials leave their own high ground, seeking greater ease among those who without circumcision are reaching toward heavenly things; for sweet and blessed as the " well of vision " is, it does not exempt us from trials of faith, and other difficulties. Then the temptation is strong to descend to lower ground, to seek shelter in the things of sense, and in the ways of men of this world. [15] There direct revelations cease : there the Church, and the truth which it embodies, is in danger of profanation ; for worldly men, like Abimelech, and that with pure intentions, will seek carnally to know what, as worldlings, never can be theirs. Sons of God yet think too lightly of the shame and peril incurred here ; but did not the Lord Himself most graciously interfere, such a course would bring only worse judgment upon the world, and disgrace on God's children. Nevertheless on this ground bread is found, and wells are dug ; though envy assails us for the one, while against the other there is open opposition. "The bread is my flesh : he that eateth me, even he

---

[14] 1 Tim. vi. 20. The notes on chap. xx. have already shewn the views of the Fathers as to the spiritual import of the "Philistine." I may add the following : — " Iste Abimelech non semper pacem habet cum Isaac, sed aliquando dissidet, aliquando pacem requirit. . . . . Philosophia enim neque in omnibus legi Dei contraria est, neque in omnibus consona. . . . . Sed et duo alii cum Abimelech venerint, id est Ochozach,

gener ejus, et Ficol, dux exercitûs ejus. Interpretatur autem Ochozach ' tenens,' et Ficol, ' os omnium.' Ipse autem Abimelech, ' pater meus rex.' Qui tres, ut ego arbitror, imaginem totius philosophiæ tenent, quæ in tres partes dividitur, logicam, physicam, ethicam," &c.—*Orig. Hom.* xiv. *in Gen.* xxvi. He pursues the subject at considerable length.

[15] Compare the scene, chap. xx.

shall live by me:" and again, "The water which I will give, shall be in you a well of water, springing up into everlasting life." Bread is the outward form of the word of truth: water is its quickening and refreshing spirit.[16] The chief strife is ever for the waters. The "staff of bread"[17] may be grudged, but it is not destroyed; but the waters are actually choked; Philistines, who never worked to dig wells, will gladly work to stop them. Out of the world we may dig as we please, and sweet and calm are the hours spent at the "well of the oath," or beside the "well of vision." There no envying hand mars the joy by fouling the spiritual stream. It is far otherwise when we are among Philistines. Philistine herdsmen count wells an evil: they are deep and dangerous pits: not only sheep, but men also,—so they judge,—may perish in them. Have not some souls, while pretending or attempting to dig for hidden fountains, hurt themselves or others by leading them, from the firm ground of the letter, into uncertain and slippery quagmires of mystic nonsense, or into dry depths which yielded no water? Some have slipped: the well is therefore to be stopped, and the stagnant pool preferred, lest some blind leader of the blind should fall into it. Who is there that in the faith of the "deep which coucheth beneath,"[18] reckoning on a vein of living water, out of sight perhaps, but yet not far off from them that seek it, has dug below the surface, and brought into view the hidden streams of the Spirit's pure and living waters, but has met with strife at the hand of Philistines for the waters, clear and refreshing though they be, which he has opened out. And the strife is from "herdsmen"

[16] John vii. 39.   [17] Psalm cv. 16.   [18] Deut. xxxiii. 13.

who have charge of flocks, and who should know the value
of living waters. But they know it not. And like the
Scribes, they "take away the key:" they "neither enter
themselves, and those who would enter in, they hinder."[19]
Thus are the Isaacs troubled still, and God's most precious
gifts, given for our cleansing and refreshment, are made
occasions of contention; so that such words as *hatred* and
strife become, even in the mouths of the elect, almost
synonymes for these pure wells of living waters,[20] till they
return from this low ground and communion with worldlings
to the ground of promise where men of this world care not
to come. There the Lord again appears in peace: the
"well of the oath" is safe from the distractions which
infest us among the men of this world. There the uncircumcised must see that God is with the pilgrim, and though
they will not walk with him there, they cease to fight
against him. He offers them a feast of fat things: they
may grudge and strive with him; he will return them love
for their hatred. Another age may shew yet other fulfilments, when the pilgrimage among the Gentiles being
ended, the opposing world shall seek and find peace. Then

---

[19] Luke xi. 52. "Unusquisque
nostrum, qui verbum Dei ministrat,
puteum fodit, et aquam vivam quærit,
ex quâ reficiat auditores. Si ergo
veterum dicta discutere conatus fuero,
et sensum in eis quærere spiritalem,
et velamen legis amovere, fodio quidem puteos, sed statim mihi move-
bunt calumnias amici literæ, et in-
sidiabuntur mihi, et persecutiones
parabunt," &c.—*Orig. Hom.* xiii. *in
Gen.* So also Gregory the Great:—
"Puteos quos Isaac foderat terræ
congerie replebant. Hos enim nos
nimirum puteos fodimus, cùm in
Scripturæ sacræ abditis sensibus alta

penetramus, quos tamen occultè re-
plent Allophyli, quando nobis ad
alta tendentibus immundi spiritus
terrenas cogitationes ingerunt, et
quasi inventam divinæ scientiæ
aquam tollunt." — *Moral. in Job*,
l. xvi. c. 18, § 23. Ambrose dwells
on the spiritual import of each of
the wells named here, *De Isaac et
Animâ*, c. iv. § 20-22.

[20] "Isaac called the name of the
well Esek, or *contention*, because
they strove with him. And they
digged another well, and strove for
that also: and he called it Sitnah,"
or *hatred*.—Chap. xxvi. 20, 21.

shall the earth be glad, and the sons of God shall dwell by living waters where none can harass them. Lord, Thou only canst bring us to that rest. Bring us thither, whom Thou hast redeemed with thy most precious blood. Amen.

Such is Isaac's course, that is the path and experience of the spirit of sonship in us; very different to the energies of faith, freed from the peculiar struggles which mark each stage of Abraham's history; differing widely too from Jacob's path, knowing nothing of that long toil for flocks and children in the far country; but coming in at once to rich blessing, as Abraham's heir inheriting all faith's good things; yet with its special blessings having special trials of its own, first mocked and laughed at, then called to be a sacrifice, to give up as an obedient son its own will in everything, to be even as a lamb appointed unto death, only in the act of perfect self-sacrifice to find deliverance; then, when fruitful, to be pained, at home by its own seed, abroad by seeing the living waters which faith had opened choked by aliens; such is the path; for there is no form of spiritual life which in its progress towards the perfect man must not be tried to the uttermost. The form of the trial varies with the growing form of the elect life, for that which tries us at first is not the trial of the riper and more advanced spirit; but a cross and trial there must be at every stage, to purify the elect from the hereditary evil which still so perseveringly cleaves to him. Many therefore are the inward groans and deaths, which must be passed through in the journey towards perfection. For as the vine draws its sap from the impure earth, and so yields a fluid fruit, first sour, then sweet, which, being crushed in the wine-press, is then turned into wine by fermentation, and thus by successive changes spiritualised and advanced into a more powerful and enduring form of being ; so in the great change of man's renewal unto God, the new life, growing out of and in part and for a season sustained by the defiled and earthly nature, is dissolved and purified by successive changes and ferments, till it is transformed and rectified into that which is immortal. But many stages are there in the labour, and many times does nature halt before this final rest. And often do we think the work is done, and the promised rest is come, while yet we are far indeed from seeing it. But it shall come at last to those who by grace yield themselves to God in everything.

PART 6

JACOB, OR THE SPIRIT OF SERVICE

Chapters 27-36

" Jacob served for a wife, and kept sheep."— Hos. xii. 12.

" Surely there is no enchantment against Jacob, neither is there any divination against Israel: according to this time it shall be said of Jacob and of Israel, What hath God wrought ! "—Numb. xxiii. 23.

JACOB, OR THE SPIRIT OF SERVICE

Chapters 27-36

We come now to another form of life. Five great stages we have already passed. Jacob is the sixth, in whom is shewn a further very distinct development of the same spiritual life. Essentially they are alike, as root, and shoot, and leaf, and bud, and flower, and fruit, and seed, are all the same life; they differ in form, each being a fresh manifestation of that sevenfold Spirit which indeed is yet one.[1]

Jacob, as we have already seen,[2] represents that spirit of service, which is not the first and natural, but the spiritual fruit of true sonship; which from the first is distinguished by using its hand; "laying hold," and labouring to bring the first-born, and what is akin to the first-born, into subjection to a higher life. The figure is most distinct, and stands in striking contrast to all the forms of life which we have already gone through. Abraham, the spirit of faith, goes forth from the ground of the outward man to walk with God beyond Jordan. He leaves his

---

[1] Rev. i. 4, and 1 Cor. xii. 4, 11.   [2] See on chap. xxv. 24–34.

kindred behind, coming out from Mesopotamia, that is the ground between tradition and reasoning,[3] forsaking the outer world to walk with God, and to stand in His strength upon the heavenly ground of promise. This is the life of faith, to pass from earthly into heavenly things. And Abraham's experience is all in keeping with this beginning. For faith, having turned its back on the outward man, returns to it no more, but abides beyond Jordan. Isaac lives yet more completely in Canaan; for our walk as sons of God is not with the natural man or in the outward world. Isaac's life begins and ends beyond Jordan. A son and heir, he dwells in peace in heavenly places. Once only through trial he nearly leaves this ground, driven to its very borders, in the direction of the Philistine. But his life is a life in Canaan. In Jacob the view presented to us is very different. Here the elect is seen, not as coming by faith from the ground of the outward man, nor as Isaac dwelling in Canaan in peace by wells of water; but rather going down from thence to the ground of the outward man, from which the spirit of faith has come up and separated itself, there to serve for a bride and flocks, whom it may bring, as the fruit of service, back with it into heavenly places. Jacob's life is service throughout; a life, beginning in the midst of the blessings of the elect in heavenly places, which yet goes down thence to toil in outward things, to bring under the power of the spiritual life in us faculties which till now have only served the outward man; a form of life which only comes after sonship is known, which is indeed its fruit, though most unlike it; for it goes down from heavenly

---

[3] Respecting these rivers, from which Mesopotamia, or Aram Na-haraim, took its name, see on chapter ii.

things to earthly, to labours amongst the unclean, from whom God's elect have been separated.[4]

Such a life may seem to undo what has been done, for Jacob goes down to the very ground which Abraham had forsaken : yet are the paths in substance one ; and both, unlike as they appear, are but different parts of one and the same series; both are the same life at different stages; now rising like a plant to hold its fruit above the earth in air and sunshine, now again casting its fruit into the earth, in both pursuing only one end. For life is growth, and involves a constant change. Hence the same life, which at one stage, as Abrahams, draws us away from outward things, at another stage, as Jacobs, brings us back to them. Being life, it cannot preserve a dead consistency. The elect change, because they are alive. Hence the fact, of their having once and for ever by faith forsaken outward things, shall by no means keep them from going back in service to toil for that which by faith they have forsaken. Besides, things are safe at one stage which are dangerous at another; as Egypt, which was a snare to Abraham, is none to Joseph, but becomes the scene of all his glory.

I.—JACOB'S CARNAL MEANS TO GAIN GOD'S ENDS

Chapter 27

FIRST we see how Jacob attempts to supplant the flesh or first-born. His mode of action is fully shewn, and the results, which leave Esau, without the blessing indeed,

---

[4] Ambrose thus points out the distinction between these lives : — "In Abraham didicistis impigram fidei devotionem, in Isaac sinceræ mentis puritatem, in Jacob singularem laborum tolerantiam," &c. — *De Joseph.* c. i. § 1.

but yet " my lord Esau." The more excellent way comes
out in Joseph. There the victory over the first-born is
won, not by striving or supplanting, but by suffering.
Not the strength of nature, not doing but dying, in a
word the cross, is the elect's true sceptre over the flesh
and outward world. But this is not known at this stage.
Here we see the first ways by which the younger strives
to overcome the elder, namely by craft and energy.

Three men appear in this scene, who yet live, and still
repeat the same acts in the elect house.

First Isaac seeks to bless Esau. He will, if possible,
give the blessing to the first-born or natural life. " Isaac
called his elder son, and said unto him, My son, make me
savoury meat, that I may eat and bless thee." [1] But this
first-born is slow in bringing what is asked ; and the
blessing, spite of Isaac's inclination, passes according to a
higher purpose upon the younger son.

And so the spirit of sonship in us struggles, if it might
be so, to make the flesh blessed. Spite of our knowledge
that flesh must fail, we yet would make it the heir, and
bless it, though we know it cannot be. In vain have Cain
and Terah lived and died : in vain has the spirit of faith
struggled to save Ishmael : the same desire remains when
Isaac is old, stronger now perhaps than at any former
stage. For Abraham only prays for Ishmael, but Isaac
determines himself to bless the first-born. But flesh and
blood cannot inherit the kingdom. [2] The sons of God may
excite the flesh to seek the blessing. It is in vain. The
true kingdom is in and of the spirit, in things which the
flesh loves not, and where it cannot come.

And Isaac, foiled in his purpose, at once and without

---

[1] Chap. xxvii. 4.   [2] 1 Cor. xv. 50.

hesitation confirms the blessing upon the head of Jacob. He answers, " I have blessed him, and he shall be blessed;"[3] nor do Esau's cries for a moment change this deep conviction. He "trembles" indeed, for the struggle of his own with God's will moves him exceedingly; but his judgment is untouched; the blessing is fixed: he neither can nor will reverse it. So now, spite of our wish to bless the flesh, through its delays we find our purpose set aside. Then instead of seeking to reverse the gift, we fully acquiesce in the fact, that the spirit is the true possessor of it. The spirit of sonship confirms the rejection of the flesh. It receives a blessing, but it cannot have the inheritance.

But Jacob is the chief figure here. Elect, unbroken, still Jacob, not yet transformed into Israel, the man whose own hand is at work, not yet a prince with God, as he becomes afterwards,—just as he is, young and eager to be blessed, without a thought of his own unfitness to use the blessing he longs for, not fearing Esau, as he does in later days, he seeks at once by craft to supplant him, and take the blessing. Thus the spirit of service in us at the first, loving the blessing, and intent at once to rule the carnal old man, little thinks of its own unchastened state, or of the flesh's power, if it be roused by opposition, but pursues the same old plan to be blessed, making itself as much like the rejected first-born as possible, putting skins on its hands and neck to be rough, then taking Esau's raiment, then personating Esau. Instead of waiting God's time, it will by roughness and guile, contrary to the better nature within, attempt to rule the flesh or first-born, putting on the manners and appearance of the carnal seed, to gain by

[3] Chap. xxvii. 33.

roughness what roughness has no claim to. For because he was such as he was, Esau fails; and yet Jacob will make himself like this thereby to gain the blessing. But he cannot do this without compunction. He says, " I shall bring a curse upon me, and not a blessing."[4] Nevertheless " he puts the skins of the kids upon him."[5] The flesh's roughness is put on, to gain what we think will be lost, if we walk on in humble quietness.

This part of the figure is most striking. When Adam fell, God gave him a " coat of skins,"[6] a witness of death, and yet a covering through the slain Lamb. In like manner the prophets wore hairy garments,[7] testifying the same truth of a fallen nature and its remedy. This Jacob uses to be more flesh-like. He wears the rough garment, like false prophets, to deceive.[8] The death of the creature is made his cloak, to be more like that creature, whose doom is sealed by that which covers him. Even thus is the gospel abused. The fact that the lamb was slain, the very pledge that our flesh must not be lived in, is used at first by the spirit of service in us as a means to make us more like Esau, more rough, and more beast-like. And this especially when we would serve. As sons of God, our dangers and temptations meet us on another side; but as workers we try fleshly means, even when the desire of our heart is to overcome the flesh, and to live and walk in the spirit.

This was not done by Jacob alone. His mother,

---

[4] Chap. xxvii. 12.
[5] Chap. xxvii. 16.
[6] Chap. iii. 21.
[7] 2 Kings i. 8, and Matt. iii. 4.
[8] Zech. xiii. 4, " Quid est quod idem Jacob manus ac brachia et collum hædinis pellibus texit, nisi quod hædus pro peccato offerri consuevit," &c. — *Greg. M. in Ezech.* l. i. h. 6. He does not notice that Jacob did this to make himself like Esau.

Rebekah, moved him to practise this deception.[9]   Rebekah is that form of truth which the spirit of sonship loves;[10] and this truth, acting on the spirit of service in us, through our impatience and tendency to trust ourselves, excites, and so tempts us.   Thus it was in Abraham's case.   Sarah herself stirred him up to seek seed by the bondwoman.[11] So even spiritual truth may mislead, if, instead of keeping us in hope and patience, it excites us to godless haste and carnal policy.   In service especially we are prone to this, in the efforts which we first make to overcome the elder son. The truth itself excites us to steps, which shew our zeal, but practically deny the zeal of the Lord of Hosts.[12]   The result is always chastening.   We learn at last that we only mar God's work when we attempt to do it for Him, and that if we do wrong, we must also suffer wrong.

Nevertheless Jacob is blessed.   The grace, which before his birth gave him the promise, abides " without repentance." [13]   God's purpose is not turned aside.   This " worm Jacob " [14] must be chastened, yet He blesses him.   " And Isaac said, The smell of my son is as the smell of a field which the Lord hath blessed." [15]   The " image of God " is not yet come, but the " herb and fruit tree " is yielding fruit and odour after its kind.   And sweet is the smell of this spirit of service in us, spite of all its haste and imperfections.   It is " even as a very fruitful field ; " not heaven, but earth fair and sweet to look upon.   Sweet is the field, though much is unripe there.   Sweet is the vine, when its sour and " tender grape gives a good smell." [16]   Sweet is the olive, while as yet it yields no oil, for the wounds of

[9] Chap. xxvii. 6–10.
[10] See on chap. xxiv. and chap. xxv. 12–23.
[11] See on chap. xvi.
[12] Isa. ix. 7.
[13] Rom. xi. 29.
[14] Isa. xli. 14.
[15] Chap. xxvii. 27.
[16] Cant. ii. 13.

man, or for the light on God's candlestick.[17] Sweet is
the rose, though but a prickly brier, with tokens in its
thorns of a curse still working in it. Sweet is the lowly
lily, which toils not and spins not, a witness of the beauty
which the Lord delights to put on meek and pure natures.
Sweet is the violet, hiding itself, of choice preferring shade,
and loving the quiet low ground ; not feigning humility as
a step to grandeur here, but content if only it can reflect
the hue of heaven in its humble blossoms. Sweet again is
the corn as it comes to the growth ; not yet bread-corn,
ready to be bruised, but still unripe and growing. Such
is this son, whose early life, spite of its faults, is, "as the
smell of a full field, which the Lord blesses ; " not fit for
the garner, but growing and green ; freed at least from
thickets and stones and pools of stagnant water ; where
instead of the thorn may come up the fir tree, instead of
the brier the myrtle tree, to be unto the Lord for a praise
and a name, even for an everlasting sign, which shall not
be cut off.[18]

Thus Esau still without, while Jacob is already come
with savoury meat, loses the inheritance. When he comes
it is too late. Then he cries, "Bless me, even me also, O
my father." For the flesh, though stirred up to seek the
blessing, loses it by tarrying so long in pursuing outward
things. Then it cries with a loud and bitter cry. But the
hope of glory is gone ; though a lower blessing, if sought,

---

[17] Exod. xxvii. 20 ; Luke x. 34.

[18] Isa. lv. 13. Gregory the Great
interprets all these varied flowers :—
" Odor filii, odor est agri pleni.
Aliter namque olet flos uvæ, quia
magna est virtus prædicatorum, qui
inebriant mentes audientium. Aliter
flos olivæ, quia suave est opus misericordiæ, quod more olei refovet et
lucet. Aliter flos rosæ, quia mira

est fragrantia quæ rutilat et redolet
ex cruore martyrum. Aliter flos
lilii, quia candida vita carnis est de in-
corruptione virginitatis. Aliter flos
violæ, quia magna est virtus hu-
milium, qui ex desiderio loca ultima
tenentes, cœlestis regni purpuram in
mente servant," &c.—*In Ezech*. l. i.
h. 6, § 3. Ambrose alludes to the
same subject, *Hex*. l. iii. c. 8, § 36.

is not denied to it. Then it " lives by its sword," delighting in strife, and in its struggles with the spirit at times has the dominion over it. But it cannot be the heir. The coming world and the inheritance is for ever forfeited.

Such is the scene within, so far at least as it is given me to utter it. Outwardly too it is fulfilled. Abraham's sons, who pursue external things in the field of this world, much as the Son may wish to bless them, lose the blessing, while the spiritual seed, though seeking very carnally, press in and seek and make it theirs. And who is it, even to this present day, that stirs up the heirs of promise, to make themselves like carnal men ? Alas, it is Mother Church, that body which is the outward form of spiritual truth. She it is who moves her best-loved sons, making them rough men to gain what rough men cannot have. Therefore must she lose her sons. Her craft and carnal means to obtain holy ends,—and the haste and impatience of those she loves, in and by themselves and in their own strength to seize the blessing,—ere long divide the mother from her sons, while in sore travail through many days they suffer long discipline. The Esaus stay behind : the Jacobs go forth to toil, to win flocks and herds. Even the carnal and rejected sons receive some blessing. They, no less than their spiritual brothers, have the " fatness of the earth and the dew of heaven " promised them. What is " of the earth," sacramental forms, they put in the first place. The " dew of heaven" is with them the second and lower blessing.[19] It comes indeed on all alike, on tares and wheat, but each uses it to strengthen its proper life ; the

[19] Compare the order of the respective blessings, vv. 28 and 39. Augustine, who constantly quotes Isaac's two sons as the figure of the double seed, the carnal and spiritual, in the Christian Church, goes at great length into this : — " Duo filii benedicuntur, quia duo genera bene-

one drinking in the dew to nourish thorns, the other by the same dew " out of an honest and good heart " to bring forth good things. But I need not pursue this; for in this view the fulfilment to our shame is around us everywhere.

The dispensations too reflect the scene. The Divine Word, the true Son, produced a double seed. Then He looked for refreshment of heart from him, who, as being the first-born, possessed the first claim. But this son, the Jew, yet tarries without, and comes not until the younger son has gone in, and the word is fulfilled, " A people whom I have not known, they have served me." [20] In this view, Esau's raiment, which Jacob put on, without which Esau approached his father, is full of significance. That robe of righteousness [21] which the Jew should have had on, but had not, is worn by the Gentile church, even while it misuses the doctrine of the cross, to make itself resemble the carnal seed. For the Church has sought to be rough like

dicit Ecclesia. Quomodo duos peperit Rebecca, generantur in utero Ecclesiæ duo, unus pilosus, alter lenis. . . . Sunt mali in Ecclesiâ pertinentes ad Esau, pilosi in peccatis carnalibus perseverantes. . . . Habent a rore cœli et a fertilitate terræ ; a rore cœli, omnes Scripturas, omnem sermonem divinum ; a fertilitate vero terræ, omnia visibilia sacramenta, visibile enim sacramentum ad terram pertinet," &c.—*Serm.* iv. *Class.* 1, *De Jacob et Esau,* §§ 14, 31. Some would do well to mark the place here given by Augustine to sacraments. Compare the passage quoted above from his *Confessions,* note 5, p. 28.

[20] Psalm xviii. 43.
[21] Jewish tradition tells us that this raiment of Esau's was the ensign of primogeniture, transmitted from father to son. Ambrose thus expounds the dispensational application if it :—" Hanc stolam Ecclesiæ typo Rebecca protulit, et dedit filio juniori stolam veteris testamenti. . . Dedit populo Christiano, qui uti amictu sciret accepto, quoniam populus Judæorum eam sine usu habebat, et proprios nesciebat ornatus. Jacebat hæc stola in umbrâ abjecta et neglecta. Obscurabatur enim tenebrosâ impietatis caligine, nec in angusto corde populi Judaici latius poterat explicari. Induit eam Christianus populus, et refulsit," &c.—*De Jacob,* &c., l. ii. c. 2, § 9. Gregory the Great gives the same interpretation, *In Ezech.* l. i. h. 6, § 3.

the Jew, using the very death of the Lamb, to make itself carnal rather than spiritual. Yet the blessing remains with the Church, in an order exactly the reverse of that granted to the elder son. To Esau the word is, earth first, then heaven. To Jacob, heaven first, then the blessings of this world. To Jacob, thus;—" God give thee of the dew of heaven, and of the fatness of the earth, and plenty of corn and wine." To Esau, thus;— " Behold, thy dwelling shall be the fatness of the earth, and of the dew of heaven from above." For the Jew seeks first a rest on earth; the Church, a rest in heaven now, and God's will on earth, when the kingdom of God shall be in the earth even as it is in heaven.[22]

So the last shall be first, and the first shall be last; and by strength shall no man prevail.

---

[22] Tertullian, tracing this fulfilment, calls especial notice to the varying order in the two blessings: —" Isaac benedicens Jacob filium suum, 'Det,' ait, 'tibi Deus de rore cœli, et de opimitate terræ.' Nonne utriusque indulgentiæ exempla sunt? Denique animadvertenda est hic etiam structura benedictionis ipsius. Nam circa Jacob, qui quidem posterioris et prælatioris populi figura est, id est nostri, prima promissio cœlestis est roris; secunda, terrenæ opimitatis. Nos enim primo ad cœlestia invitamur, cùm a sæculo avellimur, et ita postea invenimur etiam terrena consecuturi. . . . Ceterum ad Esau promittit benedictionem terrenam, et subjicit cœlestem; ' De opimitate terræ (dicens) erit inhabitatio tua, et a rore cœli.' Judæorum enim dispositio in Esau, a terrenis bonis imbuta per legem, postea ad cœlestia per Evangelium credendo deducitur." —*Adv. Marcion.* l. iii. c. ult. But this dispensational application is given by nearly all the Fathers; by Irenæus, *Contr. Hær.* l. iv. c. 21; (*al.* 38;) by Hippolytus, as quoted by Jerome, *Epist. Crit.* 125, *ad Damasum*; by Augustine, *Serm.* iv. *Class.* 1, *De Jacob et Esau,* and elsewhere; by Origen, *Hom.* xiv. *in Gen.*; by Gregory the Great, *In Ezech. Hom.* 6; and by others. Some not only see the Church in Jacob, but Christ also, the Church's Head, like Jacob standing in the first-born or old man's place, and obtaining the blessing by putting on the likeness of sinful flesh for us, figured in the kids' skins. So Augustine, *Lib. contr. Mendac.* c. x. § 24, and *Serm.* 79 *de Tempore.* (*al.* 11, *Append.*) and Irenæus, *Contr. Hær.* l. iv. c. 21. (*al.* 38.) But in this deeper sense, which, indeed, is to be traced all through Genesis, we touch on things unspeakable.

II.—The Motives to Service and Encouragements by the Way

Chapter 28

We have seen Jacob in the promised land, by craft and energy rather than by patience seeking to overcome the elder son. We have seen the result,—only greater opposition. The elder is not brought to serve the younger by such policy. We now see Jacob flying before his brother, going down from the ground of promise to toil in Laban's house, a course in which he is blessed,—for by it he reaches others whom he brings back with him to the promised land,—but which never conquers Esau: the victory over the first-born is won by a very different wrestling.

Esau and Laban are both forms of the flesh;[1] the one being the carnal mind as it grows out of a true son; the other, our outward natural man. These differ, though both are of the flesh; as Abraham, Isaac, and Jacob differ, though forms of one spirit. Esau is the loveliest form of the flesh, the carnal mind as it grows in us after the spirit of sonship is our ruling life, stirred at times even to seek for heavenly things, yet at heart profane, and loving this present world. Laban is our outward natural man, which dwells in outward things, and is content to dwell there. Each of these in turn tries us. At one stage the outward man is our greatest difficulty. At another it is the carnal mind within, growing up in closest connection with spiritual things, which, because more inward, is far more dangerous and much harder to overcome. Jacob here learns the strength of each. As worker, he strives, not to be

---

[1] For Esau, see on chap. xxv. 24–34. For Laban on chap. xxiv.

ruled, but to rule over these. But Esau is yet so strong that Jacob is forced for awhile to give way and fly before him ; while Laban, so far from serving, is served, though at length much that was once in his power follows a better guide. Esau too must yield at last, but not till hasty Jacob has become halting Israel.

At the stage before us Jacob flees to Laban. His motives and encouragements here are both laid open to us. We see the mixture of motive which there is in truest service ; how little credit the elect can take to themselves either for what they do or suffer.

Three distinct influences were at work upon Jacob, all uniting to urge him down to Laban's house.

First, Rebekah urges the step, through fear of Esau.[2] In this view Jacob's service appears the result, not of longing for fruit, but simply of Esau's violence. And God only knows how much we are led to busy ourselves in attempts to subdue the faculties and affections of the outward man, by the fact of a carnal mind still strong within from which we flee to toil in outward things. Some affection of the outward man, some natural faculty which is engaged in outward things,— Laban's daughters and flocks,—are sought and won. Is not this good ? Surely, very good. Nevertheless it may result from the power of the carnal mind within, which distresses the spirit, and forces it, with a vague hope of thus acquiring power, into efforts to rule our outward man. But not thus is Esau overcome. Our zeal to subdue the faculties and affections of the outward man, blessed as such service is, and much as it enriches us,—for Jacob wins both wives and flocks and herds from Laban,—will never make Jacob Esau's lord. We may have toiled with Laban, and be increased, and possess his goods as our rightful portion, earned by hard labour; yet this will not master Esau: after this, Esau is yet " my lord Esau." This is learnt as we advance. Here we see that Jacob's service to Laban in one view is a result of Esau's violence. The very strength of the carnal mind within drives the spirit in us to efforts to subdue the outward man.

Another motive is desire for fruit. Isaac says, " Arise, go down to Padan-Aram, and take a wife thence of the daughters of Laban, thy mother's brother; and God Almighty bless thee, and make thee fruitful, and multiply thee, that thou mayest be a multitude of people." [3] In this view our service aims to bring forth fruit. The spirit of sonship urges us on to attempt to subdue natural affections, that we may increase spiritually. Thus our service is not urged on through fear only; there is also a pure desire for increased fruitfulness. On this motive, I need not dwell; all know it, in whom the spirit of service has come and grown strong.

Jacob's service has yet another end. If Rebekah, and Isaac have each their purpose in it, no less has God His, to work something in Jacob as well as by him, to chasten his spirit, and wean him from his self-confidence. For the spirit of service needs breaking in. If when first awakened to the prospect of overcoming that in us which is of the flesh and " first and natural," it could effect this at once and in its own strength, it would thereby most surely be a loser. Self-will would come in, and self-satisfaction, making the very victory a worse defeat. It would be our kingdom rather than God's; and our spirit, unbroken and

[3] Chap. xxviii. 2, 3.

unchastened, could not be truly blest. For not by strength, but in weakness, does God's kingdom come; not in obtaining our will, but in His will. It is only by the death of all our hopes in self, and this after we have tried our energies to the uttermost, that we are brought really to rest in God. In the walk of faith and sonship we have already proved this. In the effort to subdue our carnal mind and outward man, that is, as Jacobs, the same lesson must be learnt again. Only by sad experience is the spirit of service purged from its tendency to self-confidence and self-exaltation.

Thus Jacob goes forth to toil. Meanwhile, Esau, hearing Isaac's charge to Jacob, that he should not take a wife of the daughters of the Canaanites, now takes to himself another wife, a daughter of Ishmael, Abraham's carnal son. Thus Jacob's course affects Esau, no less than Esau's violence had affected Jacob. We read " when Esau saw that Isaac had sent Jacob into Padan-Aram, to take a wife from thence, and that as he blessed him he gave him a charge, saying, Thou shalt not take a wife of the daughters of Canaan, and that Jacob obeyed his father and his mother, and was gone to Padan-Aram; Esau, seeing that the daughters of Canaan (whom he had already married [4]) pleased not Isaac his father, went unto Ishmael, and took unto the wives which he had Mahalath, the daughter of Ishmael, Abraham's son, the sister of Nebajoth, to be his wife." [5] This yet is Esau's way. The carnal mind, having been excited by the elect to seek the blessing, and having failed to obtain it, learning that Canaanitish wives, the evil principles which it has embraced, are obnoxious to the spirit, and seeing the spirit bent on obtaining better fruit, does not, indeed, put

---

[4] Chap. xxvi. 34, 35, and xxvii. 46. [5] Chap. xxviii. 6-9.

away the former wives, but adds to them another from Abraham's carnal seed, that is, some principle, which has sprung from the union of faith with law, and which, though Abraham's or faith's seed, is yet its carnal seed. Thus does Esau seek better fruit; and this act shews a desire for some measure of reformation. But spite of its aim, it is a mistake. The carnal mind will never be improved by adopting principles which are only the carnal fruit of true faith. The elder cannot be heir; flesh is flesh, and, improved as it may be, cannot inherit heavenly things.

To return to Jacob, his way seems hard enough. Alone, with a staff in his hands, but all unused to journeying, he turns his face towards Laban's house. Night comes on, and he lies down to sleep, with stones for pillows. In the darkness God is near. If He chastens with one hand, He sustains with the other. So Jacob sees a vision, such as our Lord promises to an Israelite indeed in whom is no guile.[6] He sees heaven opened, and angels of God ascending and descending upon a son of man. He sees how one chastened for sin, in darkness, still weaker than the first-born, and to be yet more humbled, is yet the care of God. Earth is shut, but heaven is opened; there is a path, linking the seen with the unseen, leading upward, and assuring present help. The Lord is not seen to come down, as afterwards,—for at a later stage, we read, "He went up, after He had talked with him,"[7]—but the promise is heard, and the Lord appears "above the ladder;" above, yet in communication with him. Then the sevenfold promise again is heard, "Behold, I am with thee, and will help thee in all places whither thou goest, for I will not leave thee until I have done that which I have spoken to thee of."[8]

[6] Chap. xxviii. 12, and John i. 51.

[7] Chap. xxxv. 13.

[8] Chap. xxviii. 13–15.

The spirit of service is yet thus refreshed. It needs, and must receive, correction, but a hand of love administers it. Solitude and darkness may be its lot; but in the darkness the Lord brings into view and opens heavenly things.[9] Light shines out, and fills the soul. Fears, enmities, and sorrows, for a season at least are lost to view. God fills the eye. And afterwards as our spirit journeys on, faint and travel-stained, through the appointed pilgrimage, the recollection of that hour of conscious communion comes back to us as a point of light and joy to cheer and strengthen us. Such moments are memorable indeed. We go far in the strength of that communion. We may, indeed, meet such a revelation, not with the strong grasp of faith, but like Jacob, with a half-fearing cry, " How terrible is this place!" Our surprise may shew how unaccustomed we are to see the Lord. Our language, " If God will be with me," may betray our feeble faith, which can utter an " if," in reply to God's unfailing " I will." But the vision is never to be forgotten. Our spirit " lifts up its feet," and journeys on with fresh alacrity.[10]

It is the same story without. God's servants go forth to service with very mixed and different ends. The desire for fruit is not our only motive. Our service may

---

[9] The Fathers call especial notice to the stone which Jacob took for a pillow: — " Notandum est, quod ille dormiens angelos conspicit, qui in lapide caput ponit. Quia nimirum ipse ab exterioribus operibus cessans æterna penetrat, qui intentâ mente, quæ principale est hominis, imitationem sui Redemptoris observat. Caput quippe in lapide ponere, est mente Christo inhærere. Qui enim a præsentis vitæ actione remoti sunt, sed ad superna nullo amore rapiuntur, dormire possunt, (id est, in dierum libentium cursu ab appetitu visibilium mentis oculos claudere,) sed videre angelos nequeunt, quia caput in lapide tenere contemnunt." — *Greg. M. Moral. in Job*, l. v. c. 31, § 54. Augustine gives the same interpretation, *In Johan. Tract.* vii. § 23.

[10] Jacob " lifted up his feet," &c., chap. xxix. 1, margin. Heb. יִשָּׂא רַגְלָיו. The Samaritan, Chaldee, and LXX. versions, all translate this verbatim.

be also a result of the opposition of carnal men within the Church. Christ may be "preached of strife," as well as of "love;" [11] and even our truest attempts to shew love be mixed with much that is selfish and uncharitable. Such poor worms are we at the best. In seeking to be catholic, we are often most sectarian. So in seeking to be loving and to win souls to Christ, we are too often unchristlike and unloving. But we learn even by our mistakes, — by falling, to walk upright — by many sad blots, at last to write fairly. And so out of our mixed motives God brings forth good ; for far above our thoughts He is working something in, as well as by, His servants. If none else are served, the Lord's servants themselves should be served and profited by their own ministry. Who would have thought that a course of toil could be both a labour of love, voluntarily entered upon, and bringing its own reward, and at the same time an appointed means to humble us. All our Christian path is such ; but this stage above all others shews, that our most devoted service, undertaken to please God, and to bear fruit to the praise of His faithfulness, in another aspect may be God's disciplining rod. Those especially who have engaged in service, and have spent their lives, willingly, but at great cost to themselves, in some peculiar and trying toil and testimony, will on looking back on their path, as they draw towards its close, feel how the trials of their way have been precisely that discipline which their souls most needed. I believe all suffering will on one side be found to be corrective, even though it comes upon us in the course of the most willing and holy and accepted service. The service may be blessed, the reward great, yet in its sorrows, in those very crosses for which we shall

[11] Phil. i. 16, 17.

receive a full reward, God may be teaching us obedience by the things which we suffer. Thus God's servants start, and in darkness find how near He is, and that there is a ladder joining earth to heaven, the seen to the unseen, by which their spirits can rise to Him, be they where they may, and His Spirit in return come down upon them. This is seen when we would serve. Not Abraham, or even Isaac, but Jacob beholds this ladder reared up. For the spirit of faith, and even sonship, are slow to learn what the Incarnation means. But God's servants could never serve at all in outward things, if in some measure at least this vision were not vouchsafed to them. Therefore, as they go forth to serve, they are shewn what Christ's flesh means, and what a link between highest and lowest, the outermost and innermost, is everlastingly assured to us thereby. [12] Do the angels descend as well as ascend? Has the Lord of angels Himself by His flesh come down,

---

[12] Augustine several times alludes to this, explaining this ladder by our Lord's words to Nathaniel, John i. 51. " In somnis vidit scalam. . . . Somnium hominis nod scriberetur nisi magnum in illo aliquid figuraretur mysterium," &c.--*Serm.* 122, § 2. The way in which he proceeds in another place to apply this vision, as an example of ministry, which, after the pattern of the angels and of Christ's Incarnation, should come down to earth as well as rise to heaven, is most striking:—" Quid autem vidit tunc in scalis? Adscendentes et descendentes angelos. Sic est et Ecclesia. Angeli Dei, boni prædicatores, prædicantes Christum; hoc est super Filium hominis adscendunt et descendunt. Quomodo adscendunt, et quomodo descendunt? Ex uno habemus exemplum. Audi Apostolum Paulum: quod in ipso invenerimus, hoc de cæteris veritatis prædicatoribus credamus. Vide Paulum adscendentem; 'Scio hominem in Christo raptum fuisse usque in tertium cœlum,' &c. Descendentem audite; 'Non potui loqui vobis quasi spiritalibus, sed quasi carnalibus: quasi parvulis in Christo lac vobis potum dedi, non escam.' . . . 'Factus sum parvulus,' inquit, 'in medio vestrûm, tanquam si nutrix foveat filios suos.' Videmus enim et nutrices et matres descendere ad parvulos, ... et disertus aliquis pater . . . si habeat parvulum filium, . . . linguâ puerili descendit ad parvulum. . . . Si ipse Dominus adscendit et descendit, manifestum est, quia prædicatores ipsius adscendunt imitatione, descendunt prædicatione." — *In Johan. Tract.* vii. § 23.

and been made a Jew to gain the Jews? Then His
servants too may come down to earth, and may leave their
own high and heavenly ground to win earthly souls; may
assume a fleshly form for fleshly souls, and become as Jews
to Jews, and as babes to babes, for others,[13] in the assurance that everything and anything on earth may be
sanctified by the word of God and prayer and thanksgiving. Henceforth every spot is holy ground. We cannot
call any man, however outward, common or unclean.
For heaven is linked with earth. Shall we then, who are
of the earth, count any on earth alien to us? Rather
with Jacob we say even of the untilled field, " Surely the
Lord is in this place, and I knew it not." [14] Not till
this is seen are we fitted for service in the outward world.

III. — The Service for Wives and Flocks

Chapter 29 and 30

We now come to the service in Padan-Aram. Evangelic
service is here photographed; for the Light Himself has
drawn each minutest particular, the trials, mistakes,
successes, and results, as none but light could draw them.
Jacob is seen in Laban's house, toiling there, first to gain
his daughters, then his flocks and herds. First, the
daughters of Laban are won; that is, certain affections or
truths, which by nature are akin and subject to our
outward man, are embraced by the spirit, and so become
fruitful. Then Laban's flocks and herds are gained; that
is, the animal faculties and emotions, which hitherto have
been altogether under the power of the outward man,

---

[13] 1 Cor. ix. 19, 20.   [14] Chap. xxviii. 16.

henceforth obey the spirit, and follow, though still animal and irrational, the directions of the spirit rather than of the outward man. This is not done without long toil. Many a night does Jacob watch, and many a weary day. "In the day the drought consumes him, and the frost by night: sleep departs from his eyes, and slumber from his eyelids."[1] But the work is done at last. Laban's daughters and flocks and herds serve Jacob, and he "increases exceedingly."

Such is the scene, and the outline is clear: the details need a man's, not to say an angel's, eye. For service is pictured here. Ministering spirits, therefore, according to their measure, will understand this. To others, because the reality is unknown, the picture must needs be more or less a puzzle.

We are first shewn Laban's state, when Jacob comes; then the service rendered to him; and lastly, the results of it. We may trace it within and without. The outward fulfilment will, as ever, be clearest to earthly eyes.

First, to trace it within. Laban's state is seen, that is the state of the outward man, when Jacob or the spirit of service begins to act on him. In reply to the question, "Is he well?" the answer given is, "He is well;"[2] for the natural man, till by dealings with the elect it begins to know itself, is ever self-satisfied. And yet, "it was not much he had before Jacob came."[3] A well, some sheep, and two daughters, were the better part of his possessions. And the water was scarce, for as a rule the well was closed; while his fairest daughter was occupied with the cattle, in outward more than inward things.[4] These figures are

---

[1] Chap. xxxi. 40.
[2] Chap. xxix. 6.
[3] Chap. xxx. 30.
[4] Chap. xxix. 1–9.

all familiar to us. Wells, and sheep, and daughters have again and again passed before our eyes.[5] Women are affections; but, as our principles are ever what our affections are, they also figure certain principles. Hagar, Sarah, and others, have made this clear. Here two women are seen; the elder, the first and outward affection or principle of the natural man; the younger, the later more inward principle: and of these even the fairest is yet in outward things. Nevertheless Laban welcomes Jacob: — "He ran to meet him, and brought him into his house."[6] For the outward man at first is glad to be served, and for awhile is strengthened, though in the end weakened and impoverished, by the efforts of Jacob, the spiritual inward man.

Jacob's service then begins by assisting Rachel, the younger daughter, to open the covered well. Then he gives drink to Laban's flocks. After this, he proceeds to serve with a fixed aim, first for the daughters, then the flocks, of Laban. The course and results of this service are most significant.

Laban's daughters are toiled for first, more strictly the younger daughter, though Jacob in fact obtains both. "Leah was tender or weak-eyed,[7] but Rachel was beautiful and well-favoured. And Jacob loved Rachel, and said, I will serve thee seven years for Rachel thy younger daughter."[8] He wishes for Rachel alone; but at length, after seven years' service, and when he hopes to have her, he is deceived by Laban, and put off with Leah. "It

---

[5] For "wells," see on chap. xxi., xxv. 1–11, and xxvi. For "flocks," on chap. i. xiii. and xxii. For "daughters," on chap. vi. and xvi., and elsewhere.

[6] Chap. xxix. 13.

[7] Our version, "tender-eyed," is not very plain. The LXX. translate, $\dot{o}\phi\theta\alpha\lambda\mu o\grave{\iota}$ $\dot{\alpha}\sigma\theta\epsilon\nu\epsilon\hat{\iota}s$: the Vulgate, "lippis oculis."

[8] Chap. xxix. 15–18.

came to pass in the evening, that Laban took Leah, and brought her to Jacob, and he went in unto her. And in the morning, behold, it was Leah. And he said to Laban, What is this that thou hast done unto me? Did I not serve thee for Rachel? Wherefore then hast thou beguiled me? And Laban said, It must not be so done in our country, to give the younger before the first-born." Jacob gets Rachel after all; but against his will and unknown to him he first embraces Leah. It must be so. " It is not so done in that country to give the younger before the first-born."

Laban's daughters as we have seen, are the affections or principles of the outward man. At each stage, as believer, or son, or servant, the elect spirit embraces one or more of these. Like seed, it finds a soil: it does not make it; and that soil is throughout human and natural. Thus is our fallen nature laid hold of by the Spirit, and out of its affections, earthly as they are, good fruit is borne to God's glory. The mystery of the Incarnation is the outward witness of this. And He who abhorred not the Virgin's womb,— who said, " I will dwell in you and walk in you,"—who took our nature and our infirmities upon Him,— out of the woman in us yet brings forth spiritual fruit. But the elect's aim is to gain, not the elder or first-born, but the younger or more inward and spiritual affection of the natural man. The first-born has few or no attractions for him. The spirit desires rather to gain what is lovely and spiritual of the outward man. Seven years he labours for this, and " they seemed but a few days for the love he had unto her; " [9] for when the spirit is full of love, time is nothing: love makes our life, like that of the angels, wholly out of time. But there is a sort of necessity

[9] Chap. xxix. 20.

for taking the first and natural before the spiritual. While we only desire the inward, we are put off with the outward, which we do not love. We may think we have got Rachel, but it is Leah. The old man has been too cunning for us. For we are in the dark,[10] and know not what we are doing. When, however, light breaks in, we learn how, with all our love for the younger, we have been deceived. Oh, how many, who have only got Leah, think it is Rachel, simply because they are in the dark. If they love Rachel, she too shall be theirs. In due time, after our carnal haste has been met by what is first and natural, we shall obtain the spiritual. But action precedes contemplation; a life on outward principles must come before an inward life; and the outward though not so fair, is more fruitful: not by one alone, but by both of these, is Israel built up.[11]

Surely there is a "needs be" for this. Laban could not

---

[10] " It came to pass in the evening," &c., chap. xxix. 23, Respecting the "evening," see on chap. ii.

[11] Augustine, Gregory the Great, Bernard, and others, agree substantially in this interpretation. Augustine pursues the subject at very great length, *Contra Faustum Man.* l. xxii. cc. 51–58. Gregory the Great writes briefly thus : — " Has utrasque vitas, (*i.e.* the outward and inward,) sicut et ante nos dictum est, duæ beati Jacob mulieres significaverunt, Lia videlicet et Rachel. Lia quippe interpretatur ' laboriosa;' Rachel vero ' ovis' vel ' visum principium.' Activa autem vita laboriosa est, quia desudat in opere : contemplativa vero simplex ad solum videndum principium anhelat. . . Beatus autem Jacob Rachel quidem concupierat, sed in nocte accepit Liam ; quia videlicet omnis qui ad Dominum convertitur contemplativam vitam desiderat, . . . sed prius necesse est ut in nocte vitæ præsentis desudet in labore. . . Erat autem Rachel videns et sterilis Lia autem lippa sed fœcunda ; quia nimirum mens cùm contemplando otia appetit, plus videt, sed minus filios Deo generat, cùm vero ad laborem se prædicationis dirigit, minus videt, sed amplius parit. . . . Post Liæ complexum ad Rachelem Jacob pervenit, quia perfectus quisque ante activæ vitæ ad fœcunditatem jungitur, et post contemplativæ ad requiem copulatur." — *In Ezech.* l. ii. h. 2, § 10. Bernard gives a similar exposition, *Lib. de Modo bene vivendi, ad Sororem,* c. 53. Compare the passage above from the *Catena Aurea,* on chap. xii. p. 160.

have crossed Jacob's purpose, had not God permitted it. Unwearied love is watching Jacob's steps. Not chance but love gives him weak-eyed but fruitful Leah, as well as fair Rachel; love to Laban, to win yet more of his seed, to win the outward as well as the inward affections of the natural man; love to Jacob, for he is unfit for the best things: an outward principle is the only one by which at present he can bear fruit. We may wish for the best things, like Jacob here; but for our profit we are at first united to outward principles. It was but now that we made ourselves rough like the first-born: justly therefore are we put off with Laban's first-born. When we are more spiritual, the spiritual shall be within our reach.[12] Thus do the principles which we receive,—and mere head-knowledge is not reception, for as Jacob loved and was acquainted with Rachel long before he got her, so is there an acquaintance with truth, which precedes that union with it which results in fruitfulness,— thus do the principles we hold shew what we are. Happy is it, when being spiritual we can bear spiritual things. But far safer is it for us, and a pledge of God's true loving-kindness, that while we are yet carnal we should only reach carnal things.

Jacob next serves for Laban's flocks, until, after six

---

[12] Augustine is so diffuse here that one can scarcely make a satisfactory extract, but the following is striking: — " Hanc (*i. e.* Leah) sustinet, ut ad illam (*i. e.* Rachel) perveniat, si perseveranter amat, acceptis illis septem præceptis; ac si dicatur ei, 'Servi alios septem annos pro Rachel,' ut sit pauper spiritu, mitis, lugens, esuriens sitiensque justitiam, misericors, mundicors, pacificus. Vellet enim homo, si fieri posset sine ullâ tolerantiâ laboris, (*i. e.* Leah,) quæ in agendo patiendoque amplectenda est, statim ad pulchræ atque perfectæ sapientiæ delicias, (*i. e.* Rachel,) pervenire. Sed hoc non potest in terrâ morientium. Hoc enim videtur significare, quod dictum est ad Jacob, 'Non est moris in loco nostro, ut minor nubat priusquam major,' " &c. — *Contr. Faust. Man.* l. xxii. c. 53.

years more labour, a great part of the cattle have changed masters, and are henceforth Jacob's flock. It appears that Jacob, having got Rachel, wished to leave. Then Laban answers, "I pray thee, tarry; for I have learnt by experience that the Lord hath blessed me for thy sake. And he said, What shall I give thee? And Jacob said, Thou shalt not give me anything: if thou wilt do this for me, I will again feed and keep thy flock. I will pass through thy flock, removing thence all the speckled and spotted cattle, and of such shall my hire be. And Laban said, Behold, I would it might be according to thy word." [13] The bargain is that Jacob is to have the "speckled and spotted," and of these ere long by his art he gains the larger and stronger flock. Out of flocks of one colour, he gets others speckled and ring-straked; and the flocks change masters only by changing colours. "Jacob took rods of poplar and almond and chestnut tree, and peeled white strakes in them, and made the white appear which was in the rods. And he set the rods which he peeled before the flocks in the gutters, in the watering troughs when they came to drink, that they should conceive when they came to drink. And the flocks conceived before the rods, and brought forth cattle, ring-straked, speckled, and spotted." [14]

Even so are the flocks yet won. Those animal emotions, which hitherto have been altogether under the power of our outward man, by the spirit's efforts receive another hue, and shew in their very appearance the spirit's handywork. Animal emotions of course are animal to the end, but on them a great outward change has passed, so that even the old man must confess they do not look as they used to look. Jacob has changed their hue. This is done by setting rods

[13] Chap. **xxx.** 31–34.   [14] Chap. **xxx.** 37–39.

of varied colours before their eyes. These "rods" are portions of the Word;[15] and like that, which, when stretched out over the sea, opened a path for Israel,[16] or that, which, though dry, when laid up before the Lord, budded and blossomed and brought forth almonds,[17] these feeble rods effect great things: by them, as by "the rod out of the stem of Jesse,"[18] the weak are made strong. These, partly peeled, partly unpeeled,— peeled, that is with the inward sense opened, so that what is covered and hidden within may be brought to light,— unpeeled, that is in the letter alone, with the outward covering still untouched, as at first we always see the Word,—are set before the flocks, where the living streams are opened, that the offspring or fruit may take another hue.[19] The animal in us is only thus won; nor can the spirit claim anything

---

[15] See what is said of the trees of knowledge and life, on chap. ii.

[16] Exod. xiv. 16.

[17] Numb. xvii. 8.

[18] Isa. xi. 1.

[19] Gregory the Great thus explains these rods:—"Quid est virgas virides et amygdalinas atque ex platanis ante oculos gregum ponere, nisi per Scripturæ Sacræ seriem antiquorum patrum vitas atque sententias in exemplum præbere. Quæ nimirum quia juxta rationis examen rectæ sunt, virgæ nominantur. Quibus et ex parte corticem subtrahit, ut in his quæ exspoliantur intimus candor appareat; et ex parte corticem servat, et sicut fuerant exterius, in viriditate permaneant; variusque virgarum color efficitur, dum cortex et ex parte subtrahitur, et ex parte retinetur. Ante considerationis enim nostræ oculos præcedentium patrum. sententiæ quasi virgæ ponuntur; in quibus dum plerumque intellectum literæ fugimus, quasi corticem subtrahimus; et dum plerumque intellectum literæ sequimur, quasi corticem servamus. . .Quas bene Jacob in aquæ canalibus posuit; quia et Redemptor noster in libris eas sacræ scientiæ, quibus nos intrinsecus infundimur, fixit. Has aspicientes arietes cum ovibus coëunt, quia rationales nostri spiritus, dum in earum intentione defixi sunt, singulis quibuscumque actionibus permiscentur, ut tales fetus operum procreent, qualia exempla præcedentium in vocibus præceptorum vident, et diversum colorem proles boni operis habeat; quia et nonnunquam subtracto literæ cortice acutius interna considerat, et reservato nonnunquam historiæ tegmine bona in exterioribus format." —*Moral. in Job*, l. xxi. c. 1. Ambrose gives a similar interpretation, *De Jacob.* l. ii. c. 4, § 19. Justin Martyr too alludes to these rods, as figuring the doctrine of the cross, *Dial. c. Tryph.* c. 86.

of the old man's, save that on which it has exerted a transforming influence.

As the results of this service, Jacob obtains, not Laban's daughters and flocks only, but fruit by each of these. First he gets fruit by the daughters. These children by Leah and Rachel and the bond-maids are the different forms of life which are produced by the spirit of service in us out of different principles; Leah and Rachel representing the higher principles, outward or inward; the bondmaids, other lower principles, subservient to the former, but which are also embraced and produce their own fruit. First come four sons by Leah, whose names point out the peculiar form of life which each shadows forth; Reuben, intelligence;[20] then Simeon, obedience;[21] then Levi, service;[22] then Judah, rule.[23] Then come the sons of Rachel's maid; first Dan, that is "judgment" or justice; then Naphtali, that is victorious "strugglings." After this the fruit of Leah's maid; first Gad, a "troop" or power; then Asher, or "happiness." Then Leah herself again has sons;

---

[20] Reuben, *i. e.* "filius visionis." Jerome, *Nom. Heb.* "Seeing" is the common figure for intelligence. Cf. Numb. xxi. 8, 9, and John iii. 14, 15; Luke xxiv. 31; John vi. 36, 40, 46, 47.

[21] Simeon, *i. e.* "auditio." Jerome, *Nom. Heb.* "Hearing," or "hearkening," is synonymous with obedience. See 1 Sam. xv. 22; John x. 2, 3, 16, 27, xviii. 37; Isa. lv. 2; Jer. vii. 23, 24, 26.

[22] Levi, *i. e.* "conjunctio." Jerome, *Nom. Heb.* The force of this name, "joining," as representing service, may be seen in many Scriptures: — Isa. lvi. 3, 6; Numb. xviii. 2; Mat. vi. 24; Jer l. 5; Zech. ii. 15. See also Gen. ii. 24, and Mat. xix. 5, where the word "joining" shews

the very intimate and sanctified service connected with the marriage tie.

[23] Judah, *i. e.* "confessio." See Psalm c. 1–5. This and the succeeding names need no illustration. I may add here, that in the naming of Leah's first four sons, she connects the fruitfulness with "*the Lord*," saying, "I will praise the Lord," &c.; while in the naming of the last two she speaks of "*God*," saying, "God hath given me my hire," &c. Compare chap. xxix. 32, 33, 35, with chap. xxx. 18, 20. See also chap. xxx. 24, where Rachel says, "The *Lord* shall add," &c. This is not without a reason. We have noticed a similar change in the 1st and 2nd chapters.

Issachar, or a "reward," representing the actual joy of labour, as the Psalmist says, "In keeping thy commandments there is great reward;" then Zebulon, "dwelling together," or communion ; then Dinah, whose name signifies the same as Dan, but in whom, as a daughter, justice is seen as a principle rather than an active life.   After this Rachel brings forth a son, the lovely fruit of a life of patient suffering; "And she said, God hath taken away my reproach : and she called his name Joseph," that is "addition " or increase.   All these are the fruits of service in us, some better than others, some destined to cause grief; all needing rule and culture, yet owned and formed by the Lord to shew forth his praise.[24]

Jacob's service gained more than this.   Laban's flocks, as well as his daughters, come at last into Jacob's hands. Not only do the affections and principles of the natural man come under the spirit's government, and produce spiritual fruit, but even the animal emotions after long watchings are gained, and out of them also there is much increase to God's glory.

The results of this on Laban are, that he is increased at first,[25] but impoverished in the long run.[26]   When the spirit of service comes to deal with the natural man, and works with him and for him, for a season the outward man is enriched ; but further service, if it continue long enough, will as surely weaken him.   And the old man not seeing God's hand in this, that it is " God who has taken away his cattle," [27] is angry because he is made poor; but he

---

[24] The reader who cares to pursue this subject, will find it treated at great length, and with much spiritual insight, in a volume entitled, *"The Patriarchs, as setting forth the things of the Sermon on the Mount;"* being the Christian Advocate's publication for 1849, by Thomas Worsley, Master of Downing College, Cambridge.

[25] Chap. xxx. 27-30.

[26] Chap. xxxi. 1.

[27] Chap xxxi. 9.

cannot hurt the inward man, and all his wrath only hastens the further accomplishment of the Lord's promise.

I have thus traced this scene within, because if this inward view be known, the other more outward fulfilment of it will of course be manifest. But some will see it without, better than within. Without, Jacob's service sets forth the labour of those, who, though heirs, seek to win out of the far country, and from the power of the natural man, children and flocks whom they may take back to a better land. They come down to Laban's ground; for only thus, by coming down among natural men, can elect servants reach those whom they are looking for. Here they toil for children and flocks. Like Jacob, they would fain have Rachel only, that is a spiritual church; but in the world, and while serving there, they find that they must have outward principles also and an outward church. As Isaacs, or sons, we may have Rebekah only, though even by her we have a twofold seed; but if we come to be servants, whose "hand must take hold," we shall find that we must take blear-eyed Leah as well as fair Rachel. Those who know only sonship may judge as carnal the Jacobs who have been led on by grace to reach a further stage; but if they advance to apprehend what they are apprehended for, they themselves may, and surely will, attain to Jacob's life. Then will they find that, even when they think to pass by the elder, in the outward world and in service it is impossible. In service we must have the two wives; an outward church, and outward and natural principles, as well as spiritual. We may wish to escape this, but in the result we shall not be able to boast over our father Jacob. I speak that which I know, and testify what I have seen; and I know that though at first it would be more in accordance with the mind of true servants not to have Leah, there is a stage when she too is needful and fitting, and therefore not without divine permission is given to us; and not she alone, but the two handmaids also, that is, even lower and yet more servile principles.[28] So we serve, and the Lord builds the house: sons are given, very diverse, though sprung from one common father, and heirs of one inheritance; some are Reubens, good mediums for light, like water, but "unstable as water," excitable and prone to defile their father's bed;[29] some are Simeons, quick to give ear, but apt, in their zeal for obedience, to perform cruel things;[30] some are Levis, joined to the Lord in service, entering into His presence with oblations presented

---

[28] Augustine, whose comment throughout is striking, thus interprets the handmaids:—"Rachel autem . . . . dolet potius currere homines ad eam virtutem, quâ eorum infirmitatibus necessitatibusque consulitur, (viz. Leah, the outward principle,) quàm ad illam unde divinum et incommutabile aliquid discitur. Hic dolor figuratus videtur in eo quod scriptum est 'Et zelavit Rachel sororem suam.' Proinde quia liquidus purusque intellectus de illâ substantiâ quæ corpus non est, ac per hoc ad carnis sensum non pertinet, verbis carne editis exprimi non potest, eligit doctrina sapientiæ per quaslibet corporeas imagines et similitudines utcumque cogitanda insinuare divina, quàm ab officio talia docendi cessare; sicut elegit Rachel ex viro suo et ancillâ suscipere liberos, quàm sine filiis omnino remanere. Bala quippe interpretari dicitur 'Inveterata:' hanc habuit ancillam Rachel. De vetere quippe vitâ carnalibus sensibus deditâ corporeæ concitantur imagines, etiam

cum aliquid de spiritali et incommunicabili substantiâ divinitùs auditur. Suscipit et Lia de ancillâ suâ filios. . . . Invenimus autem Zelpham ejus ancillam interpretari 'Os hians.' Quapropter in prædicationem fidei evangelicæ, quorum os hiat, et cor non hiat, cùm in Scripturis adverterimus, hæc intelligitur ancilla Liæ. Scriptum est enim de quibusdam, 'Populus hic labiis me honorat, cor autem eorum longè est a me.' . . Verumtamen ut etiam per hanc conditionem libera illa uxor Jacob laborans filios hæredes regni suscipiat, ideo Dominus dicit, 'Quæ dicunt, facite; quæ autem faciunt, facere nolite.' Unde in labore vinculorum vita Apostolica, 'Sive,' inquit, 'occasione, sive veritate Christus annuntietur, et in hoc gaudeo, sed et gaudebo;' tanquam et ancillâ pariente de prole numerosiore lætata."—*Contr. Faustum,* l. xxii. c. 55.

[29] Chap. xlix. 4.

[30] Chap. xlix. 5, 6.

for their more outward brethren;[31] some are Judahs, gifted for rule, and to be praised, because their hand shall be upon the neck of all their enemies;[32] some are Dans, ready to judge Israel;[33] some Naphtalis, satisfied with favour, and full of the blessing of the Lord;[34] some are Gads, overcome at first, but strong at last;[35] some Ashers, who dip their feet in oil, and are acceptable to their brethren;[36] some Issachars, crouching down between their burdens;[37] some Zebuluns, occupied with the outward things and commerce of the great salt sea of this world;[38] some the children of Rachel, like Joseph, sorely shot at, but whose bow abides in strength, because the arms of their hands are made strong by the hands of the mighty God of Jacob.[39] The fairest come the last; but all, better or worse, make up one house of Israel.

This service further wins flocks. We serve to gain even animal and irrational natures, whose colour is changed indeed, but who remain to the end rough and animal; not true sons, but needing to be fed and led by such; who nevertheless, speckled and spotted though they be, under the Spirit's guidance may be brought safely into a better land. At first we feed a flock which is not ours; but in due time, not without long toil, those, who once obeyed and served the world, obey a better guide. True servants labour night and day: by night the frost, and by day the drought, consumes them. Some of the flock at times are torn by beasts, and they bear the loss;[40] but at last a flock is won whose change of colour shews the

---

[31] Deut. xxxiii. 10.
[32] Chap. xlix. 8, 10.
[33] Chap. xlix. 16.
[34] Deut. xxxiii. 23.
[35] Chap. xlix. 19.

[36] Deut. xxxiii. 24.
[37] Chap. xlix. 14.
[38] Chap. xlix. 13.
[39] Chap. xlix. 23, 24.
[40] Chap. xxxi. 39, 40.

presence of more than human skill.[41]   And the colour of
the flocks is changed, now as of old, by that which is set
before their eyes, where the living waters are poured forth.
Men yet become like what they look at.   "We all, with
open face, beholding as in a glass the glory of the Lord,
are changed into the same image:"[42] and at last, "We shall
be like Him, for we shall see Him as He is."[43]   But the
world, like Laban's sons, cannot perceive God's hand in
this; they say "Jacob hath taken away all that was our
father's:" while true servants confess that the work is
God's, saying, "God hath taken away the cattle of your
father, and given them to me."[44]

The dispensations too reflect this scene.   In this view
we have here the experience of Christ's Spirit as servant in
this world.   He comes into the outward world to serve.
When He comes water is scarce : then He opens the well,
and feeds the flocks, and seeks union with the seed of the
natural man.   Fain would He have the younger daughter
alone ; but He must, such are the requirements of the
natural man, first take the elder or first-born.   So Leah or
law comes first : and then Rachel, that is the gospel dispensation.   Leah is fruitful, while Rachel has yet no son.
But at length the Gospel yields fruit ; and then the old or
natural man, who had been improved while Jacob had
children by Leah, that is, throughout the Jewish age, is
much impoverished and loses his wealth, after Rachel is
fruitful, that is, in gospel days.   In a word, as Sarah and
Hagar prefigure these two dispensations in their connection

---

[41] Jacob's words, chap. xxxi. 8–
12, shew that the means he used to
change the colour of the flocks were
shewn him in "a vision."

[42] 2 Cor. iii. 18.
[43] 1 John iii. 2.
[44] Chap. xxxi. 1, 9.

with the spirit of faith, and thus in reference to heavenly things, Jacob's wives set forth the same dispensations, in connection with the spirit of service, and so in reference to earthly things.[45]

Surely it is a wondrous tale, respecting which many unspeakable words remain, which it is not possible to utter here.

IV.—THE DEPARTURE FROM LABAN

Chapter 31

WE are now to see the efforts of Jacob to lead what he has won in Mesopotamia into Canaan, with Laban's attempts to hinder it. As fulfilled within, we have here the travail of the spirit to set our affections on things above, and not on earthly things,[1] and the hindrance to this which the old man offers, the open opposition or secret craft, by which he would keep our affections, which are by nature akin to him, still bound in outward things. As fulfilled without, we see the toil of true servants to lead those whom they have gained out of the world into a better land, and all the hindrance which worldlings throw in their way, the seductions held out, and the reasons which are urged, to keep them in outward things. It is a scene known to all who have toiled long in the world, and at length have set

---

[45] This dispensational view is common to many of the Fathers:— Ambrose says, "Ipse autem est qui præfigurabatur in Jacob, Dominus Jesus, sponsus duorum conjugiorum, hoc est legis et gratiæ, que virginem Rachel ante dilexit, et prædestinatam sibi in conjugium pio amabat affectu. Sed quoniam Lia tanquam lex subintravit, et oculis infirmior obrepsit tanquam synagoga, ... superabundavit gratia sanctæ Rachel," &c.—*De Jacob.* l. ii. c. 5, § 25. Gregory the Great gives the same interpretation:—"Per Rachel, quippe quæ et ovis dicitur, Ecclesia figuratur," &c.—*Moral. in Job.* l. xxx. c. 25, § 72. So too Irenæus, *Adv. Hær.* l. iv. c. 21, (al. 38,) § 3.

[1] Col. iii. 2.

their face to go with what they have won into the better land.

As fulfilled within, some parts of this scene, through our ignorance of the inward world, may be beyond our intelligence. Our lack also of fitting words prevents anything like a perfect interpretation to the understanding, although the spirit may see all.[2] But the scene is still fulfilled wherever souls have laboured for fruit, and are striving to come from outward to inward things. Laban envies Jacob's wealth, and attempts in one way or another to get it back again. For the old man in us, though strengthened at first and improved for awhile by the labours of our inward and spiritual man, finds at length that the spirit's work, if continued, instead of strengthening, rather weakens it. It is vexed to see the power the spirit has gained over so many of the affections and emotions of the outward man; that Jacob rules where Laban once did. Thus a strife now manifests itself between our outward and inward man.[3] The old man's ways perplex the inward man. For our spirit, like Jacob, when it begins to work upon the old man, is not at all aware what the result will be. We sincerely hope by service to improve the old man. But though Laban's daughters are won, though the affections or principles of the natural man are subjected and united to the inward man, the old man remains unchanged, to the end ever ready to play us false and to deceive us.[4] And painful as this is, so it must be. The Lord would not have our spirit remain for ever bound to the outward man or to outward things in their present state; for the outward man and the ground he dwells on are yet unpurged, and though the

[2] 1 Cor. xiv. 14, 15.   [3] Chap. xxxi. 1, 2.   [4] Chap. xxxi. 7.

spirit may win much there, it cannot purge that ground or save the outward man. In due time we learn this. Then a voice is heard, saying to our spirit, "Return to the land, and I will be with thee." [5] Thus at one stage having served the old man and outward things, at another we are called again to inward and spiritual things. Knowing this, let us leave souls to walk with God, instead of making, as we are so prone to do, our present standard the one rule. For have not we ourselves in faith been led now to give up and leave all outward things, again in service to seek them, and then again to leave them, to set our affections, where our faith has long since been set, on heavenly things.

But Rachel, though willing to go to Canaan, takes some idols with her, " her father's images;" [6] not the gods representing the powers of nature, such as " the star of your god Remphan," [7] Baal, or Ashtaroth; but rather household gods, [8] forms of departed kindred, which, though at first regarded only as patterns and memorials of honoured forefathers, were soon turned into idols, as guides and precedents to be obeyed and followed instead of the true God. Our inward affections yet cling to such, even when drawn by grace to seek better things; not indeed to the grosser outward idols, but to household idols of pride of birth, past greatness, gentility, custom, fashion, or such like. In other words, our principles, even the best, are not at once wholly purged from all the evils which belong to the outward man. Some of these are still taken with us, although the spirit knows that, not only they cannot help, but are even a shame to us.

---

[5] Chap. xxxi. 3.
[6] Chap. xxxi. 19, 30.
[7] Acts vii. 43.

[8] Heb. תרפים, answering to the Latin *Penates*.

The old man meanwhile does all he can to hinder the affections being set on heavenly things ; just as Laban attempted to stop Jacob, saying, " Wherefore didst thou flee ? Thou hast now done foolishly. Wherefore didst thou not tell me, that I might have sent thee away with mirth and harp and tabrets ?"[9] So the old man argues. Why leave him ? At all events, why not accept his assistance on the way to heavenly things? Can he not make music and laughter for us, and cheer us on by his pipes and harps and tabrets? No. By these he may yet keep us where he is ; they will not help our spirit to heavenly things. Yet the old man fairly asks, — " And now, though thou wouldest needs be gone, yet wherefore hast thou stolen my teraphim ?"[10] Why do the affections, while even reaching towards heaven, yet cling so fast to idol vanities? We shall see how these idols, though hid from Laban, cannot be hid from God, and must be put away before Jacob can come to worship and dwell at Bethel.[11]

As for Laban, he still is unchanged, and dies, as he has lived, in Mesopotamia. Henceforth he may not hinder Jacob, but neither may Jacob seek to hurt him in any way.[12] Each returns to his place. The old man, poorer than at first, settles down again in outward things ; while the inward man, enriched by his labour, journeys on afresh, with what he has gained, to heavenly things.

If we turn now to look without, we shall see the more manifest workings of these same opposing minds ; Laban figuring those in whom the outward man, Jacob, those in whom the spirit of service, is the ruling life. The Jacobs

---

[9] Chap. xxxi. 23–28.
[10] Chap. xxxi. 30.

[11] Chap. xxxv. 1–4.
[12] Chap. xxxi. 44–55.

have won flocks and herds; and this stirs up the wrath
and ill-will of worldly men. But their anger serves God's
end. By it the elect are forced to seek a better land. So
true servants lead the way, and those, who are already
"counted strangers" in the world, follow them;[13] not
wholly blameless, for, unknown to its guides, the Church
takes some of the idols of the world with it, as if these
could succour it.[14] Laban meanwhile is busy too. He
yet possesses flocks, the colour of which remains unchanged
spite of Jacob's art. And while Jacob is fleeing, Laban
is shearing. The one thing here recorded of him is that
"he was shearing sheep."[15] So do outward men yet
count "sheep-shearing" pleasant work. The Jacobs and
Davids feed the flock: the Labans and Nabals and
Absaloms prefer shearing them.[16] Worldlings, like the
king of Moab, may be "sheep-masters,"[17] but they have
not a pastor's heart: the fleece, and not the flock, is what
they care for; and their zeal for the fleece opens a door
for true servants like Jacob to flee away heavenward.
Then comes the world's pursuit. Vexed as they are at
the power gained by the elect, they are more vexed to see
them go, and the way they go thence. Why should they
think of seeking any other land? but after all, if people

---

[13] Chap. xxxi. 15.

[14] Chap. xxxi. 32. Theodoret,
who sees in Jacob's departure the
flight of the church out of the world,
and whose comment in substance is
that given above, thinks that Rachel
stole the idols to free her father from
his superstitions. *In Gen. Qu.* 90.
Ambrose too hints the same, saying,
"Beata Rachel, quæ abscondit cul-
tus, erroresque Gentilium, quæ simu-
lacra eorum plena esse immunditiæ
declaravit," &c. — *De Jacob.* l. ii.

c. 5, § 25. But God's command
respecting these idols, chap. xxxv.
2, implies that they were yet objects
of idolatrous reverence to some in
Jacob's house. Chrysostom regards
this theft of the idols as an instance
of the force of bad habit, even in
true souls. *Hom.* lvii. *in Gen.*

[15] Chap. xxxi. 19.

[16] 1 Sam. xxv. 2, 4 ; 2 Sam. xiii.
23, 24.

[17] 2 Kings iii. 4.

must go, why not accept all the assistance which might be rendered them? Why not have some music and mirth? Why go in a way so unlike the fashions of that land? Thus natural men would stop the elect, or at least would have them go toward heavenly things with their aid and forms and pageantries; and those who go not thus are "foolish;"[18] but Jacob can seek his true home without Laban's aid. All that worldlings can do to help our way is as useful or as useless as Laban's pipes and harps. So true servants depart. God by them has visited the Gentiles, to take out of them a people for His name.[19] This done, the elect journey on; while the world, unchanged by what has been done for it, goes back to its old ground and again settles there.[20]

A voice yet cries, " Hearken, O daughter, and consider; forget thine own people and thy father's house. Then instead of thy fathers shall be thy children, whom thou mayest make princes in all the earth."[21]

V.— THE JOURNEY TO CANAAN, AND CHANGE OF NAME

Chapter 32 and 33:1-16

JACOB's departure from Padan-Aram is an important step, and yet but a step, towards entering the promised land. After Laban is left, it still remains in the face of Esau to go up over Jordan. Leaving outward things is not

---

[18] Chap. xxxi. 27, 28.

[19] Acts xv. 14.

[20] Gregory the Great thus gives the outward view:— "Potest per Laban mundus hic exprimi, qui cum furore Jacob persequitur, quia electos quosque, qui Redemptoris nostri membra sunt, persequendo oppri-

mere conatur. Hujus filiam Jacob abstulit, cum sibi Christus Ecclesiam ex gentilitate conjunxit, quam et de domo patris abstulit, qui ei per prophetam dicit, ' Obliviscere populum tuum, et domum patris tui,' " &c. — *Moral. in Job.* l. xxx. c. 25, § 72.

[21] Psalm xlv. 10, 16.

possessing heavenly things. Not a few have left the world, who are not come to the good land; and yet forsaking the outward world is one stage, and most necessary, for all who at last attain to heavenly things.

Here Jacob, escaped from Laban, is seen, hastening with his children and flocks to enter the promised land. At this point Esau again appears, as determined to stop his entrance into Canaan, as Laban had been to oppose his departure out of Mesopotamia. As fulfilled within, the scene represents the opposition which is offered by the carnal mind to the efforts of the spirit to set our affection on things above: as fulfilled without, it shews the resistance of carnal professors to the efforts of true servants to bring those whom they have won out of the world into the enjoyment of heavenly things. It is a scene of deepest interest; for here, in, and partly by, this trial, in sore wrestlings of spirit Jacob becomes Israel; and the man, whose "hand laid hold," at last in weakness is made a "prince with God."

The opposition here proceeds from Esau. Laban had been the hindrance to Jacob's leaving Mesopotamia; for it is our outward man which stands in the way of our spirit's departure from outward things; but it is the carnal mind within which threatens to stop our attempts to enter heavenly things.[1] And thus after we have turned from the outward man, and have left his old ground tradition and reasoning, another opponent, more closely related to our spirit, remains, in that carnal mind, which grows within us even out of the true elect. And this Esau now threatens our way, if he can, to oppose our possessing the promised land.

---

[1] Respecting Laban and Esau, that they are the outward man and carnal mind, respectively, see on chap. xxviii. p. 324.

To prepare the spirit for such opposition, the Lord here vouchsafes a vision of angel guards. "Jacob went on his way, and the angels of God met him; and Jacob said, This is God's host." [2] Some such perception of heavenly help is yet vouchsafed to make us persevere. But the vision soon fades away, and the unseen hosts, because out of sight, are in measure out of mind; while the strength which is against us is felt distinctly, and the fact, that, spite of the spirit's fruitfulness, the carnal mind is yet strong. We cannot journey this path without most painfully feeling that the flesh as Esau is yet "my lord Esau." In outward things this may be forgotten. The fact meets us in its painful reality as soon as we are set on entering heavenly things; and our spirit, which should rejoice, if not in the hosts of the Lord, yet in the Lord of hosts, is cast down by the evil which is so sorely felt, and which outweighs at times the fact of heavenly help. Hence the elect is perplexed and full of fears. He knows not how, with such an unwearying enemy so near him, he shall ever find rest. "Jacob was greatly distressed." Again and again he repeats the bitter words, "My lord Esau." [3]

This, coming here, is very striking. Why should he, who at an earlier stage neither feared nor courted Esau, now feel such dread of him? Because in the first joy of learning God's purpose, believing the promise that "the elder shall serve the younger," our spirit never fears the flesh, not knowing its own weakness or the might of the carnal mind. If we can get the blessing, we think that we can use it. It never occurs to us that a certain preparation of spirit is needed for the right enjoyment of what God has promised us. Esau therefore, though he may affect our course, is not thought of. We have yet to learn the

[2] Chap. xxxii. 1, 2.   [3] Chap. xxxii. 4, 5, 18, 19, &c.

difference between "apprehending" and "being apprehended."[4] So we go and toil to subdue the outward man, and as we toil we learn our weakness and foolishness. We are forced to confess that Esau is lord. Our fruitfulness has not given us power over the carnal mind. The elder does not yet serve the younger. To effect this, planning Jacob must become halting Israel.

Yet it is here, in painful, abject weakness,—when we most feel the power of the flesh, and that our spirit cannot govern it,—here, when Esau most clearly is the stronger, —here in self-despair is Jacob made a "prince of God:" not while toiling in outward things,—not until the humiliating fact is plain past all question, that the carnal mind is far too strong for us,—not till this is confessed, openly confessed once and again, and this while spite of all opposition we yet press on to heavenly things,—is our spirit out of weakness made strong, and we learn that to have God's power we must ourselves be powerless.

So much for the time of this change. For the means, the greatest of all is prayer, persevering, wrestling prayer. Jacob does indeed what he can by prudence to escape and calm down Esau's enmity, giving up to Esau some of the flocks,[5] that is, allowing some of the animal emotions which have been won from the outward man to fall under the power of the carnal mind,—a step, the faith of which I will not judge,—but his hope is not in this, but simply in God alone. So he prays, "O God of my father Abraham, and God of my father Isaac, the Lord which saidst unto me, Return unto thy country and to thy kindred, and I will deal well with thee; I am not worthy of the least of all the mercies, and of all the truth which thou hast shewed to thy servant; for with my staff I passed over this Jordan,

---

[4] See Phil. iii. 12.   [5] Chap. xxxiii. 13–20.

and now I am become two bands. Deliver me, I pray thee, from the hand of my brother, from the hand of Esau, for I fear him, lest he will come and smite me and the mother with the children. And thou saidst, I will surely do thee good, and make thy seed as the sand of the sea, which cannot be numbered for multitude."[6] Thus he prays, and turns again to prayer, wrestling alone in spirit until the shadows flee away;[7] taking God's word against all that seems like opposition, saying, "I will not let thee go, except thou bless me." For God had said, "I will surely bless thee;" and Jacob, with his will for God's will, holds God to this His own will.

This is the trial yet,—Can we believe, that when He says, "I will surely do thee good," He really wills it? Can we back this His "I will" by our "I will," in the confidence that when we will with Him we must be conquerors? Then, though we may have much to ask, even of the name of Him whom we would not let go except He blessed us;[8] and we wake up, as the darkness breaks, to think how little we have known of Him whom we have wrestled with, and who has given Himself into our hands "in the likeness of man,"[9] and that He may have a new name involving far more than anything which has as yet been revealed to us;[10] though we may feel all this, the change is wrought: Jacob is now Israel, for "as a prince we have power with God and man, and have prevailed."[11]

[6] Chap. xxxii. 9–12.

[7] Chap. xxxii. 24.

[8] Chap. xxxii. 29.

[9] "There wrestled a man with him," v. 24. Cf. Phil. ii. 7.

[10] Rev. iii. 12. Augustine dwells much on this, taking the words, "Let me go," as meaning, "Let me go in the form you have known me, that you may know me in a higher and more spiritual way: — "Ille autem dicebat, 'Dimitte me,' carna-liter; 'quia ecce jam mane est,' ut spiritaliter illumineris, &c. . . . . Sed ille quod dixit? 'Non te dimittam, nisi me benedixeris.' Quia per car-nem nos prius benedicit Dominus," &c. — *Serm.* v. *Class.* 1, § 6.

[11] "Primitus fuit vocatus Jacob postea Israel, ... et nos primitus

But a price has to be paid for this. Jacob, to have God's strength, must lose his own strength. The man "whose hand lays hold" is not a "prince of God," until the hollow of his thigh is out of joint.[12] When he is weak, then is he strong. The power of Christ only rests on him in his infirmities.[13] Who has learnt this lesson of the cross? Are there not souls, who have toiled and accomplished much as respects their outward man, who have served for Laban's flocks, yet are conscious that Esau, the carnal mind, not only lives,—for he will yet live,—but is keeping their spirit from the full enjoyment of heavenly things? Will their fruits give them the power they lack? Never. Would we be Israels? These are the conditions,—to go up over Jordan, and wrestle alone, and be smitten in the fleshly part, and lamed, and halting; so shall we have power with God and man; and because so few will submit to this, there are many Jacobs, but few Israels.[14]

Such is this stage as known within. Without, it is the experience of those who are toiling on, to take their flocks and children into the promised land. The world now is left behind. Its pursuit has not stopped the elect, who is

debemus esse Jacob, hoc est supplantatores vitiorum, ut postea possimus esse Israel, id est animæ videntes Deum," &c.— *Hieron. in Psalm.* cxiii. "Anima videns Deum," is one of the translations which Jerome gives of the name Israel; but he confesses elsewhere, (*Quæst. Heb. in Gen.*) that our common rendering, "a prince with God," is more correct, as derived from שׂרה and אל.

[12] Chap. xxxii. 25.

[13] 2 Cor. xii. 9, 10.

[14] "Magna est mentis contentio, cum sese ad cœlestia erigit, cum transgredi nititur omne quod cor-

poraliter videtur, cum sese angustat ut dilatet. . . . Quod benè sacra historia designat, quæ beatum Jacob cum angelo luctatum narrat. . . . . Notandum quòd idem victus angelus nervum femoris Jacob tetigit, eumque marcescere statim fecit, atque ab eo tempore Jacob uno claudicavit pede; quia scilicet omnipotens Deus cùm jam per desiderium cognoscitur, omnem in nobis voluptatem carnis arefacit. . . . Si ergo tenemus angelum, uno claudicamus pede; quia dum crescit in nobis fortitudo amoris intimi, infirmatur proculdubio fortitudo carnis," &c.— *Greg. M. in Ezech.* l. ii. h. 2, § 12.

now close to heavenly things. Then fleshly professors arise, false brethren, like Esau, born in the house of the Son, and yet like him profane men, whose very wrath drives the elect in self-despair to God, till from Jacobs they are transformed into Israels. The details in this view I need not repeat: — how the elect divide the flocks, by such division hoping to go more safely; — how, spite of this, some of the rough and animal natures we have won, though freed from the world, are given into the hand of carnal brethren, in the hope that thus the true heirs may be saved; — how such planning cannot give us rest; — how prayer is the true and unfailing means of strength; — how wrestling and darkness must be our experience;— how in feebleness and pain we meet our carnal brethren; — how those, who have once bitterly opposed, receive us graciously; — how the proffered aid of such is declined, lest the babes and flocks be overdriven; for "if men should overdrive them one day, all the flock would die;" [15] — all this and much more here is known to those, who have attempted to guide flocks out of the world into heavenly places. The way remains the same as of old; and the just shall walk in it safely, though transgressors fall therein.

VI.— THE SOJOURN IN SUCCOTH, AND DINAH'S FALL

Chapter 33:17-20 and 34

AT this stage, after so many labours and prayers, escaped from Laban and Esau, and standing on the ground of promise as "a prince of God," Jacob might have expected that he and his would now be permitted to rest in quietness. But at this point new foes appear, by whom the

[15] Chap. xxxiii. 13.

worker is severely wounded, when he least expects, and where he most acutely feels it. For the virgin daughter of Jacob now falls, seduced by the Hivite who yet is in the land.

We see here the special snare which assails the elect, when, having escaped from the dominion of the world and the flesh, he now has entered heavenly things. Wicked spirits assail some of our best affections, and succeed in corrupting what the world and the flesh had not corrupted. For no ground is exempt from snares; nay, more, the higher and better the ground, the more grievous may be the failure there. Satan rages most against the best. He will go into swine, if cast out of men;[1] but he would rather stay in men, and still more in an angel, if it were possible. He will go into earth, if cast out from heaven; but he struggles hard to dwell in heavenly things.[2] And yet we act as though attainment made us secure; as though, because we have forsaken the outward man, and are changed from Jacob into Israel, and have been delivered from the power and dominion of the flesh, no further peril still awaited us; whereas, here, out of the reach of the flesh and outward man, our purest affections may be defiled by other more devilish, because more inward, forms of evil. This is the lesson learnt by Jacob here, as we too often learn it, by actual failure and shameful humiliation.

First to mark what led to this fall. Jacob yields to the temptation, peculiar to this stage, of resting in his attainments instead of still pressing on. He seems to think, that, being now free from Laban and Esau, and come to the borders of Canaan, he has advanced far enough. He settles where he is. He "builds a house," and "buys a field,"[3] and thus prepares the way for Dinah's ruin. And

[1] Matt. viii. 31.   [2] Rev. xii. 7–12.   [3] Chap. xxxiii. 17, 19.

the soul which by grace has come thus far, and has escaped from the dominion of the carnal mind and outward man, is tempted to think, that, because " a prince of God," it is now safe; that therefore it may sit down, and rest secure in its attainments. But not in attainments, but in attaining, are we safe. Thus even the strivings of our flesh, grievous as they are, may serve our spirit, by keeping us from resting before the time, while our gifts and blessings may be as snares to us. We are apt to think that our flesh is only a dead weight, while we regard all freedom of spirit as good and to be coveted. Longer experience teaches us to be thankful for all, for the strivings of the flesh, as well as for the grace of the inward man; for cold and heat, for strifes and peace, for falls and risings, yea for all things; to rejoice in infirmities, and distresses, and fightings and fears within, as well as in visions of the Lord and revelations;[4] to be watchful in times of blessing and rest; above all, to be humble at every fresh gift, knowing that it is in gifts and attainments we fail most signally. We know this, and yet no sooner have we attained some blessing, than we attempt to rest in it, and so by our own act prepare the way for fresh disquietudes.

For this settling led to Dinah's fall. If Jacob may buy a field and settle there, his daughter will go and see the daughters of the land. The result is, she is defiled; for " Shechem, the son of Hamor, the Hivite, saw her; and he took and lay with her, and defiled her."[5]

Dinah, the daughter of Leah, represents those affections of the elect, which spring from outward principles.[6] The Hivite is an evil spirit of Canaan's seed; if I do not err, the spirit of religious formalism. For Canaan was the

---

[4] 2 Cor. xii. 1, 10.   [5] Chap. xxxiv. 1, 2.   [6] See on chap. xxx.

spirit of mere external worship;[7] and the Hivite is the same spirit, only at a further stage.[8] This spirit, which lives "till the redemption of the purchased possession,"[9] is sure to appear whenever we come to heavenly things. Then, if we rest in attainments, formalism creeps in, and by it some of our purest affections are defiled.[10] This leads to bitter inward conflict, which, though from zeal for God, is not approved of Him. For polluted affections cannot be cleansed by anger. Dinah is fallen, though Jacob's sons may rage. In the next place, there may be a kind of anger against sin which in God's sight is worse than the sin and fall which occasions it; and of which, at a further stage, like Jacob, we learn to say, "Cursed be their anger, for it was cruel."[11] God knows how much of inward conflict is the result of pride; mere vexation at seeing how easily we may be defiled. Zeal and judgment are easier than confession. But violence with ourselves on account of failure will not amend it. We need as much patience towards the failure within us, as towards the evil which is without us in the different forms of worldliness.

---

[7] See on chap. x.

[8] Chap. x. 15–17.

[9] Eph. i. 14.

[10] Gregory the Great thus alludes to this inward fulfilment:—"Dina, ut mulieres videat alienæ regionis, egreditur, quando mens sua studia negligens, actiones alienas curans, extra ordinem proprium evagatur. Quam Sichem, princeps terræ, opprimit, quia inventam in curis exterioribus diabolus corrumpit, et conglutinata est anima ejus cum eâ, quia unitam sibi per iniquitatem respicit. Et quia cùm mens a culpa resipiscere atque admissum flere conatur, corruptor autem spes ac securitates vacuas ante oculos revocat, quatenus utilitatem tristitiæ subtrahat, rectè illic adjungitur, 'Tristemque blanditiis delinivit,'" &c. — *Reg. Past.* pt. iii. c. 29, admon. 30.

[11] Chap. xlix. 7. In the history of Saul, Hivites again appear in a scene similar to this, in which they are judged by one who is zealous for the house of Israel, while his judgment of them is pronounced cursed. Saul, "in his zeal to the children of Israel, slew the Gibeonites," who were Hivites, (Josh. ix. 3, 7,) and for this mistaken zeal a curse comes on his house. See the history, 2 Sam. xxi. 1-14.

Such are the fruits of resting in attainments, and of supposing that because the world and flesh are left, and we are Israels, we may be secure. Often have I beheld this scene, not only in the inward experience of souls, who have gone far and laboured long and well, but in the failure of more than one true congregation, which, delivered from the world and carnal men, has been seduced by worse spirits. Heavenly places are no defence from such a fall. It is when we already stand on the ground of promise that Canaan's seed harass us.

But the outward fulfilment here may to some be more striking; and in this view most important is the lesson, not only to halting Jacobs, but to zealous Levis. Jacob has now reached the promised land. True servants have brought those whom they have won into heavenly places. The outward world has long since been left. Carnal brethren too, who like Esau have sought to stop us, by grace are overcome. At this stage, so sweet is the rest, that the elect settles where he is instead of pressing onwards. Then the virgin of Israel falls. Some body, which is the outward expression of a truth, and the fruit of loving service, is found to be corrupted and seduced by wicked deceivers. Formalism creeps into the church,[12] the natural result of settling down and resting in attainments. Would any congregation be seduced, if the fathers and young men toiled and journeyed on? But the church halts and is seduced; then, as a first step, the seducers are admitted to certain holy ordinances; for a fallen church always brings in many to such forms, although they are

---

[12] It is to be remembered that Dinah is Leah's daughter, not Rachel's, and so figures a congregation which is the offspring of outward truth. See on chap. xxix.

confessedly submitted to for wrong and selfish ends ; and
then some of the true heirs of promise, grieved to the
heart at such awful profanation of the church and things
of God, finding judgment easier than confession, arise with
cruel zeal to judge and cut off the seducers. Instead of
asking of the Lord how the fallen can be helped, they take
the iron sword of truth, and rage with it bitterly.[13]   The
fiercest wrath which I have ever seen has been that of
brethren judging the evil.   But such zeal does not cleanse
a fallen church, and much of the wrath is against facts, as
if Dinah had not fallen, to save their own credit.   Alas !
such zeal, common as it is, profits not at all ; and at length
we learn that such judgment is " cursed," and that confession would befit us far better.   Yet how many count it
holy zeal to contend against the defilers of a fallen church,
even when her whoredom has been manifest.[14]

Is the sword then never to be used—is there to be no
cutting off, no judgment or excommunication of offenders ?
Judgment surely there must be at times, and divine zeal
against evil, as we see in Abraham ; [15] but not to maintain
a fiction, as though a harlot could again be made a chaste
virgin ; far less to supersede that confession which becomes
us for that fall of the church which is our common shame.

---

[13] Respecting iron, see on chap.
iv. 22.

[14] I have met with very little on
the spiritual sense of this chapter
among the Fathers ; probably for
the same reason that they say so
little of Noah's fall, or of Nimrod,
or Babylon ; namely, that the scene
described was not familiar to them.
They had not seen, as we have, the
fall of the Church and the useless
wrath of some of Jacob's sons.   The
Glossa Ordinaria here is as follows :

—" Duo fratres Dinæ, per quos significantur prædicatores Evangelii, qui
ad prædicandum mittuntur com-
binati,   arreptis   duobus   gladiis,
scilicet oratione et prædicatione, in-
vadunt civitatem diaboli, et sic tollunt sororem suam de domo Sichem,
id est diaboli," &c.   Augustine is
quoted as giving the same interpretation ; but I have not been able
to find the passage.

[15] Chap. xiv. 14.

Nevertheless out of this wretched scene the Lord can work His own purpose. Even by such distresses as this are the elect rescued from resting in attainments and hastened on to Bethel. And the Simeons and Levis, though their wrath is cursed, are blessed; their ways are a reproach to the truth, and " make them to stink among the inhabitants of the land;"[16] their haste to judge also carries its own judgment with it: " I will," says the Spirit of God, " divide them in Jacob, and scatter them in Israel;"[17]—a lot which always overtakes such spirits;—but the grace, which redeemed them, keeps them, and through many trials saves them at last.

The same act comes out in the dispensations. Israel ceased to be a pilgrim, and so the first wife's daughter fell. The virgin of Israel plainly was defiled. Nevertheless the Pharisees and Scribes, the Simeons and Levis of their day, instead of confessing, raged against the shame, cutting off and judging those who had corrupted Israel. Thus Pharisaism was " the concision," not " the circumcision."[18] But the fallen daughter of Israel could not by such means be restored. The Spirit of the Lord went not with such zealots, but said,—all Christ's life was saying it,—" Cursed is their anger, for it was fierce, and their wrath, for it was cruel." For such judgment answered no end, save to make poor Israel to stink among the nations. " They pleased not God, and were contrary to all men."[19] What a lesson for all succeeding generations! When shall we learn that Pharisaic judging helps no one? When shall we, not possess only, but be possessed by, the Spirit of the Lord?

---

[16] Chap. xxxiv. 30.
[17] Chap. xlix. 7.

[18] Phil. iii. 2, 3.
[19] 1 Thess. ii. 15.

VII.—The Return to Bethel

Chapter 35:1-22

We have seen how attainments, through resting in them, may become a snare to the elect, and lead to grievous defilement. Now again we see how falls may help us on. Jacob's rest brought shame: the shame advanced and freed him. Such is our path, and such the grace of God, that our falls and mistakes may be a means to nurture our true growth; as a tree extracts fresh strength from the soil which is enriched by its own decaying leaves and fallen blossoms. In this way are we led on; by blessings learning our weakness; by weakness, the riches of our God.

Thus Dinah's fall advanced Jacob. He could not, amidst such shame and conflict, rest longer where he was. And by this self-same thing, what zeal is wrought in us, what vehement desire and clearing of ourselves, yea, what fear and carefulness ! [1] But Jacob is helped by other means. God's word comes directly commanding him to go up to Bethel.[2] Such a word of God comes, often as we are faint and fail, and, by recalling God's purpose, effects a change, first in ourselves, then in our position. For "Jacob said to his household, and to all that were with him, Put away the strange gods that are among you, and be clean, and change your garments; and let us arise and go up to Bethel, and I will make there an altar unto God who answered me in the day of my distress, and was with me in the way which I went. And they gave to Jacob all the strange gods which were in their hands, and Jacob hid them under the oak which was by Shechem." [3] So the word

---

[1] 2 Cor. vii. 11.   [2] Chap. xxxv. 1.   [3] Chap. xxxv. 2-4.

both leads us on and sanctifies. The uncleansed cannot advance, for certain stages are only reached as we are sanctified. But by the word true servants judge themselves. Before God speaks, idols may be suffered : when His voice is heard, they are confessed and put away.

The progress now is very marked. There is advance in reference to each of the blessings enjoyed by the elect servant. Of these the first is " the everlasting hills " of promise, and in these " the blessings of heaven above and of the deep which lieth under : " the second is " the wife of youth," " blessings of the breasts and womb," the fountain from whence springs forth the stream of Israel : the third is the Lord Himself, " the God of thy fathers, even the Almighty who shall help and bless thee." [4] Here there is advance respecting each of these, involving trial and grief, yet real blessing also.

First, Jacob's advance opens to his view lengths and breadths of the land as yet unknown.[5] There is true progress in the knowledge and possession of what the Lord has promised him ; not without apparent danger, but " the terror of the Lord was upon the cities that were round about them, and they did not pursue after the sons of Jacob." [6] Thus, when, under a sense of failure and defilement, we again press on, fields on fields of promise open to us, which we have heard of, but till now have never realised. The Canaanite is indeed upon this ground, that is false spirituality, ready to assail and wound us in the way.[7] But God preserves His own. " So Jacob came to Bethel, he and all the people with him, and built an altar, and called the place El-bethel." So far from losing by

---

[4] Chap. xlix. 25, 26.
[5] Chap. xxxv. 6, 16, 21.
[6] Chap. xxxv. 5.

[7] For the Canaanite, see above, on chap. xxxiv.

his advance, it gives him deeper acquaintance with and insight into the treasures of the " everlasting hills."

Here, on the ground where he had seen earth joined to heaven, with angels of God ascending and descending upon man, the elect receives fresh revelations. " The Lord appeared," saying " I am God Almighty," and promising afresh possession of the land, not to Jacob only, but to his seed after him.[8]   In struggles of spirit, Jacob had met the Lord, and had asked to know the name of Him who wrestled with him.[9]   But until now, that name, revealed to faith,[10] in the toil of service had not been apprehended. " God Almighty " had not " appeared " to Jacob.   Now He appears, revealing Himself by the name which alone could quiet the busy worker.   And as Abraham, hearing this name, was content at once to give up the strength of the flesh, and to judge himself by circumcision ; so Jacob by the same blessed name is freed : henceforth his hand ceases to lay hold, to allow the Almighty to effect and order all for him.

Then at this stage three women are removed, whose life directly or indirectly had affected Jacob more than any others.   Deborah, Rachel, and Bilhah, the first the nurse, the second the wife, the third the handmaid, are all now taken from him.   The first two die ; the last is defiled ; for Reuben, Leah's first-born, " went and lay with Bilhah, his father's concubine." [11]

What has been said of Sarah's death will explain the inward fact expressed by the death of these women.[12] Men are always certain minds : the women, the affections or principles of truth with which they are united.   These,

---

[8] Chap. xxxv. 9–12.

[9] Chap. xxxii. 27.

[10] Chap. xvii. 1.

[11] Chap. xxxv. 8, 18, 22.

[12] See on chap. xxiii.

whether men or women, all die out; that is, they pass away
as outward forms, thereby to be more spiritualised.   This is
what now takes place with Jacob's nurse and wife.   Those
truths or affections, which are set forth by these women,
now as outward forms die and pass away; not to perish,
for truth never perishes, but through the dissolution of the
outward form to exist in a higher and purer way ; while
Bilhah, Rachel's maid, who represents that lower and
servile principle, by which nevertheless some good fruit
has been brought forth, is now defiled by Jacob's first-born,
that is, by the unlawful workings of other fruits of true
service.[13]   Deborah, the nurse, dies first.   A nurse is one
whose office it is to care for babes and sucklings.   Deborah therefore is that which serves such as have need
of milk.   As having belonged too to Laban's house,
and been engaged with Rebekah before she left Padan-
Aram, Deborah would partake of the character of that
land, and so be rather outward and natural, such truth in
fact as babes and sucklings need.   Now, having fulfilled
her work, she passes away.   Rachel too, as an outward
form, now departs in bearing fruit; even as that spiritual
principle, which she represents, is changed from an earthly
form to a spirit through its very fruitfulness; giving birth
to another form of life, which is indeed " a child of
strength," though at first it seems " a child of sorrow." [14]

Few, however, will apprehend this.   Adam's way, in
trusting the creature more than God, in listening to the
tempter, in choosing knowledge more than life, in hiding
from God, or in laying the blame on some other, will be

---

[13] See on chap. xxix. respecting
Bilhah and Reuben. These things
are all but ineffable, and cannot
fully be expressed.

[14] Benoni, the name which Rachel
gave to her son, means, " son of my
sorrow;" but his father called him
Benjamin, that is, " son of the right
hand."   As to the "right hand,"
compare Psalm lxxx. 17, and cx. 1.

known by all who have come to themselves; for old Adam
is in all his progeny. The picture therefore will be plain.
But the form of life set forth in Jacob is not in all, much
less that stage of it which is here presented to us. Still
this stage, though attained by few, is to be reached. Let
us not judge it impossible, simply because as yet it is
beyond us. Rather let us press on that we may know it;
and such as cannot follow here now may follow hereafter.

Such is this scene within. Without, the details will to
not a few be more manifest. In this view we see how the
very fall of the Church awakens some to further progress.
True servants cannot rest where pollution is made manifest. Then comes some word of God, recalling His purpose, which leads to the putting away of idols and un-
cleannesses. Thus are the elect stirred up afresh, and pass
on to know yet more of God and of their own privileges.
Then comes fresh grief, for surely it is a grief to find
bodies we have loved, and which in different ways have
helped us, as outward bodies ready to be dissolved, or,
what is worse, to be defiled by some in Israel. Yet this
too must be known by true servants, when they come to some
of the higher stages in heavenly things. The outward
Church is found to be corrupted by the first-born sons, who
should have been its help and safeguard; who, puffed up
with pride, usurp another's place, to their own great loss
and to the shame of all in Israel; [15] while the true Church
is seen as an outward form to die, only to live a higher

---

[15] "Per Reuben, qui interpretatur
'visionis filius,' intelligitur vir lite-
ratus, qui super alios in aliquâ gratiâ
elevatus; eo quod Reuben fuit pri-
mogenitus, et hoc sive talis vir secu-
laris fuerit, sive religiosus; et ex
gratiâ sibi datâ aliquando erigitur
in superbiam, et vult cognoscere
patris sui uxorem, id est, usurpare
sibi ecclesiam, vel dignitatem ejus,
et per hoc machinatur ad ejus de-
positionem."—*Gloss. Ordin.* in loco.

life with God and in God. Some true servants have seen and known all this. It is well, that, ere they see it, they are from Jacobs made Israels, and know the Lord as " God Almighty."

The dispensations too reflect this scene. After the defilement of the first wife's daughter, that is, the Jewish dispensation, the Spirit of Christ as Worker led on the elect to greater knowledge and enjoyment of heavenly places. There Rachel, the beloved wife, dies; that is, the Church, as an outward form, in due time is seen to pass away; while the Worker yet survives through many griefs to see Joseph's glory and dominion over all the land of Egypt.

A little while, and our eyes shall see that glory, and the things which now distract us shall for ever pass away. As we can bear it, bring us into that day, O Lord; and while darkness is yet safer for us, be Thou, yea, and for ever, our everlasting dwelling-place.

VIII.—The Seeds of Jacob and Esau

Chapter 35:23-29 and 36

As a fit conclusion to Jacob's course, we have his seed summed up,[1] in contrast to Esau's generations.[2] Here are the results of these two lives; Jacob's sons setting forth the fruits of that spirit of service, which springs from true sonship; Esau's line, the fruits of the flesh or carnal mind, as it appears at this stage of man's development.[3] Each form of life can only bear its proper fruit. That of the flesh still fleshly, and that of the spirit spiritual.

---

[1] Chap. xxxv. 23-29.   [2] Chap. xxxvi. 1-43.
[3] See on chap. xxv. 24-34.

Jacob's fruit in all is twelve sons, six by Leah, two by Rachel, and two by each of the handmaids; all fruits of the same elect spirit, but differing according to the principle or affection which produces them ; the sons of Leah, the first-born, representing those fruits which are produced by the elect from forms of outward truth, such as understanding, obedience, service, rule, joy, and communion, for so the names are interpreted : Rachel's children, those later fruits of patience and long-suffering with joyfulness, which grow from the contemplative life; the handmaids' sons, the fruits of those more servile principles, which, as they are owned and blessed of God, bear justice, conflict, power, or happiness.[4]   The spirit of service bears all these, and in them, spite of many errors and imperfections, the Lord is glorified.

Esau's line is then displayed, first his sons by Canaanitish wives, and then his fruit by Ishmael's daughter.   The names of his immediate sons all express some good quality ; for the fruit of the flesh. in its Esau form is good in its way, though not good as measured by the divine standard. For " all flesh is grass ; "[5] and grass at the best is soon dried up and withered.   But some of their names imply polish at least, if not a recognition of God and respect for His protection.   Eliphaz, and Reuel, and Korah, and Jaalam, express in their names good things which even the elect might wish for."[6]   In the grandsons there is a falling off : Omar, Gatam, and Kenaz, describe a worse condi-

[4] For the names of these sons, and their interpretation, see on chap. xxix. and xxx.

[5] 1 Pet. i. 24.

[6] Jerome interprets all these names, (*Nom. Heb.*) but it is difficult to speak with certainty of all.

I do not therefore give them; but the following seem to be beyond dispute :—Eliphaz, " *God is my endeavour* ;" Reuel, "*the friend of God* ;" Korah, "*smooth*" or "*polished* ;" Jaalam, "*hidden*" or "*protected.*"

tion;[7] while the names of the subsequent kings of this race, as Bela, Jobab, and Husham, are all variations of misery.[8] Such are the fruits of the religious flesh, at first in measure good, but soon degenerating, till their corruption proves that religious flesh is but flesh, and fair Edom only a variation of old Adam.

Nevertheless this line is great in the world. Even in the first generation, the children of one wife, Aholibamah, all become "dukes;"[9] the grandsons all have this title,[10] which, only varied with that of "king," is kept through all this genealogy. So is it yet within. The fruits of the true spirit are little valued in the world. The carnal fruits which grow out of the elect are such as, being in measure of the world, the world can appreciate: with just so much of outward goodness as the flesh when trained and taught by the spirit can appreciate, and yet enough of the world to please the world, with a zeal for seen and present things. Such fruits must be great in the world: they may even be counted good fruit, but their end will shew their true nature; for by them the things of the house of the elect are taken to make a kingdom for self out of the land of Canaan.[11]

This is better seen without. In this view the sons of Esau and Jacob set forth in figure the further growth of those opposing seeds, which, though born in the house of the Son, and from one common mother, end far apart, the one as kings in Mount Seir, the other as keepers of sheep upon the ground of promise. Jacob's sons are not all alike; the elect, as they grow, develope many differences;

---

[7] Omar, "*a speaker;*" Gatam, "*their clamour;*" Kenaz, "*a hunter*" or "*drinker.*"

[8] Bela, "*a devourer;*" Jobab, "*a*

howling;" Husham, "*raging.*"

[9] Chap. xxxvi. 18.

[10] Chap. xxxvi. 15–17.

[11] Chap. xxxvi. 6–8.

some Reubens, some Judahs, some Dans, but all making one Israel, who return after long toil to dwell in heavenly places. Esau's children differ as much: even as the carnal seed out of the Son exhibit great variety, one common mark, however, being upon them all, that sooner or later they all attain to rule of some sort, building up a kingdom out of the land, while the elect remain to the end as humble shepherds in Canaan. "Eight kings in succession reigned in Edom, before any king reigned over the children of Israel." [12] St. Paul marks this of the Church's carnal seed: "Now ye are full, now ye are rich, ye have reigned as kings without us;" [13] for carnal brethren want a kingdom now, and the desire and need of rule is sooner felt, and rule is sooner developed with them, and, as they think, perfected, than with the spiritual. Thus are they great in the world; their course in almost all things being in direct contrast to that of the elect. The one leaves Canaan to dwell in Mount Seir; the other comes back from toil in the world, to dwell in Canaan. Jacob brings all the souls he has gotten, and "comes to Isaac his father to Mamre, which is Hebron." [14] "Esau took his wives, and all that he had gotten in the land of Canaan, and went and dwelt in Mount Seir." [15] The elect, having felt the power of the world far more than carnal brethren ever feel it, (for the carnal seed never try to win it,) come back with what they have won to rest in heavenly places; while the Esaus, born in the house of the Son, and enriched with so much of its truth as they can use for self exaltation, go forth never to return, preferring in their own strength to establish an earthly kingdom.

---

[12] Chap. xxxvi. 31–39.

[13] 1 Cor. iv. 8–12.

[14] Chap. xxxv. 27.

[15] Chap. xxxvi. 6–8. The LXX. read here, καὶ ἐπορεύθη ἐκ τῆς γῆς Χαναάν.

Thus Esau dwelt in Mount Seir.[16] This ground had for long been the stronghold of gigantic Horims, against whom the king of Shinar had come up, and smote them, without dispossessing them; [17] but " the children of Esau destroyed them before them, and dwelt in their stead even to this day." [18] Hither Esau seems to have been drawn by his marriage with Aholibamah, for she was one of Seir's daughters; [19] and here, having dispossessed Seir's sons, Esau reigns in the kingdom of that ungodly line to which he had allied himself. The Church's carnal seed have just done this. Having first formed an alliance with the world, they end by taking its kingdom; driving out certain gigantic evils, against which Babylon the great had struggled unsuccessfully, to found a kingdom of bloodshed and force, which, though famed far and near for its strength and terribleness,[20] and destined even to give a king to Israel by whom the true King shall be mocked and set at nought,[21] is doomed to be destroyed, as it is written,—" For his violence against his brother Jacob shame shall cover him, and he shall be cut off for ever." [22]

Of this kingdom much might be said. The names of the sons of Seir, whom Esau dispossessed, and whose names and acts are not recorded in vain, shew the forms of evil which are opposed and can be destroyed even by carnal Christians. The names I cannot touch here;[23] but I may observe that to one act peculiar prominence is given. Mules,

---

[16] Chap. xxxvi. 8.

[17] Chap. xiv. 5, 6.

[18] Deut. ii. 12, 22.

[19] Esau's wife Aholibamah was " the daughter of Anah, the daughter," or (as the Samaritan version, the LXX., and other ancient versions read), "the son of Zibeon;" chap. xxvi. 2. In verses 20-24, we read

that " Anah, the son of Zibeon," was one of the " sons of Seir, the Horite, who inhabited the land."

[20] See Jer. xlix. 16; Obad. 3.

[21] Luke xxiii. 11.

[22] Obad. 10.

[23] Jerome (*Nom. Heb.*) has attempted an interpretation.

we are told, were discovered by one of Seir's race :—" Anah found mules, as he fed the asses of Zibeon his father in the wilderness." [24] This mixture of seeds so opposed to nature,[25] and law,[26] but which soon found such favour that king's sons used mules by way of distinction,[27] began among the sons of Seir. Not by chance is the fact recorded in their genealogy. Not in vain is it linked with Esau's seed, as characteristic of the race to which he had allied himself.

I cannot say more of these lines, though I am assured that every point contains a lesson for us. I will only add a few facts, which are plain and standing types of what has been and must be. Under David's rule, Edom was subject to Israel.[28] In the days of the failure of the kingdom, even before Babylon led Israel captive, Edom rebelled.[29] Later on, towards the end of the dispensation, a son of Edom was ruling in Jerusalem, and Edomites were reckoned Jews.[30] The elect had fallen so low, that the rule of the carnal seed was scarcely felt to be a degradation. How far the carnal seed of the Church is now confounded on all hands with the spiritual,—how busy it is to build the temple,—how it rules, and seeks to slay the Heir,—how instead it only destroys the Innocents,— how spite of its crimes for a while it seems to prosper,— how all these things shew where we are,—I leave for

---

[24] Chap. xxxvi. 24. Our authorised version, after all objections to it, seems to be correct. The LXX. do not translate the word, which we render "*mules*," but simply read ἰαμείν, which is the Hebrew, ימם written in Greek letters. Aquila and Symmachus do the same. The Rabbins explain the word to mean *mules*. So does the Arabic version.

[25] Gen. i. 24.

[26] Lev. xix. 19; Deut. xxii. 9–11.

[27] 2 Sam. xiii. 29, xviii. 9.

[28] 2 Sam. viii. 14.

[29] 2 Kings viii. 20, 22.

[30] Herod was an Edomite or Idumæan. For proof of the Edomites being considered Jews, see Josephus, *Antiq.* l. xiii. c. 9, § 1, and Whiston's note on the passage.

others, whose eyes by grace are opened, to weigh and consider.

Such then is Jacob's course, for every age the type of that evangelic service which is the fruit of faith and sonship; too full of human craft at first, "laying hold with its hand," to perform the work by human energy; but schooled through much grief and many disappointments, to learn its own faults and weakness and insufficiency, till, lame and smitten in the flesh, at length it becomes a "prince of God," and prevails mightily. Such service is dear to God. No form of life more represents the ways and mind of heaven; for it stoops, like angels, to serve; yea, like the Lord of angels, it comes down from the hills and wells of Canaan to outward men to save some of them. In all this, much failure comes out; and the worker, like every sower of seed, has his feet defiled in the miry ways of the field of this world; yet he works on, sowing the seed with tears, to return at length in joy, bearing his sheaves with him. Mark again what is, and what is not, Jacob's work. He serves, and so wins flocks and children, whom he may lead to Canaan. He does not attack or dispossess the monstrous Horims; for the opposition to gigantic evils in the world, though it may be the work of some of the children of the True Son, is Esau's labour, not Jacob's. He that hath ears to hear, let him hear. There yet are souls, whose only idea of service is to grapple, like Esau, with the monstrous evils which have grown up in this world, and to set up some rule or order instead, in which the things of Isaac's house are taken to make a kingdom in Seir, out of the land of Canaan. Such work must not be judged. Israel may not meddle with Esau's children, who have dispossessed the Horims.[31] But this

---

[31] Deut. ii. 4, 5, 12.

is not Jacob's work. He serves to bring souls from the ground midway between tradition and reasoning to know the ground of promise,—work, which to carnal eyes seems less and meaner than Esau's, but which is only accomplished by a wrestling which the carnal seed know nothing of. But what Esau ever doubted that the kingdom in Seir was far grander and better than the tents and flocks of Jacob in Canaan?

But it is time we should pass on from Jacob to Joseph, in whom a still further development of the elect appears.

PART 7

JOSEPH, OR SUFFERING AND GLORY

Chapters 37-50

" The afflictions of Joseph."—AMOS vi. 6.

" Heirs of God, and joint heirs with Christ; if so be we suffer with Him, that we may be also glorified together."— ROM. viii. 17.

JOSEPH, OR SUFFERING AND GLORY

Chapters 37-50

HERE begins the story of Joseph, in whom the fairest form
of human life is seen. Six stages have passed, in which we
have traced how Israel, a Prince of God, grows out of old
Adam. We have seen human nature, and flesh and spirit,
and regeneration, and faith, and sonship, and service. Now
comes the last form of life,—a life which from the first
dreams of rule, and which attains it through suffering; a
wonderful change from naked Adam; and yet an outcome
from him, brought forth by God's ingrafting. Joseph does
not leave his home, to walk in simple faith, he knows not
whither; nor can he rest in peace, a son and heir, by
wells of water enjoying the sweets of sonship; nor does he
serve night and day to win flocks and herds, who may be
led up out of the world to Canaan. Joseph is none of
these, but a life which surely follows these; never seen
but where faith has brought forth sonship, and sonship
service; itself the fruit of service, one of its last and fairest
fruits; which from the first has dreams, not of service, but
rule; which yet, spite of its dreams, is called to suffer many
things; which suffers long, and is sorely tried, but at last
out of suffering attains to rule all things; the world and

brethren bowed at its feet, forced to confess the might of that they once ridiculed.

We have nothing like this before. In Abraham the elect forsakes the world to walk in heavenly places. At this faith stage, Egypt, so far from being ruled, is rather a snare to the believer. Nor can Isaac rule this land : the spirit of sonship is content to rest at peace in heavenly places. In Jacob or service something is done in outward things ; some flocks and herds are won there. But Egypt, the ground of sense, is not subdued : service is not sufficient for such an achievement. But in Joseph, the spirit opposed, and fettered, and bound, conquers by passive power, and is at length exalted over all things. Joseph stands where Abraham falls. The ground which is a snare to mere believers, is none to patient sufferers. Suffering conquers that which tries our faith, and by it, and by it alone, the ground of sense is ruled at last.

Such as live and walk in the spirit know that we too are called with this calling,—to rule, not to be ruled by, sense, that the kingdom may be in the earth even as it is in heaven ; for Christ our Head has reached to this, and we as His members are predestined to be conformed to Him. But few get beyond faith or sonship ; few reach to service, and fewer still to glory in tribulation, by the cross to rule the world, and to walk among the things of sense, confessedly superior to them all. Some unknown, yet well-known, have done it ; and others, who yet are captive to sense, cannot forget the dreams, once divinely given, by which their hearts and hopes were stirred to look and wait for perfect victory. Let such abide their time. They shall shew that if we suffer with Christ we also shall with Him be glorified.[1]   The whole path is here set forth : how

---

[1] Rom. viii. 17.

it goes with man in this path,—how his very brethren mock him,—how the world deals with him before he rules it,—how trials increase the more he walks with God,—how the battle is won at length,—all this is told, as none but God, whose own work it is, could tell it. Being is proved to be far more than doing. And, like the light, which serves us by simply being light, the spirit which beareth all things, by the virtue that flows forth from it unconsciously, commands a place and power which is felt by all to be of God. And indeed there is no service like this unconscious service, which naturally flows from what we are through the divine indwelling.

I.—Joseph's Dreams, and Suffering from his Brethren

Chapter 37

First, we see the reception this new life meets from Jacob's sons :—" They hated Joseph because his father loved him more than all his sons." [1] All know the story : how Joseph's brethren plot against his life, and strip him, and mock him, and sell him into Egypt. The same life still is treated thus, as we may see, within, and without, and in the dispensations.

To trace it first within. We are here shewn how our purest inward life for a while is crossed and hindered, not so much by worldly things, as by other activities which are the fruit of true service. It is Jacob's sons who sell Joseph. These sons are the varied fruits which are brought forth by the elect,—whether knowledge, or service, or rule, or the like,—by union with Leah, that is by outward principles.[2] These fruits are forms of active life, and these,

---

[1] Chap. xxxvii. 3, 4.   [2] See on chap. xxix.

if ungoverned are prone to cause confusion, and to oppress and hinder the higher aspirations of that pure and passive life in us, which now begins to dream of rule. The young Christian may not understand this. He can see how the old man, as Terah, or the religious flesh, as Esau, may hinder our path; but how true service can yield any fruits which oppose the highest life in us, is at first incomprehensible. But so it is. The fruits of an active life may cross a yet more inward life, and the mind which Joseph represents be opposed, as he was, by other activities, which, though true fruits of the spirit, need to be ruled rather than to rule. Thus Joseph is sold into Egypt. And so this spirit in us for a while is sorely overborne, forced under the bondage of sense, while it is thought that some beast or evil spirit has destroyed that life, whose early promise was so lovely. But it cannot be thus destroyed. It may be bound in deepest dungeons; at last it must be free.

Such is the scene within. Without, it shews the path of souls whose passive character, so unlike the ways of Jacob's house, is for the fall and rising again of many in Israel, and for a sign which shall be spoken against, that the thoughts of many hearts may be revealed, judging all around them, even while they are judged, and, though sorely grieved, in the end made stronger than all. Such souls, as they hinder God less, gain power which others never know; though the same passivity, which makes them open to God, lays them open to peculiar trial from their more active brethren. First, they see evil among brethren:—" Joseph brought unto his father their evil report; "[3] and this involves double trouble; he who sees the evil is judged for seeing, and hated for reproving it.

[3] Chap. xxxvii. 2.

This of itself is no little cross, to outrun sympathy, to grieve friends, to offend brethren. Yet such is the price which must be paid for light; such the penalty of being faithful beyond the measure of our brethren. Then a coat of many colours is given him, for which his brethren hate him more and more,[4] not seeing that if they too walked in obedience, they also might be adorned like him. But they feel that he is preferred, and the secret sense of their inferiority, instead of humbling, only enrages them. If we walk with God in truth, and turn from evil, not afraid to rebuke it even among our brethren, a fair robe will soon be put upon us, not only, as in Adam, to hide our shame and nakedness, but to clothe us in "garments of glory and beauty," even that "fine linen which is the righteousness of saints."[5] The "many colours" will all be there; for colours are but the various shades and reflections of light, and he who walks in the light must needs reflect it, giving back each ray that is not lost and absorbed. In the priests, the garment was perfect white; and upon the Mount, One was seen "whose raiment was shining, so as no fuller on earth could whiten it;"[6] but the many colours, if not so heavenly, may better reveal to human eyes the wondrous fulness which there is in light.[7] The Josephs are yet thus adorned, and for this are the more hated by their brethren who are not with Jacob.[8] "They could not

---

[4] Chap. xxxvii. 3.

[5] Exod. xxviii. 2 ; Rev. xix. 8.

[6] Mark ix. 3.

[7] In this "coat of many colours," Bernard sees the varied gifts of the Spirit:—"Non sum tam hebes, ut non agnoscam tunicam Joseph polymitam. . . . . Audi quomodo polymitam. 'Divisiones (ait) gratiarum sunt.' . . . . Deinde diversis enume-ratis charismatibus, tanquam variis tunicæ coloribus, quibus constat eam esse polymitam, adjungit, 'Hæc autem operatur unus atque idem Spiritus.'" —*Apol. de vit. Rel.* c. 3.

[8] It is plain, from the narrative, and from Jacob's command to Joseph to "go and see how his brethren were," that they were absent from their father; he at Hebron,

speak peaceably unto him." "They hated him yet the more, because of his words."

Then comes the well-known dream of power one day to be enjoyed;[9] for the passive life, which lives near God, from its very nature is prone to dream, and can receive far more than active souls of heavenly mysteries. And for this they who live this life are always reproached as "dreamers," enthusiastic mystics, and I know not what else. Are not many dreams uncertain, and are not many of the things which this dreamer sees, or professes to see, just such uncertainties? Who can with confidence speak of a dream, or prove that these mystic views, so derogatory to the glory of those who now are strongest, are anything but fancies? "Art thou greater than our father Jacob?" Can any new form of life be superior, or accomplish more than has been already done in the good old path of service? So ask the elder sons, and not waiting for an answer at once they mock the "dreamer." They "will see what will become of his dreams."[10] And they do see, though not at all as they expected.

Meanwhile the Josephs are fettered and bound. Instead of ruling or serving, they are shut up where they can help no one; while Ishmaelites, the carnal seed of men of faith, are used to do the dirty work, which the elect have planned but dare not perpetrate.[11] Their coat is dipped in blood, and a tale is told, as if some wild beast or devil had overcome them; a falsehood which in itself is trial, as some

they at Shechem and Dotham'; verses 12–17. These places, like all the rest, are significant.

[9] Chap. xxxvii. 6–10.

[10] Chap. xxxvii. 19, 20.

[11] Chap. xxxvii. 28. The Ishmaelites and Midianites were those sons of Abraham whom he sent away from Isaac. See chap. xxv. 6. Ishmael was Hagar's son; Midian, Keturah's. We see from Judges viii. 12 and 24, that the Midianites were called Ishmaelites, or confounded with them, in Gideon's days.

have learnt who have suffered under false reports, by which their best friends are deceived. Such suffering at the time looks despicable enough. All martyrdoms are said to have looked but meanly, when they were suffered. For stripping and bonds are ever shameful; and the elect are stripped and bound;—" when we see him, there is no beauty that we should desire him." But though cast out, they yet are blessed, some eyes discerning that the Lord Himself is with them, if brethren are not; while within there is the peace of God, for none can rob the true soul of that inward satisfaction which the truth itself ministers. This is the appointed way, the high road of the holy cross,—suffering first, and then a kingdom; to be wronged, misrepresented, punished, cast out; and then to have every secret wrong redressed, and every deed of truth and love manifested;—this is yet the royal way, the end of which is assured even from its beginning : while to do as others do, even of the elect, (for where is worse sin than among the sons of Israel?) though they who walk thus may be "saved so as by fire," involves sure chastening, self-reproach, and humiliation.

The dispensations too reflect the scene. We know how the sons of the first wife rejected the second wife's Firstborn. How the sons of Israel mocked the Heir,—how Egypt, that is the Gentile world, received its future Lord, —how, spite of all, He could not be hid, but was exalted to be head over the kingdom, while His brethren believe Him to be dead,—all this, and much more, is figured here of the life of Him who was " separated from His brethren ; ". who said, " They hated me without a cause ; "[12] " Me they hate, because I testify against them that their works are

[12] John xv. 25.

evil." [13] He came unto His own,[14] toiling in the field of this world, finding no rest there, yet seeking lost brethren. And He found them, and was rejected. He uttered similitudes of His kingdom, but His words to them were as dreams. Their answer was, "We will not have this man to reign over us." [15] They that passed by railed on Him, wagging their heads.[16] They stripped Him of His robe,[17] and sold Him for silver,[18] and sat down to eat, even while they prepare to make away with Him.[19]

So must His members suffer; and though at times the way seems long, He, who hath begun the good work, will surely finish it; [20] for One in a certain place has testified of man, "Thou hast put all things under his feet;" and this covenant cannot be broken.[21]

II.—JUDAH'S HISTORY

Chapter 38

AT this stage in Joseph's course, while that pure life, spite of its dreams of rule, is yet rejected, Judah's path is shewn in contrast, in whom we have the whole story of rule as it springs out of the first and natural principle. If the spirit of service produces fruit in us, the mind to rule will in due time be developed. Other fruits will first be

---

[13] John vii. 7.
[14] John i. 11.
[15] Luke xix. 14.
[16] Mark xv. 29.
[17] Matt. xxvii. 28.
[18] Matt. xxvi. 15.
[19] John xviii. 28. The Fathers are full of allusions to Joseph as a type of Christ. Ephrem Syrus, *De laud. Patr. Jos.*, traces at length the application of the history to the first

and second comings of Christ. So too Ambrose, *De Joseph, passim* ; Tertullian, *Adv. Judæos*, c. xi. ; Augustine, *Qu. in Gen.* l. i. n. 123 and 148, and *Ep. ad Hesych.* cl. 3, n. 199; Chrysostom, *Hom.* 62, *in Gên.* ; and many others. But this figure speaks for itself.

[20] Phil. i. 6.
[21] Heb. ii. 8.

seen, such as Reuben, and Simeon, and Levi, but then comes Judah or rule;[1] a mind in us which attempts some rule, but which, being the fruit of Leah, is outward rather than purely spiritual. I feel that words are lacking here; yet some must know how at a certain stage a mind is born in us, which seeks to rule our other powers. Here, as ever, the natural comes before the spiritual. Joseph is Rachel's son, in whom we see that rule which springs out of the spiritual principle; and which, "by pureness, by knowledge, by long-suffering, by love unfeigned,"[2] shews that a passive life is indeed of all the strongest. Judah is rule as it springs out of Leah, that is, from first and outward principles; strong at first, but forced to bow to Joseph at last; for though "Judah prevailed over his brethren, and of him came the first ruler, the birthright was Joseph's."[3] Yet for a season Judah prevails, while Joseph must wait in weakness till Judah's shame is seen.

The story is full of shame, so much so that some look upon its insertion as a blot in Holy Scripture. But a mirror contracts nothing of the uncleanness which it reflects. The sun is not defiled by shining alike on stye and palace. Besides, "in a great house there are not only vessels of gold, but also of wood and of earth, and some to honour, and some to dishonour."[4] And Judah's life is one of these, which as much as others, perhaps above all others, contains a moral never to be forgotten.

Like all the rest, this story must be fulfilled, within, and without, and in the dispensations.

Within, we see in Judah, that mind intent to rule, which springs up in us from outward principles. Such a mind, if we could see within, yet refulfils all Judah's

---

[1] See on chap. xxix.
[2] 2 Cor. vi. 6.
[3] 1 Chron. v. 2.
[4] 2 Tim. ii. 20.

course. It "goes down," and "turns aside," and "takes to wife the daughter of a certain Canaanite;" that is, it embraces some mere formal and outward principle.[5] But such an attachment to outward forms does little in ruling the elect; the fruit is judged as evil, though an attempt is made to improve it by union with Thamar, who, as the second wife, is the figure of spiritual principles.[6] This attempt does not succeed. The fruits of such forms are evil, and ere long come to their end; while spiritual truth is regarded with fear and suspicion, as if it were the cause of the judgment on what is evil in us. Yet after all this very truth bears fruit, and by it, through awful corruptions, another form of life is brought forth. Who can tell what confusions and falls within accompany the first attempts we make to rule ourselves? We may know perhaps that forms are first embraced, and that these bear wretched fruit, which God in mercy takes away; but who can tell the confusions which then are wrought within, and all the profanation and adulteration which the eye of God witnesses? Yet out of this too can He bring forth good, and by Judah's fall prepare the way for purer rule and better discipline.

But this inward view is "hard to be uttered." We may perhaps learn more by tracing the outward fulfilment.

In this view we see in Judah's course the story of rule in the Church, as it grows from outward principles; for Judah is Leah's son, and Leah is the outward Church, that is, the form of outward principles, which to her other

---

[5] Chap. xxxviii. 1, 2; and compare chap. x. 6, and xii. 6.
[6] Verses 6–9. Respecting the younger or second wife, see on chapters xvi. and xxix.

children adds rulers also, whose ways, though they may be "praised by brethren," [7] demand the deepest self-abasement. This is their course:—they take a Canaanitish wife, that is, the principle of mere external worship,[8] thereby to build up the kingdom. By this they bring forth sons, whom God judges, after an attempt has been made to improve them by introducing a younger wife, that is, the spiritual principle. But this line have little love for spiritual truth: ere long it is an object of fear and suspicion, if not of loathing, to them. Rulers of this stock instinctively feel that there is in spiritual truth and in a spiritual Church something which does not suit them. At first they hoped better things from it, but they have tried it, and in their hands at least it does not answer. Yet even while they reject it, they speak it fair: it would not do to declare their thoughts to all on such matters. They promise therefore that it shall again be tried, but at present Judah's sons are not prepared for such a helpmeet. Spiritual truth therefore is put away. Meanwhile the old system of formal worship is found to be lifeless;[9] to console themselves for which the rulers turn to "sheepshearing:" for this comfort remains to them, that, let what will be dead, the fleece at least remains theirs. And here, not knowing what they are doing, the rulers of the outward Church accidentally meet and lay hold on spiritual truth; and against their will the succession of rule is continued, as the fruit of those more spiritual principles, which they themselves had put away. God knows how often this has been done,—how often the true Church, which is the body of spiritual truth, has erred, just as Thamar erred here. She feels her rejection by that old

---

[7] Chap. xlix. 8. [8] Respecting the Canaanite, see on chap. x. 15–17.
[9] Chap. xxxviii. 12.

line, out of which men looked to see the kingdom. She likes not to trust in God alone, continuing as a widow night and day in prayers and supplications; but seeks by carnal policy such a connection with the old rulers, as may make her sons their heirs and true successors. The result is, Judah has seed by Thamar, that is, the old line of rule is continued in connection with spiritual principles. Thus does the rejected Church get apostolic succession, and bear in the line of rule the twofold seed again; though in this case there is a special mystery; something of the younger being seen, even before the firstborn is brought forth.[10] In other cases the carnal seed comes fully first: in outward rule, when it is brought forth from spiritual principles, the spiritual just appears, and then is forced to give place to what is carnal. He that hath ears to hear, let him hear. He that hath eyes, let him look around at the fruit of outward rule by spiritual principles; and he shall see that there is yet always first a glimpse of the spiritual, and then the firstborn or carnal seed breaks forth and supersedes it.[11] But the old line of rulers disown the offspring. The mother shall be burnt. As for the children, they know nothing of them. But their wrath is vain. Proofs are forthcoming, whose the seed is. The " signet, and bracelets, and staff," [12] spite of the rage of the old rulers, declare the parentage. The lineage is very manifest. Those

---

[10] Chap. xxxviii. 27–30.

[11] Ambrose, at very great length, goes into the mystery of this birth by Thamar: — " Cur autem alter manum præmisit ex utero, alter genitali præcessit exortu ; nisi quia per geminorum mysterium gemina describitur vita, una secundum legem, altera secundum fidem, una secundum literam, altera secundum gratiam," &c.—*In Luc.* l. iii. § 20–29. He only traces the fulfilment, as it is seen in the dispensations ; but of course it has its manifestation on every platform. Irenæus, also, *Contr. Hær.* l. iv. c. 25, *al.* 42, gives the same interpretation.

[12] Chap. xxxviii. 25.

spiritual churches which have desired the " succession "
of the outward kingdom, and have got it, though not
legitimately, can shew by indisputable proofs, by the very
ornaments which are in their possession, the stock from
which their children spring.

The dispensations even more clearly reflect this scene.
In this aspect, Judah, the son of Leah, sets forth the fruit
of the Jewish dispensation, regarded as a kingdom. Leah,
the first wife, was that dispensation, which, after law and
priesthood, bore Judah, that is, the kingdom, also. This
Judah took a Canaanite to wife. " Thy birth," said the
prophet to Jerusalem, " and thy nativity is of the land of
Canaan." [13] That kingdom was allied to forms, and grew,
loving an external worship in which was no spirit. An
evil seed was the result, who either could not or would not
have fruit by spiritual principles, when these were offered
to them. For even of old the spiritual Church was offered
to the Jew. In prophets and righteous men it came near
to them, but they would not receive it. [14] So Thamar, the
younger wife, was put away: the sons of the first wife
would not be built up by her. Then Judah's wife, that is
the old dispensation, died and came to its end; her sons
having first been cut off for sin by sore judgments. Then
by Judah's fall the Church is made fruitful, not without
some failure perhaps on her part, from a too great looking
to Judah as the only source from which the kingdom could

[13] Ezek. xvi. 3.

[14] Just as, in the type of Jacob,
Rachel was loved long before she was
fruitful, and, during all the years
while Leah had her children, was,
though without children, yet in
Jacob's house; so here Thamar lives
and is introduced to Judah's house,
before she has any fruit by Judah or
his sons. Augustine therefore rightly
says, "Res ipsa, quæ nunc Christiana
religio nuncupatur, erat apud anti-
quos, nec defuit ab initio humani
generis."—*Retract.* i. 13. And again,
" Viri sancti et justi, qui licet illo
tempore fuerint, ad novum tamen
pertinent testamentum." —*Contr.
Faust.* l. xxii. c. 84.

be continued.[15] Yet Judah knows it not. As Paul declares, " God hath given them the spirit of slumber, eyes that they should not see, and ears that they should not hear, unto this day. And David saith, Let their eyes be darkened that they may not see, and bow down their back alway." [16] But " their fall is the riches of the world." " Through their fall salvation is come unto the Gentiles, to provoke them to jealousy." [17] A seed has sprung out of Judah, which, when it is conceived, Judah judges, not suspecting that it is his own offspring. Yea, he is ready to destroy it with the mother ; but proof is at hand that it is Abraham's seed. The " signet" and " staff," though Judah may rage, will prove beyond all contradiction the lineage of the Church's children. Then again appears the twofold line, which in this case, as the fruit of rule, is developed with certain remarkable peculiarities ; something of the younger or spiritual line being seen here for a moment before the first-born or carnal breaks forth and supersedes it.[18] But I have said enough of this. The story is

---

[15] How little the early Church at Jerusalem saw of the distinct glories of this dispensation, how it clung to circumcision and the law, might be shewn from many scriptures. It was some time before even the Apostles were clear respecting the call of the Gentiles. Their thoughts still hung upon the Jewish line. See Acts xi. xv. &c.

[16] Rom. xi. 8, 9.

[17] Rom. xi 10–17.

[18] Augustine goes at great length into the dispensational fulfilment of this story. The following are the leading points in his comment:—
" De tribu Judâ reges tanquam mariti Thamar adhibebantur. . . . Duo autem genera principum, qui non rectè operabantur, significantur in duobus filiis Judæ. . . . Deus tamen ambos occidisse dictus est, ubi figuratur regnum talibus hominibus abstulisse. Tertius vero filius Judæ, . . . significat tempus ex quo reges plebi Judæorum cœperunt de tribu Judâ non fieri. . . . . Illo ergo tempore quo jam de tribu Judæ regnum defuerat, veniendum est Christo, vero Salvatori nostro. . . . . Jam Thamar habitum mutat, . . . typum quippe jam Ecclesiæ gerit Thamar, sedens cum hoc habitu ad portam Enaiim, quod interpretatur 'fontes.' Cucurrit enim velut cervus ad fontes aquarum, pervenire ad semen Abrahæ ; illic a non agnoscente fetatur, quia de illâ prædictum est, 'Populus quem non cognovi, servivit mihi.' Accepit in occulto annu-

throughout a mystery of the kingdom; and as such is alluded to in that Gospel, which is peculiarly devoted to set forth our Lord in connection with the kingdom,[19] shewing how the line of heirs should change, while yet the kingdom should be continued to Judah's sons and Abraham's seed.

Such is Judah's course. And yet in every age Judah's sons have been ready to boast, "We were not born of fornication."[20] The Jew said so, and since then the Church has been forward to repeat the boast with just as little ground for glorying. Those who know her story best must own, that, if the true seed of the kingdom has sprung out of her, there have been also most awful confusions. I know God's grace can master all; and Judah's fall, even as Adam's, may give occasion to bring in better things. Out of the adulterer's lust may grow the living child, in its bodily perfections displaying God's wisdom, and in its soul's salvation His love, which delights to save to the uttermost. But in each case sin is judged as sin. Our place is, not to boast,—for God knows, we have cause for deepest self-abasement,—but to walk humbly with God, that He may forgive and deliver us from our own and also our fathers' sins.

lum, monile, et virgam. . . . . Postea vero publicis signis, annuli, monilis, et virgæ, vicit temerè judicantes Judæos, quorum jam personam Judas ipse gestabat, qui hodie quoque dicunt non hunc esse populum Christi, nec habere nos Abrahæ semen. Sed prolatis certissimis documentis nostræ vocationis, justificationis, et glorificationis, confunduntur, et nos magis quam se justificatos esse fatebuntur."—*Contr. Faust.* l. xxii. cc. 84–86. Chrysostom also, *Hom.* 62 *in Gen.*, refers to the mystery here.

[19] Matt. i. 3.

[20] John viii. 41.

III.—Joseph in Potiphar's House

Chapter 39

THE fruits of outward rule having now been seen in Judah,
we return to that more inward and spiritual life, which at
last attains to rule all things. Joseph, rejected by his
brethren, is here " brought down to Egypt." [1]   That pure
life, oppressed and crushed by other more outward fruits
of true service, that is, by Jacob's elder children, is now
enslaved in things of sense, for Egypt is the ground of
sense, and Joseph is now brought down here. [2]   The tree
is destined to be both high and wide; its root is therefore
laid deep in the earth: it is to bloom in bright sunshine,
but it is first reared in deep shadow; and at this stage
shade is safer than sun, while the very shadow proves that
there is sunshine not far off. So the mind which dreams
of rule must serve, and first know the bondage to sense in
all its bitterness. In this way, and thus alone, does our
spirit obtain the longed-for power over natural things.
Those only who have felt the bondage ever reach the true
deliverance.

First to trace the scene within. That mind in us which
waits to rule by pureness and long-suffering, already
crossed by other fruits of service, now feels the power of the
things of sense, and ere long is sorely tempted by them.
Against its will it is brought down to Egypt, and there is
bound and sold as a slave, like Joseph. [3]   The sensual mind
overrules the spirit; and sense, instead of being governed,
still holds the spirit captive. Can the spirit hope for rule
after this? Is not such bondage a token of the final

---

[1] Chap. xxxix. 1.   [2] Respecting Egypt, see on chap. xii.
[3] Chap. xxxix. 1.

triumph of the flesh or natural man? Not so. God Himself appoints this way:— "It was not you, but God, that sent me hither, to save your lives by a great deliverance." [4] He first empties, that He may fill; for the spirit to the end requires such discipline. Joseph does not, indeed, like Jacob, use carnal means to gain his ends; but his way of telling his dreams shews that as yet he lacks that self-despair and brokenness which God waits for. Besides, God loves the world. He will have the kingdom in our earth even as it is in heaven. Egypt may be Egypt to the end, yet in it the Lord will shew what He can accomplish. Our spirit therefore is brought down and bound, and made to feel how little, spite of faith and sonship and service, the ground of sense is overcome; that at last the evil there, having been felt, may be subdued, the spirit meanwhile by the trial being yet more chastened and purified.

This state is open to special trial. The spirit cannot feel the power of the natural man, without being subject to temptation through its affections. So the Egyptian's wife sought to corrupt Joseph; [5] that is, some natural affection, the exact character of which we are not told, for her name is not given us, is felt within, seeking to seduce the spirit. Some affections of nature may indeed be won and blessed: Joseph himself at a later stage has an Egyptian wife, who bears him good fruit.[6] The evil here is that this affection, which now tempts the elect, is wedded to the natural man, and as such seeks only to corrupt the spirit, not at all to obey or serve it. Very sifting is this trial. Secret, repeated, even violent are the solicitations, which assail us in the very duties we owe to the natural man,

---

[4] Chap. xlv. 7, 8. [5] Chap. xxxix. 7–12. [6] Chap. xli. 50–52.

tempting us to embrace some worldly principle, and so to
give up the narrow path of holy separateness. But the
seductions of natural affection by grace are overcome,
though it costs us a struggle to escape their importunity.
Then the immediate result is worse bondage. The spirit,
like Joseph, is charged with acts for which the flesh is answerable; and there is that within us, like the Egyptian,
which believes the charge, and at once condemns the
spirit as an evil-doer.

Some can trace all these confusions within. We ask
our Lord that we may know the power of His resurrection,
and the fellowship of His sufferings. He draws us by
His Spirit thus to pray. A dream of power over self and
sin flits before our inward man. We think a few short
stages will bring us to the end,—that His love, who has
promised, will quickly give us victory. Instead of this, we
discover fresh evil. The flesh, in forms strange and as yet
unknown, assails and holds us captive. But we will not
yield to nature and its affections. What then? Our sorrow is increased. We are thrust still lower, and a voice
within untruly blames the spirit, charging its bondage on
it as the result of its unfaithfulness. Could we then hear
the Lord, He would tell us, all was well,—that this discipline, painful as it is, is really indispensable. Had Joseph
been happy with the Egyptian, he would not so soon have
ruled Egypt. Were the flesh never to rise against the
spirit, its evil would remain undiscovered, and therefore
unsubdued. In men whose nature is rough and strong,
how often the very strength of the flesh forces the spirit
to rise to overcome it; while weaker natures, whose evil
comes out less, remain less changed, because less conscious
of the evil. The elect therefore must feel the evil. Only
thus do they obtain the full deliverance.

But let us look now at this scene without. Here is set forth a stage of the early experience of those who by patience and pureness look for spiritual power. Such souls have many griefs. Not only are they rejected by their brethren, they also must suffer in the world. They are there, but not by choice. Far rather would they abide in heavenly places. But the sin of the elect forces them away; and the very world, bad as it is, is kinder to them than brethren. Then in the world such souls are made a blessing:—" The Lord blessed the Egyptian's house for Joseph's sake." [7] Their character makes itself felt. Ere long they exercise some power even in that worldly circle. Then comes the temptation to swerve from holy separateness. The principle (women are principles) of that society in which they are forced to move becomes a tempter to them; or, to put it more outwardly, that body, which is the outward form or expression of some worldly principle, seeks with open arms to gain and lead them astray. What peculiar form of worldliness this is, we are not told; for, as I have already observed, the name of this Egyptian woman is not here given us. It may be any worldly principle, whether that which animates the literary world, or the musical world, or the fashionable world, or the mercantile world, or the scientific world, or any of those other many minor worlds, which, like the households of Egypt, are all constituent parts of the one great world of sense which Egypt represents. That body, to which the elect stands in nearest contact, will be his tempter; assailing him peculiarly while he is engaged about his business in the world. It would make our outward calling an occasion to undo us. It is very urgent,

[7] Chap. xxxix. 5.

and will not be denied. But a voice has said, " Love not the world, neither the things that are in the world : if any man love the world, the love of the Father is not in him. For all that is in the world, the lust of the flesh, and the lust of the eyes, and the pride of life, is not of the Father, but is of the world. And the world passeth away, and the lust thereof; but he that doeth the will of God abideth for ever." [8] The Josephs therefore will not be drawn aside : in holy truth they reject all those advances which would seduce them from their integrity; and for this the world now hates them more, and, to save its credit, stirs up its acknowledged masters to judge what it cannot corrupt. The elect are accused of wishing to loose the bonds of society, and under this false charge for a while are shut up as evil-doers. But " in all things they approve themselves, in much patience, in afflictions, in stripes, in imprisonments, in tumults; by pureness, by knowledge, by long-suffering, by kindness, by the word of truth, by the armour of righteousness on the right hand and on the left; by honour and dishonour ; by evil report and good report; as deceivers, and yet true; as unknown, yet well-known ; as chastened, and not killed; as sorrowful, yet always rejoicing ; as poor, yet making many rich ; as having nothing, and yet possessing all things." [9]

Dispensationally too this scene has been fulfilled. The Spirit of Christ, as a patient sufferer in the world, suffered, served, was blessed, and made a blessing. The world, with its offers of love, sought to seduce it in vain. The Spirit of Christ in His true Church could not be thus corrupted. So it was basely slandered and falsely accused;

and the lords of this world, misinformed of the elect's acts and purpose, opposed and grieved and bound them. Those, who know the story of the coming of this Spirit into the world, will at once recognise the details of this dispensational fulfilment.[10]

Thus journey on the Lord's beloved. Happy are they who have learnt, not only to trace these journeys, but to be partakers of them. Then, while they look to the things unseen, the light affliction, which is but for a moment, worketh for them a far more exceeding and eternal weight of glory. Faithfulness cannot go unrewarded. The blessing may seem to tarry, but for every delay there shall be the largest interest.

IV.—JOSEPH IN PRISON

Chapter 40

HERE follow yet further temptations, through which the spirit in us is yet more perfected. If it resists the solicitations of natural affection, the natural man is stirred up against it, and the spirit is more than ever straitened. Like Joseph, it is sorely bound. Then, in its bonds, it is brought into contact with certain servants of Pharaoh, that is, certain forms or powers of the natural man, which by it are served, and even in some degree disciplined. Inwardly, we see here how certain natural activities are subdued, while the spirit is yet shut up in grievous bondage: outwardly, how certain natural men are schooled and taught

---

[10] On the spiritual sense of this chapter I have found but little in the Fathers. Ambrose, (*De Joseph*, c. 6, § 31,) and Gregory the Great, (*Moral. in Job*, l. ii. c. 36, § 59,) just allude to Joseph's temptation here, as a figure of what Christ suffered on earth. It is, however, but an allusion.

by the elect while the world neglects or frowns upon them.

Of this work within I can say but little here, because of our dim perception of that immense complexness of thought and being, which go to make up man. Adam's path may be clearly seen by us, and some of the earlier stages of man's development; while the later steps, which are more inward and deal with the many varieties of the carnal and spiritual mind, may be beyond our vision. Even if seen, the nice distinction between these varied forms of thought and life is hard to be uttered, in our present state and with our imperfect language. Without, our eyes can see the immense variety of tribes which have come forth from Adam, all of which are but various forms or manifestations of man or human nature. But within, though secret and hidden, the outcome is the same. Old Adam in us brings forth as many different minds, each of which throughout this book is figured and set before us in some son of Adam, or Noah, or Shem, or Ham, or Japhet; some outward, some inward, some sensual, some natural, some spiritual, and this in different measures; the elect all representing some form of the spiritual mind in us; the non-elect, some form of that mind which is earthly, sensual, devilish.

Now Egypt is the ground of sense, and Pharaoh, king of Egypt, the highest part or ruling power of the natural man;[1] his servants being those inferior or subordinate activities, whose office it is to serve this natural man. I do not pretend to interpret with perfect precision here, but we shall not be far wrong if we regard these servants as the senses; for the natural man (I do not mean the body) imbibes, receives, and digests the things the senses give

---

[1] See on chap. xii.

him. But these senses at a certain stage are felt to need restraint. They have been useful in their place, but something occurs which makes the natural man perceive that they require discipline. He finds that his servants are not wholly trustworthy: their fallacies begin to be discerned. Hence they are restrained, and thus brought into contact with the spirit, which in its bondage instructs them, and so prepares them to instruct the natural man. For now they learn that there is a power to know God's mind above their own; their lot too is shewn, that some will be restored to serve the natural man, and others must be mortified; while a way is thus opened by which the natural man, through its own servants, may in due time receive an intimation of that higher faculty, which as yet is shut up and bound within.

But this fulfilment within can hardly be uttered. Let us therefore look at the same scene as it is very manifestly fulfilled in the wider sphere of the outward world around us.

In this view, we see here the griefs and works of those, who, while looking for spiritual power, because they will not be corrupted by the world, are for a season shut up from outward usefulness. Neither Abraham, Isaac, nor Jacob, ever suffered thus. Faith, sonship, and service, with all their trials, are not so pressed as the pure and loving soul which dreams of rule. The Josephs are mocked and sold even by brethren. Then, in the world, they are first tempted, and, if they will not yield, are made to suffer grievous bondage. What the elect feels at this stage, none know but God. To get even a glimpse of this sorrow needs an instructed eye. Such a path may appear to be free from all doubtings, a course which throughout shall be so plain as to cost us little exercise. In vain we read the Psalms: in vain we see "John in prison" doubting what "John baptizing" never questioned.[2] We too at last are shut up. Till we have felt it, we cannot conceive that sickness of heart, which at times will steal upon the patient sufferer; that sense of loneliness, that faintness of soul, which comes from hopes deferred and wishes unshared, from the selfishness of brethren, and the heartlessness of the world. We ask ourselves, If the Lord were with me, should I suffer thus, not only the scorn of the learned and the contempt of the great, but even the indifference and neglect of those whom I have served, who yet forget me? So Joseph might have asked; and so till now may the elect ask, as they stand alone without man's encouragement or sympathy, not turned aside by falsehood or scorn, with their face set as a flint, yet deeply feeling what it costs them.

In this trial the elect meets other men.[3] The spiritual are not the only sufferers. The world at times must judge its own children, and worldling and Christian may both be under its frown. Here, as on Calvary, we have before us three sufferers, alike rejected by the world, though most unlike each other. God's elect fall in with just two sorts of men, both Egyptians, and both sufferers, whose end is very different; the one after a brief term of bondage being released and blessed; the other remaining in bondage, till suddenly they are cut off. To outward eyes there is little difference between them. The world, if it think of them, passes one common judgment on all. Those who are shut up must doubtless deserve punishment. Besides, who has not heard of the attempts of the elect to loose the bonds

---

[2] Compare Matt. xi. 2, 3, with John i. 28, 29.
[3] Chap. xl. 1–4.

of society, and thus to subvert the world's happiness? So the precious are mingled with the vile. Then some, who in their prosperity would never have met or thought of Joseph, in their sorrow learn the might of truth and grace, as they see a man of like passions with themselves, and in the same affliction, shedding the sunshine of his own peace on all around, bound, yet free, and poor, yet making many rich, without a murmur, forgetting himself and his own griefs, in loving efforts to serve and comfort others.

But Joseph does more. He interprets their dreams, and makes them understand the thoughts of their hearts and what the Lord is saying to them.[4] Not in their bright days, but in hours of darkness and grief, does the Lord's voice come home with power to the men of this world. Some dream,—it may be of the day,—some inward consciousness of a voice from God,—reaches even sensual men, when all is dark around, which, with an authority which cannot be stifled or silenced, though they cannot explain it, with strange light flashes in upon them, forcing them to feel that God Himself is speaking. Then they need an interpreter to expound to them their thoughts; and God's elect, long schooled to know God's voice, help the perplexed ones to solve their own secret. They declare that if He speaks, He will also interpret;[5] and that worldlings, though often they cannot understand, are never left without a witness; for He speaks not only to His own, but to all, that all may learn, and all may be comforted. The word differs indeed to each, for the revelation must be according to our state, but to each the Lord has some message; which in our sunny days may not be heard, but will come with power to our souls in our dark hours and

nights of heaviness. To Jacob there is a dream of protection in service, a ladder uniting the rough and untilled
earth to highest heaven, testifying that God and His
angels come down from highest to lowest, and that true
servants with Him may go anywhere. To Joseph, dreams
of glory and might; to the butler, a dream of restoration
and blessing; to the baker, of losing what he had wrought.
And as the dream is, so is the fulfilment. I cannot but
think, that, to a degree few suppose, the impressions which
reach us from another world, are often true forebodings to
men of what is about to come upon them. Doubtless
Satan, as an angel of light, in this as elsewhere to discredit
God, seeks at times to deceive us with wrong and false
suggestions. But I speak of the settled and growing
conviction, which makes to some their calling and election
sure, and to others seems already to forestall the day of
judgment. Be this as it may, revelations from the Lord
depend upon our state, and each receives that message
which is best suited to him. The faithful sufferer has
visions of glory, well understood; Egyptians have visions
of mercy or judgment, both awhile a riddle to them, till
the elect, without fear or favour to either, interprets to each
their deep and awful significance.

As to these dreams, which are of everlasting truth, they
shew the fate and end of those two classes, into which the
slaves of this world may be divided. In this view, worldlings make up two classes, and but two, the saved and lost.
The thoughts and ways, may I not say, the inward life of
each, is here remarkably displayed. Before the one, a
vine is set, which appears to bud, and blossom, and bring
forth clusters. He does not plant it or make it to grow;
but his eyes are turned and feast upon its beauty. As he
looks it seems to grow. Then he takes of its fruit, and,

not content to have it for himself alone, he ministers it to others near him. Thus one class of worldlings, in their hour of trouble, have an eye opened to behold Christ as " the Vine which cheereth God and man."[6] As they look, the Vine they are intent on seems to grow before them ; one beauty after another opens out to their astonished view; first the blossoms, and then the clusters, and then the precious wine, which with glad hearts they take and give to other worldlings. What can they render to the Lord for all His mercies ? They will take the cup of salvation, and confess they owe their all to Him. And yet, with an eye open to see the Vine, and a hand stretched out to grasp it, and to give its cheering blood to all around, the man is yet in sadness and fear, not seeing that such a vision is the certain pledge of life and liberty. Then God's elect explain the dream. If such things are seen, the prisoner may be of good cheer. He that sees this Vine on " the third day " shall go forth free. Soon shall his bondage cease, and in the power of the resurrection he shall live to serve others.[7]

How different the scene before the other's eyes. He sees himself, carrying on his head baked meats, the work of his own hands. He has toiled to make " all manner of things for Pharaoh," but none for God. Carelessly he exposes the produce of his toil where it may be stolen from him. It is " on his head," not in his hands; " in baskets full of holes,"[8] whence the birds of the air can come and

---

[6] John xv. 1 ; Judges ix. 13.

[7] Chap. xl. 20. The " third day " is always connected with resurrection. See p. 21.

[8] Heb. סלי חרי, translated in the text of the authorised version "*white* baskets;" but in the margin " baskets *full of holes*." The Hebrew root, חור, is a *hole* or *perforation*, evidently expressing the holes or interstices between the twigs, of which the baskets were made. Jarchi explains it of wicker-baskets, made of twigs which were white from having the bark peeled off.

steal away his labours. While some poor worldlings in their fears behold the Vine, others are occupied and burdened with what they themselves have wrought to please the world. They see their work, not for God, but for the world. As they look, they see their treasure is in danger, for it has been " put into a bag with holes ; "[9] and ere long evil spirits, (so our Lord Himself explains the " birds,"[10]) deprive them of the fruits of all their labour. One would have thought that such things would need no interpreter. But it is not so. The poor prisoner looks with fear, but he understands not. What must the elect say to such ? Can he say, Peace, Peace, where there is no peace ? What can he say, but that, if no change comes, " the end of such things is death."[11]

Thus even in his bondage does the elect shew out God's thoughts, cheering some of the slaves of this world, if he can only warn others. Those he comforts in due time are freed, and in their joy forget the man through whom the comfort reached them.[12] The Lord's prisoners differ greatly. Some there are, who hear the truth, and go forth from bondage, and yet are not spiritual. Such men never suffer like purer souls. They could not bear it; therefore it is not laid upon them. For the vessel of wood, it is enough that it be washed with water : the precious gold can bear, and therefore must be purged by, fire; for it is written, " Every thing that may abide the fire, ye shall make it go through the fire, and it shall be clean ; and all that abideth not the fire, ye shall make go through the water." [13] Thus, while these are freed, the beloved of the Lord remains in bonds ; fitted for service or rule, and yet

[9] Haggai i. 6.
[10] Matt. xiii. 4, 19.
[11] Rom. vi. 21.

[12] Chap. xl. 23.
[13] Numbers xxxi. 23, and Lev. xv. 12.

cut off from it. It seems as if Joseph thought the butler would help him; but many weary days elapse before he remembers Joseph. Let spiritual souls understand their calling. They may comfort others: let them not think they shall therefore be remembered in the world.

Dispensationally too this is fulfilled. In this view, Joseph in an Egyptian prison is Christ come into the world, where He can meet the two peoples, that is, the Jew and Gentile. The Jews, even as we, need many figures to represent all the different aspects or relations in which they may be seen. As the brethren of Christ in the flesh, who reject and sell Him, they are again and again set forth in the sons of the first wife. As the line of the kingdom, they are seen in Judah and his sons. As a sensual people, uncircumcised in heart,[14] and ignorant of God's secrets, even when He speaks, an Egyptian captive awaiting judgment is their appointed figure. Christ, the true Joseph, meets these two peoples, Jew and Gentile. In former days they had each served Egypt or the world with meat and drink in different measures. When He comes, they are shut up, unable to serve others. God has spoken to both, but they cannot understand.[15] For the book of prophecy and God's purpose, though given by Him to men, was not opened rightly till the Spirit of Christ opened it. In these visions or dreams, one people saw a vine, and gathered,

[14] See Jer. ix. 26.

[15] Those who are familiar with the early Fathers know how confidently they spoke to the Gentiles, as men who ought to have had better thoughts of God, even from their own poets, and the voice of nature. See Justin Martyr's *Cohortatio ad Græcos*, § 14, and the following sections; also his *De Monarchiâ*, § 2, &c. The *Pedagogue* of Clement is full of this thought throughout, that the Divine Word was the invisible teacher of men at all periods and in all lands. St. Paul seems to express the same thought, Acts xiv. 15–17, and xvii. 23–28, and Rom. i. 19, 20.

and then presented, its precious juice to others. This people, which is the Gentile, though for a while shut up, shall be released, and bear forth the cup of blessing to the world; while the other people, though burdened and toiling, shall be robbed of the bread they have prepared, —this is the Jew,—and then be judged and cast out. But the Gentile people, though freed, ill requite Joseph. In their joy they forget that, though they are free, He does not rule yet where He surely must rule. They seem to think their service to Pharaoh will suffice, till, by the discovery of their own impotence to solve his difficulties, they are forced to remember Him to whom all in heaven and earth shall bow. When will Gentile Christendom awake to the fact that there is One, who has served them, and waits to rule? When will they welcome Him to judge all things? [16]

V.—Joseph exalted over all Egypt

Chapter 41

WE come now to the exaltation of the elect. After long suffering, first from the ungoverned violence of activities which spring from true service,[1] then through temptations

---

[16] The Ordinary Gloss thus sums up the substance of this chapter:— "Per carcerem istum intelligitur pœnalitas vitæ præsentis, in quâ fuerunt Gentiles et Judæi. Per Joseph autem, qui fuit cum eis, propter ejus innocentiam, intelligitur Christus. . . . . Ipse vero, quantum homo, fuit in carcere pœnalitatis prædictæ, quam assumpsit voluntariè; et ipse prædixit vocationem gentium ad fidem, quæ per pincer-nam significantur, et reprobationem Judæorum, qui significantur per pistorem," &c. The Interlinear Gloss adds, as to the dreams, " Clausa fuit prophetia donec venit Christus, qui aperuit librum, et solvit signacula ejus. . . . Vitis autem visa in somnis Dominus est, qui de seipso dixit, 'Ego sum vitis vera.' . . . . . Qui calicem Domini accepit, liberari meruit," &c.—*In loco.*

[1] Chap. xxxvii.

from the affections of the natural man,[2] then through bondage and pain,[3] the spirit is freed and glorified. All Egypt bows to Joseph. He counsels its prince, and in due times arranges all its doings.

Of the inward fulfilment I can write but little, though in each detail this scene deserves the closest attention. This, however, I may say, that we are here shewn how the natural man is subdued at last, and in all its parts is governed by the spirit. The steps detailed are briefly these. Pharaoh, that is, the highest faculty of the natural man,[4] is now greatly disturbed by visions. He dreams that all his strength is swallowed up. He sees lean kine devouring fat ones, while the lean are none the better for it. He sees thin ears consuming the full, till nought remains. He feels assured, though he cannot read the riddle, that it portends evil.[5] Cattle and corn are two great gifts for man's blessing, namely, the animal faculties which may be used or abused, and the fruits which are the result of the cultivation of the creature.[6] Here the natural man begins to perceive that these may perish, and leave their present possessor in utter misery. By the elect these creatures were offered to God; but in Egypt they are never so offered, but beast eats beast, and none is better for it. The fruits of the earth, too, (and where is it cultivated as in Egypt?) are seen now consuming one another. Surely it is an awful sight. In this juncture the wisdom of Egypt is summoned to aid, but it can render no assistance. Then from the butler, that is, some sense which serves the natural man,[7] the natural man himself learns of one who is near and can unravel such difficulties. The

---

[2] Chap. xxxix.
[3] Chap. xl.
[4] See on chap. xii. and xl.

[5] Chap. xli. 17–24.
[6] See on chap. viii. and ix.
[7] See above on chap. xl.

spirit's witness is heard with awe, and its counsel at once is obeyed through fear of coming judgment. Wherever the natural man is to be governed, this must be known. It invariably occurs wherever the spirit is destined to be the ruler. Egypt's pride must bow. Troubles, therefore, which it is not able to avert, press on it. The natural man is brought into perplexity, that it may submit itself and hear the spirit's teachings. The details I cannot open here; for it is one thing to see, another to utter such mysteries. I will only note that Joseph now receives a wife;[8] that is, certain natural affections or principles are embraced and rendered subject to the spirit; while some of the riches which God so wondrously bestows are treasured up, as a means of at least abating and better meeting the impending judgment.[9]

As fulfilled without, this scene is open to all; and in this view we are here shewn the means by which worldlings are brought to allow the exaltation of the spiritual. Sooner or later the great of this world stand by their river, that is, watch the transient course of earthly blessings, and thereby are grieved with sad visions, as they see the good destroyed and preyed on by the evil. But they cannot understand their own riddle, much less devise a remedy which shall suffice to meet the crisis; till, at the suggestion of some who have already profited by their wisdom, the Lord's beloved are found, not mere men of faith, or sons of God, or zealous servants only, but men who have long since dreamt of rule, and then for their truth and grace been separated from their brethren, and falsely charged, and sold, and shut up; who by all this have been prepared of

[8] Chap. xli. 45.   [9] Chap. xli. 47–49.

God in due time to enlighten and guide and help many. By such both blessings and judgments are used to save the world. Egypt does not become Canaan, but a wondrous change is effected throughout its length and breadth; while some are united to them by a nearer and dearer tie, as a beloved Church, in which children are begotten who shall inherit Canaan. I do not care to dwell on historic applications; but I may say, that the christianising of Europe, through the influence which saintly souls exercised on a violent age, is one example of the outward fulfilment here; after which came that awful famine of the word of the Lord, which, had not abundant treasures been laid up, would have consumed the world.[10] But the same story is fulfilling every day; and those who at one stage are mocked as dreamers, and misrepresented, and shut up, and cast out by brethren, end by ruling those whom their brethren cannot rule, and by saving and serving those who mocked them.

Dispensationally the fulfilment here concerns us much. We saw how in this view the saved butler prefigured Gentile Christendom.[11] Here we see how this liberated people, whose eyes were opened to behold the Vine, even while ministering it to the world, unfaithfully keeps to itself the secret of what the true Joseph has done for it. But a time comes, in the providence of God, when the rulers of this world, represented in Pharaoh, begin to be

---

[10] "Joseph, qui typum Christi (vel spiritûs Christi) gerebat, accepit potestatem prædicandi et judicandi. Congregavit per septem annos omnem frugum abundantiam, id est, frumenta fidei, sanctorum horreis condens, ut cum septem anni inopiæ cœperint, id est, cum iniquitas occur-rerit septem capitalium criminum sub Antichristo, quando fames fidei fuerit et salutis, tunc sancti habeant copiosam justitiæ frugem, ne fides eorum inopiâ sermonis deficiat," &c. — *Gloss Ord.* in loco.

[11] See on chap. xl.

sorely troubled. Visions haunt rulers, of weak things destroying strong, of hungry creatures eating up the fat and flourishing. The oxen strong to labour are seen to be consumed; and, what is worse, the thin and hungry ones are none the fatter for it. The seven good ears, of which it is twice noticed that "they came up upon one stalk," [12] are devoured by the poor and weak, in whom is seen no bond of union. The strong and good, having union among themselves, are destroyed by those who are alike in misery, but have no bond of fellowship. Surely it is an awful dream, which the world's rulers are beginning to see, and not without perplexity. What does it portend? Such is the question this day with some to whom the butler has given the cup, but who do not know Joseph. It portends a trouble, which the world unaided cannot meet; one for which the learning and counsels of Egypt will find no remedy. For God Himself shall bring all Egypt to such self-despair, as will render the need of His Elect Servant's presence and help plain to all. At this day a million men in Europe are needed to keep order; to keep, while it may be so, the weak and hungry from devouring the strong before them. Sooner or later, spite of all its boastings, the world will discover that it needs Christ; that neither its present rulers nor magicians can solve their own riddle. Sooner or later they must confess their own weakness, and admit that a power not in them,—the government of Christ and His Spirit,—alone can save the world. Blessed be God, the day is at hand, when the Despised One shall rule: the night has been dark, but the light of day cannot be far off. When the night is darkest, the morning is at hand; and the child is born, when the travail pains are sharpest. The world has long travailed and been in pain,

[12] Chap. xli. 5, 22. Nothing like this is seen in "*the thin ears.*"

waiting for the manifestation of the Son of God, and the redemption of the body. His day shall surely come. Then, while earth bows itself, shall His Virgin Bride be given to Him. Then shall the earth be glad, for He cometh to judge the world with equity, and the people with His truth. Through judgment shall the world be saved. His wisdom shall rescue it, even while it passes through "the consumption which is decreed on all the earth." [13]

Holy, Holy, Holy, Lord God of Hosts, who is like unto Thee, who dwellest on high, yet humblest Thyself to behold the things which are in heaven and in earth; who takest the poor from the dust, and the needy from the dunghill, to set them with princes, even with the princes of Thy people? The whole earth shall be full of Thy glory. Glory be to Thee, O Lord Most High.

Here, for the present, I conclude these Notes, unable to write of that glory which shall ere long be manifested. The works of Christ cannot be fully written yet. If they should be written every one, I suppose that even the world itself could not contain the books that should be written. But the part of His work here written, (for it is He who works in us,) may shew how great is that transformation, which He is able and willing to perform in those who yield their will to Him. Only let us give ourselves to Him, and wait for Him. For it is love which keeps us so long waiting for the powers of the world to come, lest being used in self-hood they should be a curse, and so increase

---

[13] Isa. xxviii. 22. Ambrose, (*De Joseph*, c. 7, § 40,) and Augustine, (*Enar. in Ps.* lxxx. § 8,) both allude to this dispensational fulfilment.

our condemnation. There have been some, who, having
received some special gift or energy, have in self-will
denied the gift its true development, and, substituting
their own hasty purpose for that of Him who called them,
have used the spirit to their own private ends, thus injur-
ing themselves unspeakably. Therefore let each humbly
submit himself in all things to God, that He may fulfil
His will and work as He pleases. O Lord, through life
and death fulfil Thy work in us, that to us to live may be
Christ, according to Thy pleasure, that so Thou mayest be
seen and rest in us, and we be hid and rest in Thee, for
ever. Amen.

INDEX

Abel, the spiritual mind, 88; a type of Christ, 99.

Abraham, the spirit of faith, 160; import of the change of name from Abram to Abraham, 221; a type of God the Father, 250, *note* 2.

Abraham's servant, who seeks the bride for the Son, the figure of the ministers of the house of faith, 268.

Active life, figured in Japhet, 132; and in Jacob, 336, 337; may degenerate into mere worldliness, 137, 139.

Adam, human nature, 63; his way, 69; though fallen, raised up in the woman's seed, 81.

Analogy between days of creation and stages of man's progress, 57.

Antinomianism, shews itself after regeneration, 163; a reaction from legalism, 217.

Apostasy, course of, figured in the building of Babel, 150, 151; in Nimrod's kingdom, 147, 148; and in Esau's kingdom in Seir, 372, 373.

Apostolic succession, connected with rule in the church, 390.

Ark, figure of the cross, 109; and of the church, 113; three stories of, 114; a remnant of beasts saved in, 110, 116.

Ascetic life, figured by Keturah, 279; its fruits easily corrupted, 280; cannot produce spirit of sonship, 281.

Ass, to be left in Isaac's sacrifice, 260, and *note* 4.

Asshur or *Assyria*, the ground of reasoning, 176, 177, and *note* 31. See *Euphrates*.

Attainments, no pledge of security, 358.

Aurora Borealis, not the true morning, 46.

Babylon, built by those who pass the baptismal waters, 135; the work of Ham's seed, 138; built of brick, 152; full of imitations of God's true work, 154; connected with the revelation of Jesus Christ, 155.

Baptism, the way through the waters, or regeneration, figured in Noah, 104, 114, 121, *note* 22; of fire, 117.

Barrenness, for a while the trial of the elect, 203; of Abram, 204; of Isaac, 285.

Beasts, moving creatures, or emotions, of the will, 37, 262; clean and unclean, 33; need ruling, 39; after fall, sacrificed, 95; by regeneration stilled, 110; and ruled,

125, 126; an object of worship in Egypt, 187.

Birds, moving creatures, or emotions, 33, *note* 13 ; of the understanding, 34, 35, 36 ; very various, 36 ; distractions to worship of faith, 208.

Birth, the first and second, of human nature, figured in Cain and Abel, 88.

Blessings are trials, 202.

Brick, man's imitation of God's work, 152 ; Babel and Nineveh built of, 152 ; brick-making common in Egypt, 152 ; examples of brick for stone, 154.

Bride, found by the well, 272 ; how recognised, 273; arrayed in gold and fine linen, 273, 275 ; borne upon camels, 277.

Cain, the carnal mind, 88 ; his religion the cultivation of the fallen creature, 95 ; a type of the Jew, 99.

Call of God, contains promise and exhortation, 165 ; how obeyed by faith, 167.

Camels, used to bring the bride home, 269.

Canaanite, the, false outward religion, 133, 135, 175, 359, 365. See *Ham* and *Hivite*.

Carnal mind, the first fruit of Adam or human nature, 88.

Catholic unity, may be wrongly sought, as in building Babel, 153; the true ground and means of it seen at Pentecost, 153.

Change of name, in Abram to Abraham, 221; in Jacob to Israel, 354.

Cherubim, the divine in creature-form, 79 ; figuring the Incarnation, 79, *note* 11.

Christ, works in many, rests in few, 42 ; figured in Adam, 82; in Abel, 99 ; in Noah, 130; in Isaac, 250, *note* 2, and 264 ; in Joseph, 379,

412 ; His fullness such that no one type can reveal Him, 33.

Church, unity of, 151 ; varieties in, 134 ; place of discipline, 130 ; contains both good and bad, 135 ; contains both an outward and inward element, 290; and therefore has a double seed, like chaff and wheat, 290, 372 ; its worst enemies nursed in its own bosom, 135, 136 ; produces a seed which builds Great Babylon, 135 ; its development and divisions foreshadowed in Noah's seed, 136, 142 ; its failure, in Noah's fall, 145, in Nimrod's domination, 148, and in the building of Babel, 150; its blessings unlike those of the Jews, 323 ; even when fallen, rich in forms of truth, 154 ; when fallen and corrupted, admits formalists to holy things, 361 ; figured in Eve, the mother of all living, 83 ; in Abel, giving a life to God, 99 ; in Noah, 134 ; in Rebekah, 271, 290, 321.

Circumcision, the putting away of the filth of the flesh, 224 ; not our righteousness, but a seal of it, 225 ; why on the eighth day, 226.

Cities, systems or polities, 149 ; unlike primitive dwellings, 149.

Communion, different measures of, 233.

Conscience, acquired in the fall, 76.

Consistency, of worldlings, 173.

Contemplative life, one fruit of regeneration, 132 ; figured in Shem, 132 ; degenerates into mere reasonings, 136, 139.

Covenant, the old and new, 128 ; the token of, 129.

Creation, seven days of, a type of the new creation, 4 ; progressive, 7.

Creature, state of the, when God begins to work on it, 5 ; change in it, wrought by God's word, 6.

Cross, the, figured in Abel's lamb, 95; in Noah's ark, 109; in Isaac's sacrifice, 259; the key to all mysteries, 207; witnessed to even in nature, 242.

Darkness, called Night, or deviation, 13; brings into view God's work in heavenly places, 29; ruled on the fourth day, 32.

Day, means movement, 13; first day's work, 11; second day, 14; third day, 18; a type of resurrection, 21; fourth day, 25; fifth day, 32; sixth day, 36; seventh day, 42; has no evening, 45; the seven days a figure of all God's work, 4, 57; eighth day, the resurrection, 226.

Development, true theory of, 136; through discoveries of failure, 162.

Dreams, Jacob's, 328, 329; Joseph's, 384; the butler's and baker's, 403, 405; Pharaoh's, 409.

Earth, dry land called, 22; figures the will, 15, 18, 36; rises above the waters on the third day, 18.

East, advancing light, 48.

Eden, pleasure, 48.

Egypt, the ground of sense, 176; beasts worshipped in, 187; an enchanting land, 177; a snare to faith, 177; taught and ruled by the patient sufferer, 401, 410.

Eighth day, resurrection, 226.

Elohim, God known as, in days of labour, as Jehovah on day of rest, 46, 47; the serpent substitutes Elohim for Jehovah, in the temptation of Eve, 70, *note* 2.

Emotions, good in themselves, become evil through self-will, 34; the best need ruling, 39; won from the power of the old man by the spirit of service, 338.

Esau, the flesh in its fairest form, 291, 324; his works and fruit, 372, 373.

Euphrates, reasoning, 50, 51.

Eve, that is life, so called by Adam, 67; a type of the church, 83. See *Woman*.

Evening, decline of light, 44; none on the seventh day, 44.

Faith, the spirit of, figured in Abraham, 160; is first moved by the call of God, 164, 174; every act of, brings the elect into greater trials, 176; overcomes what reason cannot, 194; is stirred by the promise to seek fruit from its own energies and from law, 215; is afterwards fruitful by grace, 219; fails in Egypt, 178; and in the Philistines' land, 239; is enriched by knowledge, 242; unmortified at first, 252; is succeeded by the spirit of understanding, 281, 282, *note* 12; first fruits of, are carnal, and opposed to purer life, 215, 253.

Faithfulness, the results of, 383.

Fall, the, not man's normal state, 62; details of, 64; the way to better things, 107, 109.

Famine, the experience of Abraham, 175; of Isaac, 302.

Five, connected with the senses, 193, *note* 3, and 240, *note* 6.

Flesh, the, can be religious, 89; its worship, 89; has many forms, 291, 324; opposes some monstrous forms of evil, 373; is very fair in some of its forms, 293.

Flocks, strife for, between herdsmen, 189; won from the world by changing their colour, 344.

Formalism, figured in the Hivite, 360. See *Canaanite*. Creeps into the church and defiles it, 360, 361.

Fruit, order of, in creation, 22, 23; having seed in itself, 24; variety of, 23.

Fruitfulness, follows the bounding of the waters or lusts, 22.

Genesis, special object of, to reveal development of human nature, 3.

Giants, monstrous forms of life, the result of the union of the sons of God and the daughters of men, 113 ; fought against by the king of Shinar, 194 ; dispossessed by Esau, 373.

Gifts, need ruling, 39 ; an occasion of strife between brethren, 189.

Gihon, or Nile, sense, 50, 51.

God's life, reflected in the saints, 250, *note* 2, and 264.

Gold, higher forms of truth, 91 ; possessed by Abraham, 184 ; jewels of, put on Rebekah, 273. See *Metals*.

Gospels, the four, figured by the four cherubic faces, 38, *note* 5 ; and in the rivers of Paradise, 52, *note* 34.

Gospel dispensation, figured in Sarah, comes to an end, and then many sons in Abraham's house, 284.

Hagar, the affection of outward truth, 210 ; typically, the law, 210.

Hair, the strength and beauty of the flesh, 293 ; to be cut off by priests at consecration, 293 ; and by leper at cleansing, 293 ; Esau marked by, 293.

Ham, the life of mere doctrine, 132 ; the type of those who cultivate false inward religion, 135, 139 : fruits of, 138 ; most numerous, 137 ; but subserve a good end, 140.

Heaven, or expanse, formed on second day, 15 ; means arranger, 16, 17 ; represents the understanding opened, 15 ; comes before fruits, 17.

Heresy, the lineage of all, 136.

Hiddekel, or Tigris, tradition, 50, 51.

Hivite, religious formalism, 359, 360. See *Canaanite*.

Idols, clung to, even by our best affections, 348.

Incarnation, the, God's way for man's redemption, 79 ; reasons of, 244 ; figured in Jacob's ladder, 331.

Instability, before firmness, 18.

Iron, most useful in this world, 91. See *Metals, Gold, Silver*.

Isaac, the spirit of sonship, 249 ; sacrifice of, 259 ; type of God, the Son, 250, *note* 2, and 268.

Ishmael, carnal seed of faith, 256 ; cast out, 256 ; multiplies greatly, 286.

Jacob, the spirit of service, 294, 295, 313, &c. ; a type of God, the Holy Ghost, 250, *note* 2 ; import of change of name to Israel, 356.

Japhet, the active life, 132 ; the figure of those who cultivate true outward religion, 135 ; his blessing, 141.

Jehovah, God is known as Jehovah on the day of rest, 46 ; mystery of the name, 221, *note* 6.

Jew, the, figured in Cain, with mark set on him, lest he be slain, 99, 100 ; in Ishmael, the son of the bond-woman, who is cast out when Isaac comes, 257 ; in Esau, 300, 322 ; in Judah, 391, 392 ; in Pharaoh's baker, 407, 408 ; in Jacob's sons rejecting the son of the younger wife, 385.

John, St., the type of the life of vision, 134, *note* 6.

Jordan, the stream of judgement, 169.

Joseph, the spirit of patient suffering, whose end is glory, 379, &c.

Keturah, practical truth, 279 ; cannot produce the spirit of sonship, 281.

Kingdom, first in the hand of the Jew, 391 ; fails in that line, 392 ; raised up in the younger wife, who has witness of her children's parentage, 392; figured in Joseph's glory, 412, 413.

Kings, in Edom, before any in Israel, 372.

Knowledge, cannot possess the things of faith, 241 ; or of sonship, 304 ; may enrich faith, 242 ; danger of, 244.

Laban, the old or natural life, 324.

Lahai-roi, the well of vision, 282.

Lamech, both in Cain's and Seth's line, 99.

Law, figured by Hagar, 210; a bondmaid, 212; is embraced by the spirit of faith, 215 ; is cast out when the spirit of sonship comes, 254.

Leah, the first and natural affection of the outward man, 335.

Light, the first step in the new creation, 12 ; is called Day, or movement, 13 ; peril of, 244.

Lights, on the fourth day, 27, 28 ; for signs, 30 ; for seasons, 31.

Lion, Christ and Satan, each represented as a, 34, and *note* 11.

Lot, a form of the natural man, 170, 229 ; goes some distance with Abraham, 182; his preaching, 236; and prayers, 237; produces an evil seed, 238.

Man, a world in himself, 4 ; created male and female, the figure of the understanding and the will, 40, 41, *note* 10, 52, 53, *note* 35, and 63, *note* 2 ; his food, 41 ; his fall, 64 ; and remedy, 80 ; his food after the flood, 126 ; the new man or seed of the woman, how formed, 66, 67.

Marriages, of Patriarchs, a mystery, 280, *note* 5.

Mesopotamia, the land between Tigris and Euphrates, *i. e.* Tradition and Reasoning, 164. See *Tigris* and *Euphrates*. Abraham, or the spirit of faith, starts from hence,

164 ; the bride of the Son is brought hence, 270 ; Jacob, or the spirit of service, goes down to serve here, 314, 315; the home of Laban, or the natural man, 349.

Metals, truths, 91. See *Gold, Iron.*

Ministry, figured in Abraham's servant seeking the bride for the Son, 268 ; uses rough and unclean things, like camels, 270 ; provided with the goods of the house of faith, 269 ; in Jacob's service also, for wives and flocks, 332.

Moon, trumpet to be blown at the new, 31; paschal lamb eaten at the full, 31 ; weak when in sun's place, 30.

Morning, growing light, 7, 45.

Movement, the first, by the Spirit of God, 6.

Moving creature, on fifth and sixth days, emotions of the understanding and will, 35, 37.

Mules, discovered by Seir's seed, 373, 374.

National churches, their contrast to the earlier form, 149.

Natural life, the stages of, a figure of spiritual things, 159.

Nimrod, the lawless one, 147 ; his rule over brethren, 141.

Night, means deviation, 13.

Noah, the figure of regeneration, 104; and of the regenerate, 114 ; a type of Christ, 130.

Numbers, contain mysteries, 119, *note* 17, and 191, *note* 3. See *Third* and *Eighth day.*

Omissions, of Scripture, significant, 45, *note* 9.

Outward things, keep us from knowing ourselves, 190.

Paradise, exclusion from, one of the results of the fall, 78.

Passions, popularly represented by beasts, 37.

Paul, St., a tentmaker, not a builder of cities, 149, and *note* 15.

Peter, St., the type of the life of faith and conflict, 134, *note* 6.

Philistine, the son of Mizraim or Egypt, knowledge derived from the senses, 240, 241. See *Egypt*. Unknown before regeneration, 301; a trial to faith, 239; and to the spirit of sonship, 301; famed for giants, 241: labours to choke wells, 307.

Pilgrimage, the common experience of the elect, 171; brings to view weaknesses of the elect, not seen in worldlings, 172.

Pison, intuition, 51.

Progress, in the spiritual life, through apparent retrogressions, 162, 310, 315.

Protestantism, the lineage of, 136 and 134, *note* 6.

Purification, through experience of corruption, 109, 310.

Rachel, the spiritual affection of the natural man, 335, 336.

Raiment, outward habits, 276.

Regeneration, a state subsequent to spiritual quickening, 103, 159; not the improvement, but the judgment, of the old man, 106; not reached but through the discovery of the ruin of the old man, 107; figured by the third day, 21; and by Noah's passage through the waters, 104; stages of, 105, 115; mystery of, as experienced within, 108; does not wholly take away or abolish the evil of the old nature, 110; leaves a mind which revives the ways of the old man, 135; in it the fall of Adam is repaired, 111; sealed in baptism, 114, 122; blessings of, 123, &c.; produces more than one form of life, 131; and so far from ending all man's wickedness, discovers in man new forms of evil, 155.

Rest, on seventh day, and only in a perfect work, 43; reveals God in a new character, 46.

Resurrection, figured in third day, 21; and in eighth, 226.

Revelations, of God to man, according to man's state, 230.

Rivers, of Paradise, channels of truth, 50. See *Euphrates, Gihon, Pison, Hiddekel*.

Rule, secret of, 38; carnal, figured in Judah, 386, 389; spiritual, in Joseph, 387.

Sabbath, or rest of God, only in a perfect work, 43.

Sacraments, God's method for fallen man, and figured in the cherubim at the gate of Eden, 79; are, according to Augustine, parts of the lesser light, 28, *note* 5; and of the earth, 322, *note* 19; yet put in the first place by the carnal seed of the church, 321.

Sacrifice, the key to many perplexities, 207.

Sarah, the affection of spiritual truth, 177; typically, the Gospel, 210; is denied in Egypt, 178; and in the Philistines' land, 239; stirs Abraham to take Hagar, 214.

Schism, the result of gift abused, 189.

Seas, mean agitations, 22.

Seed of the Woman, its lineage, 66, 67.

Seeing good, characteristic of the good, 8, 146.

Serpent, the, still the tempter, 63, and *note* 1.

Service, the spirit of, the fruit of sonship, 313, 369; seems to reverse the path of faith, 314; descends as well as ascends, 331, and *note* 12; its errors, 317; and motives, 325, 330; is pleasant to God, 319, 375; wins flocks out of the world, 332; must embrace natural as well as spiritual principles, 335, 336, 342; its fruits, 340; some of which may oppose a yet more perfect form of life, 382.

Sheep-shearing, a favourite occupation of the old man, 350; and of carnal rulers, 389.

Shem, the contemplative life, 132; the figure of those who cultivate true inward religion, 135.

Silver, higher forms of truth, 91. See *Gold, Iron*.

Sin, not the law of our being, 62.

Sodom, self-love, 229.

Son of Man, the new man, 81, *note* 3.

Sonship, the spirit of, the fruit of faith, 249; chastened from the first, 252; opposed by carnal fruits of faith, 253; leads to the casting out of the spirit of bondage, 254; is weaned, 253; is a sacrifice, 261; cannot embrace law to be fruitful, 288; would bless the fleshly seed, 299, 316.

Spirit, one, under many varied forms, 33, 250.

Spiritual, the, suffer here, 406.

Spiritual mind, the second birth of human nature, 88; different from the spirit of sonship, 161, *note* 2.

Suffering, power of, 380; the way to glory, 385.

Temptation, Adam's, the figure of man's temptation in every age, 70; resisted in one form, meets the elect in another, 199.

Tents, elect live in, 171; Paul a tentmaker, 149, *note* 15; results of leaving the tent for the city, seen in Asshur, who built Nineveh, 149; in Lot, who went down to Sodom, 197, 231; and in Jacob, at Shechem, 361.

Third day, resurrection, 21.

Truth, four sources or channels of, 50; comes to man in forms suited to his state, 266, 278; with these forms of truth, fallacies of the senses are connected, 288, 289; forms of truth may pass away, while the truth yet lives, 267, 278.

Unity, desire for, may mislead, 153.

Waters, figures the desires, 15; first divided by a heaven, 15; bounded on the third day, 16; called seas or agitations, 22.

Weaning, of the spiritual seed, provokes the mockery of the carnal, 252, 256.

Wells, the springs of living water, 272; the bride found by, 272; choked by Philistines, 307.

Will, the, figured by the woman, 41, *note* 10, and 63, *note* 2; its agency in the fall, 64; is the mother of all living, 67.

Woman, the, figure of the will, 53, and *note* 35; the agent in the fall, 64; the channel of the promised seed, 66. See *Man*.

Word of God, the new creation wrought by the, 6.

Work, of the new creation, progressive, 7; first dividing, then adorning, 9, 10; though imperfect, good in God's eyes, 8.

World, religious and irreligious, figured in Babylon and Egypt, 196, and *note* 8; cannot as such possess the things of faith, 243; many forms of, 397.

Worship, of the carnal and spiritual seeds, 95; of the elect an abomination to worldlings, 187; distractions of true worship, 208.

Zealots, scattered in Israel, 363.